GATEWAY
OF THE
GODS

KEVIN,
ENJOY THE BOOK!
"SQUARE THE CIRCLE"

Craig Hines
8-4-07

GATEWAY OF THE GODS

An Investigation of Fallen Angels, the Nephilim, Alchemy, Climate Change, and the Secret Destiny of the Human Race

CRAIG HINES

NUMINA™
MEDIA • ARTS

Murrysville, Pennsylvania

Cover artwork, book design, typesetting, and illustrations by Craig Hines. Edited by Matthew Heilman.

"Numina Media Arts" and design are trademarks of Numina Media Arts, LLC.

Publisher's Cataloging-in-Publication
(Provided by Quality Books, Inc.)
Hines, Craig.
    Gateway of the gods : an investigation of fallen angels, the nephilim, alchemy,
    climate change, and the secret destiny of the human race / Craig Hines.
    — 1st ed.
        p. cm.
    Includes bibliographical references and index.
    LCCN 2006905626
    ISBN-13: 978-0-9785591-0-6
    ISBN-10: 0-9785591-0-X

        1. Civilization, Ancient—Extraterrestrial influences. 2. Angels—Miscellanea.
    3. Christianity and other religions. 4. Physics—Philosophy. 5. Apocalyptic
    literature—History and criticism. I. Title.

        CB156.H56 2006   001.942
                                  QBI06-600265

Published by
Numina Media Arts, LLC

www.NuminaMediaArts.com
www.GatewayoftheGods.com

Printed in the United States of America on acid-free paper.
09 08 07   10 9 8 7 6 5 4 3

For Amy, with all my love.
None of this would have been possible without you.
Thank you for your patience and understanding.

The most beautiful experience we can have is the mysterious. It is the fundamental emotion that stands at the cradle of true art and true science. Whoever does not know it and can no longer wonder, no longer marvel, is as good as dead, and his eyes are dimmed.

—Albert Einstein
"The World As I See It" (1931)

CONTENTS

ACKNOWLEDGMENTS

To BEGIN, I WOULD LIKE TO THANK MY FRIENDS AND FAMILY for their support and encouragement while researching and writing this book. I appreciate the joint efforts of Rich and Dave for commenting on my earliest manuscripts and for the many wonderful conversations about not only my theories, but our obsessions with films, television, and life in general—it certainly helped to break up the monotony. I would also like to thank my dear friend and editor, Matthew Heilman, who devoted countless hours to this project. His masterful command of the English language has elevated the quality of my writing considerably.

I cannot even begin to offer enough thanks to my beautiful and loving fiancée, Amy, for her endless patience with both myself and my work. She has seen this project through from the beginning, and without her help it may have never reached completion. Thank you for understanding my late night ramblings and for translating them into coherent thoughts; for knowing when to finish my sentences and getting "to the point" during so many long-winded discussions; and most importantly, for never letting me feel like I was alone throughout everything that has transpired. There is certainly so much more to thank you for, but this is just a start.

I would also like to thank several musicians for providing the appropriate musical scores while I slaved away researching, writing, and pondering the many questions that fill my head. Most notably, I would like to thank Trent Reznor of Nine Inch Nails, who is "right where he belongs;" Maynard James Keenan of Tool, A Perfect Circle, and Puscifer; Ronan Harris and Mark Jackson of VNV Nation; Artaud Seth of Garden of Delight; Iskandar Hasnawi and Renaud Tschirner of Elend; and the ever-so influential Carl McCoy of Fields of the Nephilim/Nefilim. Their contributions and inspirations have made the experience of writing and researching much more enjoyable.

INTRODUCTION

I think now that the simplest questions are not only the hardest to answer, but the most important to ask...

—Northrop Frye[1]

THE SYNTHESIS OF IDEAS AND CONTENT PRESENTED in this book will not only alter our understanding of the past, but it may affect the course of the future as well. Fundamental questions such as *"Why are we here?" "Do God and heaven exist?" "What happens when we die?"* and *"What is the answer to the Ultimate Question of Life, the Universe, and Everything?"* have kept theologians busy for millennia.[2] My own attempts to discover the answers to these questions inevitably led to more questions—and usually questions that are more puzzling and mysterious than their predecessors. My theory proposes that we should not continue asking *"Why are we here?"* but rather, *"What are we going to do about it?"*

I might not be the first person to present such an extensive exploration of the variety of topics at hand, but I do believe that this is the first time that such a cohesive theory has ever been presented that unifies all of them. Numerous authors have discussed the topics explored throughout these pages, and some of their theories have been similar to my own, but unfortunately, I found that most of their arguments were not particularly convincing. The problems with other similar explorations usually result from large gaps in logic, while some important subjects or ideas were not addressed at all—whether it was because the author was unaware of the information or if in fact it was omitted intentionally, I do not know—but it was information that would have significantly changed their theory.

But the problem that I have encountered most often is that some authors and researchers are purposefully misleading with their work, and some of the most popular names in alternative research are *not* what they claim to be.

Their research may appear scholarly on the surface, but their conclusions are flawed and contrived to fit their ideology. All too often, minor investigations into these topics reveal that important facts have been manipulated to fit new interpretations by these authors. Unfortunately, most readers do not put in the time or the effort to verify these details for themselves.

This brings me to a point that I consider extremely important, and I would like to be upfront about it to avoid any unnecessary arguments or confusion. I am *not* a credentialed scholar of any kind, nor do I hold degrees from any prestigious universities. However, I believe that good scholarship is paramount when reviewing any work and claims—and it should be to you as well. For this reason, I have tried to use only authentic and scholarly sources endorsed by mainstream academia to support my theories related to ancient languages and modern science whenever possible.[3] In situations where I have relied on other types of sources, it is noted either within the body of the text or in the notes.[4] Surprisingly, it seems that example after example of words and definitions from these accepted sources already fit with my proposed ideas. There has never been any reason to change them or radically re-interpret their meanings.

For instance, scholars of the Sumerian[5] and other Middle Eastern languages understand the meanings of the ancient tongues because the scribes left behind many multi-lingual dictionaries. One of these dictionaries might have the Sumerian cuneiform writing on one side, and then state its reference in a comparable language, such as Akkadian, on the other side. These "dictionaries" have tremendously aided in the deciphering of long-forgotten languages because their native speakers have shown us the exact meanings of these words. This alone makes me question the credibility of some modern authors who hold their own reinterpretations of words as more credible than those of the ancient scribes.

On the other hand, there also seems to be a "knowledge filter" in mainstream academia. This has even been admitted by some people who work in fields such as ancient language studies, among others. Some ancient language scholars are very strict in their interpretations of words, yet they often relegate the stories to the realm of pure myth. Some of these scholars (but not all) have a tendency to scoff at the notion that myths may contain historical truths and consider such ideas to be foolish. Sadly, these biases may very well have denied the rest of us the chance to fully appreciate and understand the messages left behind by our ancestors from the distant past.

Furthermore, some scholars and researchers claim to be skeptical but are in fact quite cynical. Important data is often manipulated and ignored to reflect *their* concepts of truth. Sometimes this is intentional on the part of the researcher and other times it is not. However, true skepticism is not a bad thing and it should be encouraged. In fact, skepticism is a valuable tool that becomes *essential* when we are asked to look into any claim that sounds incredible. Undoubtedly, the nature of the material explored throughout this book easily falls under such a categorical listing. I have tried to take a skeptical approach to these topics, but perhaps it won't be skeptical *enough* for others. I simply know that I have found enough evidence to convince myself, and if I've done my job properly then most readers should find it convincing as well. All that I can ask of my readers is that they shed their agendas and approach this body of knowledge with an open willingness to understand. No matter how controversial or bizarre a theory might be, true skeptics should be willing to change their views in accordance with the data when they have been presented with enough evidence.

With that being said, I hope that I have piqued your interest in my theory. Although it is actually quite simple, it is intricately woven between the complex threads of ancient mythology, language, symbolism, and theoretical physics, to name just a few of the disciplines I will be exploring. After connecting these (seemingly) unrelated topics, I have come to the following conclusion:

Thousands of years ago, intelligent beings from another realm developed inter-dimensional "gateways" to transfer themselves to our world. While here, they were able to physically interact with our ancient ancestors and many specific accounts concerning "the gods" and "angels" have been passed down in legends and myths. Sometime later, these beings returned (or were forced to return) to their place of origin and the gateways were deactivated. However, they left behind clues and symbols that would withstand the trials of time so that a future civilization might decipher their message and understand how to reactivate the gateways. They also recognized that eventually the earth's climate and ability to support a large population would fail, accelerating the possibility of extinction for many species (including humans). Therefore, the human race is expected to rediscover the gateway technology so that we can reunite the realms as well as transform ourselves into advanced inter-dimensional beings.

As I have already acknowledged, the theory is "incredible" and therefore depends upon a considerable amount of speculation. However, hundreds of writings and archaeological discoveries reinforce my claims. Additionally, I have tried to harmonize them with the latest investigations and scientific speculations regarding the nature of reality. While my proposal is certainly not the Holy Grail "Theory of Everything," it does provide an explanation for many historical anomalies in a straightforward manner. Many readers may quickly discover that they have problems accepting my theory—not because it's necessarily wrong or does not make sense—but rather, because parts of it will clash with what they previously believed to be "true." Most of the time, this is because many of these anomalies were explained by people that did not understand the significance of what was before their eyes because all of the context clues had been removed. What I have simply done is provide the context clues so that the path connecting these issues becomes apparent.

Unfortunately, the nature of my proposal must be classified as a *construct* at this time (instead of a *hypothesis*) because it is non-falsifiable. What this means is that it can neither be proved nor disproved and will be considered "pseudoscience" by mainstream academia. However, there is still a chance that the proper technology and experimentation will be developed at some point in the future so that it can be tested. Therefore, the purpose of this book is to encourage scientists to fairly and objectively consider these possibilities and investigate the likelihood of inhabitable dimensions beyond what we commonly recognize. It is my hope that it will provide some kind of framework or guide for scientists to develop suitable methods to test it.

The speculative nature of my theory suggests that it should be relegated to the realm of the unknown and the "fringe" borderlands of science (as *Skeptic* magazine publisher Michael Shermer would put it). However, these borderlands are frequently home to some of the most amazing discoveries. The people who dare to reach into these areas, where the ideas flirt between the ordinary and the extraordinary, are the ones that discover the radical new theories and technologies that serve as milestones in history.

For example, most scientists and astronomers doubt that we are being visited by extraterrestrial beings in UFOs because they find the majority of evidence unconvincing. Yet, there is almost a unanimous belief among them that life must exist elsewhere in the universe, as evidenced in such programs as SETI (Search for Extraterrestrial Intelligence). This belief fuels their quest even though no hard evidence exists to support it. This demonstrates that programs such as SETI are actually borderland sciences (although they are arguably much closer to the inner-fringe of accepted scientific thought than my proposal). These scientists have studied enough ancillary data to develop meaningful speculation and insight to follow their "gut-feelings" about where to look for evidence.

But what if we're looking in the wrong places?

What if we should be looking much closer to home?

After many years of studying the myths and legends presented in this book, I believe that I have been able to develop similar meaningful speculation and insight. I am convinced that those records point to something worthy of closer study—something that has gone largely unnoticed until now. I don't have answers for everything and I won't even pretend to understand how it all works. However, I cannot ignore the feeling that keeps shouting, "Look over here!"

It does not seem unreasonable to believe that the human race has encountered an advanced extraterrestrial civilization far in the past. An overwhelming number of ancient records point to such a conclusion. But the problem might be that we are not looking at the evidence in the right way, and therefore it will only make sense if we change our perspective. We have preconceived notions about what an "extraterrestrial" would have been like, how their technology functioned, or how they may have communicated. My ideas will expand upon all of these areas. Most importantly, I will suggest that symbolism plays a highly important role in how this advanced race of beings communicated concepts and messages that would be understandable to a culture living thousands of years later.

Additionally, for those who demand physical evidence I will suggest that you do not need to look any further than the world around you. The existence of churches, temples, mosques, and even ancient structures like the pyramids all share a common origin. Most of the world's religions refer to "gods" or divine beings that interacted with the human race a long time ago. The effects of this "contact experience" have rippled throughout history. Wars have been waged and monuments have been built. It seems unlikely that the *entire* world suffered from a "mass delusion" that caused them to believe so passionately in these things.

So why do I think that I am qualified to present this new idea? It is because I have tried to take a step back and look at the larger picture—to see what others have been missing. Please do not misunderstand this and think that I am saying my ideas are more valid than established scholars and scientists. I truly value and depend on their contributions greatly. However, one of the major problems I've noticed with modern scientific discoveries is how professionals tend to "specialize" in certain fields. This is understandable because there is a great deal of knowledge out there and a person could easily spend a lifetime devoted to just one subject. The problem is that the people who specialize in one field may be completely unaware of astonishing new discoveries in a different one that echo a commonality. It is then up to people like myself to notice and make connections between these points of data.

It will take some very brave souls and bold thinking to develop serious tests for the topics covered in this book. However, if true, these theories will have far-reaching implications for the world that could prove devastating to ignore. Therefore, I ask that you seriously and objectively study the subject matter covered in the following pages. Our future may depend on it.

I have divided the book into five parts. The first part reveals my background and the interests that drove me to pursue this research. It also establishes the accepted rules of the scientific community regarding evidence and evaluates some of the pros and cons of how this system relates to my research.

The second part introduces readers to many of the ancient legends concerning angelic beings known as the Watchers and their offspring, the Nephilim. I will also provide detailed explanations regarding the many terms and names that are pertinent to the investigation. Descriptions of these beings are also used to show their striking cross-culture similarities as well as to put forth a new idea that encourages scientists to consider that these beings may have once existed on our planet.

The third part explores the gateway technology described in the ancient texts. The proposed nature of this technology is that it may have allowed inter-dimensional travel by adjusting the molecular structure of matter. Although there are many differences, fans of science fiction will find this concept comparable to the transporter technology of *Star Trek* or the wormhole portals used in the movie *Stargate* and its spin-off television series. Seeing as how some scientists consider that some semblance of this technology may be viable one day in the not too distant future, I am confident enough to suggest that my model of these gateways could be as well.

The fourth part of this book describes the ancient world views regarding the heavenly realms and the afterlife, and then compares it to modern ideas and research in paranormal investigation. The pros and cons of different technologies are covered as well as specific investigation techniques. Readers are then encouraged to experiment on their own as a method of confirming such phenomena, as well as for the purpose of providing a wider field of data to analyze. In addition, some of the latest theories in quantum physics will be discussed, particularly concerning discoveries which relate to the idea of parallel or multi-dimensional universes.

The fifth part of the book covers the unfolding environmental collapse and the impact it will have on the planet. The human race is facing a disaster unlike any we have ever encountered before, and we must make quick, but educated decisions about how to solve this problem. Next, my investigation moves into a new field of research regarding modern alchemy that, if proven true, could show amazing promise in the ability to reactivate the aforementioned gateways. If we learn how to harness the power of these inter-dimensional devices, the human race may have a viable plan to escape its impending extinction. Finally, I conclude the investigation by coalescing all of the previous material and symbolism under my proposed construct. You will then understand how the long-forgotten potential of the human race will once again emerge from the deepest recesses of our consciousness.

I have also included appendices that further elaborate upon the above material. In fairness, I recommend that everyone read Appendix A, where I describe many of the potential problems inherent to my theories and speculations. It is meant to demonstrate how there is still a great deal of information missing from my research and how specific issues such as the lack of physical evidence, the trouble of hoaxers, and other ideas should be addressed. Appendix B offers a *purely speculative* concept of how the gateway technology *might* have operated and is intended for readers who want further insight into the devices or still have major doubts about their functionality. Additionally, Appendix C has been included as a brief effort to inform readers about a few of the flawed theories being perpetuated by so-called "experts," so that readers may become more discerning of such material. The remaining appendices involve step-by-step tutorials of how researchers can further test and attempt to verify information for themselves.

Something that may come as a shock to readers is that I do *not* believe in the supernatural. Why do I say this? It is because I consider the term "supernatural" to be a misnomer; it infers that things are "above" or "outside" the normal laws of the natural world. Instead, my argument is that these things are only violating *manmade* laws—laws that are severely limited by our understanding and biases. I believe that phenomena attributed to the realm of the supernatural will eventually be explained by science. Then, it will only be a matter of moving it from the "unknown" into the "known" category. For reader clarity, however, I will continue to use the terms "supernatural" and "paranormal" because of their familiarity to audiences interested in such topics.

Now, I invite you to accompany me on a fascinating journey into the world of our ancient ancestors, to face their gods and demons, understand their myth and symbolism, and complete the task that they have given to us.

PART 1

A SMALL, QUIET VOICE

We create the world in which we live; if that world becomes unfit for human life, it is because we tire of our responsibility.

—Cyril Connolly[1]

In My Dreams

IN THE BEGINNING, I HADN'T THE SLIGHTEST IDEA that I would be writing this book (or any book for that matter). While growing up, I planned to pursue a career somewhere in the broad field of multimedia. As a small boy, I had a talent for drawing and by the time I was eight years of age, I began teaching myself how to create computer graphics. At that time, computer games were still in their infancy but making tremendous breakthroughs in design and graphics. I was in love with the idea of being able to use my talents for projects such as computer and video games or animating some creature for the next big Hollywood blockbuster.

Those dreams changed very little over the years and my experience continued to grow. I was a straight-A student in school, involved in both the junior and senior high school video production crews, and just about everyone who knew me thought that I was going to be doing something big with games or movies someday. There was even a computer game company located near my home—a somewhat rare occurrence for the northeastern part of the U.S.—and I intended to work there.

I was awarded a two-year scholarship to a local college at the end of my senior year. It seemed like the right thing to do since there were only a few schools specifically dealing with game design at that time and most of them were too far away for my liking. I looked into art schools—but I had heard far too many horror stories from people who attended them and paid huge tuitions, only to go out into the working world and find that much of what they learned either wasn't practical for that type of work, or studios were not inclined to hire inexperienced students fresh out of college. Additionally, since I had spent so many years learning on my own and pouring through just about every book and magazine I could get my hands on, much of what was being taught at those schools had already been in my bag of tricks for years. I had my plan and was well on my way.[2]

Something I learned quickly at the close of 1999 was to expect the unexpected—and that *my plans* do not always work out with the plans that *someone else* might have for me.

You see, I am one of those few people who usually claim that they do not dream. I realize that some people will say that it is impossible for me not to dream, and instead, I am simply not remembering the majority of my dreams. To that end, I really cannot argue differently—it's probably true. Some people seem to recall their dreams all of the time and with little difficulty—I'm simply not one of those people. However, on the rare occasion that I do remember, I have always been able to clearly discriminate between the dream and what happens during my waking life. So if I do recall a dream, it usually tends to stick with me.

Throughout the months of October and November, I began having some rather disturbing dreams involving a dark, shadowy entity that seemed to be stalking me. These felt different from regular dreams, though. There was something strange about them, like there was actually something else in my head making its presence known. Then, in the very early hours of a cold December morning, at 3:04 a.m. to be precise, it seemed as if the thing actually *came out* of those dreams! The event that happened in those early hours was one of those life-altering moments that you *never* forget—even if you try. While no physical harm was inflicted upon me, it did leave quite an emotional mark.

I have chosen not to go into the details about my experience, even though many people will certainly be curious about further details. I am still not exactly comfortable discussing them at this time and I hope this is understandable. Additionally, I would prefer not to focus on the darker side of my experience for the following two reasons. First, despite having an unnerving effect on me, this particular event was of minor significance within the broader context of what I would soon discover. Second, many people tend to dwell on the more frightening aspects of such phenomena and regrettably fail to see the larger message. Nevertheless, I wouldn't have mentioned it if

I felt that there was no relationship to what I'm about to describe. Therefore, I will explain the subsequent unfolding of events as I understand them.

Throughout the next day, I was somewhat shaken up but generally felt okay. It was only when the time arrived to go to bed that I grew rather anxious. Never before in my entire life had I felt scared by such a simple thing as falling asleep. I told myself it was just an irrational fear and my mind was simply playing tricks on me—everything was going to be okay. After lying in bed for what seemed like an eternity, I eventually drifted off to sleep. I do not recall having any dreams, but at 3:04 a.m.—the exact same time as the night before—I snapped awake. Despite what transpired exactly twenty-four hours earlier, I still wasn't prepared for the sight that was now before my eyes. To my complete amazement, my room was… shimmering?

A soft blue glow filled the entire room, but there was no discernable light source. I remember looking at the walls and seeing the dancing reflection of light all over them, much like the reflection of water from an indoor pool. I do not recall any odd sounds or noises—it was astonishingly quiet. I sat upright in my bed, completely amazed at the sight before my eyes. I looked over at my clock to check the time and then back around the room. There was also a thin silver glow coming from around my bedroom door, but it was nothing like the light that seeps through the openings from the hallway light. I also had the overwhelming feeling of another presence in the room with me, but I was not frightened like before. Rather, I felt very protected and safe enough to go back to sleep—and so I did.

Now, I know that many people will find this hard to believe and I can't expect them to believe it. They will want more proof, or say, "Well, why didn't you try to get some pictures of it or some form of physical documentation?" Honestly, I would definitely like to have something like that too. All that I can say is that when things like this actually happen to you, it's as if documenting it doesn't really matter. I know it may seem like a poor excuse, but I cannot quite explain it any other way. When I awoke to this glowing vision—as amazing as it was to see—it also felt completely natural to me. The thought of *I need to document this!* never crossed my mind until the next day.

I am also sure that some people will say that it was just the product of an overactive imagination and none of it was real. Perhaps they are right, but it is difficult for me to accept this because I was the one who actually experienced it. Granted, I am involved in the type of work that greatly depends upon my skills of imagination. However, I must admit that I often grow frustrated because I have fantastic ideas or visions that I cannot satisfactorily translate onto paper or computer. I sometimes like to blame part of this on my being a little too grounded in the real world and my knack for occasionally over-analyzing something to death.

I am also my own worst enemy when it comes to self-criticism. I have gone over it a million times in my head, thinking such things as: *Am I losing my mind? Was I really asleep even though it seemed that I was awake? Could I simply have misinterpreted common lighting effects coming in through the windows?* The list went on and on, further adding to my confusion. I should also point out to critics that I am not a drug user, nor was I under the influence of any medications or substances at *any* of these times (or any other time, for that matter).

The most common explanation for my experiences would be that I was suffering from "sleep paralysis," but this was not the case. I was aware of the symptoms of sleep paralysis before this ever happened to me, and I would have recognized it immediately. While there are some overlapping similarities between my experience and those of "night terrors" described by other people, there were too many differences for me to accept this as the explanation. Most importantly, I never felt paralyzed—I could freely move around and I was fully awake.

However, a more specific explanation closely related to sleep paralysis is that I was having a "hypnopompic hallucination." This occurs most often when a person suddenly awakens from REM (Rapid-Eye-Movement) sleep. In this state, the person has the feeling of being completely awake, but they are still technically producing brain waves as if they were asleep. The person may have both auditory hallucinations (e.g. strange mechanical noises, pulses, hums, footsteps, indistinct voices, etc.) and visual hallucinations (e.g. "shadow people," angels, demons, or other creatures). To the person experiencing these "hallucinations," the event can seem unquestionably real.[3]

So, was this what happened to me or not? I do not know. It does seem to be the most plausible explanation and includes most of the symptoms I described. However, even if I accept this, I am still at a loss to explain some other details. For instance, while many people may describe seeing strange lights accompanied by the feeling of another presence within the room, they usually describe these lights very differently than what I experienced. Perhaps my situation was just rarer than those of other people.

Another problem that I have is that it does not explain how I awoke at exactly the same time (to the minute) two nights in a row. I understand how our bodies become accustomed to certain schedules and develop what is often described as an "internal clock," but it never seems to be *that* precise. In addition, I am aware that people with irregular sleeping schedules or even sleep deprivation often experience hypnopompic hallucinations. While I am certainly the type of person who is a "night-owl" and frequently has irregular sleeping patterns, it should be noted that I was accustomed to a much more regular schedule at the time because of my college classes. If irregular sleeping patterns were a major culprit, the occurrence of these hallucinations should have increased within the last few years rather than back in 1999. Whatever the case, I have not experienced any similar disturbances since that time. However, that does not mean that weird things suddenly ceased happening around me—not at all. Even if I accepted that the above situations had been hallucinatory, I am still at a loss to explain the next series of events that began to occur.

Over the next several months, I had the feeling that someone or something was guiding me—but I did not understand why or for what purpose. On occasion, I would even seem to hear a voice that should not be there. It is not completely correct to say that I was *hearing* a voice, but rather *sensing a foreign thought*. What I mean by this is that it seemed that there was someone else in my head either responding to a question I had been thinking about or telling me to look at something, or various other things of that nature. Regardless, it was *noticeably* different from my own thoughts.

These thoughts did not occur often, and never became overpowering enough that it bothered me. As I explained a moment ago, it was more like I was simply being guided to things but still had my own free will in how I chose to act and respond. Most often, this guide would "activate" when I was near a bookstore and I would get these distinct impressions such as "Get this book" or "Part of the answer is in here." (I even joked with my girlfriend that it was a plot cooked up by Barnes and Noble and that she should hold onto my wallet!) It never came right out and told me anything specific—it only encouraged my exploration in a wide variety of subjects. As I read more and more, and looked to other sources besides books, it seemed like I was finally starting to get a bigger picture in my head and I could see the lines connecting the dots that this guide wanted me to discover.

I do not remember exactly when these "thoughts" stopped—only that it has been a few years now.[4] Nevertheless, the last message is certainly one that stuck with me, because at the time, it made absolutely no sense and I did not recall ever hearing the term before. The voice said, "Square the circle."

Square the circle? What did *that* mean? I did a little bit of research regarding the phrase and found that it was a mathematical problem with many connections to alchemy. Alchemy? Was I supposed to be turning lead into gold? I seriously doubted that! I certainly hoped that I had not spent all of this time, energy and money listening to this guide, only to be duped into trying to turn lead into gold. I knew enough high school chemistry to recognize that it had its origins in alchemy, but grew into a specific science that did away with all of that superstitious nonsense. *Right?*

However, as far as the mathematical problem is concerned, it is *impossible* to solve. The concept is to have the area of a circle equal that of a square. That sounds simple enough. Any geometry student could tell you that to find the area of a square or rectangle you multiply the length times the height (area = l x h). However, the problem arises that to find the area of a circle, you must multiply the number Pi with the squared radius of the circle (area = πr^2). Since Pi is a potentially infinite number with no discernable pattern ($\pi \approx 3.1415926535\ldots$), we can never give a definite answer for the area of a circle; it must always be approximate.

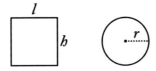

Not sure what to do with this, I simply filed that little message about squaring the circle away into the back of my thoughts and moved onto other things. If it ever came up again, I would know where to find it.

Now, let's fast forward to April of 2003, when I purchased *The Key* by Whitley Strieber. I was new to Strieber's work, although I was familiar enough with his name and the story tied to him. He is an author that alleges to have been abducted by aliens, or "visitors" as he calls them, made famous by his book, *Communion: A True Story* (William Morrow & Company, Inc., 1987). I had been listening for a short while to *Dreamland*, his weekly internet radio program, and was intrigued by the subject of *The Key*.

I was in for quite a shock.

The Revelation

The Key is an account of a conversation that took place between Strieber and a stranger that entered his hotel room at three o'clock in the morning on June 6, 1998.[5] Thinking at first the knock on the door might be room service, Strieber opened his door to a man with pale skin and sharp features, dressed completely in black, with a rim of white hair around his head.[6] Before Strieber could even assess what was happening, the man proceeded into the room, turned around to face him, and then politely smiled. Thinking that this might be another case of a stalker or obsessed fan, Strieber asked him to leave immediately—but what the man said surprised him—and something told him to listen to what he had to say.

"You know perfectly well who I am," he told Strieber after being asked to identify himself.

"Why are you here?"

"You're chained to the ground."

"Excuse me?"

"I am here on behalf of the good. Please give me some time," he responded.

Now intrigued, Strieber grabbed a yellow notepad and began taking notes, eager to discover where the conversation would lead him.[7]

The stranger quickly began referring to mankind's ascension and how the human race was trapped on the planet, unable to escape a sequence of devastating events that would soon begin taking place. The "Master of the Key," as Strieber later referred to him, went on to describe how there is an "undiscovered country" behind a veil that's waiting to fall. Mankind has been invited to join this place—but only if we prove we have earned it.[8]

What struck me as extremely important, if somewhat hidden within the words of the Master of the Key, was the reference to what we must do to save ourselves from extinction. Strieber is told that all of the events taking place concerning UFOs, government secrecy and climate change are purposeful and intended as "part of the plan of your evolution." He continued by saying, "Pisces, the little fish, will be poured out onto dry land by the stream of Aquarius. Then, how will you live? How will you breathe? You will make a leap of evolution. You will *square the circle* or die"[9] (Emphasis added).

There it was right in front of me! By this point in 2003, I had nearly forgotten about it—and now it practically plowed into me like a runaway freight train! However, this was not the only time it was mentioned. Later in the conversation, the role of the human race in achieving the impossible is again stated and our purpose is to "square the circle."[10]

Why was the Master of the Key referring to this as the solution? What could it possibly mean? I still did not understand at the time, but I knew there was something here for me to use—I only needed to dig deeper. Now, I had an idea that squaring the circle was referring to some kind of evolutionary leap or change in humanity, and a new door opened for my research. I went back over my previous resources and sought out new ones, but this time with the new perspective—everything changed for me.

I also realized at this time just how important this clue might be. Prophecies about the end of the world or large-scale social and economic problems are nothing new, and there will always be a large number of people willing to believe them. I remember sitting back and politely smiling as Y2K hysteria swept across our culture. I believed that it was nothing to fret over, and yet people were on edge. They also worried about the start of the "millennium"—even though it did not officially begin until 2001. All of the world's computers were going to crash and Jesus was scheduled to return.

Nothing happened.

Maybe Jesus missed the memo?

Perhaps the boy has cried wolf too many times and now people won't want to listen. But what if there really *is* something going on with our planet—something on a grand scale that we're not prepared to handle? The Master of the Key explained the sequence of events that would create storms of a magnitude unrecorded in human history—storms so severe that they could bring the human race to extinction.[11] The details of this were enough to convince Strieber to look into the matter. The result was the book titled *The Coming Global Superstorm* (Pocket Books, 1999), which he co-authored with Art Bell, a close friend and host of the popular late night radio show *Coast to Coast AM. Superstorm* was later adapted into the mega-blockbuster 2004 film *The Day After Tomorrow,* and ignited controversy regarding the implications of global warming.

When Strieber asked what he or anyone else could do about this kind of disaster, he was told, "You can write. Use your tool."[12] The results were two books and a Hollywood movie. That is a pretty remarkable outcome for simply listening to what a stranger had to say.[13] By writing those books, he was able to spread the message. Within that message were clues for others to discover—clues intended for people such as myself, perhaps?

What you are looking at right now is the product of those clues. In these pages are what I have managed to put together by connecting the dots and trying to form a more complete image. Maybe I'm wrong in my interpretations. It would certainly be more pleasant to think so. In any case, I know what brought me to this point, and I feel that publishing my findings has become my responsibility. Perhaps this book will be the catalyst for someone else to make the next great discovery that will finally enable all of us to square the circle.

What I cannot stress enough throughout this book is how much I do not want you to merely take my word, or that of anyone else, as being the final answer and absolute truth to the great mysteries of our world. If the whole purpose of this "exercise" is to see humanity grow above our (mostly) self-imposed limitations, then we should stop blindly accepting everything that we are told—no matter how comfortably it may satisfy our worldviews, or justify our beliefs—and start asking bold questions. We must walk forward, eyes open, and critically analyze every shred of evidence along the way. Maintain a believer's heart, if you like, but keep a skeptic's mind.

EVALUATING THE EVIDENCE

The supernatural is the natural not yet understood.
—Elbert Green Hubbard[1]

IF WE ARE TO KEEP A SKEPTIC'S MIND about the world and its happenings, we should examine a framework for processing that evidence. To accomplish this task, a set of standards have been developed to help separate the wheat from the chaff, and to ensure the scientific community that we are serious about our methods and studies. Generally, these rules serve extremely well for most situations. However, they are not without their limitations and so we must learn when to apply them and when they are impractical for proper evaluation of certain data.

Setting the Rules

There are typically three established rules that non-conventional theories must pass to satisfy the skeptical community. Investigator Joe Nickell, a member of CSICOP (Committee for the Scientific Investigation of Claims of the Paranormal), states that these rules are:

1. Extraordinary claims require extraordinary proof.
2. The burden of proof is on the advocate of a claim, not on anyone who would question it.
3. The simplest tenable explanation—that is, the one with the fewest assumptions—is most likely to be correct. (This principle is commonly known as "Occam's Razor.")[2]

The first two items involve the existence or absence of proof. What is typically meant by "extraordinary proof" is the presentation of physical evidence that equally matches the claim. An example would be if someone claimed to have handled wreckage from a crashed UFO. If so, then having a piece of this wreckage suitable for scientific analysis, as well anything else from the crash site that could be measured or scrutinized, would certainly aid in determining the truthfulness of such a claim. If no physical evidence exists, proving the authenticity of the claim becomes more difficult.

Determining exactly what physical evidence should be considered proof for the claims of this book is difficult—to say the least. This is mostly due to the passage of so much time between when these ancient cultures existed and the present day. Much like how a crime scene investigator has a better chance of collecting untainted evidence the sooner they arrive at a crime scene, in order to most efficiently evaluate the evidence discussed in this book, it would be necessary to return to the "crime scenes" of the ancient past. Thus, without the aid of a time machine, our only recourse is to carefully reconstruct the events of the past and objectively interpret the details to the best of our abilities.

It is a fact that immense stone structures were built sometime in the remote past and many still stand today, such as the Great Pyramid of Giza. Other structures have been destroyed by the ravages of time or the hands of man, and only vestiges remain. We know that the people and cultures existed because we have found their skeletons and items such as pottery and weapons. These people also left behind writings on thousands of stone and clay tablets and paper. These writings are what bring us to another point.

Unless we are to believe what the ancient people of the world communicated in their writings, we really have no other viable explanation exactly how or why so many of these stone monuments were constructed. A brief survey shows that there are not only the pyramids of Egypt, but also pyramid-like structures from as far west as North and South America to as far east as China. According to the writings of our ancestors, these monuments were built to serve as gateways for the gods. Although most accounts describe the ways in which the gods aided humanity, some legends describe malevolent interactions attributed to "fallen" gods. In either case, after the gods had completed their tasks, they returned to their places of origin. The legends also said that they would return sometime in the future.

Most skeptics argue that these stories were the product of superstition and a lack of sophistication and knowledge. Such stories are merely myths, for gods never literally came down from heaven. Yet again, aside from building a time machine to travel back into the past, there is no definitive way to successfully argue with any certainty that there were *not* gods walking the earth in remote ages. This argument demonstrates an inherent fallibility to the application of the three rules listed above. While I agree that such rules are generally good enough to test most modern claims, their effectiveness when applied to very old claims quickly falls apart the further we reach back in time.

Complete acceptance of the skeptical view that all such stories grew out of simple superstitions also leads to an interesting conundrum. We must explain how so many of our distant ancestors came to tell extremely similar stories even though they were on different continents separated by vast oceans. Why were they obsessed with building pyramid-like structures and identifying them as gateways to the heavens? The traditional historical model teaches that they were not in communication at those times and that such similarities are due to coincidences, the result of trying to explain the same types of phenomena, or the influence of migrating people from other cultures.

While these explanations may be reasonable, they do not adequately explain enough of the ancient records. For example, consider that Christian missionaries might have influenced Native Americans, causing them to adapt specific Biblical stories into their own culture. This explanation seems appropriate enough—until we consider that the Native Americans spoke of specific things in their legends that were not likely spread by the missionaries—things based on heretical ideas and banned books that the missionaries themselves probably did not know or would never want to reveal.

Instead of focusing on all of the minor differences in the stories, such as how a god in one story is similar to another but with a seemingly different name, careful examination often shows that the core is homogenous. It should be expected that over time subtle differences would eventually creep into the stories, especially as people grew more distant from the original events and modified the stories to have new meanings for the times. However, even though different words and names are applied to these beings, the amazing fact is that these words often end up translating across cultural divides to roughly the same meanings.

Another hurdle to overcome involves demonstrating how the large stone monuments were built. There are various theories, but not a single group has been able to successfully erect even a scaled down version of these structures, such as the Great Pyramid, without using some type of modern shortcut. If someone insists that they know how it was achieved, then the burden of proof is on them. Therefore, according to the rules stated above, even the skeptical community should be able to build an exact replica of the same dimensions using only the tools thought to be available to the people at that time if they ever hope to fully dismiss alternative theories. Until this task is accomplished, the question relating to its origin must remain open. Someone or some*thing* obviously accomplished this feat in the past, or else structures such as the Great Pyramid would not exist today. Of course, a counter argument could be made that even though the structures exist, it does not necessarily mean they functioned as the ancients claimed.

We must also consider another type of evidence involved in this kind of research. It is information deduced from the evidence that was unknown to the person making the claim. Consistent descriptions provided by people who have never met helps to increase the likelihood that the claim is genuine. Of course, when dealing with the Biblical texts it is not unfair to reason that many "consistencies" are in fact due to the copying and the retelling of commonly known stories. However, this does not explain why two different cultures that did not know of each other at the time, such as the Hebrews and the Native Americans, would have similar descriptions of the angels and their offspring. The ancients rarely attempted to explain why these beings appeared the way that they did—they just described them as they saw them. Later in this book, we will examine these physical descriptions and show how modern science may finally be able to explain and validate the claims.

It is my personal belief that language has provided an important link to the past that should not be overlooked as valuable evidence. Monuments and archives may crumble to dust, but we've never stopped talking. By tracing the use of words back through history, we *are* effectively using a time machine that allows a glimpse into ancient worlds and the mindsets of the people inhabiting the past. Of course, our understanding of these ideas can be severely limited if they seem completely foreign or "alien" to us today. Nevertheless, language and symbolism are still some of the best tools we have to communicate ideas and information effectively (even across time and space). Referring back to the third rule of CSICOP mentioned earlier, it states that sometimes the simplest answer most likely explains the unknown. If we take the ancient people's stories seriously and consider it in context of other evidence, perhaps the simplest answer is that they *were* in contact with otherworldly beings.

Something else important to consider in research is to not "throw the baby out with the bathwater." Some people will debunk one claim, and expect everyone to assume that everything else must be bogus, too. However, just because one facet of a theory can be disproved does not mean that every other bit of data is also false. A true skeptic follows the facts and scientific process to arrive at their conclusions by systematically proving or disproving each separate element in a claim.

Myth vs. History

Researchers of ancient mythology must develop the ability to distinguish passages that are intended to be the literal truth from those that are meant to be read as allegory. For instance, when a story tells about battles between gods or mythical creatures in the heavens, it should probably be understood as an allegorical teaching about celestial events. Unfortunately, far too many people get carried away with the story and would really like to think that it is retelling actual heroic battles between the gods. They will even begin grafting new concepts onto these stories that weren't there, such as flying saucers and atomic weapons.

The evaluations of ancient myths by researchers such as Ralph Ellis illustrate how allegory often functions in these types of text. Ellis' example concerns the ancient tale known as the *Epic of Gilgamesh*. In the story, it describes Gilgamesh's companion, called "Enkidu," as a stellar object:

> This <u>star of heaven</u> which descended like <u>a meteor from the sky</u>; which you tried to lift, but found too heavy ... This is the strong comrade, the one who brings help to his friend in need.[3]

Ellis states that possibly Enkidu represents the star Sirius, which is a companion to the constellation Orion (Gilgamesh).[4] However, I propose it could also be that Enkidu is simply meant to represent an important comet. To elaborate, Enkidu is described as being a wild man whose entire body "was shaggy with hair."[5] Comets are stellar objects often described with "tails." The word "comet" is derived from the Latin *(stella) cometa,* meaning "long haired (star), which is from the Greek *(aster) cometes,* with a similar meaning. It was not uncommon for comets to be called "hairy stars." The comparison between a comet and Enkidu becomes rather obvious at this point.

Ellis goes on to show how Gilgamesh's description matches the constellation Orion, the hunter, as he arms himself for a great battle:

> Gilgamesh took the <u>axe</u>, he slung the quiver from his shoulder, and the <u>bow</u> of Anshan, and buckled the <u>sword</u> to his <u>belt</u>; and so they were armed and ready for the journey.[6]

Enkidu, as a comet, leads Gilgamesh to battle. The story is teaching about the end of one zodiacal age and the transition into another. The figure of Orion has his bow aimed at Taurus. In this case, Gilgamesh (Orion) is to battle against the Bull of Heaven (Taurus) to usher in the Age of Aries (the Ram). Before this can happen, though, Gilgamesh encounters a strange beast called Humbaba by the Akkadians (or Huwawa to the Sumerians).

> The <u>watchman</u> ... has put on the first of his <u>seven splendours</u> but not yet the other six, let us trap him before he is armed ... At the first stroke Humbaba blazed out, but still they advanced ... and <u>seven times</u> Humbaba loosed his glory upon them ... At the third blow Humbaba fell ... Now the mountains were moved and all the hills, for the guardian of the forest was killed ... the <u>seven splendours</u> of Humbaba were extinguished.[7]

The fearsome creature was the guardian of the Bull of Heaven, and in astrological terms, the "seven splendours" is a reference to the Pleiades star cluster—a grouping of seven stars on the back of Taurus that is visible to the naked eye and nicknamed the "seven sisters." After Humbaba was slain, the back of Taurus was exposed and it was easy for Gilgamesh to kill the Bull of Heaven:

> 'Now thrust in your sword between the nape and the horns.' So Gilgamesh followed the Bull, he seized the thick of its tail, he thrust the sword between the nape and the horns and slew the Bull. When they had killed the <u>Bull of Heaven</u> they cut out its heart and gave it to Shamash (the Sun), and the brothers rested.[8]

The premise of the story takes on new meaning when the characters and symbols are interpreted allegorically as I have shown. However, this does not work for all "myths." Some of them do not seem to have any particular stellar correspondences, and may be literal events that require further in-

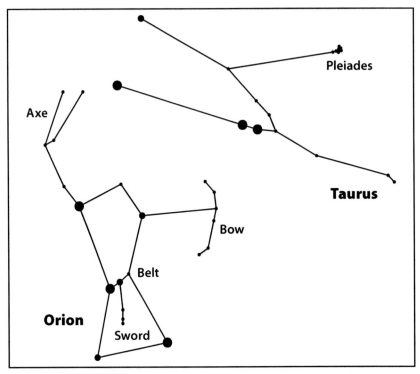

vestigation. For instance, there do not appear to be any immediate ways to interpret the stories of gods coming from heaven and mating with human women as being based on the stellar symbolism of the constellations and zodiac. Many times, these gods are called "stars" in the writings, but this seems to have been more of a title or method of recognition than an actual description—much like how we refer to major celebrities as "stars" today. In fact, this modern association may even be derived from the ancient beliefs. Lastly, while the people who recorded these events seemed to know that some of the stories were only mystery teachings to higher initiates, it is important to recognize that they believed that these gods were physical flesh and blood beings. To the modern mind, however, this seems difficult to believe and has been dismissed as mere superstition.

Today, many people believe in guardian angels and spirit guides, but without recognizing how very different they are from the awesome beings described thousands of years ago. This is not meant to deny the personal experiences of these people with what they believe are angels, but to illustrate the difference in thinking. It is highly likely that some people have misinterpreted ordinary events and wrongly attributed them to "angels." This would seem especially true since the majority of people have gotten their concepts of angels from inspirational stories and popular culture. Were they truly smiling cherubs, or fearsome creatures that inspired awe and fear? Only those who have seen them "in the flesh" would be able to answer these questions for sure.

Summary

❖ The theory presented in this book can go no further until it is properly tested and evaluated by people with the capabilities to do so.

❖ A rational, skeptical view is recommended when further researching the topics covered in this book and by other authors. However, remember to consider all possibilities, no matter how unlikely, and rule out only those that have the least amount of support based on the available evidence.

❖ It is important to understand that some stories were meant as allegorical teachings, usually involving celestial bodies and events. Other stories that do not fit into this view may be referring to literal events in history.

PART 2

The Evolution of Cuneiform Writing

Uruk IV c. 3100	Sumerian c. 2500	Old Babylonian c. 1800	Neo-Babylonian c. 600 B.C.E.	SUMERIAN *Babylonian*
				AN / DINGIR *anu* god, heaven
				APIN *epinnu* plough
				GUD *alpu* ox
				KI *ersetu* earth
				KU(A) *nūnu* fish
				KUR *šadû* mountain
				ŠAR *kirû* orchard
				ŠE *še'u* grain

The writing system used in Mesopotamia began as a pictographic and ideographic system, meaning that the earliest signs were pictures which represented objects and ideas. Over time, the scribes began using a reed stylus with a triangular tip to write on clay tablets, known as cuneiform (wedge-shaped) writing. Sometime later, the scribes found that it was more convenient to turn the clay tablets in such a way that the pictographs were rotated onto their sides. Eventually, the writing system became too unweildy because of the numerous symbols required to represent so many different concepts, so the language and writing system became conventionalized and simplified.

"Touched" by an Angel

You were born with wings. Why prefer to crawl through life?
—Jalaluddin Rumi[1]

MANY GREAT MINDS HAVE FOUND THEMSELVES ENTERTAINED by the rhetorical question concerning how many angels could dance on the end of a pin. For centuries, the answer was usually explained as "infinitely many," because angels are spiritual beings and therefore do not take up any physical amount of space. However, while this presents a great philosophical challenge, it is hardly in keeping with the ancient worldview of angels. But how did the concept of angels become so skewed? As our investigation continues, we will learn how religious authorities were able to *easily* reshape the populace's impression of such topics to their own ideology by omitting and withholding important information.

On a Wing and a Prayer

For most people, the existence of angels as purely spiritual beings is entirely acceptable within their belief systems. After all, we do not see angels flying in the sky, walking down the street, blowing their trumpets, or singing praises to God in our modern world. Yet people still choose to believe in them, and recall stories they have heard about other people's experiences with so-called angels and spirit guides. To them, it is simply a matter of faith.

In fact, the re-emergence of angels into our culture has exploded over the last thirty years. When Billy Graham published his book *Angels: God's Secret Agents* in 1975, it reintroduced the heavenly host to mainstream audiences in a heartfelt and popular way. Considered by many people to be the definitive work on angels, Graham's book has sold over three million copies worldwide since its first publication. However, these modern portrayals of angels introduced by Graham are hardly accurate when compared to the original descriptions recorded by ancient scribes, and other contemporary authors have helped to further popularize such misleading views.

Numerous books about angels soared to the religious best-seller lists shortly thereafter and have sustained the public's attention ever since. At times, publishers could scarcely keep books on store shelves—such as: Eileen Elias Freeman's *Touched by Angels,* Joan Wester Anderson's *Where Angels Walk,* Sophy Burnham's *Book of Angels* (which sold over half a million copies between 1990 and 1993), as well as Alma Daniel, Timothy Wyllie, and Andre Rahmer's *Ask Your Angels.*[2]

The belief in angels was further popularized by the New Age movement. Soon, angel focus groups and angel workshops were organized for people wanting to learn more about their heavenly brothers and sisters. Merchandisers were quick to seize the opportunity and worked together with places like the Angel Collectors Club of America to offer a seemingly unlimited supply of angel inspired collectible products, such as: "angel statues, dolls, rings, pins, watches, calendars, T-shirts, napkin rings, thank-you notes, greeting cards, plates..." and many other things.[3]

What has perhaps contributed most to the popular appeal of angels have been the heartwarming stories which share the personal encounters and experiences people have had with angels. One such story appeared in Billy Graham's *Angels: God's Secret Agents* (and later a slightly condensed version in Joan Weston Anderson's *Where Angels Walk).* It tells about a young girl desperately seeking medical help for her sick mother. Graham's account goes as such:

> Dr. S.W. Mitchell, a celebrated Philadelphia neurologist, had gone to bed after an exceptionally tiring day. Suddenly he was awakened by someone knocking on his door. Opening it he found a little girl, poorly dressed and deeply upset. She told him her mother was very sick and asked him if he would please come with her. It was a bitterly cold, snowy night, but though he was bone tired, Dr. Mitchell dressed and followed the girl...
>
> As *Reader's Digest* reports the story, he found the mother desperately ill with pneumonia. After arranging for medical care, he complimented the sick woman on the intelligence and persistence of her little daughter. The woman looked at him strangely and then said, "My daughter died a month ago." She added, "Her shoes

and coat are in the clothes closet there." Dr. Mitchell, amazed and perplexed, went to the closet and opened the door. There hung the very coat worn by the little girl who had brought him to tend to her mother. It was warm and dry and could not possibly have been out in the wintry night…

Could the doctor have been called in the hour of desperate need by an angel who appeared as this woman's young daughter? Was this the work of God's angels on behalf of the sick woman?[4]

This is truly a touching story—if it were true. Unfortunately, it is nothing more than a repackaging of the common "mysterious stranger" and "phantom hitchhiker" tales usually told around campfires. Graham offers no source other than a mention of *Reader's Digest.* Investigator Joe Nickell discovered that the story appeared almost verbatim in Margaret Ronan's *Strange Unsolved Mysteries* a whole year before Graham's book was published. Compare Graham's statement that the doctor "was awakened by someone knocking on his door" to Ronan's version that "the doorbell downstairs was ringing violently." The most notable difference was how Ronan's version suggested the young girl was a ghost, writing that she looked "almost wraithlike in the whirling snow," and that "at times she seemed to vanish into the storm…" Instead, Graham's version removes any of these references and implies that the girl was really an angel in disguise. Both versions mention that the girl had passed away a month earlier, however the mother in Graham's version says, "Her shoes and coat are in the clothes closet there." Ronan's account, on the other hand, has her say, "All I have left to remember her by are those clothes hanging on that peg over there."[5]

Like many other urban myths and legends, the two stories clearly share a number of similarities. In both stories, the clothes of the deceased little girl are presented as physical evidence to validate the encounters. Additionally, the stories attempt to sound credible by having a medical doctor as the key witness. However, none of these factors enhance the credibility of the stories or convincingly prove the existence of angels or the heavenly realms. The real intention of the story is to repackage a tale that was originally designed to frighten its audience so that it can instead become a story that inspires a very warm and comforting message assuring that everything is going to be just fine.

Other highly popular stories involving angels are known as "mysterious stranger" encounters (similar to the above story) and a subgroup called "roadside rescues." In fact, this particular genre has become clichéd due to its popularity. You may have heard similar stories, such as when devastating car accidents are prevented by the intervention of an invisible force, which yanks the steering wheel of a dozing driver at the last moment. Rosemary Ellen Guiley provides other similar scenarios, explaining, "In the roadside rescue, the mysterious stranger arrives to help the motorist stranded on a lonely road at night, or who is injured in an accident in an isolated spot. Or, human beings arrive just in the nick of time."[6] She goes on to describe a testimonial from "angel channeler and author" Jane M. Howard:

> One night, the gas pedal in Janie's car became stuck, and she ran off the freeway near Baltimore. She stopped the car by throwing the transmission into park. It would not restart, and she began to panic. It was ten P.M. and she was miles from the nearest exit. She prayed to the angels for help, and within minutes, a van pulled up, carrying a man and a woman.... The woman rolled down her window and told Janie not to be frightened, for they were Christians. Even so, many people would have been wary of strangers at night. But the angels gave Janie assurances, and she accepted a ride to a gas station. She discovered that the couple lived in a town near hers, and knew her family. They pulled off to help Janie, they said, because they had a daughter, and they hoped that if their daughter ever was in distress, she, too, would be aided.[7]

Investigator Joe Nickell poses a valid question regarding stories like those above: "Why assume that *angels,* or anything of a supernatural order, had something to do with such a mundane event?" To be fair, he recognizes that most stories like this provide some kind of "preternatural occurrence" as proof of their authenticity, such as the sudden disappearance of the stranger.[8] He then cites a woman's story about her visit to an electronics store with her son, and the mysterious young man who was able to offer some technical advice:

> I was just dumbfounded. The young man wished us a nice day and left the store. A couple of seconds later, I rushed out the door to thank him, but he was gone. He literally disappeared. The store is in the middle of the block, so you would still be able to see someone

walking down the sidewalk. Obviously, this was not an ordinary human. I still get chills when I think about it.[9]

Nickell once again points out a major flaw with this story. He asks whether or not it was really only "a couple of seconds later" or if enough time had passed for the man to enter a waiting car or neighboring store?[10] If it were truly only a few seconds later, the woman should have been able to yell or get his attention somehow before he ever reached the doors. If more time had passed, and he did get in a vehicle or go to another store, there is certainly no reason to attribute his vanishing act to someone that "was not an ordinary human." There also seems to be no reason to associate this young man with the qualities of an angelic being. I mean no insult, but it would seem to me that things must be rather boring in heaven if this alleged "angel" had nothing better to do than offer technical advice in an electronics store! An even simpler refutation of this claim is possible on account of the fact that people that frequently shop in electronic stores tend to be very well-versed in the subject of technology (sometimes even more so than the staff). For instance, if I am in an electronics store (or just as often in a book store) and I overhear someone debating with themselves about purchasing a product, or if they seem like they are searching for something, I will often ask if I can help or offer any of my expertise to them. From now on, maybe I should try to quickly vanish into thin air, too.

By now, you may be wondering why I am going through all of this trouble to disprove these "true" accounts of angels. It is simply because these stories do not match the original descriptions of angels from the ancient texts very well. Rosemary Ellen Guiley put it best when she wrote: "Popular culture portrays angels as anthropomorphic 'best friends,' which is in stark contrast to the awesome, impartial, unknowable beings of Jewish angelology and early Christian lore."[11]

Stories such as these appear to be projections of people's hopes and wishes reinterpreted in modern ways, probably to keep their faith alive. Even worse, most of these accounts cannot be verified or wrongly attribute supernatural forces (i.e. angels) to situations without proper cause. Can I prove that angels were not involved? No, I cannot. However, citing these stories as undeniable "proof" for their existence does not help the argument. If nothing else, they harm the credibility of any legitimate claim that might exist because they are promoting fiction as fact.

So, exactly how have the concepts of angels changed over time? To answer this question we'll begin with a very brief examination of what the ancient world thought of angels. This will lead us into an exploration of a book that was nearly forgotten. The book was first held in high esteem amongst various religious sects, but was later condemned as heresy when its content no longer suited their beliefs and agendas.

See No Evil, Read No Evil

The term *angel* is derived from Latin, *angelus,* which is itself derived from the Greek *ángelos* (ἄγγελος), meaning "messenger" (the double gamma "γγ" is pronounced "ng" in Greek). These messengers could be of divine or human origin. The Persians similarly referred to them as *angaros,* meaning "courier." The closest equivalent in the Old Testament Hebrew is *malak* (מלאך), which can also mean "messenger." This term is related to the Hebrew word *Melek* or *Molech* (מלך), meaning "king." Therefore, angels were known by various titles, including "kings," "princes," and "messengers." The plural form would have been *malakim* (the "-im" ending designates a plural in ancient Hebrew).

However, even though the term *could* apply to a human being, many of these "messengers" displayed characteristics and abilities that were beyond those of normal humans. This distinction will allow us to discard the cases describing ordinary people as "messengers" of God and focus our attention more closely on this other group of super-human beings. They were often identified as "holy ones,"[12] the "host of heaven,"[13] and the "sons of God,"[14] amongst many other titles.

It is important to note that these divine beings were not believed to be some kind of unseen collective merely residing in the heavenly realm. The Bible and other ancient texts clearly indicate that they were able to manifest real flesh-and-blood bodies and walk amongst humanity. More often than not, they are portrayed as males within Biblical texts. However, I tend to think that there is some gender bias at work here—mostly due to the countless descriptions of "goddesses" found in other cultures. Angels were able to sit down and eat meals,[15] carry on conversations, wrestle,[16] and even engage in sexual acts.[17] This latter behavior is highly significant and a topic that we will be investigating throughout this book.

Most people will find the concept of angels partaking in physical desires with human beings shocking or even blasphemous. After all, Jesus said that angels do not exhibit such behavior, particularly pertaining to marriage

(Matthew 22:30). However, this is a misunderstanding of the passage. Jesus only said that the angels no longer marry, but never said that they are incapable of having sex (or bearing offspring, for that matter). In fact, the context of this verse implies that the angels are no longer allowed to indulge in such human behaviors due to a highly significant event in their past. The confusion revolving around this issue is understandable, though, because it has been suppressed for a better portion of the past two-thousand years.

Where did all of this controversy originate? It was from an obscure reference in Genesis as well as from supplemental texts and teachings that expound upon it. Genesis records that "When people began to multiply on the face of the ground, and daughters were born to them, the <u>sons of God</u> saw that they were fair; and <u>they took wives for themselves</u> of all that they chose" (6:1–2). Another ancient text, now identified as the *Book of Enoch*, greatly elaborated on this ordeal.

The *Book of Enoch* (also known as *1 Enoch)* is considered to be a pseudopigraphal book (meaning that it was attributed to Enoch but not penned by him) and apocryphal (because it was not included as part of the accepted canon). It was written sometime between the third (or second) century BCE (Before the Common Era) and the first century CE in either Hebrew or Aramaic (perhaps a combination of both, but recent findings favor the latter). At that time, it was largely popular among the Jewish, early Christian, and Essene communities. The book is actually composed of several smaller books:

- *The Book of Watchers* (1 Enoch 1–36).
- *The Book of Parables* (1 Enoch 37–71) (Also known as *Similitudes of Enoch).*
- *The Book of the Heavenly Luminaries* (1 Enoch 72–82) (Also known as the *Book of Luminaries* or the *Astronomical Book).*
- *The Dream Visions* (1 Enoch 83–90) (Also called the *Book of Dreams).*
- *The Epistle of Enoch* (1 Enoch 91–105).
- *The Book of Noah* (a separate fragment often included with 1 Enoch).
- *The Book of Giants* (not included in 1 Enoch, but some scholars argue that it was originally part of it).

Fragments of *1 Enoch* have even been discovered among the Dead Sea Scrolls, verifying not only its antiquity, but also that it was held in high regard by the ancient people. In fact, nearly all of the early church fathers knew of and quoted from *Enoch* (apparently from a Greek translation of the text). Some of these people were Justin Martyr, Irenaeus, Athenagoras, Origen, Clement of Alexandria and Tertullian.[18] They accepted the authenticity of *Enoch* because of a quote in The Epistle of Jude:

> It was also about these that Enoch, in the seventh generation from Adam, prophesied, saying, "See, the Lord is coming with ten thousands of his holy ones, to execute judgment on all, and to convict everyone of all the deeds of ungodliness that they have committed in such an ungodly way, and of all the harsh things that ungodly sinners have spoken against him."
>
> Jude 14–15 NRSV

Now, compare it to a translation of the *Book of Enoch:*

> And behold! He cometh with ten thousands of His holy ones, To execute judgement upon all, And to destroy all the ungodly: And to convict all flesh, Of all the works of their ungodliness which they have ungodly committed, And of all the hard things which ungodly sinners have spoken against Him.
>
> 1 Enoch 1:9
> R.H. Charles Translation[19]

52

However, one brief quotation is not enough to merit any major support for the book. In fact, some later church fathers did not approve of the subject matter throughout *Enoch* and even tried to strip Jude of its canonical status just because it referenced an "apocryphal" work. Nevertheless, as our investigation unfolds, you will see how the ideas introduced in *Enoch* have permeated many important areas of the Bible and other religious texts.

But what was it within *Enoch* that made so many of the church fathers uncomfortable? It was because the book made implications that were contrary to their accepted doctrines—notably that angels were able to take physical form and have sexual relations with humans. Also, they had been teaching for quite some time that the "fallen angels" were cast out of heaven with Satan because of their pride.[20] Instead, the texts of *Enoch* recorded that the figure of Satan had nothing to do with the fall, and it was instead on account of the angels' physical lusts that they were exiled from heaven.

By the fourth century CE, the Church found that was it much easier to teach that fallen angels were shadowy, non-physical beings capable of tempting humans into sinful behavior merely by whispering evil thoughts into their ears. However, by putting a face on this dark force of evil—like the *Book of Enoch* did—the psychological effect conjured by the church fathers became jeopardized. The "Big Bad" was much more effective if people believed that it was lurking just around every corner.[21]

Filastrius, the bishop of Brescia, openly condemned the *Book of Enoch* as heresy,[22] and it became discredited after the Council of Laodicea in 364 CE. Even before that, the rabbinical community had begun to denounce the text and its views of angels. In fact, during the second century CE, the Rabbi Simeon ben Jochai actually declared a curse upon anyone who believed that *Enoch's* account involved "real" angels—let alone angels that could have sex![23] This was despite the fact that the Septuagint (the Greek translation of the Old Testament that was popular at the time), specifically used the term *angelos* in place of "sons of God."

The demand grew for an alternative theory that could serve double duty: it had to discredit the prevailing account of the fallen angels as described in *Enoch,* and it still had to fit the accepted scriptures plausibly. It was found within the arguments of Julius Africanus (c. 200–245 CE), who preferred to believe that the incident in Genesis 6 did not involve angels at all—merely human beings. Instead, he reasoned that the "sons of God" were really men from the righteous line of Seth (the third son of Adam and Eve after Cain murdered Abel). Therefore, the "daughters of men" were from the ungodly line of Cain. This became known as the "Sethite and Cainite explanation." Ironically, this view created *many* significant contradictions and theological problems—a mistake that Julius should have certainly realized. Nevertheless, since the view satisfied the above conditions it gained widespread acceptance from other Church leaders.

The war against the *Book of Enoch* was in full effect between the fourth and fifth centuries. The Church Father Chrysostom (c. 346–407 CE) vented his outrage against anyone who believed such absurd lies:

> Here is, first, the most audacious idea, of which we are going to show you the absurdity, by presenting to your meditation the true meaning of the Scripture, so that you do not listen to those who utter such blasphemy…. They say that it is not men that are referred to here, but angels, and that it is the angels that are called "sons of God."… It would be folly to accept such insane blasphemy, saying that an incorporeal and spiritual nature could have united itself to human bodies!
>
> Saint Chrysostom, "Homelies sur la Genèse"[24]

Chrysostom demonstrated through this rant that his real problem was not what the sons of God purportedly did, but that it was "insane blasphemy" to think that angels could ever have physical bodies like humans. Chrysostom's opinion found favor with other officials, such as Caesarius of Arles.[25]

As we have previously noted, acceptance of the Sethite explanation produced many problems. Some of these are very easy to expose. First, nowhere within the Bible does it directly associate the "sons of God" with the "sons of Seth." This view must be imposed upon the text.[26] Occasionally, there may be instances where regular humans are referred to as "sons of God," but these are rare. More often than not, the phrase is designated for divine beings. Second, the Bible clearly says "daughters of men [humankind]"— not "daughters of Cain." It would have been much more effective to write "daughters of Cain" if that is what the author intended (or "sons of Seth" for that matter).

Most importantly, the Sethite view attempts to strip the story of any supernatural overtones. This creates a tremendous self-contradiction within the text. Not only does it try to remove the angels from the story, it does not even offer a viable explanation for the resulting offspring of these unions. Genesis 6:4 records that the offspring of these unions were giants! Additionally, it contradicts other passages in the New Testament that clearly accept the supernatural version.[27] After going to such great lengths to disprove the *Book of Enoch's* version of events, the Sethite version falls embarrassingly short of explaining why human-to-human marriages would result in children that were notoriously non-human.

Despite these problems (among others), this view gained widespread acceptance as the answer to the problem created by *1 Enoch.* By the fifth century, the final steps were taken to ban the "heretical" book and all copies that remained in libraries and churches were either lost or destroyed so that it could never be read again.

It worked… for a while.

The Rediscovery of the Forbidden Tome

For over a thousand years, the book remained forgotten by the general population. From time to time, whispers would surface about a secret book—one that was quoted in Jude and by early church fathers. However, such books most often turned out to be fakes or texts other than the elusive *Book of Enoch.*

The book's name alone conjured a great desire within scholars and mystics alike to discover it. The Elizabethan astrologer, alchemist and scientist, Dr. John Dee, even hired an alleged psychic, Edward Kelley, in an attempt to learn the secrets of the book from the angels themselves. Through Kelley's mediumship, Dee did end up with a pseudo *"Book of Enoch"* and an "Enochian language of the angels"—but this was not the authentic book that he had been seeking.

Nearly two centuries later, a Scottish explorer by the name of James Bruce had learned of some convincing evidence that *Enoch* had been preserved in Ethiopia. He was a very tall man and highly intelligent.[28] He also spoke several different languages, including Aramaic, Hebrew, and *Ge'ez,* the written language of ancient Ethiopia. He delighted in researching ancient history and frequently visited parts of Europe, North Africa, and the Holy Land.[29] Following up on the rumors, Bruce spent a great amount of time and effort questioning the monks and abbots of the Ethiopian monasteries. He was greatly rewarded for his diligence, however, because he learned that the Ethiopic Church had indeed preserved the banned book. In fact, he was able to secure not one but *three* copies, which he brought back to Europe in

1773. One was on consignment to the National Library of Paris, another was donated to Oxford's Bodleian Library, and the third found its "proper home" "...amongst the books of Scripture," according to Bruce's own words.[30]

Excitement and news of the discovery quickly spread and steps were taken to immediately begin translation of the copy in Paris. However, no translation from the *Ge'ez* text came into existence until *forty-eight years later!* Unfortunately, the influence of Newtonian science and the Industrial Revolution during the late eighteenth and early nineteenth centuries greatly diminished the popularity of the church in England. The majority of people were no longer interested in church matters—and even less in the folly of angels. Sadly, this delay meant that Bruce never got to see a translation of the text available to the public before his own death in 1794.[31]

Finally, in 1821, the University of Oxford released the first English translation by the professor and Reverend Richard Laurence. The professor labored for hundreds of hours, painstakingly translating the *Ge'ez* language into suitable English from the copy available at the Bodleian Library. His work also required careful comparisons and cross-referencing with all of the known fragments that were in Greek.[32]

After the release, the *Book of Enoch* caused quite a sensation and had everyone from scholars to the general public discussing it. The subject matter of fallen angels lusting after mortal women particularly caught the attention of Romantic writers, who quickly seized upon the opportunity to incorporate such details into their own works. These included such works as *Heaven and Earth – A Mystery* by George Gordon, Lord Byron in 1821, and *The Love of the Angels – A Poem, with Memoir* by the Irish poet, Thomas Moore, in 1823. It probably even had an influence on Bram Stoker's classic horror story *Dracula* (1897), among many other pieces of literature and art.[33]

The popularity of *Enoch* continued to increase and scholars began finding more fragments hidden away in long forgotten places. New translations were made in both English and German. An alleged "sequel" known as the *Book of the Secrets of Enoch* (or *2 Enoch)* was even discovered in Russia and translated in 1894. Then, R.H. Charles released the authoritative English translation in 1912.[34]

Despite the efforts of the Church to suppress the teachings of *Enoch,* it has managed to survive—unwilling to be silenced. However, most people are largely unaware of this priceless historical work. It touches upon many topics that are cornerstones of major religions such as Judaism and Christianity, but is largely unrecognized. In fact, for some time it was widely believed that the *Book of Enoch* must have been written much later than first thought, because the content of the book contained so many Christian elements—but *before* the existence of Christianity! However, the fragments that have been discovered—primarily those of the Dead Sea Scrolls—have proven just the opposite. The Bible did not influence the *Book of Enoch*—it was *Enoch* that influenced the Bible.

The original story of the fallen angels may have been nearly forgotten if it had not been reintroduced by the discovery of the *Book of Enoch*. These angels revealed to the human race things previously hidden from the world of mortals. They mated with our people, producing mutant offspring of giant stature and ferocity. We are told that the angels were punished for their misdeeds, but their influence can still be felt in today's religions. The implications of such legends lead to many unsettling questions: What were they, exactly? How did they get here? And most importantly, could it ever happen again?

Summary

❖ Popular views of angels suggest that they are spiritual "best friends" that live in heaven and occasionally come to the aid of a person that is in trouble. However, this is in stark contrast to the ancient worldview of angels, which believed that angels were physical flesh-and-blood beings that possessed superhuman powers and sometimes even frightening physical appearances.

❖ The term "angel" (ἄγγελος) is derived from words that referred to a being that was a "messenger," as well as a "king" or a "prince." These beings were not merely unseen spiritual forces, but the physical representatives of God on the earth.

❖ The *Book of Enoch* described events that transpired between "fallen" angels and humans—a theme common throughout many ancient cultures. This view was predominant for several centuries until Church Officials declared such accounts to be blasphemous because they refused to believe that angels could appear to humans in physical forms as portrayed within the writings of *Enoch*.

❖ After being nearly destroyed and forgotten, the *Book of Enoch* was rediscovered in the late eighteenth-century by the explorer James Bruce. The translation of *Enoch* into modern English revealed a significant influence upon the authors of the Bible. Additionally, many important concepts regarding angels and other Biblical themes have been misunderstood for centuries because they lacked the proper context provided by *Enoch*.

THE FALLEN ONES

Qui custodiet ipsos custodes?
Who watches the watchers?

—Juvenal[1]

THE *BOOK OF ENOCH* IS NOT THE ONLY ANCIENT SOURCE you can turn to for further information concerning "the fallen ones." Throughout most of the world, ancient cultures have described gods or god-like beings that came to earth and taught them about agriculture and the ways of civilization. But who or what were these beings and what happened to them? Did they have humanity's best interests at heart—or was there a more sinister agenda? Our investigation now turns to a group of beings virtually unheard of by a majority of people, even though they were the backbone of most world religions. Until recently, their names were only whispered within small circles—and their deeds have haunted the minds of those who study the ancient past.

The Watchers

For as the days of Noah were, so will be the coming of the Son of Man. For as in those days before the flood they were eating and drinking, marrying and giving in marriage, until the day Noah entered the ark, and they knew nothing until the flood came and swept them all away, so too will be the coming of the Son of Man.

Matthew 24:37–39 NRSV

Most people are familiar with the story of Noah's Ark and the flood that destroyed all living creatures except for those saved by Noah and his family. However, most people are unaware *why* everything was destroyed. The

Bible simply states that humanity was "wicked," but offers very little explanation about what caused this condition or why the world was deserving
of such punishment.

The reason becomes clear when the Bible is compared to similar myths
from other cultures. It was because "fallen" angels had come to earth and
began producing offspring with human beings. This very small and obscure
section of the Bible is often skipped over by many people—others merely
read it without understanding. These passages have been highly censored
and repeatedly misrepresented; however, they may prove crucial to not
only the history of humanity, but our understanding of the future as well.
We have already examined part of this myth in the previous chapter, but
now we are going to dig much, much deeper. The passage shortly preceding the flood story reads:

> When people began to multiply on the face of the ground, and
> daughters were born unto them, the <u>sons of God</u> saw that they were
> fair; and they <u>took wives for themselves</u> of all that they chose. Then
> the LORD said, "My spirit shall not abide in mortals forever, for
> they are flesh; their days shall be one hundred twenty years." The
> <u>Nephilim</u> were on the earth in those days—and also afterward—
> when the <u>sons of God</u> went in to the daughters of humans, who
> bore children to them. These were the <u>heroes</u> that were of old, war-
> riors of renown.
>
> Genesis 6:1–4 NRSV

Most biblical scholars believe that the sons of God are heavenly angels, which
was the original intention of this passage. This is supported elsewhere in the
biblical texts,[2] as well as in apocryphal sources such as the *Book of Enoch.*
However, as the last chapter has demonstrated, the belief that angelic beings could take on physical bodies and have sexual relations with humans
soon fell into disfavor with church officials.

Sons of God in the Hebrew language is rendered as *bene ha'elohim*
(בני האלהים pronounced "beney-ha-el-o-heem").[3] They are the heavenly
angels that desired to "know" mortal women (and possibly men).[4] These
angels are the same beings referred to as the Watchers in the *Book of Enoch.*
According to the ancient lore collected by Raven Grimassi, the Watchers
once had physical bodies of matter, but evolved into non-physical Beings

of Light long before humankind came into existence. The Watchers were associated with the stars, and perhaps had even come from the stars in the very remote past. Later, some Stellar cults even considered them to be "stars" who had descended to earth.[5]

So where do the Nephilim figure into the story? The accepted view of academia is that the Nephilim are the offspring of these angels—but that may be only partially correct. In the King James Version of the Bible, the word "Nephilim" is translated as "giants." The reason is attributed to legends stating that the union of angels and humans produced gigantic offspring, often of a malevolent nature, and could be partially based on the Greek myth of the Titans. In some later translations of the Bible, the original Hebrew word has been restored because it does not seem to directly translate as "giants," and scholars cannot agree on its exact meaning. Therefore, the word remains un-translated in most modern Bibles.

In Hebrew, Nephilim is found written in the Bible two ways as נפילים and נפלים (pronounced "ne-fee-leem"), and is often translated as "giants." However, some Biblical scholars prefer to translate the word as "fallen ones." But what was the word meant to convey to its audience? To find out, we should look into its origins.

It is generally agreed that Nephilim is derived from the root verb *nephal* (נפל). Michael S. Heiser, an ancient language scholar, has demonstrated that a subtle difference in the spelling of Nephilim (נפילים in Numbers 13:33 has an additional *yod* "י") indicates that the original root must have been the *Aramaic* form of nephal, rather than Hebrew. This means that the original Aramaic word would have been *"Nephilin"* (נפילין) pronounced "ne-fee-leen"). Since the standard plural ending "-in" was for nouns of Aramaic origin, the editors of the Hebrew texts substituted the "-im" ending when it was adapted into Hebrew. The significance of this detail will be discussed shortly.[6]

The most common meanings of nephal are:

1. To fall (to the ground)
2. To fall (as in battle)
3. To be cast down
4. To desert a location
5. To fail[7]

More than likely, this is where the reference to "fallen angels" originated. But which meaning or meanings are most appropriate and do they apply to the angelic parents or the hybrid offspring? Usually, the term "fallen" is meant to imply angelic beings that have turned towards darkness and evil. However, that does not exactly fit the above definitions. The first example implies a fall or descent to the ground—but if it meant to imply a descent from a high location to a lower one, or a journey of some kind, the proper term *yarad* (יָרַד) would suit better, not Nephilim.

The second example refers to warriors who "fall" in battle and die. The problem at this point in the story is that the Bible doesn't state that these are *dead* warriors.[8] In fact, it points out that both the angels and their offspring were *living* and able to reproduce more of their kind. Another possibility is that the "dead" meaning has been applied to these beings *after* their physical bodies have been destroyed. Then, when the tales were written down much later, everyone recognized them as the spirits of "dead warriors."

The third meaning of being "cast down" is the closest in the sense of referring to evil angels cast down by God from heaven. But it is debatable if this should be the *primary* meaning because it suggests a negative experience, yet many cultures spoke positively of these angels. The fourth definition concerns the desertion of a location, which fits with other descriptions of these angels when we are told that they willingly chose to leave their "home" or "domain," as you will see shortly.[9] Finally, the last meaning of failure can be stretched to fit the idea that the angels failed to obey their commands and is supported by texts such as the *Book of Jubilees*.[10]

There is another yet inherent problem with the term Nephilim. As Heiser has demonstrated in his papers, the above examples would require modified spellings of Nephilim depending on their usage. For instance, some research-ers have interpreted the term as "to fall upon" (i.e. attack) in battle—but this would require it to be rendered "Nophelim." This spelling, however, is not found anywhere in the ancient texts. Others argue that it was meant as a passive term for "those who are fallen" (through some outside force), but the construction of this form would be "Nephulim." This is also incorrect, but Heiser notes that the meaning is *possible* if the root was the Aramaic form of nephal, as we have already observed. If correct, this means that the term was intended to mean "those who fell/were fallen." Hence, the implication is that these beings were "spiritually fallen," and therefore "evil."[11]

However, I must respectfully disagree with Heiser's conclusion—at least partially. While it is plainly evident that the Nephilim were often considered to be the bad guys of yore, it seems wrong to insist that *all* of them were truly evil incarnate—especially because of a single word associated with them. For instance, the description of the sons of God and the Nephilim in Genesis 6 seems mostly neutral (however, the story *is* directly preceding the onset of the Flood). Also, and perhaps more importantly, our investigation of these beings in other cultures will show that many of them were considered benevolent. There is good and bad in everything, and it is through the actions of an individual (even an angel) that determines their nature.

I believe that the word Nephilim is best defined as a race of beings that abandoned their heavenly realm and "fell" or descended to earth—some of whom chose to violate the rules set forth by God, and whose punishments were consequently applied to their offspring. Essentially, the word Nephilim was intended to encompass multiple meanings instead of only one. After examining some of the previously mentioned stories and other ones throughout this investigation, it appears that the ancient scribes also understood it this way.

So, how can I justify that the title "fallen" does not necessarily imply that the subjects in question are purely evil? It is really quite simple after studying the surrounding issues regarding this matter. Most names in the Bible are actually descriptive titles or clues to a character's function in a story. For instance, the name *Adam* (אדם) simply means "man" and *Eve* (חוה) means "life" or "life-giver"—all of which are correspondent titles. Quite often, merely observing the meaning of a name or title given to a character will reveal their purpose in the story.

But if the title of Nephilim encompasses multiple meanings and can be broadly understood as "the fallen ones," or "those who were cast down," or even "the deserters," what could that have meant in the ancient world? Many mystical teachings describe the earthly plane as being in the midst of several different levels or layers of a heavenly realm. These levels are interconnected, but appear separate because they are operating on different "vibratory frequencies." As a result, a higher vibration frequency might be considered "up," while a lower vibration frequency would be "down." The following example will better explain this concept by using some basic scientific observations.

Imagine tiny particles of matter that are gently vibrating in their neutral state. If we continually decrease the surrounding temperature, the particles will begin to slow down and eventually "stop" in a frozen state. Conversely, applying heat will make the particles react by increasing their speed and making their motion more erratic. Now, consider that the neutral state would be matter that is present in the earthly realm. The "lower" realms would consist of the lesser vibratory particles, whereas the frantic hot particles would be "higher."

We can take this analogy a step further by comparing it to the different states of water. It is a liquid while in the neutral state. The reduction in temperature will eventually result in a transition to a "solid" state (ice), while boiling will spread the molecules apart so that it turns into a gas (water vapor). Throughout the entire process, it is still H_2O, but it is able to transition between these different states of matter. Now, imagine that these different states of matter were actually transitioning into alternate realms of existence. Perhaps this is the message that the ancient texts were trying to convey about the angels?

Applying this kind of thinking shows that the "sons of God" and the "Nephilim" may be the same beings, but with different titles. Both terms are thrown together in the same verse, seemingly as if they are separate. However, if we understand this as a change in title, it makes more sense. The "sons of God" is a title reserved for angels when in their heavenly domain ("up")—but when they "descend" or "fall" to earth, they are lowering their vibratory frequency and the new title of Nephilim, or "fallen ones" applies.[12] An example of a single person having their name changed to reflect their role in the story is that of *Jacob* (יעקב) being renamed *Israel* (ישראל) after wrestling with an angel.[13]

While this view is certainly at odds with traditional academia, it does make logical sense when partnered with surrounding evidence. A single person or group can obviously have different names or labels applied to them depending on what characteristics are intended to be shown. After all, the Bible contains numerous different names and descriptions that are used to express the many different aspects of God.

This also explains the seemingly odd contradiction of why only Noah's family and the animals in the ark were supposed to survive, and yet the Nephilim apparently weren't wiped out as intended. The verse concerning the Nephilim states: *"The Nephilim were on* [some read: in] *the earth in those days—and also afterward—when the sons of God went in to the daughters of humans, who bore children to them"* (Genesis 6:3).[14] The alleged reason for the flood was that God was upset with the wickedness of mankind (instigated by some of the angels), and perhaps much of the human race even contained angelic bloodlines.[15] Noah was instructed to build an ark and to save two of every species of animal, and seven of every "clean" species of animal, while everything else was left to perish. However, the Bible clearly states that the Nephilim were on the earth both *before* the flood as well as *after* it! Apparently, the near total genocide of an entire planet was an exercise in futility if the eradication of these beings was the reason for the flood.[16] As you will see later, the Watchers and/or Nephilim were able to return to the earthly realm because they were able to escape the devastation. Curiously, there is also another interesting note concerning this passage. It states that the "Nephilim were *on the earth* in those days," but some translations state that they were "in" the earth. Perhaps this means that they were living under the ground. In light of my new explanation, though, perhaps it suggests they were *in* the earthly dimension.

Nevertheless, this is all still such a very small part of the Bible that most people may feel it is insignificant. After all, if it was so important, then shouldn't there be more information about it? Why didn't they learn this in Sunday School? Well, there is more information, and it's contained in the apocryphal *Book of Enoch* mentioned earlier. This book was regarded very highly among the ancient priesthoods and is referenced or quoted numerous times both in the Old and New Testaments. The concept of angelic beings from heaven becoming flesh and blood on earth was also well understood at the time this book was in circulation. It was only after the church fathers began to object to the idea of angels engaging in sexual relations that the book fell out of favor. The comparison between *1 Enoch* and chapter six of Genesis is apparent immediately from the following passage:

> And it came to pass when the children of men had multiplied that in those days were born unto them beautiful and comely daughters. And the <u>angels</u>, the <u>children of heaven</u>, saw and lusted after them, and said to one another: "Come, let us choose us wives from among the children of men and beget us children." And <u>Semjâzâ</u>, who was their leader, said unto them: "I fear ye will not indeed agree to do this deed, and I alone shall have to pay the penalty of a great sin." And they all answered him and said: "Let us all swear an oath, and all bind ourselves by mutual imprecations not to abandon this plan but do this thing." Then sware they all together and bound themselves by mutual imprecations upon it. And they

were in all two hundred; who <u>descended</u> (in the days) of <u>Jared</u> on the summit of <u>Mount Hermon</u>, and they called it Mount Hermon, because they had sworn and bound themselves by mutual imprecations upon it.

1 Enoch 6:1–6

R.H. Charles Translation

Obviously, this is the same situation described in Genesis, except with more detail. Now, we actually have a name for the angelic leader, as well as a little more insight into their intentions—not to mention that about two hundred individuals were involved. In addition, this passage clearly states that the beings were *angels,* and not humans as the later church fathers taught using the Sethite and Cainite view. The angels are also referred to as the "children of heaven," which is synonymous with "sons of God."

The name of the angelic leader is *Semjâzâ* (שמעזיז or שמהזאי pronounced "Shem-yaw-za"). The alternate spelling *Shemyaza* will be used throughout this text to help clarify which angel is being referenced, since there are several other variations of the name given in the texts. We also learn from this passage that Shemyaza is having second thoughts about their mission. However, once all of the other angels agree to the oath, he proceeds as intended.

It is also of great importance to point out that the *Book of Enoch* specifically states that the angels *descended*—even going so far as to mention that it happened during the "days of Jared." What might not be immediately apparent is that the name *Jared* ("Yarad" ירד), which refers to the father of Enoch, literally means "descent." In fact, the *Book of Jubilees* states that Jared was named "descent" for the very reason that during his time the angels descended to the earth.[17] The passage also mentions that the angels descended on the "summit of Mount Hermon." *Hermon* (חרמון) is sometimes transliterated as *Chermown* (pronounced "kher-mone"). Generally, it can mean "sanctuary," but we also find that it offers a multitude of implications upon further inspection. Since it is derived from the primitive root "Charam," the word can also infer that Mount Hermon was dedicated to *destruction, extermination,* or *to place a curse upon something.*

After the angels descended and women gave birth to their offspring, the *Book of Enoch* describes how the earth had become full of wickedness, bloodshed and anarchy. The souls of human beings killed by the angels and their children cried out to the gates of heaven and the holy angels addressed the Lord of heaven:[18]

> Thou seest what <u>Azâzêl</u> hath done, who hath taught all unrighteousness on earth and <u>revealed the eternal secrets which were (preserved) in heaven, which men were striving to learn</u>: And Semjâzâ, to whom Thou has given authority to bear rule over his associates. And they have gone to the daughters of men upon the earth, and have slept with the women, and have defiled themselves, and <u>revealed to them all kinds of sins</u>.
>
> 1 Enoch 9:6–8

Just what were these "eternal secrets" that the angels taught to humanity? The *Book of Jubilees* states that the reason the angels were sent to earth was to instruct mankind and to teach them, but instead they got carried away and became infatuated with the lovely mortal women.[19] It is also very intriguing that the "sins" revealed to humans were common knowledge *recognized* in heaven and reserved for *use in heaven!* Therefore, the implication is that these secrets were not bad—only that they were not supposed to be revealed to humanity until a later time.

The following is a list compiled from the *Book of Enoch* (8:1–4) describing the main fallen angels and what they taught to mankind:

1. 'Armârôs – Taught the resolving of enchantments.
2. Araqiêl (Arakiel) – Taught the signs of the earth.
3. Azâzêl – Taught the making of knives, swords, shields, and breastplates; the skills of metalworking, antimony, the creation of bracelets and ornaments, coloring tinctures for the beautification of women, etc.
4. Barâqîjâl (Baraqel) – Taught astrology.
5. Ezêquêêl (Ezekeel) – Taught the knowledge of clouds.
6. Kôkabêl (Kawkabel) – Taught about the constellations.[20]
7. Sariêl – Taught the course of the moon.
8. Semjâzâ (Shemyaza) – Taught enchantments, root-cuttings.
9. Shamshiêl – Taught the signs of the sun.[21]

The "Hanging Angel" of Rosslyn Chapel. Could this be a portrayal of Shemyaza?

Most of what the angels taught humans does not appear to be evil or a "sin," with the exception of Azazel's handiwork concerning killing and warfare.[22] The focus of what the other angels taught concerned meteorology and astronomy. Even the leader, Shemyaza, seems to have been rather harmless and taught agriculture and herbalism,[23] in addition to enchantments (magick).[24] Of course, some people may consider this specific art unholy—however, it's not the purpose of this book to argue for or against such opinions.

In the *Zohar*, a Jewish book of mysticism, Shemyaza allegedly had two sons by one of Eve's daughters. These children reportedly had insatiable appetites, consisting of thousands of camels, horses, and oxen that were consumed daily.[25] When the holy archangels cast judgment on the fallen angels, Shemyaza repented for his sins and was found not deserving of punishment in hell. Ashamed, he eternally suspended himself between heaven and earth in the constellation of Orion after the gates to heaven were closed to him.[26] This is probably associated with a now lost legend concerning a mighty giant who rebelled against God but was bound and placed in the sky to be identified as Orion, the hunter.[27] There is even speculation that Shemyaza is portrayed at Rosslyn Chapel in Scotland by a mysterious stone carving at the eastern wall of an angel hanging upside down and bound in rope.[28]

In fact, the association of Shemyaza with Orion further adds to the confusion of whether the Watchers and the Nephilim should be considered separate or the same. The Aramaic root of *nephila* not only means "giant" but is also used when referring to the constellation Orion. We find the same connections in other cultures, too. The Akkadian name for Orion was *šitaddalu*, "the broad man/giant," and the Arabic name was *al-jabbâr*, also meaning "the giant."[29] In the book of Job (38:31), another reference to a giant or angel restrained in the heavens is mentioned when God rebukes Job by asking, "Can you bind the chains of the Pleiades, or loose the cords of Orion?"

However, even though Shemyaza was guilty of his crimes, Azazel seems to have been the main culprit in teaching humans how to kill and make weapons for warfare. He also continued to feed temptation by showing women how to use makeup and other cosmetic techniques, further enhancing their sex appeal to the other angels.[30] The *Book of Enoch* states that because of the severity of these sins, Azazel would be blamed for the entire crime:

> And the whole earth has been corrupted through the works that were taught by Azâzêl; to him ascribe all sin.
>
> 1 Enoch 10:8

The punishment carried out by the holy archangels against Azazel is quite severe:

> And again the Lord said to Raphael: "Bind Azâzêl hand and foot, and cast him into the darkness: and make an opening in the desert, which is in the Dûdâêl, and cast him therein. And place upon him rough and jagged rocks, and cover him with darkness, and let him abide there for ever, and cover his face that he may not see light. And on the day of the great judgment he shall be cast into the fire."
>
> 1 Enoch 10:4–6

The "darkness" that is referred to is most likely the abyss mentioned in the book of Revelation. It is the area reserved for the angels in everlasting punishment. This is very similar to the Greek myth concerning the banishment of the Titans to Tartarus, an abyss far below the realm of Hades. It also seems that the method of banishing him into the abyss is through an "opening in the desert," where he is to remain. Additionally, the Old Testament book of Leviticus describes how a sacrificial goat is offered to Azazel by sending it out into the open desert:

> He [Aaron] shall take the two goats and set them before the Lord at the entrance of the tent of meeting; and Aaron shall cast lots on the two goats, one lot for the Lord and the other lot for Azazel. Aaron shall present the goat on which the lot fell for the Lord, and offer it as a sin offering; but the goat on which the lot fell for Azazel shall be presented alive before the Lord to make atonement over it, it may be sent away into the wilderness to Azazel…Then Aaron shall lay both his hands on the head of the live goat, and confess over it

all the iniquities of the people of Israel, and all their transgressions, all their sins, putting them on the head of the goat, and <u>sending it away into the wilderness</u> by means of someone designated for the task. The goat shall bear on itself all their iniquities to a barren region; and the goat shall be set free in the wilderness.

Leviticus 16:6–10, 21–22 NRSV

This is where the term "scapegoat" originates. If a character's name or title does indeed denote their role in the story as was suggested earlier, we find that the name *Azazel* (עֲזָאזֵל pronounced "az-ah-zel") is translated as *scapegoat* in the Old Testament. This is a fitting appellation for an angel that is punished for the crimes committed by others. The ritual described above concerning the sacrificial goat further supports this theory. It should also be noted that a more literal meaning of Azazel's name is "God strengthens;"[31] and when referred to as Azza ("the strong"), he is sometimes confusingly interchanged with Shemy<u>aza</u> ("the strong name").[32]

Even though Azazel is blamed for the entire crime and punished, the rest of the Watchers are not forgiven for their transgressions. Even their children are to be destroyed before their parents' eyes:

And I Enoch was blessing the Lord of majesty and the King of the ages, and lo! the <u>Watchers</u> called me—Enoch the scribe—and said to me: "Enoch, thou scribe of righteousness, go, declare to the <u>Watchers of heaven who have left the high heaven</u>, the holy eternal place, and have defiled themselves with women, and have done as the children of earth do, and have taken unto themselves wives: 'Ye have wrought great destruction on the earth: And ye shall have no peace nor forgiveness of sin: and insamuch as they delight themselves in their children, <u>The murder of their beloved ones shall they see</u>, and over the destruction of their children shall they lament, and shall make supplication unto eternity, but mercy and peace shall ye not attain.'"

1 Enoch 12:3–6

Here, the Watchers are clearly labeled as those "who have left the high heaven." In other words, they abandoned their original dwelling place, which fits again with one of the definitions of Nephilim as "deserters." Another example is found in the New Testament:

> And the angels who did not keep their own position, but left their proper dwelling, he has kept in eternal chains [or pits] in the deepest darkness for the judgment of the great Day.
>
> Jude 6 NRSV

As stated earlier, the word Nephilim is usually reserved for the children of the Watchers. However, considerable evidence has already been shown that it may not necessarily be so. Nephilim may still indeed refer to the children, but not exclusively. It may be the result of their divine heritage that they have inherited this title. Unfortunately, there simply is not enough direct material to conclude one way or the other with absolute certainty.

Part of the reason the Nephilim are considered separate from the angels is because they are described as being gigantic in size. This may indeed have been the case. So let's consider some of the possibilities. In the book of Numbers, the spies give a report after seeing the descendents of Anak in the town:[33]

> So they brought to the Israelites an unfavorable report of the land that they had spied out, saying, "The land that we have gone through as spies is a land that devours its inhabitants; and all the people that we saw in it are of great size. There we saw the Nephilim (the Anakites come from the Nephilim); and to ourselves we seemed like grasshoppers, and so we seemed to them."
>
> Numbers 13:32–33 NRSV

According to this report, the spies apparently saw people that were very large. Exactly how large we do not know. The comparison between themselves and grasshoppers is quite imaginative, but it is difficult to accept. Another possibility is that they simply exaggerated the size to scare everyone else so that they wouldn't have to enter the land. Yet another idea to consider is that the Nephilim could have been standing guard high atop a tower, and the spies would have appeared as grasshoppers to them.

It is important to remember that the Bible itself clearly states that the Nephilim were on the earth again after the flood. Somehow, they were not completely eradicated as was intended. In fact, traces of the Watchers and Nephilim can be found in nearly every culture throughout the ancient world. This now requires us to delve deeper into the nature of angels and gods, and how they may have returned to the earthly realm.

Gods or Angels?

Recall that the term angel is derived from the Greek *ángelos* (ἄγγελος), and simply means "messenger." These messengers could be of divine or human origin. The closest equivalent in the Old Testament Hebrew is *malakim* (מלאכים), derived from the root *malak* (מלאך), which refers to a "messenger." This word is also very similar in sound to the Hebrew word *Melek* or *Molech* (מלך), meaning "king." However, there are many other words used to refer to angelic beings, none of which necessarily help to clarify whether or not they should be considered gods.

One of the many names for God in the Old Testament is *Elohim* (אלהים pronounced "el-o-heem"). It is used over two-thousand times throughout the Old Testament, and in addition to being translated as "god," it can also mean: gods, goddess, divine rulers, angels, a godlike being(s), and judge(s). The shortened form of this title is *El* (אל), which also means god, mighty man, and strength. This is also a common ending to many names in Hebrew, especially those of angels: Michael, Raphael, Uriel, Gabriel and even Azazel. El is not limited to just the Hebrew language, as it was also a common word in many of the surrounding cultures in the Middle East as well as in Europe. In fact, several fascinating connections begin to develop when various words from different areas and cultures are compared to one another.

> Sumerian *el:* "brightness" or "shining"
> Akkadian *ilu:* "radiant one"
> Babylonian *ellu:* "the shining one"
> Old Welsh *ellu:* "a shining being"
> Old Irish *aillil:* "shining"
> English *elf:* "shining being"
> Anglo-Saxon *aelf:* "radiant being"[34]

In the Akkadian language, *il* 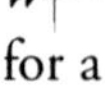 or *ilu*  was the equivalent of the Hebrew El. One of the names for a god was *ilana,*[35] which combined the shortened Il along with Ana, one of the supreme gods. This "sky" god was known as *Anu* (Babylonian) or *An* (Sumerian: ✳), which meant both "sky" and "Heaven," and was personified as being masculine.[36]

The earth was considered to be the goddess *Ki* (Sumerian: ⬦ pronounced "Kee"). Ki may have also been identified with the ancient goddess *Ninmah,* the "great queen"—and *Ninhursag,* "queen of the (cosmic) mountain."[37] Ninhursag was also recognized by other names and titles such as: Mamma, Mami and Mammitum.[38] It is from these titles that we get the words "mom" and "mommy."

According to Sumerian beliefs, the universe was called *an-ki* ✳⬦, literally "Heaven-Earth." It was believed that these two realms were united at the beginning of time. However, according to the myth referred to as the *Creation of the Pickax,* Enlil, one of the chief gods, separated An (Heaven) from Ki (Earth).[39]

Many of the gods referred to in Mesopotamian myths are known as the *Anunnaki*—a title that probably means "those of royal blood" or "princely offspring."[40] The Anunnaki were the old, chthonic (underworld) deities under the leadership of Anu (Heaven)[41] and were said to dwell on earth and in the Netherworld. Quite often, the Anunnaki are paired together with another group of gods, known as the Igigi. These are the younger generation of sky gods, led by Ellil (Enlil in Sumerian).[42] The *Igigi,* possibly meaning "those who observe" or "the Watchers,"[43] are often referred to as "the great gods" who reside in heaven. This is in opposition to the Anunnaki, who are both in heaven and earth. However, as Semitic scholar John Heise notes, there are cases where the terms Igigi and Anunnaki are interchangeable, as in the Creation epic when the god Marduk asks the Anunnaki a question but the Igigi are the ones that respond.[44]

There is, however, some slight controversy surrounding the Anunnaki in modern interpretations. This has become increasingly apparent during the last twenty years. Many people interested in the connections between UFOs and the Bible are familiar with the "ancient astronaut" theories put forth by authors such as Erich von Däniken *(Chariots of the Gods?)* and Zecharia Sitchin *(The 12th Planet).* Because of Sitchin in particular, the name of the Anunnaki has *skyrocketed* to the forefront of the UFO community. While both authors have generated a great deal of interest in this topic, I believe their work is suspect. In the beginning, I was a big fan and shared the same enthusiasm concerning their work that many other readers have experienced. Over time, though, I began to read other materials and sources, leading me to question Sitchin and von Däniken's credibility. Von Däniken has admitted to faking some of his findings in order to create interest in his books,[45] and on many occasions, Sitchin has shown a severe lack of comprehension for the very languages he claims to know.[46] For these reasons, I am wary of recommending their material and suggest that readers look at Appendix C for further explanation.

Other titles applied to the Anunnaki and Igigi throughout Mesopotamian literature reveal a common theme that is not limited to the Hebrew Bible. For instance, the angels are identified as the "sons of God," the *bene ha'elohim* (בני האלהים), but they were also known in Ugaritic texts and the Canaanite pantheon as the *banu ili* or *banu ili-mi*. These beings were also described in eighth to seventh century BCE Phoenician inscriptions and an Ammonite inscription from the ninth century that was recently discovered in Jordan.[47] The significance is that other cultures also identified these angels as *non-human* "royal ambassadors" sent to the earth by God.

When we begin to study the culture of ancient Egypt, it is not too long before we discover several curiosities. The ancient symbol for "eternal life" is the *ankh*, depicted as ☥. It is a divine symbol that represents the union between male and female, or heaven and earth. I personally have not found any other information to support the following idea, but I do find it extremely interesting that the Egyptian ankh is very similar in sound to the Sumerian word for universe: *an-ki,* and that this might be a common link in beliefs among these cultures. At the time of this writing, the only evidence of a link between the words "ankh" and "an-ki" is that sometime after 1800 BCE, the ankh symbol began to appear on Syrian seals in the Mesopotamian region, but it seldom appeared elsewhere.[48]

Even the names of Egyptian cities offer important clues for our investigation. For instance, the city commonly known as Heliopolis (Greek for "City of the Sun"), was dedicated to the Egyptian deity *On, An,* or *Onnu*. Once again, we see a connection with the name An, representing both the sun and heaven. At the city known to the Greeks as Memphis, the Egyptians founded a new capital during the First Dynasty. This capital was dedicated to the god Ptah, who was "the Greatest Craftsman" and was called *Hwt-ka-Ptah,* "Mansion of the Spirit of Ptah." Foreigners had much difficulty pronouncing this name, and so it became corrupted to *Aiguptos* in Greek. This is where the name Egypt is derived. The Egyptian people referred to their land by several different names such as *Ta Mery*, meaning "The Beloved Land," and *Kem* ◁🦅⊗, "The Black Land." The latter was because of the rich sedimentary soil in the Nile Valley.[49] Other variant spellings of Kem are *Khem* and *Khemet*. Additionally, the word "Al<u>chem</u>y" points its origin to the land of Kem (Egypt).[50]

The term used by the Egyptians to refer to a "deity" was *neter* (pronounced "net-er," or archaically as "netjer" or "nech-er"). The glyph that denoted this was a flagpole ⌐ because the ancient Egyptians used them to mark the sacred place of a god's temple.[51] Outdated resources refer to this symbol as an axe. Most Egyptologists translate neter generically (and perhaps erroneously) as "god," but they never seem to elaborate upon the meaning of the word. Perhaps this is because most Egyptologists' interpretations come from a modern western and Judaeo-Christian framework and so they do not see it as anything more than another "god" from the Egyptian pantheon. However, generalizing the term as "god" may conceal the *real* meaning behind the word—*Guardian or Watcher!*[52] Additionally, the feminine form used to represent a "goddess" is *netert,* symbolized as a cobra 🐍 , further emphasizing the serpent associations that will be prevalent later in our investigation.[53]

Moustafa Gadalla, an independent Egyptologist, defines *neteru* (the plural form of neter) as "the divine principles and functions of the One Supreme God."[54] This definition would certainly qualify as a suitable description for an angel. In the ancient world, the angels/gods were said to watch over humanity and control the forces of nature. This makes perfect sense when we observe that our modern word "Nature" is derived from the Egyptian "Neter."

There may even have been a hidden reference to the Watchers in one of the secret phrases used to gain entry to the temples of the Egyptian Mystery schools: "Though I am a child of the earth, my Race is of the stars."[55] The Watchers and other angels are commonly referred to as being "stars," the "stars of El" (כוכבי אל), or "from the stars" (usually interpreted as "heaven"), so this is not a linguistic stretch by any means. This could even be referring to how the heavenly angels had earthly offspring and created the royal bloodlines according to some researchers.

Therefore, it is likely that the Egyptians themselves understood that these celestial beings were not actually gods as most people think, but rather angels or rulers. Perhaps the common people regarded them as gods—and even worshipped them—but I believe that the literal meaning of neteru might imply that the high priests understood the true "nature" of these beings.

Over time, Western culture has become increasingly more estranged from ancient cultures; therefore contemporary scholars are more likely to misinterpret the meanings of ancient writings. It is also important to acknowledge that many people's Judaeo-Christian upbringing has influenced their perceptions of ancient cultures. For instance, the Bible repeatedly states throughout its pages how other cultures such as Egypt and Babylon worshipped "false gods." However, it is not difficult to surmise that perhaps the authors of Biblical scriptures were attempting to demonize other religions and portray theirs as the only "true" faith. As a result, many other cultures were obscured or forgotten simply because they were not privileged with the ability to promote "official" history. Another important detail to consider is that according to the Bible, God claimed Israel for Himself and *appointed* every other nation to be divided and ruled by the *other* gods.[56] Therefore, the other nations were worshipping their specific gods as commanded by the God of Israel.

In the Islamic faith, spirits known as *Djinn* (or Jinn) are said to be responsible for much of the mischief and misfortune that occurs throughout the world. It is from the word djinn that the term *genie* is derived. Islamic beliefs teach that there are three orders of beings after God: angels that were created from light; djinn that were created from fire; and humans that were formed from clay.[57] Curiously, the Koran states that the djinn weren't created from regular fire, but rather a *smokeless* fire.[58] The djinn were said to be created 2000 years before Adam and considered equal to angels. But when the angel Eblis (or Iblis), the Muslim equivalent of Satan, refused to worship the newly created human being, he was cast down from heaven along with the djinn and became demons.[59] Eblis is known as the "King of the Shaitans" (Satans, or "adversaries") and is often identified as the fallen angel Azazel.[60]

The Hebrew Bible also refers to angelic beings known as the *Seraphim* (שרפים), meaning "fiery serpents." This term is derived from the root *Seraph* (שרף), which translates as "to burn" and probably from the Egyptian *Srf* (serpent). Perhaps the seraphim are similar to the djinn, or even the same creatures? Another possible connection between the seraphim and fiery serpents is the golden cobra worn by Egyptian pharaohs on their foreheads, known as the uraeus. It was regarded as a protector because some cobras will spit venom or "fire" at enemies.[61] Additionally, many examples of Egyptian artwork depict serpents with wings, so it is not difficult to imagine how the associations emerged of angelic beings that are "fiery flying serpents."

The fallen angels described in the *Book of Enoch* and the Dead Sea Scrolls are also identified as the *Irin* (עירין pronounced "eer-een"), which is an Aramaic word that directly translates to "Watchers." The singular form is *ir* (עיר), and it occurs only three times in the book of Daniel and nowhere else in the Bible.[62] In the story, the king of Babylon, Nebuchadnezzar, explained his dream to Daniel (who is called Belteshazzar), and recalled seeing a "holy" watcher. Although references to them are scarce throughout the Bible, the Watchers were much more prominent in other writings, particularly the books devoted to Enoch as we have already discussed.

As noted above, the term Watcher was not only used to describe the fallen angels, but also good ones. The book of Daniel mentions a "holy" Watcher—

A statue of the Pharaoh Akhenaten, holding the Crook and Flail. Note the uraeus serpent on his headdress.

and *1 Enoch* refers to the seven "holy angels who watch" as Uriel, Raphael, Raguel, Michael, Saraqael, Gabriel and Remiel.[63] *2 Enoch* (also known as the *Slavonic Enoch* or *The Book of the Secrets of Enoch)* records that the fallen angels are imprisoned in the fifth heaven. *3 Enoch* states that the four great princes, called Watchers, reside in the seventh heaven opposite the throne of God. These angels are purported to sanctify the body and soul on the third Day of Judgment (after death) with lashes of fire. This is described as a method of preparing the soul for God's presence.[64]

The early priesthoods clearly accepted the idea of heavenly angels having relations with humans long before this view was suppressed. For instance, the *Damascus Document* that was discovered in Cairo has been dated to approximately 100 BCE, and refers to the sins of the Watchers:

...I will uncover your eyes that you may see and understand the works of God... that you may walk perfectly in all His ways and not follow after thoughts of the guilty inclination and after <u>eyes of lust</u>. For through them, great men have gone astray and <u>mighty heroes</u> have stumbled from former times till now. Because they walked in the stubbornness of their heart the <u>Heavenly Watchers fell</u>; they were caught because they did not keep the commandments of God. <u>And their sons also fell who were tall as cedar trees and whose bodies were like mountains</u>. All flesh on dry land perished...

4Q265–73, Manuscript A:14–20[65]

The Watchers were not limited to the regions of the Middle East and Egypt; there are references to them within the traditions of nearly every culture. The witches of Southern Europe referred to the Watchers as the *Grigori* or *Egregore* (Ἐγρήγοροι) in the Greek language. In fact, the popular name Gregory originates from this term and means *watchful* or *vigilant.* The ancient witches of Italy, known as the *Strega* (pronounced "stray-gah"), summoned the Grigori spirits in many of their magickal rituals. Strega is the Italian word for "witch"[66] and has a root in *strego,* meaning "to enchant."[67] The Strega are believed to be one of the oldest traditions associated with modern witchcraft, tracing their family lineage and beliefs back at least seven-hundred years from present day.

In Celtic[68] traditions, a belief still persists that fairies were fallen angels cast out of Heaven—but they did not necessarily commit crimes evil enough to merit punishment in Hell. According to these beliefs, the fairies took a neutral stance during the "War in Heaven" and were consequently abandoned outside the gates of Heaven, which were closed by the Archangel Michael. Yet another tradition suggests that the fairies were possibly the souls of all those drowned in Noah's flood.[69] Regardless, it is clear that there was a close association with the fairies, fallen angels, and the Watchers in Celtic lore.

Projecting further back in history, the people of ancient Ireland believed in the fairy court of the *Daoine Sidhe,* who were of the former race known as the *Tuatha de Danaan,* the people of the Mother Goddess Danu. They were described as beings of light and called "The Shining Ones."[70] Myths and legends described the Tuatha de Danaan as the old gods who constructed the megaliths of Ireland—which were regarded as gateways to the fairy realm—but were driven from the land between 3000 and 1000 BCE.[71]

The *sidhe* (pronounced "shee") was the term used to describe a fairy in both Ireland and Scotland. More often than not, they appeared as humans and were the same height, if not taller. They lived in subterranean palaces of gold and crystal and possessed many gifts and talents, which would occasionally be granted to mortals. Another connection between fairies and fallen angels can be found in the sidhe's mischievous tendency to abduct human beings to serve as their consorts.[72] Furthermore, the *bean sidhe,* which literally means "woman of the fairy," is the origin of the word *banshee,* a harbinger of death, and is one of the more familiar terms known to modern people.[73]

In Scotland, the fairy kingdom was divided into the *Seelie* and the *Unseelie Courts.* The Seelie or Blessed Court was comprised of the good fairies that oversaw the lives of mortals, offered help to them when needed, and carried out justice. The Unseelie Court was reputed to contain the unblessed dead as well as the fairies that had been banished from the Seelie Court. Most natural disasters and unfortunate events were attributed to them.[74]

The Elven kingdom played a prominent role in Viking and Germanic lore. The *Alfs* (elves) were divided into two kingdoms of the light and the dark elves, much like the Seelie and Unseelie Courts. However, the dark elves were considered more mischievous than evil. According to Viking lore, the light elves were called the *Ljossalfs* and lived in *Ljossalfsheim* or *Alfheim,* just one of nine different realms that existed at the top of the World Tree *(Yggdrasil),* which was above the realm of *Midgard,* where humans lived. The dark or black elves were known as the *Swartalfs,* and lived in *Swartalfsheim,* a realm that extended from Midgard to *Helheim,* the underworld. The dark elves were said to be expert craftsmen and their skin turned dark from the soot while they toiled in their forges.[75] Elf, Alf, and Aelf are all terms that translate as "shining" or "radiant being" and share a common link with the El and Il in the Middle Eastern region.

In Norse legends, there appeared a trickster god named *Loki,* who also happened to be a half-giant. The giants were sworn enemies of the gods, much like the Titans were the enemies of the Greek gods. Loki had three children to a giantess, all of which were considered to be of a malevolent nature. The first was *Fenris,* a great wolf. The second was the *Serpent of Midgard* (World Serpent), called *Jormungand,* and the third was *Hel,* the mistress of Death. Fearing these offspring, Odin engaged in battle with them and hurled the Midgard serpent into the ocean. However, the creature was so incredibly large that it encircled the entire world, and swallowed its own tail.[76] Hel was banished to the Land of the Dead—curiously enough known as *Niflheim*. Whether or not this term has any connection to Nefilim (an alternate spelling of Nephilim) is unknown, but it is extremely interesting that it phonetically sounds so similar and is related to a place where banished spirits of the dead were sent. Lastly, the Fenris-wolf was magically restrained on a remote island, but the gods, called the *Aesir*,[77] knew that one day it would eventually break free and attempt to devour Odin at the battle of *Ragnarok*—the end of the world.[78]

Hindu and Buddhist mythologies also refer to the *Asura*, a group of gods that used to live at the peak of Mount Meru (or Sumeru), a sacred mountain located at the center of the universe. The Asuras generally had a negative reputation within these belief systems because of their warlike and destructive inclinations. The word Asura is sometimes translated "Titan" or "giant" because of the similarities to the Greek legends of beings that warred with the other gods. It is also a cognate to the word *Ahura*, and is a designation for a class of divinity within ancient Persian mythology. For example, it is found in the title of *Ahura Mazda*, the chief deity of the Zoroastrian religion. However, in the context of Persian mythology, the title Ahura is reserved for benevolent deities.[79]

In the ancient Eastern language of Sanskrit, the term *deva* also means "shining one." In the Hindu and Buddhist belief systems, a deva is a god or spirit being that usually has close ties to nature. Unfortunately, it is from the word *deva* that *devil* got its origin and was used to describe these beings in the Judaeo-Christian framework, causing all of them to be falsely labeled as devils. Helena P. Blavatsky (also known as Madame Blavatsky), cofounder of the Theosophical Society, was responsible for introducing devas to Western occult beliefs. One of her mentors described devas as evolved spiritual beings from a previous period on Earth. These devas were said to lay dormant in the universe until humankind reached certain stages in evolution, and then they would reemerge to guide and challenge us. According to theosophical teachings, when the devas become active they can remain invisible or physically manifest as humanlike bodies of light, as well as balls and points of light. They even communicate through such means as mental impressions, intuitions and inner voices, which is entirely similar to descriptions of how angels have communicated with humanity throughout ages.[80]

Native American traditions also refer to nature spirits that physically manifested in human form to give help and guidance to various clans.

The Hopi people called these spirits *kachinas.* The kachina people taught the Hopi the skills of building a civilization, agriculture and medicine that was needed for their survival. The Hopi were instructed to build a ceremonial temple that was divided into four stories, each successively smaller to make it resemble a stepped pyramid. The first floor was where the people were taught about their history and the previous three worlds that had been destroyed. The second floor taught them how to properly respect and honor the workings of the Great Spirit in their lives. On the third floor, the kachinas showed the Hopi how to use plants to cure illnesses. Finally, the fourth floor was reserved only for initiates who had a deep understanding of nature and learned the workings of the planets and stars as well as the climate of the earth and how it all related to mankind. They were also taught about the "open door" located at the top of their heads which would allow them to speak directly with the Creator.[81]

According to some Hopi legends, one of the clans rebelled and attacked the mysterious Red City of the South[82] that the kachinas helped them to build. The kachinas decided to fend off the invaders while the other clans fled to safety through underground tunnels. They told the Hopi:

> Now we, the *kachina* people, will remain here to defend the city, while you make your escape in the darkness. The time for us to go to our far-off planets and stars has not come yet. But it is time for us to leave you. We will go by our powers to a certain high mountain,[83] which you will know, where we will await your messages of need. So whenever you need us or our help, just make your *páhos.*[84] Now another thing. We are spirit people, and we will not be seen again by you or your people. But you must remember us by wearing our masks and our costumes at the proper ceremonial times. Those who do so must be only those persons who have acquired the knowledge and the wisdom we have taught you. And these persons of flesh and blood will then bear our names and be known as the Kachina Clan.[85]

Also according to legend, the Hopi received four tablets from their kachina leader during the time of their migration. One of these tablets was given to the Fire Clan, but the kachina leader, Másaw, purposefully broke off a corner of the tablet. He told them that strange people would invade their land one day, but the Hopi were not to resist them. Instead, they were instructed to wait until the day when their lost white brother, Paháma, returned to them with the missing corner piece and deliver them from further persecution. Paháma would create a new universal brotherhood of man that would finally unite the clans and other people.[86]

Angelic beings repeatedly appear in the stories of cultures all over the world. Sometimes their names are similar sounding and other times they are related by definition only. However, what is also very fascinating is how often the physical descriptions of these beings are so much alike. Initially, someone might think that if the people themselves locally invented these gods, then they would have described the gods to be like themselves—essentially making God in man's image. However, this does not appear to be the case. Instead, they stress how *different* these beings were from humans, even though they had human appearances. These extraordinary appearances, as we'll soon see, also manifested quite differently in their offspring.

Summary

❖ Angelic beings referred to as the "sons of God," and also as The Watchers, were said to have once initiated the destruction of humanity. The Watchers began sexual relationships with the human race and taught them various skills and knowledge that had previously been withheld from humans.

❖ The two leaders of the Watchers, Shemyaza and Azazel, were both punished: Shemyaza was forced to remain in limbo until the Day of Judgment, and Azazel was cast into the deepest realms of imprisonment.

❖ Traditions from cultures around the world refer to angelic or godlike beings that at one time directly interacted with humans. Linguistic analysis of terms and words used to describe these beings cross-culturally reveals striking similarities and indicates that our ancient ancestors encountered flesh and blood "gods" that interacted directly with them.

❖ Cultures worldwide generally describe these beings as "shining" or "illumined" and often associate them with fire and light, such as the Djinn of Arabic lore. Additionally, the mischievous or evil fairies, elves and angels are usually described as being dark in appearance, and even with serpentine features, such as in the Dead Sea Scrolls.

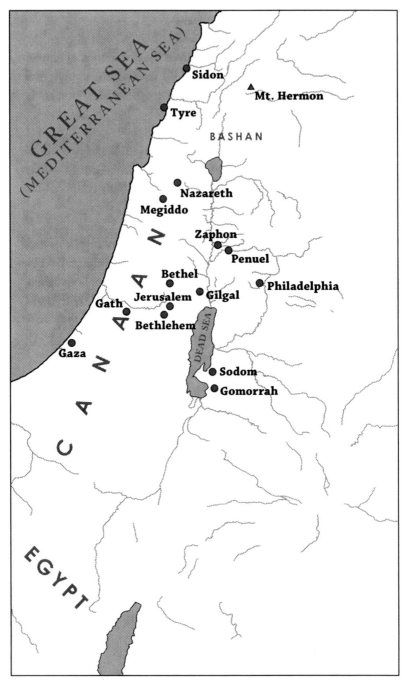

This map marks several noteworthy locations that are discussed throughout our investigation of the ancient Biblical world (c. 3,000 BCE – 100 CE).

ANGELIC BLOODLINES

I have begotten a strange son, diverse from and unlike man, and resembling the sons of the God of heaven.

Book of Noah, CVI:5

IN THE PREVIOUS CHAPTER, WE EXAMINED a variety of cultures and their traditions concerning the interaction of angels with the human race. We have learned about some of the names attributed to these angelic beings (the Watchers) as well as their progeny (the Nephilim). If the angels themselves stood out in a crowd, one must wonder what kind of commotion erupted among the people after seeing their hybrid offspring. We will now explore the physical features of these beings and the many surprisingly consistent descriptions found all across the ancient world.

The Gigantic Offspring

Our research so far has demonstrated that the ancient legends spoke of unions between the "sons of God" and human women that resulted in the creation of monstrous hybrid giants. These giants were attributed with many terrible qualities including affinities for war and cannibalism.[1] Death devoured the land wherever these monsters roamed.

We have also addressed the confusion surrounding the word Nephilim (נפילים) and its meanings as both "giants" and "fallen ones" (Genesis 6:4). The proper usage of the term has plagued Biblical scholars for ages. While scholars generally agree that Nephilim is a term designated for the offspring of the human/angel unions, a justifiable argument is that perhaps it should not be limited to *only* the offspring; they may have inherited this title from their angelic parents.

When the books of the Old Testament were being translated into the Septuagint (LXX) version, the Greek word *gigantes* (γίγαντες) replaced

A Mesopotamian depiction of a serpent-footed god with wings.

Nephilim. While the etymology of the word is uncertain, it is believed to mean "earth-born." The gigantes in Greek mythology were believed to be serpent-footed giants born from the drops of blood from the castration of Uranus (representing Heaven) that fell onto Gaea (the Earth Mother). Since the passage in Genesis is apparently describing a coupling between gods and humans, much like the stories of Greek mythology, it was only natural for the translators to select gigantes. The reference to these beings as gigantic in size therefore might have only been coincidental. Additionally, we should note that the giants were also known as the *Titans* (τιτανος), a term meaning "white earth or clay, gypsum."[2] We will discuss the significance of this particular detail shortly.

Many people are familiar with the giant known as Goliath,[3] but few realize just how many references there are to giants within the Old Testament (not to mention the numerous references by other cultures). For instance, there are the races known as the *Anakim* (עֲנָקִים),[4] the *Rephaim* (רְפָאִים)[5] and the *Emim* (אֵימִים).[6] Other encounters with giants that are mentioned include the battles with Goliath's four sons.[7] The most obvious physical characteristic of these giants was their immense size. For example, Goliath is described as follows:

> [His] height was six cubits and a span. He had a helmet of bronze on his head, and he was armed with a coat of mail; the weight of the coat was five thousand shekels of bronze. He had greaves of bronze on his legs and a javelin of bronze slung between his shoulders. The shaft of his spear was like a weaver's beam, and his spear's head weighed six hundred shekels of iron…
>
> 1 Samuel 17:4–7 NRSV

It is generally agreed by most historians that a cubit was 18 inches and a span was 9 inches. This would make Goliath nine feet, nine inches tall. A common shekel is believed to be approximately 0.4 ounces while a royal shekel is 0.8 ounces. This means that his coat weighed a minimum of 125 pounds or up to 250 pounds! That's not even including the weight for the rest of his armor and weapons, which would easily add hundreds of pounds more. Of course, if the size of Goliath is to be believed, carrying such weight would not be as cumbersome as it would be to a person of average size.

King Og of Bashan also merits a mention since his bed is described as being "nine cubits long and four cubits wide"[8]—the equivalent to thirteen and a half feet long and six feet wide. While it may be that this luxurious king just preferred to have an absolutely enormous bed, it should be pointed out that he is identified as belonging to a tribe of giants known as the Rephaim.[9] Additionally, it is noted that he came from the geographical area of *Bashan* (בָּשָׁן), the Hebrew rendering of the Ugaritic word Bathan, meaning "serpent!" The Canaanites even considered this region a type of "hell" and believed that their ancient dead kings inhabited it. It is also home to the infamous Mount Hermon, where the Watchers were said to have descended.[10]

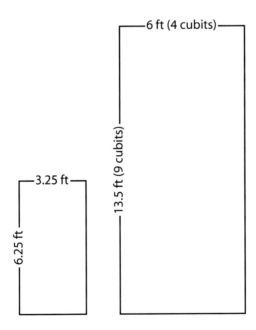

A standard twin size bed (left) compared to King Og's bed (right).

In the *Book of Enoch* it describes some of the giants reaching heights of "three thousand ells" (*1 Enoch* 7:2). An ell is considered to be either 495 or 525 millimeters.[11] The text's description of the height is probably a scribal error that has crept in over the ages. It is extremely hard to imagine a being of such size, which would be between 314 and 333 feet in height!

Trying to bring these proportions down to a more earthly size still presents other problems. Some critics will argue that these are simply exaggerated stories by primitive people who saw others suffering from the disease known as Gigantism (or Giantism). Gigantism occurs when the pituitary gland produces excessive amounts of growth hormones during adolescence and typically causes the individual to grow extremely tall, with very thick bones, large hands and feet and a heavy jaw. Continued growth of these features after puberty (a condition known as acromegaly) will cause severe health problems and even premature death.[12]

Although acromegaly is very rare, there are some well known people who have suffered from it. Among them are Robert Pershing Wadlow (1918–1940) and Andre Rene Roussimoff (1946–1993), who is more commonly known to fans as "Andre the Giant." Robert Wadlow, the tallest

human ever recorded for whom there is irrefutable evidence, was measured at eight feet and eleven inches in height. He died at the age of twenty-two from a severe infection caused by a faulty leg brace.[13] Andre Roussimoff was seven feet and five inches in height and passed away when his heart could no longer support the size of his body.[14]

While it is possible that the giants of legends were actually suffering from Gigantism, it seems very unlikely. The most obvious reason is that people with this disease often become extremely weak and their bodies cannot support them. Robert Wadlow required leg braces just to walk. However, according to the ancient legends, giants such as Goliath were incredibly strong and champion warriors.

A comparison of a fully grown man standing next to Robert Wadlow.

In the sixth chapter of the autobiography of William Cody, popularly known as "Buffalo Bill," he recounts a time when Pawnee Indians brought some large bones to his camp. At least one of the bones was examined by a surgeon and determined to be that of a giant human. The native legends about these giants were that they were three times the size of humans and "...they were so swift and strong that they could run by the side of a buffalo, and, taking the animal in one arm, could tear off a leg and eat it as they ran." Additionally, the legend tells of how these giants were full of pride, even denying that there was a "Great Spirit"—so they were punished for their sins and drowned in a devastating flood.[15]

While this may be simply nothing more than a tall tale from "Buffalo Bill," there are indeed legends about frightening giants among the native people. Yet again, they do not seem to be describing persons or beings that suffered from the physical ailments of Gigantism. In addition to their immense size, there were other characteristics attributed to these giants. Quite often, they were described as being very grotesque or with deformities. Two of the most notable deformities were six digits on each hand and foot and, in some instances, double-rows of teeth.[16]

Concerning another war between David's men and the giants, 2 Samuel 21:20 states: "there was a man of great size, who had <u>six fingers on each hand</u>, and <u>six toes on each foot</u>, twenty-four in number; he too was <u>descended from the giants</u>."[17] While there are occasional situations where people are born with a sixth finger or toe, a condition known as hexadactyly, these cases are generally rare. Also, it appears that a sixth digit has never been recorded in any medical examination of someone suffering from Gigantism. What this means is that apparently the addition of an extra digit on each hand and foot were common characteristics associated with "true" giants in the ancient past.

In addition to ancient accounts, there are many recent reports that have appeared in newspapers and documents concerning archaeological digs that have unearthed many curious things:

In 1833, soldiers digging at Lompock Rancho, California,[18] discovered a male skeleton <u>twelve feet tall</u>. The skeleton was surrounded by carved shells, stone axes, [and] other artifacts. The skeleton had <u>double rows of upper and lower teeth</u>. Unfortunately, this body was secretly buried because the local Indians became upset about the remains.[19]

Another shocking discovery of a giant with "double rows of teeth" was found off the California Coast of Santa Rosa Island sometime in the 1800s.[20] After that, three skeletons were found in Ohio in 1872, each at least eight feet tall, and each bore the strange similarity of having double rows of teeth in both their upper and lower jaws.[21] But the oddities certainly didn't stop there because seven more giant skeletons showing signs of "double dentition" were found in Clearwater, Minnesota![22]

A volunteer detachment of the U.S. Army Engineers was sent to the little island of Shemya[23] in May of 1943 to build an airstrip. They made a shocking discovery when the bulldozers began digging up layers upon layers of fossils. Within one of the layers, they found the bones and skulls of giant humans alongside those of mammoths and mastodons. Some of the skulls were apparently missing their lower jaws, and measured "from one foot ten inches to two feet long!" The bones were "emphatically human" and far enough away from the animal bones that they could not have been confused.[24]

The giant skeletons were measured and determined to be at least eighteen feet, six inches in height.[25] The informant said that all of the men involved were under strict orders not to discuss the details of their discovery, and that one of them was even threatened with court martial because he tried to smuggle out a cache of the rare bones. He also mentioned that all of the skulls had perforated holes in them from trepanation (a technique that involved cutting a hole in the skull to help relieve pressure on the brain from swelling due to a trauma). Unfortunately, it seems that these skeletons never reached a museum for proper study.[26] While the reaction of the U.S. Army to court martial the man may seem somewhat excessive, it can be understood that any media attention during a time of war would have jeopardized the airstrip to possible enemy attacks.

There are many more worldwide accounts boasting the discoveries of very large skeletons, but space is too limited for their exploration here. These are not even including the ancient legends that date back to the period when the giants were allegedly alive. Many of the giant skeletons that appear in these widespread accounts also identified them by their six fingers and other physical abnormalities.

Obviously, one should not automatically accept that the preceding accounts concerning gigantic skeletons are true. I have tried to verify the information myself and found that some of the articles' sources are circular (i.e. no other sources of information seem to exist outside of their own created loops). Additionally, some of the locations do not appear on any maps. It is not surprising that there are probably many such stories that were hoaxes or fabrications cooked up to stir national interests in unknown locales. The reason would be simple enough: people have always been fascinated by hearing tales of the strange and unknown—and that can generate money for an otherwise mundane town.

However, even if just one example was determined to be authentic, it opens up many unsettling questions about the past as well as the future. There does appear to be a genuine credibility to some of these legends because of how widespread they are—even showing common qualities such as the six fingers and toes. The most frustrating part is that if indeed these giant skeletons have been found, then what has happened to them? Unfortunately, many accounts state that when the skeletal finds were reported to the "proper authorities," such as museums or institutions like the Smithsonian, the bones were collected and conveniently disappeared. If the bones were real, then there seems to be a major archaeological cover-up going on that rivals the infamous warehouse portrayed in the Indiana Jones adventure *Raiders of the Lost Ark!* However, if the "discoveries" were merely fabrications by people trying to achieve fame and fortune, then they probably never existed in the first place.

Luckily, the invention of the camera has allowed some people with enough foresight to take pictures of their finds before they vanished. Such photos have allowed the preservation of at least some form of evidence to be scrutinized, although trickery is still possible. The photograph on the following page was originally published in *Strand Magazine* (December, 1895). It was later reprinted in W.G. Wood-Martin's book, *Traces of the Elder Faiths of Ireland.* According to the story, a fossilized giant was discovered by a Mr. Dyer, who was prospecting for iron ore in County Antrim, Ireland. The photograph was taken while the giant was located at the North-Western Railway Company's Broad Street goods station in London. The giant was first exhibited in Dublin and then moved to England and shown in Liverpool and Manchester.[27]

The article stated that the total height of the giant was 12 feet 2 inches. The girth of the chest was given as 6 feet 6 inches, while the arms were 4 feet 6 inches in length. It weighed over two tons and required six men and a powerful crane to move it into position against a railroad car for the photographer. What is most interesting is that the article also mentioned that *the right foot*

The alleged fossilized giant from Ireland was propped against a railroad car for this photo.

of the giant had six toes. Unfortunately, the giant body cannot be examined further because it mysteriously (or perhaps conveniently) disappeared.[28]

If the giant was a hoax, then the size alone was enough to attract attention. Why bother to include a sixth toe? If it was faked, and the inspiration stems from the very brief references in the Bible about six digits,[29] then why didn't the hoaxer go for "accuracy" by including six digits on both hands and feet? The reported weight of the giant (over 4,000 pounds) does seem to be excessive, however, even for a being of that size. This might indicate that the "giant" was carved from stone or some other heavy material.

Some other curiosities have appeared throughout history. While these are not necessarily associated with the skeletons of giants, there have been numerous oddly shaped skulls found all over the world. According to the accounts of ancient people, a number of the gods and even giants apparently had elongated heads. One need only to look at some of the artwork from the Egyptian civilization to see depictions of pharaohs and other people with much longer skulls than normal. Some scholars and art historians say that these were only created as an artistic style—which may partially be true—but the evidence seems to indicate that many members of the royal families had these deformities.

The most common method of achieving this look was by binding an infant's head very tightly with bandages and a wooden board so that as the bones grew, they were forced into a new shape. Most historians believe that the people did this to honor their gods, and perhaps their means of paying reverence to the gods was by emulating their physical appearance. Many people have seen images on television of the Burmese Paduang women that use brass rings to create the appearance of extended necks, which is another method of body modification meant to imitate the gods that continues to be practiced today.[30]

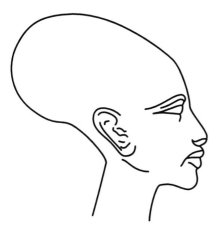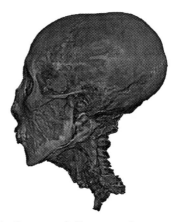

A representation of a princess—possibly Meritaten, the daughter of King Akhenaten—displaying an elongated skull. Most Egyptologists believe that this unusual family trait became exaggerated by the artistic style of the period.

A Computed Tomography scan of Tutankhamen's skull, showing an elongated deformation. *Credit: CT Scanning equipment provided by Siemens AG; Data courtesy, the Supreme Council of Antiquities, Arab Republic of Egypt; National Geographic Magazine, June 2005*

The following set of photographs show several different skulls that were discovered in Peru. This appearance is technically known as *dolichocephaly*. Also of interest is that some of these skulls have very large holes cut into them, again demonstrating the procedure known as trepanation. This ancient form of life-saving surgery was apparently very successful, as many people survived it. This is yet another example of how the ancient people were not necessarily as primitive as we've been taught to believe.

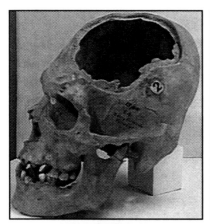
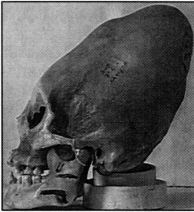
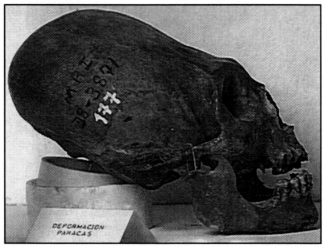

These skulls were photographed by Robert Connolly while he was researching and collecting materials about ancient civilizations. Note the elongated craniums and that the skull shown in the upper left corner demonstrates that an ancient form of brain surgery, called "trepanation," was performed while the person was still alive. Connolly published his photographs on a CD-ROM, titled *Search for Ancient Wisdom* in 1995.

In the magazine *Atlantis Rising,* Italian journalist Adriano Forgione reported that some very strange skulls had been discovered in Malta. Several of these skulls were elongated and showing other peculiarities. According to Forgione's article, the skulls were found buried along with a small statue believed to be dedicated to some form of Mother Goddess worship. The archaeologists also suspect that the statue might be associated with a relic inscribed with a serpent.[31]

Forgione noted that one skull in particular was larger than the rest and considered it to be extremely significant. "The cranium showed a very pronounced dolichocephalous," but was apparently a naturally occurring deformation, and not due to bandages or boards. Even more important was that it did not show *any* sign of median knitting (technically called "sagitta"). This is quite an amazing discovery. When medics and anatomists were questioned about this feature, they responded that it was "impossible," and that there is not a single known analogous case of this in any pathological medical literature. However, there were apparently other known examples of skulls from ancient Egypt and South America with this same exact deformity, leading Forgione to believe that perhaps this was the result of a genetic mutation caused by the mixing of two very different races of beings.[32] So that we can better understand the significance of this anomaly, we need to review how a human skull is formed.

In order to accommodate for a larger brain size, humans are born with five main sections of soft tissue in their heads, called sutures, and not with a solid skull. If the skull was completely formed, the infant's head would not fit properly through the birth canal and cause many complications, if not the death of the mother. As the child grows, these sections allow the skull to expand properly. The "knitted" patterns on the skull are the result of when these sections have fused together.[33]

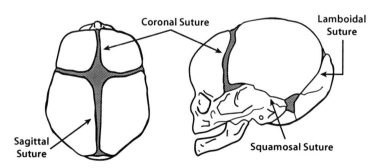

If something genetic was causing this condition, it obviously would have presented a major problem if many women were dying during childbirth. While the legend is questionable, it should be pointed out that Julius Caesar believed he was descended from the gods and that he had to be born by performing a caesarian section—hence the term. Other legends also seem to indicate that "giants" had to be born this way, too. Therefore, if a woman was pregnant with a child whose skull was not divided with the proper amount sutures, then it is quite possible that the mother would die if she did not give birth via caesarian section.

Forgione and his colleagues went on to speculate the possible origins of these ancient people. They believe the genetic traits show that they are of a different race than the natives to any of the areas such as Malta and Egypt. Forgione mentions the discoveries of the late Egyptologist, Professor Walter B. Emery (1903–1971), author of the book *Archaic Egypt,* who was involved with excavations at Saqquara in the 1930s. Emery discovered remains from a predynastic group of people and "presented a dolichocephalous skull, larger than that of the local ethnic group," and which had "fair hair and a taller, heavier build." Professor Emery also stated that he believed this group was not indigenous to Egypt but held important positions in both the priestly classes and government, usually avoiding the common people when possible and blending only with the aristocratic classes. He connected them to the priests known as the *Shemshu Hor,* or "disciples of Horus."[34]

It is interesting to see how once again there are stories about some kind of "priestly" or "heavenly" class of beings, quite possibly different from normal humans, who were involved in the building of civilizations and inter-mingling with humans. Importantly, Forgione concluded that there is a direct connection between the "long-headed" serpent priests and the fallen angels described in apocryphal literature.[35]

The evidence presented by Forgione further substantiates the possibility that a genetically different race of beings directly influenced the ancient cultures of our past. Some of these people may have actually been "giants," with distinguishing features that indicated their heavenly lineage. But how could this be possible? Are there any indications in the ancient texts and legends that would explain why these offspring would have been genetically different?

The Sons of God

In searching for possible explanations for the reports of "giants," we shall now revisit the "sons of God," the *bene ha'elohim* (בני האלהים), who were also known as the Watchers. After examining a number of texts from different cultures, it is possible to piece together what these angels may have looked like with a surprising accuracy. One of the extremely fragmented Dead Sea Scrolls found in Qumran, known as *The Testament of Amram* (4Q543–8), describes how two Watchers, one good and the other evil,[36] fight over the author:

> (I saw Watchers) in my vision, a dream vision, and behold two (of them) argued about me and said... and they were engaged in a great quarrel concerning me. I asked them: "You, what are you... thus... [about me?"] They answered and [said to me: "We have been made m]asters and rule over the sons of men." And they said to me: "Which of us do you [choose...]"
>
> I raised my eyes and saw one of them. His looks were frighten-ing [like those of a vi]per, and his [ga]rm[en]ts were multi-coloured and he was extremely dark...
>
> And afterwards I looked and behold... by his appearance and his face was like that of an adder, and he was covered with... together, and his eyes...
>
> 4Q544, fragment I[37]

It is interesting to see how the evil Watcher is described as being "extremely dark" in appearance and with the face of a snake. Unfortunately, too many other areas of the text are indecipherable to describe other attributes such his eyes and what exactly was covering his body. Since this is a dream vision, it may or may not be accurately recalling the appearance of one of these beings. For instance, in the vision, the author has been able to discern the "evil" Watcher because it looked like a snake and was "dark." Was this a subconscious manifestation, and would the angel have appeared less threatening if Amram had encountered it outside of a dream? The "multi-coloured" garment is also intriguing as it may have some connection with the "coat of many colors" associated with Joseph.

There is often a connection between angels, particularly fallen angels, and serpents. For example, everyone is familiar with the story of the snake in the Garden of Eden, yet a majority of people don't know that it wasn't a regular snake (despite the fact that it could apparently speak to Eve). According to the Jewish legends, it was a creature with a serpentine appearance but it also had arms and stood upright on two legs, with a height equal to a camel. This creature was designated as the ruler and caretaker of the garden and all of the living things in it, including Adam and Eve. However, the serpent became enamored with Eve and tried to trick her so that Adam would die by eating the fruit of the tree. As punishment for this transgression, the limbs of the serpent were hacked off,[38] a detail echoed in the Bible when God condemns the serpent with the phrase, "upon your belly you shall go" (Genesis 3:14).

This was most likely a combination of fact and fiction that blended together in the telling of the story. While it might seem very hard to believe in a bipedal reptilian creature, the serpentine appearance is common to many of the angels. Therefore, if an angel with such features had been walking the earth, it obviously would have attracted much attention and been acknowledged by the ancient scribes. The fictional side is that it partially became an "explanation story"—not only of the reason why humans "fell" from grace, but also why a snake has no legs and slithers along the ground. So, when the time came to tell the story, the authors had the ready-made link between the angels and snakes, and then added the morality lesson explaining why the snake had to lose its "legs." But what we are searching for are the common threads between these stories that keep appearing over and over again, because these details are the ones that most likely have some element of truth to them.

The Jewish legends also record that the serpent creature not only tricked Eve with the forbidden fruit, but successfully impregnated her; the result of their union was Cain. When the child was born, his appearance was described as "seraphic" (a shining serpent) and also as a "radiant figure." Later, Eve had a dream that foreshadowed the death of her second son, Abel, at the hands of Cain. She saw an alarming vision of Abel's blood flowing into Cain's hungry mouth, while Abel pitifully begged Cain to stop drinking.[39]

Not all of the accounts, however, describe these beings with serpentine features. While the *Testament of Amram* does not describe what the other Watcher looked like, we can find the possible physical characteristics in a fragment known as *The Book of Noah*, which is often included along with *1 Enoch*, and may have even preceded it. The fragment describes how Lamech, the supposed father of Noah, is gravely concerned that the child may not be his, and is instead from one of the Watchers:

And after some days my son Methuselah took a wife for his son Lamech, and she became pregnant by him and bore a son. And his <u>body was white as snow and red as the blooming of a rose</u>, and the hair of his head and his <u>long locks were white as wool</u> and his eyes beautiful. And when he opened his eyes, he lighted up the whole house like the sun, and the whole house was very bright. And thereupon he arose in the hands of the midwife, opened his mouth, and <u>conversed with the Lord of righteousness</u>. And his father Lamech was afraid of him and fled, and came to his father Methuselah. And he said unto him: "I have begotten <u>a strange son,</u> <u>diverse from and unlike man</u>, and <u>resembling the sons of the God</u> <u>of heaven</u>; and his nature is different and <u>he is not like us</u>, and his <u>eyes are as the rays of the sun</u>, and <u>his countenance glorious</u>. And it seems to me that <u>he is not sprung from me but from the angels</u>, and I fear that in his days a wonder may be wrought on the earth. And now, my father, I am here to petition thee and implore thee that thou mayest go to <u>Enoch</u>, our father, and learn from him the truth, for his dwelling-place is amongst the angels."

Fragment of the Book of Noah, CVI:1–7

R.H. Charles Translation[40]

Apparently, the baby Noah had some very interesting qualities at birth, particularly since he had the ability to speak with "the Lord of righteousness."[41] The white skin (although not necessarily "white" like that of a Caucasian person, but perhaps more like that of an albino) is also a curious clue as well as the white hair. These characteristics are commonly associated with the descriptions of the angels throughout the Bible. The possibility remains, however, that perhaps the child was simply born as an albino and an exaggerated superstition grew out of people's reactions.

Lamech's concern that the child may not be his seems justifiable, but it is very suspicious how numerous times the text describes Noah as "strange" and like a child of the Watchers. Yet Enoch, who at this point has become an angel and resides in heaven,[42] insists that Noah was really produced from the union of two humans. Could it be possible that Lamech was told that Noah was really his legitimate son to keep the child from being harmed out of fear or misunderstanding?

What if Noah was indeed the result of the union between his mother and one of the Watchers? The reason Noah was selected to be saved from the deluge was because he was determined to be "perfect in his generations" (Genesis 6:9 KJV). The word translated as "perfect" in Hebrew is *tamyim* (תמים), which means perfect or without blemish. Some researchers believe that this is referring to Noah's genes not being tainted by the intermixing of the angels and humans. But perhaps another possibility is that he was the result of a successful angel/human hybridization? The qualities describing Noah at his birth are exactly like those of the holy angels. For instance, when Enoch is translated into heaven he sees the "sons of God" and says that "their garments were white… And their faces shone like snow."[43] A short time later, Enoch is visited by God, who is referred to as the "Head of Days" and also known as the "Ancient of Days." When describing the appearance of God, Enoch observes that "His head [was] white and pure as wool, And His raiment indescribable."[44] Notice that the hair is described as being white and compared to wool, just like the hair of Noah.

In Sumerian literature, the term *melam* referred to the "brilliant, visible glamour … exuded by gods, heroes, sometimes by kings, and also by temples of great holiness and by gods' symbols and emblems." It is not well understood by scholars despite its numerous mentions in the tablets. Apparently, the melam had some association with a supernatural light and it could be "worn" like a garment or crown by the gods. It could also be "taken off" and would disappear when a god was killed. The effect of the melam on a human being in the presence of a god is called *ni,* and is described as intense terror and fear of this divine power.[45]

When Moses returns from the top of the mountain with the Ten Commandments, he is described as having a shining face after being in the presence of God. The Israelites were afraid to approach him because of how brightly his face shone, and he even wore a veil to cover his face except for when he would meet with God.[46] Compare this with the later New Testament counterpart when Jesus leads Peter, James and John to the top of a mountain (probably *Mount Hermon* according to some scholars). Once again, a transfiguration occurs and Jesus' face "shone like the sun, and his clothes became dazzling white." Moses and Elijah then make an appearance and stand beside Jesus.[47] Also, notice that both events took place at the summits of holy mountains, an important detail that will be explored in the next chapter.

When Mary Magdalene and another Mary (the mother of James) visit the tomb of Jesus after his burial, they became terrified by the awesome sight of an angel descending from heaven, "whose appearance was like lightning, and his clothing white as snow."[48] Again and again, there are similar descriptions of these angels with a shining appearance and even white skin and white clothing.

When Saint John had his revelation at the island of Patmos, he had heard a loud voice behind him and turned to see:

> ...one like the Son of Man, clothed with a long robe and with a golden sash across his chest. His head and his hair were white as white wool, white as snow; his eyes were like a flame of fire, his feet were like burnished bronze, refined as in a furnace, and his voice was like the sound of many waters. In his right hand he held seven stars, and from his mouth came a sharp, two-edged sword, and his face was like the sun shining with full force.
>
> Revelation 1:13–16 NRSV

Once again, there are direct references to white hair and skin, compared with the finest wool and pure snow—even brightly appearing eyes and a countenance that would light up a room, sounding very similar to the description of Noah's birth. The feet "like burnished bronze" could be referring to shoes of some sort, but there is also another intriguing possibility. As you will see later in our investigation, there are times when Jesus is associated with serpent imagery, such as when he is compared to the brazen serpent used by Moses.[49] The significance is that sometimes the words "brass/bronze" and "serpent" are interchangeable and intentional wordplays created by the Biblical authors. This is because the Hebrew word *nachash* (נחש), meaning "serpent," is the *same* as the Aramaic word for "bronze" (נחש). Additionally, since many of the Titans and other comparable beings in mythology were often described as being "serpent-footed," this word play becomes even more apparent since John specifically mentions that the feet of Jesus were like bronze.[50] This was probably intended as a symbolic reference to the heritage of the Watchers, while the other aspects of his description, such as the white skin and hair, were intended as physical references to this same heritage.

Both *The Book of Enoch* and the original text that contained the *Noah* fragment were obviously very influential texts upon later Biblical authors. But it shouldn't just be of concern that these texts are merely describing similar features for these angels; it wouldn't much matter if they were simply copying the description from older texts such as *1 Enoch*. What is important is *why* these angels are being described with certain features such as white skin and hair.

What kind of person might have both white skin and hair? Was it simply meant as a symbol of purity or was it something more? Although it is technically impossible according to mainstream science, let's step into the realm of science-fiction and answer the question: a person who should have these types of traits would be someone with *absolutely no genetic heritage.*

Without Father & Without Mother

The New Testament book of Hebrews contains numerous references to Jesus being of the priesthood of Melchizedek, and even likens Jesus to being another Melchizedek.[51] This is significant when you consider that the priestly line of Melchizedek was deemed superior to all of the other priesthoods, including that of Aaron.

Melchizedek (Hebrew: מלכיצדק and Greek: Μελχιζεδεκ, pronounced "Mel-kee-zeh-dek") is described as the "priest of the Most High God" and was called "king of righteousness," and the "king of peace" since he was the king of Salem (Jerusalem):

> For it is attested of him [Jesus], "You are a priest forever, according to the order of Melchizedek."
>
> Hebrews 7:17 NRSV[52]

But here is the really interesting part. When describing Melchizedek, it says that he was:

> Without father, without mother, without genealogy, having neither beginning of days nor end of life, but resembling the Son of God, he remains a priest forever.
>
> Hebrews 7:3 NRSV

What does this mean when it says that Melchizedek had no father or mother, or *any* family history for that matter? It is seemingly impossible, and probably why many scholars rarely bring up this statement. Sure, they might mention it very briefly, but the full impact never seems to be discussed any further.

Followers of the ancient astronaut theories would probably conjecture that Melchizedek was a test-tube baby, but this is unlikely and not enough evidence is provided by the texts to support that idea. He probably was not a regular human being, either. He resembled the "Son of God," which is a reference either to Jesus or to the other angels called the "sons of God." Either way, both cases point to a similar physical appearance since the book of Revelation describes the ascended Jesus with white skin and hair.[53]

So what would a person that had never been "born" actually look like? To answer this hypothetical question, we must first look into a brief overview of the science of genetics and how certain traits are inherited. This information will allow us to determine what would result from a lack of genetic traits.

Both skin and hair color are partially controlled by mutations in the MC1R (Melanocortin-1 receptor) gene. For instance, mutations in the MC1R gene are what cause some Europeans to have red hair and pale skin. This gene also causes variations in how much a person's skin may tan from exposure to UV rays.[54] We inherit our skin color from our parents. In general, micro-evolution has allowed the adaptation of our skin color to suit the regions that we live, so that people with ancestors that lived in a predominately sunny area of the world have darker skin than those that lived in areas that receive much less sunlight. The advantage of having darker skin in the areas rich in sunlight is that it helps to protect from skin cancer and prevents the destruction of the B vitamin folate, which is essential for DNA synthesis. Lighter skin color has the advantage of absorbing more sunlight, which increases the amount of vitamin D that is produced and helps with the absorption of calcium and bone growth.[55] Hair color, like our skin, is based on the amount of a pigment called melanin that is passed on from parent to child. Generally, more melanin results in darker hair color.[56] A lack of this melanin would result in white hair.

So far, it sounds like at the very least these angels might have been ordinary people who were affected by a genetic condition known as Albinism. When a person suffers from Albinism, the melanin required for color pigmentation is not present, which causes their skin to be an extremely pale shade of pink and hair color to be a flax-white. Their eye color is generally a very pale blue. They are also usually very sensitive to sunlight, which will strain their eyes and easily burn their skin.[57]

Searching through the texts, we find a peculiar clue that may indicate the angels were indeed sensitive to sunlight. When the patriarch Jacob got into a wrestling match with an angel, it was a stalemate that lasted all night. When the angel saw that the dawn was approaching, he begged Jacob to release him, but Jacob would not do so until the angel blessed him. The angel refused to reveal his name to Jacob, but is sometimes referred to as the "dark angel" since he feared the sunrise.[58]

It is possible that the angels were affected by Albinism, but this is not the most likely reason for their condition. It is probable that a hypothetical being that was created without a father, and without a mother, would also have these attributes. Assume for a moment that there was some sort of ancient device that could use a basic DNA blueprint to essentially create a generic or stock being. Perhaps "translation" through such device would be necessary for an angel to visit our realm.

For instance, if skin color is inherited as a genetic trait, but there are no genes to inherit, then there would be no reason for such a being's skin to have a pigment. Also, their "new" skin has not yet been exposed to the sun. Of course, over time they may indeed begin to show color or even tan, but not immediately. The same applies for hair and eye color. Such an idea about manufactured beings may sound very far-fetched, or scientifically impossible, but a close inspection of ancient texts appears to support this theory. Additionally, an artificial being would not need to be born, so theoretically it could be created as a full adult.

In such a scenario, the characteristics of these beings would not necessarily be subject to the laws of nature. For instance, the creature's skull may not be separated into different sutures since it never needed to fit through a birth canal. Could this be an explanation for the "impossible" characteristics of the long-headed skull from Malta mentioned earlier? If the father was an angel, and his genetics were slightly different from that of a normal human, then perhaps some of these traits would be passed onto the child— such as the skull not having the median knitting. According to science, such anomalies are considered impossible, but only if we assume that both parents were fully human. If in fact one of the parents was something not of this world, then a number of extraordinary possibilities become open for further debate.

This brings us to another important factor. Technically, only creatures belonging to similar species can interbreed. Examples would be a male donkey and female horse that create a mule hybrid. Another example would be a lion that mates with a tiger to create a "liger" or a "tigon" (depending on the gender of the parents).[59] There are natural barriers to prevent the breeding of completely different classes of animals. For instance, a dog cannot breed with a cat, and a horse could not breed with shark. And finally, as a classic episode of *South Park* has illustrated, "pig and elephant DNA just won't splice!"[60] Indeed, these might be silly examples, but they illustrate the point that such interbreeding cannot occur naturally.

However, a hotly debated topic in the news is just how far science can go with genetic experimentation, particularly when creating mixed creatures sometimes called Chimeras, referring to the mythical hybrid creatures. These crosses between animals and humans must be artificially created in a laboratory by various means.[61] They are usually created by grafting genes from one animal with the cells of another. Scientists can also bypass the natural barriers that prevent this by using powerful equipment to directly fertilize the egg of an animal or human with the sperm of something else.

Whatever the case, it seems as though such interbreeding can only occur artificially. However, if these angelic beings were genetically different, but close enough to a human, they were probably able to successfully impregnate a woman naturally, just as the texts describe. There is only one problem. Apparently, the genetics were close enough to bypass the natural barriers of a normal fertilization process, but different enough to cause major genetic mutations in the offspring. This is most likely the primary reason why the children of the Watchers had genetic deformities such as six digits or double-rows of teeth. Of course, not every one of them necessarily had these defects. Could there be a more likely reason to explain such widespread genetic abnormalities? New evidence may eventually surface that better answers these questions, but for now, this seems to be the best idea that is also supported by the ancient texts.

Leaving no stone unturned, there may still be other possibilities accounting for the existence of these particular legends. The simplest explanation would be that the Watchers and other similar beings are nothing more than metaphors intended to teach humanity moral lessons. If this is the case, then obviously the fall of the Watchers never really happened and the Watchers themselves may never have actually existed. Religious texts are always full of metaphors, such as referring to God as a gentle "Shepherd" and to people as His "flock of sheep." Ancient writings referred to the Watchers and gods as "stars" or other celestial objects—and nobody has argued that this should be interpreted literally to suggest that there were actual stars roaming about the planet.

Nonetheless, the purpose of a metaphor is to illustrate a comparison between someone or something to the attributes of a different person, thing, or idea. For example, consider when someone says, "He is such a snake!" The intention is obviously to align the unfavorable qualities of a particularly untrustworthy or unpleasant person with the equally unfavorable and negative characteristics that have been generally associated with snakes. Therefore, if we are confronted by an individual that acts in a deceitful or cunning manner, or appears to be "slimy" in their demeanor, we are reminded of the very same characteristics we have long associated with snakes. Whatever the case, no one actually believes that someone actually *is* a snake.

However tedious this lesson in semantics might seem, it is ultimately very important because in the later dream visions of Enoch, the story concerning the fall of the Watchers is deliberately *retold* using metaphorical language. Therefore, it appears as though the writer of *1 Enoch* was capable of distinguishing between metaphorical and literal techniques of storytelling, and was able to effectively utilize both methods throughout the text. Compare the following passage with the passages discussed earlier which present the story of the Watchers without the use of metaphorical language:

And again I saw with mine eyes as I slept, and I saw the heaven above, and behold <u>a star fell from heaven</u>, and it rose and eat and pastured amongst those oxen. And after that I saw the large and the black oxen, and behold they all changed their stalls and pastures and their cattle, and began to live with each other. And again I saw in the vision, and looked towards the heaven, and behold I saw <u>many stars descend and cast themselves down from heaven</u> to that first star, and <u>they became bulls amongst those cattle and pastured with them</u> [amongst them]. And I looked at them and saw, and behold they let out their privy members, like horses, and began to cover the cows of the oxen, and <u>they all became pregnant and bare elephants, camels, and asses</u>. And all the oxen feared them and were affrighted at them, and began to bite with their teeth and to devour, and to gore with their horns. And they began moreover to devour those oxen ; and behold all the children of the earth began to tremble and quake before them and to flee from them.

1 Enoch 86:1–6[62]

The first "star" that fell from heaven is Azazel,[63] the "bulls" are the Watchers, and the "cows" are the human women. The "elephants, camels, and asses" represent the giant offspring, the Nephilim, that resulted from these unions. Later chapters go on to describe how the holy angels punish the "star" and "bulls."[64] Then, an angel instructs a "white bull" (Noah) to transform into a man and build a large boat to survive the deluge.[65] These passages significantly complicate the notion that the Watchers should be considered nothing more than metaphorical representations of celestial objects. The writers were clearly using metaphors to allude to an event that they considered to be literal history. It makes absolutely no sense to use a metaphor to describe another metaphor!

———————◆———————

A brief overview of my theory up to this point might be beneficial considering the exhaustive amount of data that has been introduced: Angels became physical beings on Earth and they were described as having white skin and white hair, which substantiates the claims that they had no direct genetic lineage. Based on a basic human DNA blueprint, these angels were able to procreate with humans, but their genetics were different enough that it caused severe mutations in their offspring. These offspring came to be known as giants, and were reported in legends all over the world. The angels and some of the giants were considered to be divine rulers and taught humankind how to build civilizations. Additionally, since these beings were considered to be gods, anyone who was descended from them was believed to have the blood of the gods coursing through their veins. It was for this reason that nearly all of the powerful leaders in the ancient world claimed they were part "divine" and appointed to rule after the gods had left this world.

When Kingship Descended From Heaven

One of the oldest known civilizations in the world are the people referred to as the Sumerians. The Sumerians claimed that the gods had taught them everything they knew and helped them to establish their society. When archaeologists were discovering and deciphering the ancient stone tablets and cylinder seals belonging to these people, they came across what is known as the "Sumerian King List." What was amazing, and scoffed at by academia, was that the original kings apparently ruled for many years longer than any normal human could ever live! So the lists were regarded as mere fantasy, at least the first sections which referred to the antediluvian rulers. The following is a summary of only parts of the list; some of the kings have been removed to conserve space:

"After the kingship descended from heaven, the kingship was in Eridug. In Eridug, Alulim became king; he ruled for 28,800 years."
- Alulim of Eridug: 28,800 years
- Alalgar of Eridug: 36,000 years
- …
- Dumuzid of Bad-Tibira, the shepherd: 36,000 years
- En-Sipad-Zid-Ana of Larag: 28,800 years
- …
- Ubara-Tutu of Shuruppag: 18,600 years[66]

The life spans of these rulers are indeed quite incredible if they are to be believed, and unfortunately, it's virtually impossible to determine if they are accurate. What is intriguing is that further reading of the Sumerian's King List reveals that *after the flood* the duration of each king's reign drops off *significantly:*

"After the flood had swept over, and the kingship had descended from heaven, the kingship was in Kish."
- Jushur of Kish: 1,200 years
- Kullassina-bel of Kish: 960 years
- Nangishlishma of Kish: 670 years
- En-Tarah-Ana of Kish: 420 years
- …[67]

Although the kings continued to reign for incredibly long periods of time, it appears as though they began to live noticeably shorter lives after the flood, and in particular, during the First Dynasty of Uruk (located in what is now modern day Iraq) and after the reign of Gilgamesh:

- Gilgamesh, whose father was a "phantom", lord of Kulaba: 126 years.
- Ur-Nungal of Unug: 30 years

- Udul-Kalama of Unug: 15 years
- ...
- Mesh-He of Unug: 36 years[68]

The list seems to indicate that there was something prolonging the life of these ancient kings. But after the flood their abnormally long life spans began to diminish, perhaps because the genetically inherited traits from the gods had been weakened over time. A similar phenomenon occurs within the Old Testament, when the life spans of the Biblical patriarchs also began to shorten.

For instance, Adam lived for 930 years. His son, Seth, lived for 912 years. Later, Jared, who was supposed to have been born when the Watchers descended, lived to be 962. Enoch lived for 365 years, but did not die because God took him to heaven.[69] Methuselah, probably the most famous for his long life, died at 969. Lamech lasted 777 years and finally there was Noah, who lived for 950 years. After the flood, the lifespan of humans began to drop considerably.

Attempting to offer an alternative explanation for these long lives, some critics have argued that because people in the ancient world usually followed lunar based calendar systems, that the number of years has been miscalculated. This means that the ages given should be 13.5 times less. This would make Adam almost 69 years old and Methuselah nearly 72. While this may have been considered old since we are told that the life expectancy in the ancient world was much shorter than this, there continue to be discrepancies with this particular theory. For instance, the Bible states that Enoch's son, Methuselah, was born when Enoch was 65 years old (Genesis 5:21), which would only be about 4 years and 10 months old! Obviously, this cannot be accurate. Still, others have proposed additional ideas to explain these ages, including one theory that suggests that people lived longer because fewer ultraviolet rays were capable of reaching the earth from the sun due to a thicker atmosphere.[70]

Unfortunately, because apocryphal texts such as *1 Enoch* are largely unknown to most people, they are forced to merely speculate how the patriarchs managed to lived such long lives. Furthermore, a lack of exposure to the legends of other cultures severely limits the perception of readers that focus exclusively upon the Bible alone. Yet ancient texts from around the world repeatedly state that it was the intervention of flesh-and-blood gods that enabled humans to live longer. There is no need to invent alternative ideas when the record keepers of the past have already given an arguably more consistent explanation. But because people refuse to accept this admittedly extraordinary idea, they must resort to making up ideas that are not supported by any concrete evidence: Biblical, scientific, or otherwise. While it may be difficult to believe that angelic beings were once at large on our planet, the evidence supporting this claim is rooted in scores upon scores of unrelated documents the world over, whereas other more "rational" explanations ultimately originate within the imaginations of a select few individuals.

To further complicate matters, at some point in history the gods were either commanded to depart the earth, or decided for themselves that it was time to move on to other parts of the world. According to *1 Enoch* and other brief mentions throughout the Bible, the Watchers were punished for revealing forbidden knowledge and engaging in sexual intercourse with human beings and were said to have been imprisoned in "Darkness" until Judgment Day. Yet apparently, there were still other gods that were considered to be benevolent, for Native American legends state that these "spirit people" remained on the earth until their work was completed. Afterwards, the legends state that once they had successfully taught humankind how to survive independently, these helpful beings departed to their original homes and promised that if their assistance was ever required again, they would return to the earth.

Some cultures were so ardently convinced that their angelic guardians were going to return, that they were willing to risk their entire kingdoms. For instance, this belief led to the downfall of the Aztec empire. Their god-king was called Quetzalcoatl, the "feathered serpent," who was considered totally pure and good. Through the trickery of other gods, he fell into misfortune. Later, he redeemed himself by helping to create humans and educating them. When it came time for Quetzalcoatl to leave, a bright star dawned in the east, which the Aztecs also named Quetzalcoatl to honor their departing leader. It was later discovered that this particular star was in fact the planet Venus, the significance of which we shall discuss in greater detail in a later chapter. Nonetheless, Quetzalcoatl earned the titled "Lord of the Dawn," and according to legend, he sailed to the east on a raft of serpents but promised that he would one day return to the people he loved so much.[71] But there remains one significant detail concerning Quetzalcoatl: he was described as having *white skin and hair,* and clothed in *white robes.*

The Spanish conquistador, Hernán Cortés, learned of this legend and used it to his advantage. In November of 1519 CE, Cortés and his men invaded Tenochtitlán, modern day Mexico City, and claimed that he was the returning god Quetzalcoatl. The Aztec chief, Moctezuma, had never seen a Caucasian person before. He believed Cortés to be an emissary, if not the white-skinned god himself finally returning.[72] Thus began the demise of the Aztec civilization.[73]

From China to Europe, and North America to South America, our ancient ancestors spoke of white-skinned gods that descended from holy mountains and hills. But how and why did these gods journey to Earth? What kind of advanced technology might have been involved? To answer these questions we must explore some important ancient cities and structures, particularly those in Mesopotamia and Egypt. Ancient doctrines indicate that the gods utilized powerful "gateways" in order to swiftly move from one realm to another. While similar ideas have been a familiar staple of science-fiction stories for some time now, readers may be surprised to discover how prevalent these concepts were thousands of years ago.

Summary

❖ The Nephilim (נְפִילִים) described in the Bible are generally considered to be the giant offspring of fallen angels and human women; this was further supported by the rendering of the term into the Greek language as gigantes (γίγαντες).

❖ It is highly unlikely that the legendary giants of the ancient world were people who suffered from the medical condition known as Gigantism or Acromegaly.

❖ In addition to their size, other physical characteristics common to these giants was the appearance of a sixth finger or toe. Some reports of the alleged recovery of giant skeletons and remains have made mention of identical abnormalities as well as double-rows of teeth and other deformities (e.g. elongated heads).

❖ Ancient texts have sometimes attributed serpentine characteristics to the angels that were believed to have been on the earth, but more often, these beings are described with abnormally white skin and hair, possibly an indication that they had no genetic inheritance.

❖ Ancient lists, such as the Sumerian King List, describe how the first kings lived for significantly long periods of time, indicating that they had inherited special genetics from their angelic parents. Similar accounts are described within the Old Testament, as well as by other cultures (e.g. the Aztecs and Maya).

PART 3

Map of the Ancient Near East

THE GATEWAYS OF THE GODS

Any sufficiently advanced technology is indistinguishable from magic.
—Arthur C. Clarke[1]

SACRED PYRAMID OR PYRAMID-LIKE TEMPLES are found all over the world. The actual purposes for these structures were known only to the people that used them, but unfortunately, the ancient people took the secrets of the pyramids to their graves. Historians have long speculated why and for what purpose the pyramids were constructed. Some researchers believe that the pyramids served as monuments or tombs for kings, centers for religious rituals, astronomical observatories, and even power sources for great amounts of energy. The ancients have left very little information regarding these structures, fueling centuries of widespread speculation. However, the small amount of information that has been collected appears to be linked by a variety of common functions. Strangely, this has gone largely unnoticed by many investigators.

The Great Pyramid of Egypt

Perhaps the most famous of historical structures are the pyramids of Egypt. The Great Pyramid of Giza has inspired awe and demanded the attention of people since antiquity. It is the first and only remaining monument of the "Seven Wonders of the Ancient World"—while the others have been reduced to dust and their majesty exists only within written records. There have been many detailed books and fantastic documentaries dealing with the pyramids as well as the various theories regarding the amazing feats of engineering that enabled their construction, but for our specific purposes here, I'd like to provide a quick overview for readers that may not be familiar with some of the phenomenal skills demonstrated by the pyramid builders.

Traditional Egyptologists believe that the Great Pyramid was built approximately four and a half thousand years ago during the reign of the Pharaoh Khufu (c. 2589–c. 2566 BCE),[2] who was known to the Greeks as Cheops. Some researchers believe that recent discoveries of water erosion push the date back to 10,500 BCE, but this theory is still hotly debated. However, determining the precise construction date is not a concern of our investigation at the present time.

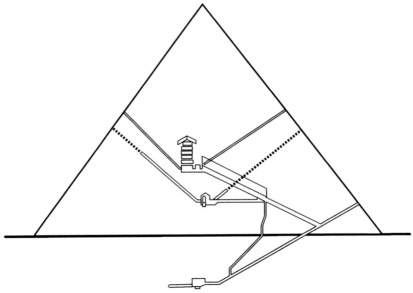

Cross-section of the Great Pyramid of Giza revealing several of the shafts and tunnels.

Until the Lincoln Cathedral was built around 1300 CE, the Great Pyramid was the tallest building on Earth, measuring nearly 481 feet (146.59 m). Each side of the base measured to be approximately 755.8 feet (230.37 m), but was reduced to only 746.4 feet (227.5 m) after the triangular blocks of pure white limestone casing were removed in the ninth century CE to construct Mosques and other buildings in the nearby city of Cairo.[3] It was once estimated that about 2.3 million blocks were used in its construction, some weighing from two to seventy tons each. These blocks were placed with such precision, that not even the blade of a knife can be inserted between them. However, more recent quarry evidence suggests that only 1.3 million blocks (some estimate even less, such as 750,000 blocks) may have been used that weighed 1.6 tons on average.[4]

The sides of the pyramid rise at an angle of 51° 52' (or more precisely as 51° 51' 14.3").[5] It is aligned to true north with such accuracy that it is only off by three minutes of a single degree, and may have been perfectly aligned when it was first constructed. Compare this with the modern Paris observatory, which is off by six minutes of a degree from true north.[6] It is interesting to note that this uncommon slope appears to be intentional and incorporates the mathematical function of Pi (π), giving support to the belief that the pyramid builders may have had advanced knowledge of mathematics and geometry well ahead of the accepted historical timeline.

In fact, the author and mechanical engineer, Christopher Dunn, notes that if the angle of the sides all equal 51° 51' 14", then the perimeter of the pyramid is in relationship to its height the same as the circumference of a circle is to its radius.[7] Some other researchers have used this to promote the idea that the pyramid itself is actually the solution for "squaring the circle." There are problems with this theory, however, because it requires some manipulation of numbers and measurements in order to make the solution work. In Appendix C, I elaborate on why I feel that these proposed solutions are flawed and why I consider it so dangerous to accept the claims of certain researchers promoting this belief.

No one has been able to confirm exactly how the pyramid builders accomplished their monumental tasks. The most obvious problem is the immense size of some of the stone blocks. Not only would they have been very cumbersome to move,[8] but some of the largest ones weren't even located at the bottom. For example, some blocks were raised 138 feet (46 meters) above the ground and moved into position with stunning precision. It has been determined that the blocks of stones did not come from local surroundings, but from a quarry over five hundred miles away in Aswan. This presents another problem as to how the huge blocks were transported over such great distances. It has been suggested that the blocks were floated along the Nile River, but modern attempts to reenact this procedure have proven unsuccessful. Another unanswered question is why the builders found it necessary to use large blocks from so far away when sufficient materials were locally available and could have been used instead. While it is still pure speculation at this point, some researchers have suggested that perhaps these particular stones were chosen because their material composition possessed certain qualities necessary for the building's function.

It is generally believed among Egyptologists that once the quarried stones were at the site of the pyramid, they were dragged along mud-brick ramps to reach the higher elevations. However, the inherent problem with this idea is that it meant the distances required to move the blocks increased even more as the ramps spiraled around the pyramid. (Have you ever noticed how many more people can fit into a line if it snakes back and forth? This is a similar concept.)

Perhaps the most perplexing issue is that the construction of the ramps themselves would have been an immense undertaking. Ramps of this type probably required even more work than the pyramid itself because they would have to be built up and then torn back down. Furthermore, the ramps would prevent the builders from spotting any alignment errors as the pyramid was being constructed, which makes the accuracy even more astonishing.

It is also important to note that no one has been able to recreate the Great Pyramid, even on a smaller scale, because of the difficulty involved in moving the large blocks without the use of modern equipment. Attempts have been made, but all have failed. In 1978, the Nippon Corporation of Japan was given the challenge to construct a sixty foot pyramid in Egypt using only the methods and tools that Egyptologists thought were used to construct the original pyramids. In the book, *Pyramid Prophecies,* Max Toth states:

> Once cut into approximate one-ton blocks, the stones could not be barged across the River Nile. Floatation apparently was not the simple answer, as had been suggested. The blocks finally had to be ferried across by steamboat.
>
> Then, teams of one hundred workers each tried to move these stones over the sand—and they could not move them even an inch! Modern construction equipment had to be resorted to, and once again, when the blocks of stone were finally brought to the building site, the teams could not lift their individual stones more than a foot or so. In the final construction step, a crane and helicopter were used to position the blocks.[9]

Other recent attempts have been made to build similar pyramids. The British television program NOVA assembled a team of people including Egyptologist Mark Lehner and stone mason Roger Hopkins to build a pyramid twenty feet high. The entire project took three weeks to complete, but involved the use of steel tools (instead of copper ones) and even front-end loaders. To look more impressive on camera, the final stones were physically dragged into place by laborers. The result was a miniature pyramid that Dr. Lehner said, "…would have fitted neatly on the top of the Great Pyramid, in whose shadow we built it."[10]

Another interesting fact about the Great Pyramid is that it is missing its capstone, also known as the "pyramidion." It's possible that one was never placed on the pyramid, but very unlikely. It is also commonly believed that the capstone was stolen, because legends tell that it was either made of solid gold or at least gold-plated. The significance of the gold capstone will be explained shortly and discussed in more detail later in our investigation.

When the Great Pyramid was completed, it was encased in white limestone that reflected the sun's light so brilliantly that the Egyptians called it the *Ikhet,* meaning "Glorious Light."[11] The pyramid shape itself is closely associated with the powers of the sun god, Re (or Ra). The Pyramid Texts (religious depictions of the afterlife that were inscribed on the interior walls of some pyramids) indicate that when the pharaoh died, the rays of the sun would be transformed into a *celestial stairway* for the deceased king to ascend to heaven.[12]

The legendary bird known as the phoenix was called the *benu* bird by the Egyptians and worshipped at Heliopolis ("City of the Sun" called *On* or *An* by the Egyptians). It was believed to be the incarnation of Re and was closely associated with the pyramid. The benu bird was said to perch upon a pyramidal mound called the *benben,* which represented the pyramids and the pyramidal point at the top of Egyptian obelisks. The benben symbolized the primordial mound in Egyptian creation legends that rose from the primeval waters, called Nun, at the beginning of time.[13] It was believed that the pharaoh would be resurrected in a new body, similar to how the phoenix or benu would die in a blazing funeral pyre and be reborn from the ashes.

Several examples of capstones, or pyramidions, have been discovered from various pyramids. Over the past few centuries, the remnants of numerous pyramidions have been discovered, and some recent evidence suggests that these

The Egyptian Benu Bird with a Sun symbol above its head.

capstones may have been gold-plated. The most famous is from the pyramid of Amenemhet III, who reigned in the Twelfth Dynasty. It was discovered in 1900 CE and is made of grey granite with inscriptions on each side addressing the gods Harakhte (the god of the rising sun), Anubis, Osiris, Ptah and Neith. According to a translation by I.E.S. Edwards, the inscription to Harakhte reads: "May the face of the king be opened so that he may see the Lord of the Horizon [Harakhte] when he crosses the sky; may he cause the king *to shine as a god,* lord of eternity and indestructible" (emphasis added).[14] Could this be a possible connection to "the shining ones"—the Watchers?

For centuries, it has been believed that the pyramids were created as gigantic tombs to house the majesty of the pharaohs. This idea has come under fire lately and is a heated debate between traditional Egyptologists and other independent researchers proposing alternative ideas. New theories suggest that long after the original functions of the pyramids went out of use, priests may have performed intrusive burials to place the bodies inside. Even Mark Lehner, an Egyptologist that strictly adheres to the "pyramid-as-tomb" theory, has admitted that "no original burials have ever been found in any Egyptian pyramids."[15]

One of the terms the Egyptians used to refer to the pyramid was *Mr* or alternatively as *Mer*.[16] Mark Lehner explains: "There seems to be no cosmic significance in the term itself. I.E.S. Edwards, the great pyramid authority, attempted to find a meaning from *m,* 'instrument' or 'place', plus *ar,* 'ascension', as 'place of ascension'. Although he himself doubted this derivation, the pyramid was indeed a place or instrument of ascension for the king after death."[17] Stephen S. Mehler writes that according to the traditions of Khemitans, a group of people believed to guard the sacred knowledge of ancient Egypt, the word for pyramid was *Per-Neter*, meaning "House of Nature" or "House of Energy."[18] It could also mean "House of God" since Neter is the term understood to refer to the Egyptian divinities.

Although some researchers may argue that one term is more valid than the other, it is interesting to see how they both can be reconciled under a revised viewpoint. For example, if *Per-Neter* meant "House of God," there is no discrepancy with traditional Egyptology because the pharaoh was considered to be a god. On the other hand, scholars who doubt the meaning "place of ascension" for the term *Mer,* might be more inclined to accept this definition if they had a more comprehensive understanding of what "ascension" meant to the Ancient Egyptians. Egyptologists also admit that these ancient people believed that the pyramids were actually "resurrection machines." In fact, Egyptologists have used this idea to "prove" that bodies were once housed in the pyramids. However, these same Egyptologists never seem to elaborate any further on how exactly a "resurrection" could have occurred, except that it might have involved the stars.

Alternative theorists trying to dismiss the "pyramid-as-tomb" idea depend upon the fact that no original burials were ever discovered inside a pyramid. Traditional Egyptologists explain that the tombs were probably robbed and the bodies removed, and while that certainly seems plausible, it also seems like a convenient excuse to dismiss alternatives. What both sides fail to realize is that *absence of evidence is not evidence of absence.* In this case, just because no original bodies were ever found in any of the tombs, it does not mean that they were never there. Likewise, even though there may not seem to be evidence of an advanced civilization or an advanced form of technology, it does not necessarily mean that it never existed.

To help explain this idea another way, consider that someone has just committed a crime. The criminal knows that leaving less evidence improves the chances of evading arrest and prosecution. They may wear gloves to avoid leaving fingerprints, or wipe up the floor to remove tracks from their shoes. If they are careful, the investigators at the crime scene will have a difficult, if not impossible time pinpointing the identity of the culprit. But this does not mean that the person was never there, only that there is no evidence of his or her presence, barring the crime itself.

So, how can these two opposing concepts be reconciled? It's quite simple, actually, and it fits with the accepted meanings of the terms for the pyramids. Let's suppose that the body of a deceased pharaoh was placed inside the Great Pyramid, but that it was not meant to be a tomb. Instead, something was contained inside the pyramid, or perhaps it was the pyramid itself, that would activate and transfer the physical body of the pharaoh to the afterlife. Remember, Egyptian legends maintain that the pharaoh was translated into the heavens through the power of the pyramid and its association with the benu bird (phoenix). This is simply one alternative view that explains the apparent absence of a body, which instead of dismissing the legends as mere superstition, actually uses and acknowledges the myths in order to support the proposed idea.

It is also important to understand that the word "pyramid" is of Greek origin and probably also holds a clue as to the function of these buildings.

The Greek word "pyramidos" contains the roots for "pyro," which refers to fire, and also "middle" or "center." Thus, it is effectively translated as "Fire in the Middle." This provides further connections to the legends about the regenerative powers of the phoenix and fire. So it would seem that the very term "pyramid" is referring to some kind of procedure that incorporates the use of fire or light in order to function as a "resurrection machine."

In fact, the papyrus texts commonly referred to as the Egyptian "Book of the Dead" should be more accurately translated as the "Book of Going Forth by Day/Light." These texts, which evolved from the earlier Coffin and Pyramid Texts, were a series of elaborate spells and rituals that were designed to assist the spirits of the recently departed dead and ensure that they properly reached heaven.[19] The Pyramid Texts were carved into the pyramid walls and frequently stated that "the king belongs to the sky."[20] They also revealed that at one time "the sky was split from the earth and the gods went to the sky,"[21] which is reminiscent of Mesopotamian legends that explain the separation of heaven from earth.

There are many other similarities between the Egyptian beliefs and those of other cultures, such as the Mesopotamians. Although the pyramids are generally thought to have functioned as elaborate tombs to house Egyptian royalty, the worldwide recurrence of common themes and terminology associated with these structures indicate that the true purpose of the pyramids may have been much more complex. Ultimately, our understanding of the pyramids may have to be significantly revised after we study other ancient structures that were believed to serve as gateways to the heavenly realm.

The Ziggurats

The land between the Tigris and Euphrates Rivers, known as Mesopotamia (now modern Iraq), also contained many pyramid-like structures. They were not "true" pyramids in their shape, but rather "stepped" or "tiered" pyramids. They were more properly called ziggurats, an Assyrian word *(ziqqurrātu)* that meant "pinnacle." The Sumerians referred to them as *unir* (𒀭𒎏𒌍). Ziggurats are most commonly believed to have been religious temples that were later used as astronomical observatories. Probably the most famous ziggurat was the "Tower of Babel" described in the Old Testament.[22]

The ziggurats were mostly constructed between 2200 and 550 BCE in southern Mesopotamia and also in the north by the Assyrians. The core was built from solid bricks of sun-dried mud and oven-baked glazed bricks were used for the outside. They generally did not have any internal rooms or spaces, except drainage shafts. Most ziggurats were either square or rectangular, with bases that averaged between approximately forty and fifty meters on each side. No complete example of a Mesopotamian ziggurat exists today, but there are still a few pieces that have managed to survive the ravages of time. The largest is located at Al-Untaš-Napiriša (modern Choga Zanbil), in Elam. It is one-hundred meters square at the base and preserved to a height of twenty-four meters, which is believed to be slightly less than half of its original height.[23]

Most ziggurats consisted of between two and seven tiers or stages, with a shrine dedicated to the local god of the city located at the building's summit. Access to the shrine was usually reached by a long stairway located on the North side of the tower. There were often two other stairways flanking

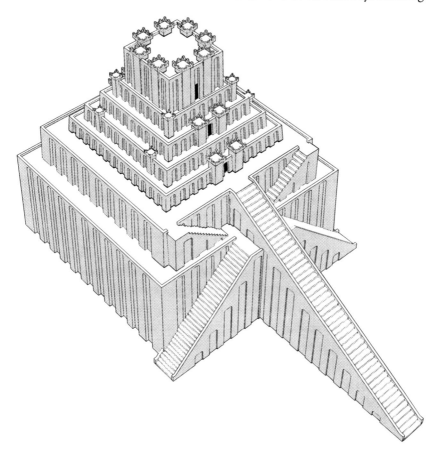

the sides of the main stairway, or perhaps a spiral stairway that followed the sides of the building. All of the walls had a slight inward slope to them and when coupled with the diminishing size of each successive tier, a person's eyes were inevitably directed toward the shrine.[24]

Glazed bricks were used for the outer walls and colored based on their cosmological significance. Evidence indicates that the four-level ziggurat at Ur-Nammu was painted black at the base level, followed by red on the next stage; the upper stage was whitewashed, and the shrine was a vibrant blue color. These colors represented the underworld, the earthly realm, the sky and finally heaven, respectively.[25] It is also possible that the roof of the shrine may have been gilded with gold, so as to represent the sun and God, and is comparable to the golden capstones of Egyptian pyramids.

According to some archaeologists, there is reason to believe that ground-level, or "lower" temples, housed the cult statues of certain gods. Such cult statues were thought to take on the authority of the gods when they were not physically present on the earth. Common rituals and offerings were left for these statues to appease them. "High" temples, such as the ziggurats, were not places intended for public worship or ceremonies, but were instead used as "a portal by a god on his visits to earth."[26]

The shrine contained a bed chamber that was used for "Sacred Marriage" ceremonies (known as *"Hieros Gamos"* in Greek). This may have sometimes involved two cult statues or even a deified king who engaged in ritual lovemaking with a priestess of Inanna (Ishtar). However, the Mesopotamians also believed that a real flesh-and-blood god from heaven would manifest here. According to Herodotus, some women awaited this visit from the god so that they could offer themselves to him.[27]

The Tower of Babylon was dedicated to the god Marduk, and called the *E-temen-an-ki*, which meant "House of the Foundation of Heaven and Earth." Similarly to how the *benben* (pyramid) was thought to represent the primeval mound that rose from the waters of chaos, the ziggurat was also considered to be a primeval mound upon which the universe was created. The ziggurats were intended to be built as cosmic axis points, and functioned as vertical "bridges" between heaven and earth as well as the underworld. They were also considered to be horizontal bridges between the lands of the earth.[28]

In the city of Nippur, the ziggurat dedicated to the god *Enlil* ("Lord of the Air") was called the *Dur-an-ki* ("Bond of Heaven and Earth"). The temple of Enlil was built adjacent to it and referred to as the *E-kur* ("Mountain House"). It was believed to have a cosmological connection with the ziggurat, where together the buildings acted as a "mooring-rope" between heaven and earth.[29]

If this is an accurate description of how these temples functioned, then it may also be describing a way of actually transferring a physical god from heaven to earth, or perhaps even the temples acted as a kind of teleportation device between other temples throughout the ancient world. These ideas are further supported by the Sumerians' cosmic images of a "mooring-rope" or "mooring-pole," that are mentioned throughout their writings. Some Mesopotamian scholars, such as Jeremy Black and Anthony Green, suggest that the Sumerians believed that the temple was "a channel of communication between earth and heaven."[30]

In fact, the very name of the city, Babylon, is derived from the Akkadian *Bab-ilim,* which translates to "gateway of god(s)." The original form was *Babil,* but the precise meaning is unknown even though it certainly seems to have the same root words of *bab* "gate" and *il* "god." Later, the plural form *Bab-ilani,* "gate of the gods" was used and became Βαβυλων (Babylon) in the Greek language.[31] In the Sumerian tongue it was known as *ka-dingir-ra* ("gate of god").

On the surface, the Biblical story about the Tower of Babel appears to be a morality lesson about overreaching our abilities and an explanation for the diversity of human language. It is a pun on the similarity between *Babel* (בבל) and the Hebrew word *bālal* (בלל) meaning, "to mix or confuse." This is where the modern word "babble" originated to describe a person's speech that isn't understandable. But there is far more than a simple play on words operating in this story:

> Then they said, "Come, let us build ourselves a city, and a <u>tower with its top in the heavens</u>, and let us <u>make a name for ourselves;</u> otherwise we shall be scattered abroad upon the face of the whole earth." The LORD came down to see the city and the tower, which mortals had built. And the LORD said, "Look, they are one people, and they have all one language; and this is only the beginning of what they will do; <u>nothing that they propose will now be impossible for them.</u> Come, <u>let us go down</u>, and <u>confuse their language there</u>, so that they will not understand one another's speech."
>
> Genesis 11:4–7 NRSV

There are a few points of interest in this passage. First, it has long been assumed that the tower would have to have been an incredibly tall structure if the people built it with the intention of reaching heaven. But if the tower itself or what was inside of it was actually the "gateway" then the extreme height was not necessary. The second point of interest is that the people wanted to "make a name" for themselves. The word for "name" in Hebrew is *shem* (שֵׁם)—a term that author Zecharia Sitchin mistranslates as "sky-borne vehicle" and "rocketship" to justify his ancient astronaut theory.[32] I will elaborate on the specifics of the term "shem" in the next chapter, along with the reason why it is important in the context of the Tower of Babylon incident. However, for the sake of clarity, I want to focus on other specific details concerning this passage at the present time.

Another important factor is that when God (or more likely the "Angel of the LORD," יְהוָה מַלְאַךְ) manifested on the earth with his fellow members of the Divine Council, they quickly put a stop to the project. Careful reading reveals some telling clues about the nature of this entity. His reasoning for ending the project does not appear to be that humans were doing anything wrong, but that they could potentially be as powerful as the gods—something that was simply not acceptable to the Divine Council.

The story is also portrayed in common Tarot decks as "The Tower" card. Other names for this card are "The House of God" and "The Lightning-Struck Tower." Most depictions of this card show lightning or divine fire striking the very top of the tower and two figures falling to their demise. Also, careful observation of the card shows many objects raining down from the sky that are actually the Hebrew letter *yod* (י). This is the first letter of the Holy Name of God, *Yahweh* (יְהוָה), and is often referred to as the "Hand of God." Since the card is the sixteenth of the Major Arcana, it is traditionally assigned the sixteenth letter of the Hebrew alphabet, which is *ayin* (ע). While it may be nothing more than a coincidence, the meaning of ayin is "eye" and its association with a tower used by the Watchers is indeed curious and was

THE TOWER

perhaps intended by the original creators of the cards.

The unfortunate incident at Babylon also bears a similarity to another event described earlier in Genesis: The "sin" of Adam and Eve. In the last chapter, I mentioned that according to Jewish legends, the serpent being that tricked Eve was probably not a snake. The being knew that Adam and Eve[33] were instructed not to eat from the "tree of knowledge of good and evil," and that they could be tricked into disobeying God. Traditional beliefs suggest that Adam and Eve would have been immortal as long as they remained in the Garden of Eden; but due to their disobedience they were banished and therefore became mortals on Earth. The *nachash* (serpent, "shining one") told Eve that to eat the fruit of the tree would open their eyes and they would "be like gods, knowing good and evil."[34] But this was only partially true, because when God discovered that they had eaten from the tree, the situation grew slightly more alarming. The reason that Adam and Eve had to be banished from Eden was stated clearly when God said to the other members of the Divine Council:

> See, <u>the man has become like one of us</u>, knowing good and evil; and now, he might reach out his hand and <u>take also from the tree of life</u>, and eat, and <u>live forever</u>.
>
> Genesis 3:22 NRSV

It is not intended here to make it seem as if the serpent was any kind of liberator for mankind. However, it does seem that God—or the being acting as the representative of God—in both the Garden of Eden incident as well as the Tower of Babel, preferred that the human race was to remain ignorant and subordinate. But why?

In various passages throughout the Bible, we are told that Yahweh came directly to the earth and interacted with the people. Quite often, though, it was understood that this was an "Angel of the LORD" (מלאך יהוה) that had physically manifested on the earthly plane. What severely complicates matters is that the ancient texts are not clear enough as to whether this "angel" was actually Yahweh incarnate, or simply an angel acting under His authority. It is this author's personal belief that the "Angel of Yahweh" was most likely a separate being (or beings) acting under the authority of God, but *not* actually God incarnate.

Gnostic beliefs held a similar view concerning this being. According to some of their popular myths, such as the *Apocryphon of John* (from the Nag Hammadi Library), a being called Yaldabaoth was born of Sophia (Greek for "Wisdom") and was described as a serpent with a lion's head. He was identified as the *Demiurge* (meaning "Artisan" or "Master Craftsman") and created other beings known as the *Archons* ("Rulers") to help him shape the foundations of the physical universe. He then declared himself to be the only god and that none other were comparable to him.[35] To the Gnostic point of view, Yaldabaoth was the wrathful Yahweh from the Old Testament. However, we must be careful about accepting the Gnostic's mythology because it is not without its own set of problems. Besides the usual discrepancies and other inaccuracies that are in most stories, much of the Gnostic beliefs were largely in opposition to traditional views. For instance, many of the Gnostics greatly detested the physical world and even considered their bodies to be impure because everything was created by an inferior being. Lastly, a great deal of Gnostic teachings are esoteric in nature and are therefore more difficult to comprehend without a well developed background regarding such topics.

Whether or not this "angel" is acting in humanity's favor is debatable. Certainly, the Gnostics viewed him as evil—and some of his actions were quite destructive (to put it mildly). However, in situations where it would seem a mortal human could attain divine status or reach heaven, these angelic beings seem to interfere. Perhaps it is in our best interest. Certainly the allure of god-like power would prove too much for many people to responsibly handle. Another reason might be that it was too early in our development for such a change. For instance, if humanity was intended to ascend to heaven and become like the gods, maybe the attempts were thwarted in the past because the time was not right. The ancient writings seem to tell us that the gods came to give human civilization a jumpstart, but then left to force us to reach the goal on our own. It would not be much of an accomplishment if we were simply given the ability to be like the gods without working for it.

The use of ziggurat temples as "gateways" to allow the gods to come and go from heaven is supported by the texts of the Bible. Most of the information has either gone largely unnoticed or has been misunderstood, therefore no one has accurately determined how these "gateways" supposedly functioned. The most famous example is one that most people don't even realize involves a ziggurat. It is the "Stairway to Heaven" seen by the patriarch Jacob in a vision:

> And he dreamed, and behold a <u>ladder</u> set up on the earth, and <u>the top of it reached to heaven</u>: and behold the <u>angels of God ascending and descending on it</u>. And, behold, <u>the LORD stood above it</u>…
>
> Genesis 28:12–13 KJV

Although commonly referred to as "Jacob's Ladder," closer investigation of the story shows that it wasn't a ladder at all. Instead, the ladder should more properly be described as a stairway or ramp, suggesting that it was a ziggurat, and many Bibles have a footnote to indicate this detail. The angels were seen walking up and down the stairs and into the shrine where the gateway was activated, and Yahweh stood on the roof.[36] Upon awaking from this dream, Jacob was terrified and exclaimed:

> How awesome is this place! This is none other than the <u>house of God</u>, and this is <u>the gate of heaven</u>.
>
> Genesis 28:17 NRSV

Before we begin to look into the operation of these gateways, it's important to remember that there are many other examples of ziggurats and pyramid-type buildings scattered all around the world, such as in South America and also Asia. The Maya civilization built the largest of the pre-Columbian cities and it was called *Chichén Itzá,* meaning "At the mouth of the wells of the Itzá people." It was also known as *Uucyabnal* ("Seven Great Rulers") in ancient chronicles.[37] There are many stepped-pyramids built in the complex, the two largest being the Pyramid of the Moon and the Pyramid of the Sun. The pyramid known as the Temple of Kukulcán (the Maya name for Quetzalcoatl) is located at the center of the city. It is referred to as "El Castillo," meaning "The Castle" in the Spanish language. It stands approximately seventy-five feet in height, and contains stairways on all four sides leading to the temple's top. The northern face is decorated with plumed serpent heads at the bottom of the steps, representing Kukulcán, and during the Spring and Fall equinoxes the sun casts shadows from the corner tiers of the pyramid that appear as a snake slowly slithering down the stairs as the day progresses.[38] An additional fact that is not well known is that the Maya incorporated the solar calendar into the physical structure of the temple. Each stairway consists of 91 steps. There is a stairway on all four sides, and the floor at the top of the temple counts as the final step. This results in 365 steps total: (91 x 4) + 1 = 365.

The the Temple of Kukulcán (Quetzalcoatl) in Mexico.
Photo Credit: Asbjorn Aakjaer / iStockphoto.com.

Quetzalcoatl (Kukulcán) also functioned as a type of phoenix myth to the native people. In the Annals of Cuauhtitlan it tells:

> When they reached the place they were searching for, now again there he [Quetzalcoatl] wept and suffered. In this year 1 Reed (so it is told, so it is said), when he had reached the ocean shore, the edge of the sky-water, he stood up, wept, took his attire and put on his plumes, his precious mask. When he was dressed, of his own accord he burned himself, he gave himself to the fire. So that where Quetzalcoatl burned himself is called the Place of Incineration.
>
> And it is said that when he burned, his ashes rose up and every kind of precious bird appeared and could be seen rising up to the sky … And after he had become ash the quetzal bird's heart rose up; it could be seen and was known to enter the sky. The old men would say he had become Venus; and it is told that when the star appeared Quetzalcoatl died. From now on he was called the Lord of the Dawn.[39]

Present day Mexico City is built over the Aztec remains of Tenochtitlán. Forty miles to the north of it there once existed the city known as Teotihuacán.

The name means "City of the Gods" or "The Place Where Men Become Gods" in the native Nahuatl language. This brings up interesting implications when considered alongside the evidence presented in this book.

Stepping Through the Gateways

The Bible and other ancient texts not only describe the use of "gateways" for these gods, but also provide some details about how they may have worked. However, if most of these gateways had been disabled or removed after the mishap that was instigated by the Watchers, such descriptions may be nothing more than "memories" that were passed down from generation to generation and later collected by the scribes. Nevertheless, while there certainly is not a detailed diagram or blueprint that shows how to build and operate a working gateway, there are enough clues in these descriptions that can help us to better understand how this technology might have functioned.

Once again, we must return to the land of Babylon. The clearest example of an active gateway is recorded in the story of King Nebuchadnezzar and the three Jewish priests: Shadrach, Meshach and Abednego. Nebuchadnezzar was said to have set up a giant golden idol to be worshipped by all of the people in the land, but the three priests refused to worship the false idol. Outraged with their disobedience, Nebuchadnezzar ordered that they be thrown into a blazing furnace—at least that's the best translation that's so far been available.

> He [Nebuchadnezzar] ordered the <u>furnace</u> heated up seven times more than was customary, and ordered some of the strongest guards in his army to bind Shadrach, Meshach, and Abednego and to throw them into the <u>furnace of blazing fire</u>. So the men were bound, still wearing their <u>tunics</u>, their <u>trousers</u>, their hats, and their other garments, and they were thrown into the <u>furnace of blazing fire</u>. Because the king's command was so urgent and the <u>furnace</u> was so overheated, <u>the raging flames killed the men who lifted Shadrach, Meshach, and Abednego</u>. But the three men, Shadrach, Meshach, and Abednego, fell down, bound, into the <u>furnace of blazing fire</u>.
>
> Daniel 3:19–23 NRSV

The word used for "fire" is *nuwr* (Aramaic: נוּר) and is from a root that means "to shine." While fire obviously provides a source of light, it is important to consider that perhaps "fire" is not the most accurate translation. Could it be that the word is referring to some otherworldly kind of light, and "fire" was the only suitable word that the translators could come up with? The story also places great emphasis on the "furnace of blazing fire" through repetition, which is a common technique employed when the author wants the audience to take notice of an important idea. The writer also stresses that the three men were bound in their clothes before being thrown into the furnace. The meanings of the words that are translated as "tunics" and "trousers" are uncertain among Bible translators and so their actual meanings are unknown. It could be possible that the men were wearing some kind of protective clothing or items, but until more detailed information can be found it is best not to speculate *too much*. The gateway motif is also supported when we are told that Nebuchadnezzar approached the "door" or "mouth" of the fiery furnace (Daniel 3:26), which is a translation of the Aramaic word, *terah* (תרע). Other meanings of this word are "gate" or "gateway."

The conventional argument is that Shadrach, Meshach, and Abednego were saved from the fire because of their faith in God, while the other men were consumed by the flames. For a long time, many people have willingly accepted this as the only lesson from the story. If that were the case, though, the three priests would only need to come out of the fire unscathed. Instead, the story becomes even more interesting and the implications of an active gateway become obvious:

> Then King Nebuchadnezzar was astonished and rose up quickly. He said to his counselors, "Was it not <u>three men</u> that we threw bound into the fire?" They answered the king, "True, O king." He replied, "But <u>I see four men unbound, walking in the middle of the fire, and they are not hurt; and the fourth has the appearance of a son of the gods</u>."
>
> Daniel 3:24–25 NRSV

It is now clear that the story is not simply relating a moral lesson about the worship of false idols and sustaining faith in God, but it also hints at an ancient technology that once existed. Christian Apologists have put forth the argument that the fourth person who appears in the fire is actually Jesus, since he is called the "Son of God," and that he was just not recognized by the people of that time. This is doubtful, because it is relying too much on changing the actual meaning of the words. It does not say specifically *the* "Son of God" or even make use of a name such as Joshua. We must hold to what the text says, and it describes a fourth being who suddenly appeared within the "fire" and looked like a "son of the gods."[40] The phrasing and words used make it more likely that the being was an angel, one of the Watchers, and *not* an appearance of Jesus long before his birth.

Another issue that we must address is why Nebuchadnezzar was "astonished" to see an angel appear in the gateway. Shouldn't he have realized that this was an actual working gateway and shouldn't he have been aware of its intended function? I can only suggest two possible explanations for these questions. First, if the original gateways had been deactivated, then perhaps Nebuchadnezzar was having difficulty figuring out how to properly use the one in his possession. Perhaps he had an idea, but without the required knowledge it was merely a guessing game, so that is why so many people were killed by this "fiery furnace." The three priests, on the other hand, might have already been initiated into the secrets regarding this technology and had been prepared to pass through the "fire" without causing harm to themselves. The other explanation, which is probably the most likely, is that this account was intended to portray Nebuchadnezzar as a buffoon since he did not know how to operate the gate. Given that the Jewish people had been held as captives in Babylon for many generations, it is not difficult to understand how this could serve as an early instance of political satire against Nebuchadnezzar and the Babylonians in general. Nevertheless, the gateway imagery is still present within the tale, especially with the emphasis placed upon divine fire.

Other similar descriptions of blazing fires and otherworldly lights are common throughout the Bible and other religious texts. Particularly, that fire or some kind of light is involved in the use of these gateways. The pyramids were intended to be "resurrection machines" and the Greek term means "fire in the middle." They were associated with the benu bird, the phoenix, which was made new again in the blazing flames of a funeral pyre.

In the world of the occult traditions, the element of fire was associated with transformation and manifestation; its designated symbol being an upright triangle . The Hebrew letter *yod* (ʼ) was assigned to it, being the first letter of the name of Yahweh and represented the Father of the Holy Family.[41] A device known as the "Triangle of the Art" or the "Triangle of Manifestation" was employed by practitioners when conjuring spirits. This tool allegedly functioned as a focus point between two realms allowing the manifestation of a spirit within the protective bounds of the triangle. If successful, it allowed interaction and communication between the occultist and the spirit.[42] However, it should be understood that this probably bears no direct relationship on the actual gateways being described in the distant past, and if it worked at all, it was not meant to give the spirits flesh and blood bodies.

In Greek mythology, the Titan Prometheus stole fire from heaven and gave it to mankind, which angered the gods. This fire symbolized important knowledge that was jealously guarded by the gods, and may have even been hinting at another kind of "fire." Also important to Greek mythology was that the gods were believed to live on Mount Olympus. Time and time again, we find that mountains are directly associated with the abode of the gods in cultures worldwide.

In fact, one of the main purposes of building the pyramids and ziggurats was to create artificial "mountains." The Sumerians referred to a "holy hill" or "holy mound" called the *Du-ku*. It was believed to be based "on the mountain of heaven and earth" and was considered to be a "world mountain" that existed before heaven was separated from earth. It was where the gods determined the destinies of humans and where the Anunnaki were said to have been created.[43] This bears an obvious resemblance to the Egyptian concept of the benben stone.

The Angel of Yahweh appeared to Moses in the burning bush at the "mountain of God" (Exodus 3:1). At another time, God appeared to Moses, Aaron, Nadab, Abihu, and seventy elders of Israel on the "mountain of God." Below his feet was a "pavement of sapphire stone" that was associated with heaven. God commanded Moses to come up to the top of the mountain to receive the Ten Commandments and a "cloud" descended onto the summit of Mount Sinai. This "cloud" was described as "a devouring fire on the top of the mountain in the sight of the people of Israel" (Exodus 24:9–18).

When Moses came down from the mountain for the second time (after the golden calf incident), his face shined brightly and all of the people were afraid of him.[44] Perhaps he was cloaked in the melam described by the Sumerians? The Transfiguration of Jesus also occurred at the top of a mountain and made Jesus radiant to those who looked upon him. Psalm 48 tells that the future holy mountain and sanctuary of Yahweh is identified as Mount Zion (1–2).

The book of Ezekiel contains a statement addressed to the king of Tyre, comparing him to the well known legend of a glorious being that fell from heaven because of his pride, usually thought to be Lucifer, but some argue that it could also apply to the fall of Adam and therefore mankind in general. Regardless, our concern is what is being described, not who it is addressing:

> You were the signet of perfection, full of wisdom and perfect in beauty. <u>You were in Eden</u>, the garden of God; every precious stone was your covering … and worked in gold were your settings and your engravings. On the day that you were created they were prepared. With an anointed cherub as guardian I placed you; you were on the <u>holy mountain of God</u>; <u>you walked among the stones of fire</u>. You were blameless in your ways from the day that you were created, until iniquity was found in you. In the abundance of your trade you were filled with violence, and you sinned; so I cast you as a profane thing from the <u>mountain of God</u>, and the guardian cherub drove you out from among <u>the stones of fire</u>.
>
> Ezekiel 28:12–16 NRSV

Upon close inspection, there is a surprising element mentioned in this passage: the Garden of Eden is also called a *mountain!* Moreover, Ezekiel 28:2 refers to this place as the "seat of the gods"—the meeting place of the Divine Council.[45] Not only does this allow us to connect Eden to the artificial "mountains" or "gateways," but it also raises incredible implications about the very location and nature of Eden.

The "stones of fire" are thought by some scholars to be the same as the "pavement of sapphire stones" that God was standing on when He appeared to Moses at Mount Sinai. However, that does not quite fit what the text seems to be describing. The word translated as "stones" is *'eben* (אֶבֶן). It is based on the root word *banah* (בָּנָה), meaning "to build" or "establish." Realizing this, it is certainly not a stretch of the imagination to consider that these verses could be referring to structures built of either common stones or precious jewels. It could therefore be rendered as "you walked among the *buildings* of fire," and could be referring to specific buildings with stones of unique qualities not like ordinary buildings.

Another connection to Egyptian legends also becomes clear. Recall that the capstone of a pyramid was also known as a *benben* and its association with the transformation of the phoenix in fire. Suddenly, the *'eben* (אֶבֶן) "stones of fire" in the Garden of Eden can be linked to structures such as the Great Pyramid that were used to translate the pharaoh to the heavens. It is possible that these "stones of fire" were contained in many of the different structures of the ancient world and provided direct links to the heavens.

We also have a potential answer to another anomaly. Recall that the Nephilim/giants were said to be on the earth both before and after the Flood. This appears to create a contradiction within the Biblical texts, though, because we are told that the flood waters were intended to wipe out all living things after they became wicked (i.e. corrupted by the angels). Yet a short time later, we find the Nephilim once again terrorizing the land but without any explanation as to how they got there. If some of their angelic parents were able to "escape" the devastation via the gateways, they could easily return to the earth after the flood waters retreated. They would once again have free reign to begin creating more hybrid offspring.

Taking all of this information into consideration, and referring back to the verses in Ezekiel, conjures up images of a great mountain or ziggurat with smaller ziggurats or temples at the summit. Each one of these would be gateways to different dimensions or locations on Earth and perhaps elsewhere—the true gateways of the gods.

One of the Dead Sea Scrolls from Qumran states:

> When the gods of knowledge enter by the doors of glory, and when the holy angels depart towards their realm, the entrance doors and the gates of exit proclaim the glory of the King, blessing and praising all the spirits of God when they depart and enter by the gates.
> 4Q405 23, i[46]

It doesn't make sense to downplay the descriptions of these "doors of glory" and "gates" by simply saying that they are common open doorways. The scroll fragment is clearly stressing that these "doors" are extraordinary. When this is coupled with a reference to the angels departing "towards their realm," it supports the theory that these are gateways to another dimension.

The *Book of Enoch* explains that the Watchers descended from the top of Mount Hermon, the "Cursed Mountain."[47] *Enoch* also states that in a lower heaven there is a "place which burns day and night, where there are seven mountains of magnificent stones" and the middle mountain "reached to heaven like the throne of God," with a "flaming fire" at the summit.[48] Beyond these mountains was "a deep abyss, with columns of heavenly fire," and past that was a void with no firmament or foundation. Seven burning stars were visible there and an angel explains:

> This place is the end of heaven and earth: this has become a prison for the stars and the host of heaven. And the stars which roll over the fire are they which have transgressed the commandment of the Lord in the beginning of their rising, because they did not come forth at their appointed times.
>
> 1 Enoch 18:14–15
> R.H. Charles Translation[49]

Notice that it states that the angels "did not come forth at their appointed times." The *Book of Jubilees* tells that the Watchers were sent to the earth to teach and instruct mankind. But the sensual pleasures of women proved to be irresistible to these angels. *1 Enoch* also explains that the angels taught people secret knowledge that was reserved for use in heaven and not on earth. This is probably the reason why it describes them coming forth before "their appointed times." We can infer from this statement then, that at some point in our history or maybe even in the near future, these angels were scheduled to appear and teach specific skills and divulge important knowledge.

Later sections of the *Book of Enoch* go into great description about the sights and workings of the heavens that were revealed to the patriarch *Enoch* (חנוך), meaning "dedicated." His was called the "Scribe of Righteousness" and interceded on behalf of the fallen Watchers before they were punished. The story of Enoch brings the investigation to another crucial point worthy of more inspection: If the gods can travel through these gateways, can humans do the same?

Walking with God

Genesis (5:18–24) tells that Enoch was of the seventh generation from Adam, and his father was Jared. As we have already seen, Jared's name (ירד) meant "descent" because he was born when the Watchers came down from the mountain. Enoch was also the father of *Methuselah* (מתושלח), the longest living patriarch of the Bible to have died a natural death. Enoch fathered Methuselah when he was 65 years old, and another 300 years passed before he was "translated" to heaven. Specifying that Enoch was 365 years old associates him with the number of days in a solar year, and therefore with a solar deity.

Enoch is one of the Biblical patriarchs that never died. Instead, the book of Genesis (5:24) says that "Enoch walked with God; then he was no more, because God took him." Unfortunately, the Bible does not provide any further details about this or the events preceding Enoch's disappearance. We must look in the apocryphal books such as *1 Enoch* for further information. In a "dream vision" that sounds very much like an "out-of-body experience," Enoch describes how he was taken to heaven:

> Behold, in the vision clouds invited me and a mist summoned me, and the course of the stars and the lightnings sped and hastened me, and the winds in the vision caused me to fly and lifted me upward, and bore me into heaven. And I went in till I drew nigh to a <u>wall which is built of crystals and surrounded by tongues</u>[50] of fire: and it began to affright me. And <u>I went into the tongues of fire</u> and drew nigh to a large house which was built of crystals: and the walls of the house were like a tesselated (sic) floor (made) of crystals, and its groundwork was of crystal. Its ceiling was like the path of the stars and the lightnings, and between them were fiery cherubim, and their heaven was (clear as) water. <u>A flaming fire surrounded the walls, and its portals blazed with fire</u>. And I entered into that house, and it was hot as fire and cold as ice: there were no delights of life therein: fear covered me, and trembling gat hold upon me. And as I quaked and trembled, I fell upon my face.
>
> 1 Enoch 14:8–14[51]

Enoch then saw a second house, similar to the first but greater in every respect and inside a portal of fire. God was seated upon a throne and surrounded by great flames and myriads of angels. God tells Enoch not to be afraid and that the requests of the Watchers will not be granted; their children will be slaughtered and their spirits will become evil demons bound to the earth that will torment mankind.[52] The angels, however, will be punished in heaven.[53] Enoch is to tell them:

"You have been in heaven, but [all] the mysteries had not yet been revealed to you, and you knew worthless ones, and these in the hardness of your hearts you have made known to the women, and through these mysteries women and men work much evil on earth." Say to them [the Watchers] therefore: "You have no peace."

1 Enoch 36:3–4[54]

Enoch is then taken on a tour of the heavens and shown beings who were "like flaming fire," but could "appear as men" when they wished. He also sees another mountain with a summit that "reached to heaven."[55] He is then shown four dark and hollow places where the souls of the dead are kept until the Day of Judgement.[56] These areas do not seem to be anything like the happy or joyous places that people have long imagined were in heaven. Instead, they appear to be like frightening "holding tanks," a concept that is in keeping with many other ancient cultures' beliefs about the afterlife and the underworld.

The "Tree of Life" is also shown to Enoch during his journey. No mortal is allowed to touch it until the Judgement, and then its fruit shall be given to the "righteous and holy." Michael was one of the angels accompanying Enoch, and told him the following in regard to the tree:

Then shall they rejoice with joy and be glad.
And into the holy place shall they enter;
And its fragrance shall be in their bones,
And they shall live a long life on earth,
Such as thy fathers lived:
And in their days shall no [sorrow or] plague
Or torment or calamity touch them.

1 Enoch 25:6[57]

The importance of the description of the Tree of Life and its fruit are explained in more detail within Chapter 12. For now, it should be understood that the tree will apparently be able to provide healing abilities and prolonged life by ingesting the fruit. Since the gods were believed to live forever, and the texts record that the first humans had prolonged life spans, it could be tied to what's called "manna" or "angel bread."

In another vision that Enoch receives, he is once again taken on a journey to the heavens. He sees the "Head of Days" (who is also sometimes referred to as the "Ancient of Days") accompanied by the "Son of Man," who is the promised Messiah.

And it came to pass after this that <u>my spirit was translated</u>[58]
And it ascended into the heavens:
And I saw the <u>holy sons of God.</u>

<u>They were stepping on flames of fire</u>:
<u>Their garments were white</u> [and their raiment],
And <u>their faces shone like snow</u>.
...
And he [the archangel Michael] <u>translated my spirit</u> into the heaven
of heavens,
And I saw there as it were a structure built of crystals,
And between those crystals tongues of living fire.
...
And Michael, and Raphael, and Gabriel, and Phanuel,
And the holy angels who are above the heavens,
Go in and out of that house.
...
And with them the Head of Days,
<u>His head white and pure as wool</u>,
And his raiment indescribable.

And I fell on my face,
<u>And my whole body became relaxed</u>,
<u>And my spirit was transfigured</u>

1 Enoch 71:1, 5, 8, 10–11[59]

Please notice that I have emphasized the next to last line of this text, which describes some kind of physical transformation that occurs to Enoch. The above is from a translation by R.H. Charles, however this particular line might be understood better when we read an alternate translation by Richard Laurence. Laurence's version is perhaps more accurate in this regard, because he renders it as "while all my flesh was *dissolved.*"[60] This is most interesting because it implies that something physically altered the body of Enoch so that his "spirit" could be "transfigured."

After Enoch's transfiguration occurs, God or one of the angels apparently addresses him as being the "Son of man who is born unto righteousness." However, a great deal of controversy surrounds this, because the title "Son of man" is thought to be used exclusively for Jesus. Some scholars, such as Laurence, have even intentionally mistranslated this phrase when used in this context as "offspring of man" to avoid any comparisons to Jesus.[61] R.H. Charles translated it as "Son of man" but believed there is a missing verse that clarifies that the speaker is telling Enoch *about* a separate being identified as the "Son of man."[62] Perhaps the most reasonable explanation, though, is that many of the Semitic cultures used this or a very similar term to simply mean "human."

The book known as *The Slavonic Apocalypse of Enoch,* or *2 Enoch,* provides further details about the transformation of Enoch. It is not certain when the book was written. Some scholars argue that it was written during the Middle Ages and not in the late first century CE as has been proposed.[63] Rosemary Ellen Guiley describes a situation when:

> God instructs Michael to "take Enoch from out of his earthly garments, and anoint him with my sweet ointment, and put him into the garments of my Glory." The oil is like sweet dew, smells like myrrh, and is like the glittering rays of the sun. Enoch takes on a shining appearance like the angels around him.[64]

While this does provide more information regarding what happened to Enoch, it does not help to clarify whether or not Enoch had been transformed into the "Son of man." The reason is because "Christ" means "anointed" and is derived from the equivalent Hebrew term "Messiah." Perhaps the best way to reconcile the argument is that the texts are comparing the transfigured Enoch to the "Son of man." This would obviously raise problems for some people because no person is supposed to be equal to the status of Jesus. For now, there is not enough imperative evidence to convincingly argue one way or the other.

The main concern of this investigation is regarding the descriptions of what happens to Enoch. His earthly garments are removed and replaced with garments of God's "Glory." The oil used to anoint him does something to his skin so that he has a "shining appearance like the angels." Enoch has essentially been turned into an angel, which bears a strong resemblance to the descriptions of what happens with the Sumerian melam garments.

In the *Hebrew Book of Enoch*, sometimes called *3 Enoch*,[65] it states that Enoch was transformed into the angel Metatron. The etymology of the name is uncertain, but some of the more likely candidates are from the Greek terms *metaturannos,* meaning "the one next to the ruler," and also *(ho) meta thronon,* which means "(the throne) next to the (divine) throne" or "the second throne." Metatron is the most powerful of the angels and second only to God in heaven. God even declares him to be "the Lesser Yahweh" before the entire court of heaven and says, "My name is in him."[66]

Metatron is a very important angel in the Merkabah and Kabbalah literature and also the Jewish Talmud. According to some sources, he is believed to stand at the top of the "Tree of Life" as the "Angel of Yahweh." He's meant to represent "both human and angelic perfection" which "enables him to be an excellent interface between the two realms." However, he is tied directly to the righteousness of people, whose good deeds will generate an energy that vitalizes him, but misdeeds render him weaker and less powerful.[67]

Another important figure who was "taken" to heaven is the prophet *Elijah* (אליה). 2 Kings 2:8–11 describes quite a remarkable scene when Elijah used his rolled up cloak to strike the river Jordan and cause it to part. Together, he and Elisha crossed the river and continued to talk when suddenly a "chariot of fire and horses of fire" appeared and separated them. Elisha watched in astonishment as Elijah "ascended in a whirlwind into heaven." The location where Elijah had been just before this spectacular event may also be significant because it was known as *Gilgal* (Hebrew and Aramaic: גלגל), meaning a "rolling wheel" or "circle" and is derived from a primitive root that can also mean "whirlwind."[68] We will return to this topic by the end of our investigation.

According to Kabbalistic lore, the translated Elijah is also turned into a powerful angel called "Sandalphon," and is said to be God's messenger throughout the world. He battles against the Angel of Death, who is unhappy that a human has been allowed to live outside of his jurisdiction. In the battle, God must hold Elijah back because he has become so powerful that he would have destroyed the Angel of Death.[69]

So what does all of this mean?

In the past, it seems that certain people achieved a favorable position with God and they were chosen to ascend into heaven and be turned into angels or even gods. They became examples of what the human race could aspire to become. This is also perhaps a reason why so many of the ancient legends seem to indicate that Satan and other fallen angels have despised humans since their creation. They knew that a lowly human had the potential to one day surpass them in every possible way and the angels were not created for any other reason than to serve God. Additionally, Paul writes in 1 Corinthians (6:3): "Do you not know that we are to judge angels…?"

In the Letter to the Hebrews, the author recalls one of the Psalms and states:

Now God did not subject the coming world, about which we are speaking, to angels. But someone has testified somewhere,
   "What are human beings that you are mindful of them,
      or mortals, that you care for them?
   You have made them for a little while lower than the angels;
      You have crowned them with glory and honor,
      Subjecting all things under their feet."
                                    Hebrews 2:5–8 NRSV[70]

Could it be possible that the purpose of the human race is to ascend and become divine beings? A re-reading of many of the ancient texts seems to indicate that this is indeed the case, and opens up a completely new understanding of the Resurrection. More evidence for all of this will be presented later.

But a new problem surfaces if this is the correct understanding of the texts. Many skeptics would quickly argue that if these gateways did indeed exist, and angelic beings or gods were coming from heaven to earth, why aren't they doing it now? Unfortunately, the answer seems to be that all of the gateways that were incorporated into these ancient temples and pyramids have been shut off or are missing. This is not intended to be a cop-out answer—simply the most plausible explanation based upon an understanding of the texts. Over time, it seems the gods abandoned or seriously limited contact in the Middle East and probably moved on to aid in the establishment of other civilizations such as the Native Americans of North and South America. We do not know how much of this technology or magick was destroyed or forgotten as cultures clashed, temples were plundered, and priceless texts were destroyed. It's possible that some of these gateways may still be active or lying dormant for the time being. But it could also be that mankind is meant to understand these ancient stories and find a way to re-create it on our own—and it does not have to be as difficult as some people might think.

The people of the ancient world were greatly in touch with nature. They understood about the balance of nature and used methods of constructing magnificent monuments that worked in harmony with nature. Many modern people automatically think that it is "primitive" to build with stone or clay and that the ancient people did the best with what they had but our modern technology far surpasses them. In many ways, I must agree that there are many perks to living in the modern age. We have wonderful inventions such as computers and convenience stores and all kinds of niceties. I honestly don't know what I would do without having my computer as a valuable asset for expressing my thoughts and artistic visions.

However, it should also be considered that despite all of our technological know-how, we still cannot figure out how the ancients built some of the structures such as the Great Pyramid—and we have yet to demonstrate that even we can do it. They have built stone structures that have lasted for thousands of years. We consider ourselves advanced to be writing on paper and using computers because we have "high technology." And yet, how long will that paper last? All of the data on a computer can be erased in the blink of an eye. Worse yet, even data stored on items such as CD-ROMs or DVDs are rendered useless unless you have the proper equipment and software to read it. The ancient people wrote down their records on seals and tablets that have survived *to this day*. That's quite an accomplishment. They obviously possessed a much higher level of intelligence than what we typically grant to them. So perhaps we should listen to what they had to say. According to their own words, they have admitted that they did not accomplish all of their great works and educational systems on their own. Instead, they claim that they received outside help from the gods.

We should seriously consider that maybe our ancient ancestors were telling the truth and not merely spreading superstitious "myths." If what they said is true, it means there is still so much more for the human race to explore and re-discover. In fact, our very future might depend on it. To ignore what might be just around the corner could prove to be an incredible injustice to all. However, there might have been another clue left for us that hints at how the gateways were activated in the past. If we look back at the Tower of Babel story, we'll recall that not only did they want to make a tower that reached heaven, but to make a "name" for themselves.

144

Summary

❖ The Great Pyramid stands as an unparalleled feat of engineering because Egyptologists have been unable to adequately explain or demonstrate how it was constructed.

❖ Numerous cultures throughout the ancient world, such as the Maya and the Mesopotamians, referred to their stepped-pyramids (ziggurats) as "gateways" that were used by the gods to travel to and from the earthly realm.

❖ Linguistic parallels between Biblical references to "stones of fire" (*'eben*) and the Egyptian pyramids *(benben)* indicate that these structures were related to the regenerative powers of the legendary phoenix *(benu bird)*.

❖ Biblical descriptions of "Jacob's Ladder" and Nebuchadnezzar's "fiery furnace" may be recollections of the original gateway technology.

❖ Jewish folklore states that Enoch never died because he was taken to heaven and then transformed into the angel known as Metatron. Thereafter, Enoch's ascension serves as the template for a recurring theme that appears throughout the Biblical texts.

WHAT'S IN A NAME?

There are more things in heaven and earth, Horatio,
Than are dreamt of in your philosophy.
—William Shakespeare, *Hamlet* Act I: Scene 5

THE SIGNIFICANCE OF EPITHETS AS NAMES to describe the function or duty of a character has been touched upon earlier in this book. In this chapter, the subject will be elaborated on to provide additional details regarding some very important names, including the most holy name of God, and the names of Jesus and Mary Magdalene. The information presented will explain why Biblical texts repeatedly placed an emphasis upon names, and will also shed light upon other significant events that have previously been shrouded in mystery.

The Power of a Name

The ancient world placed great importance on the name that was designated for a person, god, or even demon. This is emphasized in many of the stories and texts that described significant people and characters. It represented more than simply a person's title, but the very attributes and powers that they wanted to embody. For instance, when the pharaoh known as Amenhotep IV (meaning "Amen is pleased") ascended to the throne of Egypt, he decided to do away with all of the other Egyptian gods and worship only one, called the Aten. Upon his conversion to the worship of Aten, he changed his name to Akhenaten, which meant "He Who Works for Aten."[1]

A name was believed to hold the essence of that particular being, and to know the name of a deity or spirit meant that a human could invoke and command them. This was believed throughout ancient Babylonia, Assyria, and especially in Egypt.[2] However, it is likely that many of the familiar names we attribute to important figures in the Bible are not their common names after all. They are likely names that have been provided by story-tellers in order convey important messages. Names were thought to have been imbued with mystical power, and many occult traditions continue to believe that a sorcerer's knowledge of an individual or god's real name renders them vulnerable to magickal spells or incantations. A legend about Noah stressed the following belief:

> By the name Noah he was called only by his grandfather Methu-selah; his father and all others called him Menahem. His genera-tion was addicted to sorcery, and Methuselah apprehended that his grandson might be bewitched if his true name were known, wherefore he kept it a secret.[3]

Another example is recorded in the book of Judges when the "angel of Yahweh" appears to Manoah, announcing that his wife will give birth to Samson:

> And Manoah said unto the angel of the LORD, <u>What is thy name</u>, that when thy sayings come to pass we may do thee honour?
> And the angel of the LORD said unto him, <u>Why askest thou thus after my name, seeing it is secret</u>?
>
> Judges 13:17–18 KJV

The angel then uses the *fire* from the altar of a burnt offering to ascend to the heavens (13:19–20). It is likely that this is yet another reference to the otherworldly "fire" of the gateways.

Other passages in the Bible emphasize not only the importance of a name, but the *renaming* of a person. In the book of Genesis, God makes a covenant with the patriarch *Abram* (אברם) and he is renamed *Abraham* (אברהם) by inserting the letter Heh (ה) into his name (17:5). Likewise, Abra-ham's wife also receives the divine letter and is renamed from *Sarai* (שרי) to *Sarah* (שרה), meaning "princess" (17:15). Other exceptional patriarchs that contained this divine letter were *Moses* (משה) and *Solomon* (שלמה). While Jacob's name did not contain this letter, he was renamed *Israel* (ישראל) after his confrontation with an angel (Genesis 32:28).

We have seen how the Nephilim, and perhaps the Watchers, were known as "heroes that were of old, warriors of <u>renown</u>" (Genesis 6:4). But the word used for "renown" is *shem* (שם), meaning "name." And we have seen the significance of the Tower of Babel, when the builders proclaimed, "let us make a <u>name</u> for ourselves" (11:4). Once again, the word used is "shem." Most scholars have generally considered this last passage as simply referring to a way for men to build a monument that would allow them to be immortal, at least in name only. However, the previous chapter suggests that a radically new interpretation of this event is much more likely.

But why is so much significance placed on something as seemingly mundane as a name? Why are the Nephilim referred to as people of the "Name" and why did the builders at Babylon need to "make a name" so that they could reach heaven? It seems as though there is an important connection between these details that scholars have repeatedly overlooked.

The leader of the fallen angels was called *Shemyaza* (שמעזי or שמהזאי), which is most likely translated to mean "the strong name." But why was he given this title? If we examine the structure of the name, it will become clear. "Shem" (שם) translates to "name" and the root word "azaz" (עזז) means "to be strong." The name also integrates the letter "y," which is a transliteration of the Hebrew letter *Yod* ('). This is the first letter of what is sometimes known as the "Ineffable Name of God," and is often used as a shortened form of the name when referring to God. Considering this, it is likely that Shemyaza's name is probably referring to how he was in possession of—or in command of—the use of the Ineffable Name. Support for this can be found in a Jewish legend concerning the Watchers' fall from heaven:

> Shemhazai saw a maiden named Istehar [a variant spelling of Ishtar], and he lost his heart to her. She promised to surrender herself to him, if he first taught her the <u>Ineffable Name</u>, by means of which <u>he raised himself to heaven</u>. He assented to her condition. But once she knew it, she <u>pronounced the Name</u>, and herself <u>ascended to heaven</u>, without fulfilling her promise to the angel.[4]

While it is doubtful that the legend itself should be taken as a literal event, its purpose was probably to form direct associations between the characters and certain knowledge understood by the scribes. Apparently, there was something about the Name of God that allowed Shemyaza and even Ishtar (a goddess associated with Venus) to ascend to heaven. This is an important clue and likely tied to the intention of using a "name" to activate the gateways that allowed the translation of beings to and from the heavens. Exactly how this

"Name" was used as a method to ascend to the heavens, I do not know—nor do the accounts seem to shed any particular light on the matter. So in this regard, I am still at a loss for a better explanation. However, we can try to better understand the significance of names by studying the history and usage of some of the most important names found in the Bible. Since we have already been introduced to the Ineffable Name, we shall begin with it.

The Tetragrammaton

The *Tetragrammaton* is a Greek term that means "four-letter word" and is used to refer to the most holy name of God to the Jewish people. It consists of the four Hebrew letters יהוה (remembering that Hebrew is written right to left, the letters are pronounced "Yod, Heh, Vau, Heh").[5] People of the Jewish faith considered the name so holy that they forbid the pronunciation of it and simply referred to it as *ha Shem* ("the Name"). The only exception allowed was the whispering of the name by the Temple priests during the benediction (Numbers 6:22–7) and on the Day of Atonement (Leviticus 16:30). Because the ancient Hebrew language contained no vowels, the name could be written in the Torah and still hide the proper method of pronouncing it. When a Jewish person read the Holy Scriptures aloud and encountered the Ineffable Name, he substituted the word *Adonai* (אדני pronounced "Ad-o-ny"), meaning "Lord." In some instances, if both words were already written together, then *Elohim* (אלהים) was used instead to avoid saying Adonai-Adonai.[6] In most modern translations of the Bible, when the text reads the "LORD" in all capital letters it's to show that the real word is actually Yahweh.

Due to such secrecy regarding the name and the lack of vowels, the true method of pronouncing the name has been lost. Many modern scholars believe it is pronounced *Yahweh* ("Yaw-way" or "Yaw-weh"). When it was transliterated into Latin, it became IHVH (but also YHWH and JHWH). However, the name proved impossible to be written in Greek without revealing the proper way of saying it. The original classic Latin transliteration should be pronounced *Yehowah,* but over the centuries it degenerated into the common form known to most people today: *Jehovah.*[7]

The reason for this mistake is due to the fact that the European scholars of the fourteenth century were unfamiliar with Hebrew scribal methods. Since all letters in the Hebrew language are consonants, the vowels had to be indicated by putting small "points," known as diacritical marks, close to the letters. The diacritical marks for the word Adonai were placed around YHWH to indicate it should be read as Adonai instead. Since Jewish readers were well aware of this, it was unnecessary for them to put the consonants of the substituted word in the margins, as was common practice. But since the European scholars were not aware of this technique, they combined the consonants and vowel sounds of both words, which transformed it into "Jehovah."[8]

The true meaning of the name of Yahweh is also unclear, but it probably means something like "The Existing One," or the more familiar phrase "I Am." It is most likely derived from the archaic verb *hayah* (היה), meaning "to be." It has also been speculated that it could be from the root *hawah* or *havah* (הוא), which translates as "to be" or "to exist," and curiously enough, even as "to fall."[9] Yahweh also sounds similar to the names of some other gods, such as the Roman form of Jupiter, which is Jove (pronounced "Yoweh" in classical Latin)[10]—and also the Gnostic deity IAO, which relies heavily on the power of vowel sounds.[11] However, there appears to be little evidence to prove any direct connections besides their sounds.

An even greater mystery lies not in the pronunciation of the name, but in its application throughout the ages. The practice of Jewish mysticism, known as *Cabala* (pronounced "Ka-baw-la"),[12] seeks to discover hidden meanings behind words and phrases in sacred scriptures—the Tetragrammaton is no exception. Within the *Sefer Yetzirah* (Book of Formation), the oldest known book of the Cabala, we read:

> He selected three letters from among the simple ones and sealed them and formed them into a Great Name, IHV, and with this he sealed the universe in six directions. He looked above, and sealed the Height with IHV. He looked below and sealed the Depth with IVH. He looked forward, and sealed the East with HIV. He looked backward, and sealed the West with HVI. He looked to the right, and sealed the South with VIH. He looked to the left, and sealed the North with VHI.[13]

Since there are two *Hehs* (H=ה) in YHWH, there are really only three distinct letters. These three letters are all that is necessary to sufficiently describe an object within the six cardinal directions of three-dimensional space: up, down, front, back, left, and right.

Cabalists will even apply the Tetragrammaton to what is known as the *tetractys,* which is based on Pythagorean number mysticism. The tetractys is composed of ten points or letters that have been arranged in a triangular pattern. Pythagoreans considered it a very important element to their workings and would swear their most solemn oaths upon it. To them, it represented the four important disciplines of arithmetic, geometry, music, and astronomy. With the Tetragrammaton applied, a tetractys would appear as:[14]

The four letters of the Tetragrammaton have also been used to describe a "divine family" by assigning genders to each individual letter. The *Yod* (י) represents the *Father* and the element of *Fire*. The First *Heh* (ה) represents the *Mother* and the element of *Earth*. Next, the letter *Vau* (ו) stands for the *Son* and the element of *Air*. Finally, the second *Heh* (ה) is the *Daughter* and the element of *Water*. It is important to note here that these values assigned by Cabbalists differ from those assigned specifically to letters in the Hebrew alphabet. The above genders and elements are used in regards to the Tetragrammaton only. The Hebrew alphabet assigns the elements of Air, Water, and Fire to the letters *Aleph* (א), *Mem* (מ), and *Shin* (ש), respectively. There is no letter assigned the element for Earth because the alphabet is supposed to reflect a heavenly rather than earthly concept.[15] Additionally, when the Hebrew letters are written vertically, they appear to resemble a crude human body in "stick" form.[16]

The Tetragrammaton naturally lends itself to the shape of a cross. The masculine elements *Yod* (י) and *Vau* (ו) are assigned to the vertical segment of the cross, while the feminine elements are assigned to the horizontal segment. The simple shape of the cross can then be converted into a three-dimensional solid called a *tetrahedron*. A tetrahedron is the simplest solid body, which is composed of four planes or faces, using equilateral triangles, with four distinct points created from the intersection of the planes. Each letter of the Tetragrammaton is then assigned to a corresponding point. The figure below will provide a better visual description of the cross shape turning into a tetrahedron as described.[17]

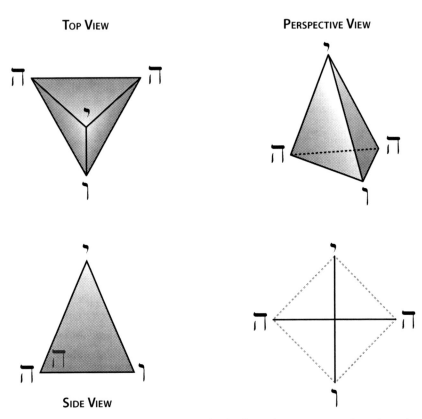

TOP VIEW

PERSPECTIVE VIEW

SIDE VIEW

Cabalists also incorporate a method of number mysticism based on the Hebrew alphabet, known as gematria. Most ancient languages were isopsephic, meaning that the letters had numerical values assigned to them. The following chart lists all of the letters and their matching value. Additionally, five of these letters have a second form when used at the end of a word, and so are repeated in the chart. These "final" letters also have different numerical values than their counterparts.[18]

By analyzing each word, a Cabalist could detect deeper or possibly hidden meanings to the scriptures. Using the following chart, the numerical value for the Tetragrammaton can be found. *Yod* (')=10, *Heh* (ה)=5, *Vau* (ו)=6, and

The Hebrew Alphabet

א	ב	ג	ד	ה	ו	ז	ח	ט
Aleph (A)	Beth (B)	Gimel (G)	Daleth (D)	Heh (H)	Vau (U, V)	Zayin (Z)	Cheth (Ch)	Teth (T)
Ox	House	Camel	Door	Window	Peg/Nail	Sword/ Weapon	Fence	Serpent
1	2	3	4	5	6	7	8	9
י	כ	ל	מ	נ	ס	ע	פ	צ
Yod (I, Y)	Kaph (K)	Lamed (L)	Mem (M)	Nun (N)	Samech (S)	Ayin (Aa)	Peh (P)	Tzaddi (Tz)
Hand	Palm of Hand	Ox-Goad	Water	Fish	Support	Eye	Mouth	Fish Hook
10	20	30	40	50	60	70	80	90
ק	ר	ש	ת	ך	ם	ן	ף	ץ
Qoph (Q)	Resh (R)	Shin (Sh)	Tau (Th)	final Kaph (K)	final Mem (M)	final Nun (N)	final Peh (P)	final Tzaddi (Tz)
Back of Head	Head	Tooth	Sign of the Cross					
100	200	300	400	500	600	700	800	900

the final *Heh* (ה)=5. So the value is: 10 + 5 + 6 + 5 = 26. What proves most interesting about this value is how it portrays Yahweh. Twenty-six is exactly *half* of the number fifty-two, which corresponds to the number of weeks in a solar year. Additionally, there are approximately thirteen full moons in a year, and twenty-six is exactly *double* the number thirteen. This identifies Yahweh as being the center of both the solar and lunar powers and of light and darkness. Yet another example of a union between the name, geometry and numbers involves the symbol of a cross enclosed by a circle ⊕. Since the Hebrew alphabet reflects a heavenly concept, the twenty-two letters can be represented by a circle. The four arms of the cross also represent earthly matters (as well as the four sides of a square). Therefore, we find that the union of Heaven and Earth can numerically be represented as: 22 + 4 = 26—demonstrating another connection to Yahweh's divine name.

There are numerous other uses and applications of the Tetragrammaton throughout the ages and there are far too many to list here. Even though the true pronunciation of the Name has been lost, it has still been incorporated into many traditions that rely on its power. For instance, the Tetragrammaton is vital to many of the ritual workings of magickal orders such as The Hermetic Order of The Golden Dawn. However, instead of trying to pronounce the name as a whole, it is instead "vibrated" letter-by-letter as Yod-Heh-Vau-Heh. The act of vibrating a name is akin to *singing* each letter, not just speaking it.

A very long tradition has carried the Tetragrammaton throughout the era of the Old Testament and even up to the present day. However, a new "Word" eventually descended from heaven to take the place of the Ineffable Name. It is a name that has been echoed all over the world for the good part of the last two-thousand years.

The Name of Jesus

The modern name of Jesus comes to us from the Latin *Iesus,* which is derived from the Greek Ιησους (Ihsous). Ιησους, pronounced "ee-ay-soos," is a transliteration of the Aramaic[19] name *Yeshua* (ישוע), a shortened form of the Hebrew name *Yehoshua* (יהושע). Yehoshua, meaning *"Yah(weh) is Salvation,"* is more commonly known today as *Joshua,* and was the name given to Moses' successor that led the Israelites to the Promised Land.[20]

According to Cabalistic thought, the name Yeshua embodied the essence of the Messiah and could be revealed just by analyzing the letters. It is spelled using the Hebrew letters *Yod* ('), symbolizing the Hand of God; *Shin* (ש), a tooth; *Vau* (ו), a *nail;* and *Ayin* (ע), which represents an eye. The hand and nail are easily recognizable as symbols of the crucifixion. The tooth is considered a symbol of transformation and renewal of the Spirit because it is used in the process of eating food that is turned into energy for the body. Finally, the eye is a symbol of understanding and the illuminating aspect of the divine.[21] For example, consider the Egyptian's frequent use of the Eye of Horus (originally the Eye of Ra) as a symbol of power and protection.

It is often forgotten or overlooked that the New Testament was actually written in Greek as opposed to Hebrew. Since many of the names were of Jewish origin, they did not always transliterate well into the Greek language and important details were unfortunately lost. The ancient scribes were aware of this problem, however, and found clever ways to include the missing information and even conceal entirely new levels of knowledge within the names.

Adapting the Aramaic and Hebrew letters of the name of Jesus into Greek posed several problems. First, the two Greek letters *Iota-Eta* (Iη) were joined to produce the sound "ee-ay," since Greek has no equivalent for the "yah" sound of the Hebrew *Yod* ('). Next, because there is no counterpart for the "sh" sound of the Hebrew letter *Shin* (ש), the *Sigma* letter (σ) was used as an "S" sound. For the Hebrew letter *Vau* (ו), the diphthong *Omicron-Upsilon* (ου) was used to produce the "oo" sound. The final letter posed yet another problem. The Hebrew *Ayin* (ע) has an "ah" sound, but this is a violation according to the rules of Greek grammar. A masculine name must never end with a vowel sound, and when it does, it should be closed with an "S," if possible. The solution that was accepted was to drop the "ah" sound and substitute the final *Sigma* (ς) to finish the name.[22]

To further add to the mystery of the name of Jesus, it was secretly encoded with special numerical values by using the Greek letters described above. Like Hebrew, the Greek alphabet used letters that also represented numerical values. Out of the total twenty-four letters, the first eight represent units (monads = 1–9), the next eight represent tens (decads = 10–80), and the last eight letters represent hundreds (hecatads = 100–800).[23] Thus, the alphabet was divided into three sections of the number eight, or 8–8–8. The chart below shows the Greek alphabet with its corresponding number values. Please note that three letters, *digamma* (6), *koppa* (90), and *sampi* (900) were considered ob-

The Greek Alphabet

A α	B β	Γ γ	Δ δ	E ε	Z ζ	H η	Θ θ
Alpha	Beta	Gamma	Delta	Epsilon	Zeta	Eta	Theta
1	2	3	4	5	7	8	9
I ι	K κ	Λ λ	M μ	N ν	Ξ ξ	O o	Π π
Iota	Kappa	Lamda	Mu	Nu	Xi	Omicron	Pi
10	20	30	40	50	60	70	80
P ρ	Σ σ ς	T τ	Y υ	Φ φ	X χ	Ψ ψ	Ω ω
Rho	Sigma	Tau	Upsilon	Phi	Chi	Psi	Omega
100	200	300	400	500	600	700	800

solete by the time the New Testament was written and discarded from the alphabet. They were retained strictly for their use as numbers.[24]

By studying the gematria of the alphabet, we can discover how these numerical "secrets" reveal deeper meanings about the characters and their roles within the Bible. If we are to add up the numeric values of the letters of the name of Jesus, the equation would look like this: 10 + 8 + 200 + 70 + 400 + 200 = 888. The name perfectly matches the triple-eight structure of the Greek alphabet! This was a subtle method employed by the New Testament scribes to show that the name expressed the entire power of the alphabet. This also adds a completely new dimension to the words uttered by Jesus when he says: "I am the Alpha and the Omega, the first and the last, the beginning and the end" (Revelation 22:13). Most people have believed that this statement was merely intended to describe the eternal and complete authority of Jesus, but now we can see a much more sophisticated word-play in operation. Interestingly enough, in musical harmony—which was a sacred science among the Pythagorean mystery schools—the value .666 is the string ratio of the perfect fifth and .888 is the ratio of the whole tone.[25] Now, it becomes clear how the numerical value of 666 that's designated for the second beast of Revelation (13:18) is used in opposition to the number 888 of the Messiah.[26]

But why should it be of any importance about the hidden meanings of these numbers? It is because they were used to deliberately pass on hidden information to people who were initiated into secret "mystery schools." It's very likely that much of what was written in the gospels were veiled or secret wisdom teachings, wrapped in appealing stories for the common people. As Jesus said, "Let anyone with ears to hear listen!"[27] This belief was even stated by Jesus when his disciples questioned his reason for speaking to the people in parables, he responded, "To you it has been given to know the *secrets* [or *mysteries*] of the kingdom of heaven, but to them it has not been given." He added, "The reason I speak to them in parables is that 'seeing they do not perceive, and hearing they do not listen, nor do they understand.'"[28]

One of the most convincing arguments for the veiled meanings associated with numbers is contained in the Gospel of John, where it describes how Jesus helped his disciples catch a miraculous amount of fish. In fact, it specifically states that they caught 153 fish.[29] It would be irrational to assume that John only wanted his readers to interpret this event as a "miracle" and nothing more. Since the gospel mentions a specific number, it indicates that there is more to be gleaned from the story.

The Pythagorean mystery school believed that 153 was a very sacred number associated with geometry. The Greek mathematician, Archimedes, referred to a mathematical ratio of 153:265 as "the measure of the fish," because when the circumference of one circle touched the center of another circle of equal size, it produced the mystical symbol known as the *vesica piscis* ("sign [or bladder] of the fish").[30]

Obviously, the fish symbol is closely associated with Jesus by the New Testament authors. He is referred to as a "fisher of men" and early Christians used the fish as a secret symbol for their faith. They also made a connection to the Greek word for fish, *Ichthys* (ΙΧΘΥΣ), which could be used as an acronym for "Ιησουσ Χριστος Θεου Υιος Σωτηρ" (Latin: *Iesous Christos Theou Huios Soter*) meaning: "Jesus Christ, Son of God, Savior."[31]

The timing of Jesus' birth creates another association with the fish. His birth is believed to have foreshadowed the dawning of the Age of Pisces

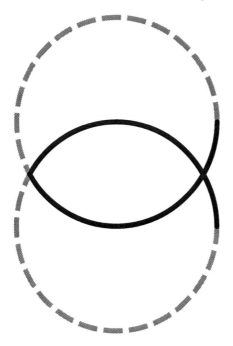

Two overlapping circles produce the sacred ratio (153:265) known as the "measure of the fish," which was a symbol closely associated with Jesus.

(which technically did not begin until sometime around 500 CE).[32] During this time, the Age of Aries was coming to an end and a popular cult worshiped the god Mithras, who symbolically celebrated the slaying of a bull (representing the previous Age of Taurus). It was a popular belief that the god of the "new age" would be "born" of (or at least connected to) the sign that was its opposite. When the signs of the zodiac are placed sequentially on a wheel, Pisces forms an astrological partnership with the opposite sign, Virgo, the Virgin. Therefore, the "fish" would be born of a "virgin."

There are also many obvious comparisons between Jesus and his Old Testament counterpart, Joshua, the successor of Moses. In fact, significant parallels can be discovered if we compare the stories of Moses and Joshua as described in Exodus, to the gospel accounts of Jesus. The following table notes some of these similarities.[33] Additionally, Old Testament authors

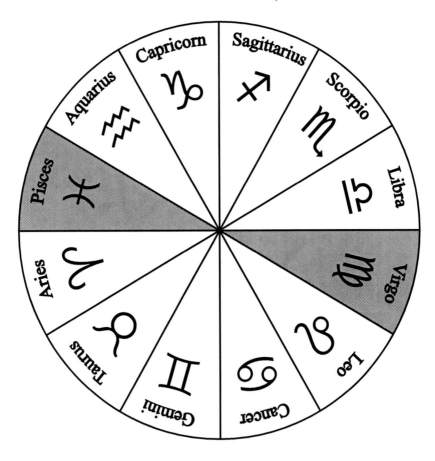

continually pointed out that Joshua was the son of Nun (נון). The Hebrew letter, *Nun* (נ and final form ן), means "fish." It is therefore no coincidence that both Jesus and Joshua were associated with fish.

Old Testament	New Testament
Pharaoh orders mass infanticide of all Hebrew males	King Herod orders the slaughter of all Hebrew males under two years of age
The baby Moses is rescued from the Nile River and then raised as royalty in Egypt	Joseph and Mary flee with Jesus to Egypt and do not reappear until several years later
The crossing of the Red Sea	Jesus is baptized by John
40 years of wandering	40 days in the wilderness
Death of Moses	Crucifixion of Jesus
Joshua replaces Moses and leads the Israelites to the Promised Land	Jesus' Resurrection and Ascension into Heaven

Furthermore, concerning the "measure of the fish" and sacred geometry, the fish shape is also understood to represent the female vulva and was referred to as the *matrix* in Greek, which meant "mother." It was also associated with the "Holy of Holies" and the "bridal chamber." Also known as the *mandorla* in Western art, it was symbolic of the Holy Spirit. Many great works of art portrayed Jesus within the ◊ shape.[34]

A mistake made by many people is that they use "Christ" as if it were the last name of Jesus, when it is actually a title. Christ is from the Greek word *Christos* (Χριστος), meaning "anointed." In Judaism, the body of the high priest or king would be anointed with perfumed oil. Christos was directly translated from the Hebrew term for "anointed," which is *Mashiyahk* (משיח), pronounced "maw-shee-awk." This is the origin of the term *Messiah*—a title applied to any priest or king who had been anointed.

The evolution of the word Messiah can be traced back to both Egypt and Mesopotamia, locations that played important roles in the history of the Jewish people. Pharaohs in ancient Egypt were anointed with the fat of a crocodile, a creature sacred to the god Sobek, who was also called a *Messeh*.[35] In Mesopotamia, Sumerian poetry praised their gods and kings by calling them *ušumgal*,[36] pronounced "oo-shoom-gal," which meant "Great Dragon." Later, in the Akkadian language, these snake-dragons were called *mušhuššu* (𒈲𒍑𒁲), pronounced "moosh-hoosh-shoo," interpreted as "furious snake,"[37] a term which evolved into "messiah."

A Mesopotamian depiction of a "Dragon" (Sumerian: ušumgal, Akkadian: mušhuššu).

But certainly the Bible wouldn't equate Jesus with serpents, would it? In fact, it does. The Hebrew word for messiah, *mashiyahk* (מְשִׁיחַ), is connected to the word for serpent, *nachash* (נָחָשׁ pronounced "naw-kawsh"), by comparing their numerical values. Adding together the values of each letter in mashiyahk derives the equation: $40 + 300 + 10 + 8 = 358$. Likewise, adding together those of the word nachash results in: $50 + 8 + 300 = 358$. This connection was well known to Biblical authors. When the Israelites were suffering from the venomous bites of serpents in the desert, God commanded Moses to form a bronze statue that looked like a snake and to place it on a pole so that anyone who looked at it would be cured (Numbers 21:4–9). This act is mentioned in the New Testament when it says, "And just as Moses lifted up the serpent in the wilderness, so must the Son of Man be lifted up" (John 3:14). John was apparently not only aware of the symbolism of

A coin from Ancient Greece depicting the crucifixion and the raised serpent.

the serpent on the pole and Jesus on the cross, but also the numerological connection between the serpent and the Messiah.[38]

Additionally, there may even be a serpent connection to the *age* of Jesus. The Gospel of Luke states that Jesus began his ministry when he was approximately thirty years of age (3:23). The New Testament does not record how long his ministry lasted, but it could have been between two and four years. Generally, most scholars believe it lasted for just over three years.[39] This would have made Jesus thirty-three years old when he was crucified. The ancient mystery schools taught that the serpent was a symbol for knowledge (recall the serpent and the tree in Eden)—called *Kundalini* by the mystics of India—and that it was coiled and dormant at the base of a person's spine. As the person works towards higher understanding, the serpent is said to travel up the spine. Intriguingly, the human spinal column consists of *thirty-three* vertebrae.[40]

Now it is becoming clear just how much power and symbolism could be contained within a name. The name and titles of Jesus encompass the entire numerical "power" of the Greek alphabet, not to mention clever wordplays and puzzles revolving around fish and serpent symbolism. However, only the name of Jesus as it appears throughout the Bible has been discussed thus far. There is yet another variation of Jesus' name, but it is important to realize that this is *different* from the official name. It is known as the Pentagrammaton.

The Pentagrammaton

Before we delve too deeply into the subject of the Pentagrammaton, I must issue an important caveat. Please understand that this derivation of Jesus' name was made up by ceremonial magicians that did not possess a solid background of the Hebrew language. Why am I still bothering to cover this topic? Even though I recognize that the origin of this particular name is suspect, it still seems as though the intention behind its use was to continue a sacred tradition from long ago.

During the time of the Renaissance, there was a rebirth of ceremonial magick due to increased interests in Cabala and Christian Mysticism. At this time, it was believed that a new name had supplanted the power and authority of the Tetragrammaton. This magickal name of Jesus was composed of the same four Hebrew letters of the Tetragrammaton so that it would contain all of its power. But there was the addition of one other Hebrew letter, *Shin* (ש), which was inserted into the middle of the Name of the Father to represent the element of heavenly *Fire* as well as *Spirit*.[41] This was believed to indicate that the Spirit of God had descended or incarnated on Earth in the midst of the four physical elements, just as it was believed Jesus was God incarnated in the flesh. This five-fold Name of the Son was *Yeheshuah* (YHShWH), written with Hebrew letters as: יהשוה, and pronounced "Yeh-heh-shu-ah."[42]

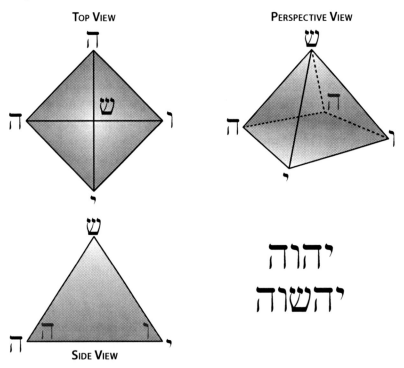

When the letter Shin (ש) is inserted into the Tetragrammaton,
each letter of the name can be placed at the points of a pyramid.

In 1486 CE, the opinion that the name YHShWH had supplanted YHWH was proposed when Giovanni Pico dell Mirandola (1463–94) published his seminal seventy-two *Conclusions* on the Cabala. In his fourteenth conclusion, he not only argued for the descent of the letter *Shin* (ש) into the Tetragrammaton, but also that the addition of this letter made the ineffable name of YHWH finally pronounceable.[43]

Earlier, we studied how the act of placing the four letters of the Tetragrammaton on the arms of an equilateral cross could then be extracted into three dimensions to form a tetrahedron. A similar technique can also be developed using the five letters of the Pentagrammaton. The difference is that now the letter Shin (ש), representing Spirit, rests at the exact center of the cross where the lines converge. However, the addition of this new point effectively transforms the tetrahedron into a new shape. Now, we can successfully render a three-dimensional pyramid—representing fire, knowledge, and transformation—simply by "raising" the "Spirit" to a higher level.

There appeared two different methods of writing the magickal name of Jesus. The first has already been discussed, and is YHShWH (יהשוה), while the other is YHWShH (יהושה), and pronounced "Ye-ho-va-shah," or "Ye-ho-wah-shah." The subtle difference is in the switching of the *Shin* (ש) and the *Vau* (ו) letters. What is the reason for the switching of these letters? It will become apparent as we examine the application of the name in magickal rituals.

Because the Pentagrammaton YHShWH consists of five letters, each point of a pentagram can be assigned a particular letter. Beginning at the lower right point, the *Yod* (י) is assigned because it represents the element of Fire. Moving counterclockwise around the pentagram, the placement falls as *Heh* (ה) for Water, *Shin* (ש) for Spirit, *Vau* (ו) for Air, and the final *Heh* (ה) for Earth.[44] The use of a counterclockwise move-ment is in accordance with specific magickal rituals intended to banish evil spirits and negative energies. A clockwise motion is used for the opposite effect of invoking, or summoning those same energies. Therefore, the Pentagrammaton functions for both banishing and invoking rituals, depending on how it is applied. The following illustration shows the placement of each letter and

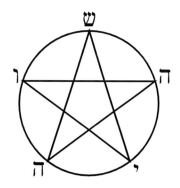

its corresponding element on the points of the pentagram.

While it is important to bear in mind that the Pentagrammaton seems to be of medieval origin, magickal associations with the name of Jesus can be found in the New Testament. The actual validity of this particular connection to the Pentagrammaton is unknown, but it appears to be of great significance.

Jesus said that others would be able to cast out demons under the authority of his name.[45] In the occult sense, this would be done by assuming the "god-form" of Jesus and using his name (the Pentagrammaton) in a counterclockwise motion on the pentagram to banish evil spirits. The key to a successful banishment was calling upon the power of the name and using it properly in the ritual. Simply saying something like, "I banish you in the name of Jesus," would not work despite what Hollywood would have us believe. However, due to the popularity of the modern name, there are some people who report that attacks from demonic entities (or even sometimes aliens) were thwarted after calling out the name of Jesus.

Donald Tyson has noted in his research that the Bible depicts the consequences of using the name of Jesus improperly, or not assuming the authority of the name. This is evidenced in the botched exorcism performed by seven priests that used the "names" of Jesus and Paul, to which the demon replied, "Jesus I know, and Paul I know; but who are you?" (Acts 19:13–16). It is both frightening and somewhat amusing to imagine the look of shock upon the exorcists' faces once they realized that they had no real power over the demon only seconds before it attacked them. They all promptly fled the house—but with *much* less clothing than when they had entered.[46]

If the Pentagrammaton was only devised as recently as the Renaissance period, then it would be logical to assume that it had no *real* connection to the name of Jesus. However, this argument is mistaken because the popularity of the Pentagrammaton merely demonstrates that it was a new way of recognizing an already established tradition. Therefore, to understand how such a connection was formed, we must explore the history and associations of the five-pointed star itself.

The Pentagram

Many Christians might be confused as well as uncomfortable with a connection between Jesus and the pentagram. Time and time again, the pentagram has been mistakenly interpreted as an emblem of evil. Much of the confusion and misunderstanding of the pentagram derives from the ongoing misappropriation of the symbol by filmmakers, novelists, and heavy-metal bands for purely sensational purposes. Additionally, Satanists such as the late Anton Szandor LaVey (1930–1997) deliberately hijacked the symbol and imposed different meanings and interpretations upon it for the sheer pleasure of mocking Christians. However, despite the last hundred years of negative at-tention, further research into the history of this symbol reveals a very different and much more interesting story.

The seal of ancient Jerusalem.

The pentagram has been used by cultures throughout the world for thousands of years as a protective symbol with the power to banish evil spirits.[47] Pentagrams have been discovered on broken pieces of clay from the region of Palestine, dated to around 4000 BCE. The Sumerian culture was certainly using it as a common symbol around 2700 BCE and it was probably from astronomical research in the Tigris-Euphrates region almost six-thousand years ago that the shape of the pentagram was derived.[48]

It has also been established with complete certainty that during the period of 300–150 BCE, the ancient city of Jerusalem used the pentagram as its official seal.[49] When a fragment of a fourth century BCE jar handle was discovered, it could be seen that it had been inscribed with a pentagram and the Hebrew/Aramaic letters ירשלם (YRShLM).[50]

The common interpretation of the name Jerusalem is "City of Peace," but there is also a very different possibility. Some Biblical scholars write that it was originally the "Foundation (of the deity) Shalem." *Shalem* (שלם) is believed to be a child of El, the Most High God, according to Ugaritic mythology (the name is also sometimes transliterated as Šalim). This deity, Shalem, is directly connected to both the Evening and Morning Star within the mythological texts, particularly the story known as "The Gracious and Beautiful Gods."[51] If Jerusalem (originally Salem) was indeed dedicated to this god, that would therefore make it the "City of the Morning/Evening Star."

The pentagram was a very important symbol used by Pythagoras (c. 570–c. 495 BCE), who was among the first of major figures in Western occult traditions. Pythagoras believed the five-pointed star[52] was an "emblem of physical and mental harmony." Additionally, the Pythagorean Brotherhood used the pentagram to identify members of their group, and used the letters of the Greek word for "health," ΥΓΕΙΑ, on each point of the star. Members of the Brotherhood even wore a signet ring bearing the pentagram symbol.[53]

The Pythagoreans also considered the pentagram as a symbol of the human body, with the points representing the head, arms, and legs.[54]

During the early Middle Ages, the pentagram became deeply entrenched in Christian symbolism. It was associated with the five books of Moses (the *Torah*), and even the five stones David had collected to be used against Goliath[55] (and the four brothers of Goliath). The epic poem *Sir Gawain and the Green Knight* describes the coat of arms for Sir Gawain as being a gold pentagram set against a red background.[56] The poem then continues to make connections between "the five points to the five wounds of Christ, the five joys of the Virgin Mary," and also "the keenness of Gawain's five senses, the strength of his five fingers, and the five knightly virtues of liberality, loving-kindness, continence, courtesy, and piety."[57]

The "Legend of the Sand Dollar" is a well known folk poem that associates the skeletal remains of the marine animal with the story of Jesus. The sand dollar forms a five-pointed star shape, and the legend links it to the five wounds suffered during the crucifixion and also the star that announced the birth of Jesus.

In the early eighteenth century, the pentagram was incorporated into Freemasonry as "the blazing star." The symbol is displayed on the eastern wall of Masonic lodges worldwide. Later, in the nineteenth century, Éliphas Lévi further altered the significance of the pentagram.[58] Éliphas Lévi, whose real name was Alphonse Louis Constant, was a French magician and author (1810–1875), and is considered to be "the single most important figure in the modern revival of ceremonial magic."[59] Due to Lévi's writings, and the incorporation of the pentagram into many magickal lodges, particularly the Golden Dawn, the pentagram became a well-known ritual tool.[60]

The skeleton of a Sand Dollar showing its five-pointed star shape.

According to most modern magickal traditions, largely influenced by the writings of Lévi, the meaning and intent of the pentagram depended on how it was depicted. If it has one point up, it is meant to be a symbol of good and the power of Spirit over the material elements. However, if it is inverted with two points upward, the meaning is the dominance of material elements over that of Spirit, and is commonly used for negative purposes.[61] Something to consider, however, is that prior to the distinction made by Lévi, there did not appear to be any negative connotation that the inverted pentagram was a symbol of evil.

While the upright pentagram naturally lends itself to the depiction of a human with arms and legs outstretched, when the symbol is inverted, the human figure is replaced by a horned goat's head. Satanists deliberately associate the horned goat with the inverted pentagram because of Christian beliefs concerning the Devil. For instance, during the Middle Ages, the Church merged the Horned God of pagan faiths with the story of the Devil, and in so doing accused "witches" of worshipping Satan. The Horned God imagery was commonly associated with a goat-man (a.k.a. "satyr"), particularly the Greek myths concerning the frolics and promiscuousness of Pan. However, it is also easy to perceive how the image of the goat became synonymous with evil on account of Azazel (the "scapegoat") and his lustful behavior toward the women of the earth when he fell with the other Watchers.

Today, modern Satanists employ the use of the inverted pentagram in their rituals. Since their beliefs stress higher importance towards material gain and empowering the Self over God, they use the inverted pentagram as

The upright and inverted pentagram as they are used in some occult rituals.

a representation of these beliefs. Most people do not pay close enough attention to notice the difference, though, and then think that *any* pentagram is Satanic. This confusion has led to many occult practitioners being wrongly associated with Satanic worship. Additionally, with this new evidence linking Christ to the pentagram, many of the negative or unholy associations are revealed to be completely unfounded.

The Morning Star

The importance of the pentagram's astronomical significance was briefly discussed in an earlier section. The people of the ancient world paid close attention to the night sky and to the stars and the planets, particularly Venus. When Venus appears, it is the brightest visible point of light in the sky (besides the sun and moon). It was known by many names, but mostly as the *Eastern Star,* the *Morning Star,* and the *Evening Star.* Because of its proximity to the sun in the sky, it is only visible on Earth just before sunrise and shortly after sunset.

Other titles for Venus throughout the ages have been: *Nindaranna* by the early Babylonians (c. 1600 BCE),[62] *Mul.Dili.Pat* by the Sumerians,[63] *Ishtar* by the Akkadians,[64] and the Chinese identified it as *Jin xing.* The Maya called it *Chak ek,* which meant "The Great Star," because it was their most important heavenly body, and they believed it represented the Mesoamerican god Quetzalcoatl (Kukulcán to the Maya). Apparently, the early Greeks considered the appearance of Venus in the morning and the evening as two separate celestial bodies. The name *Hesperus* was applied to it when it appeared in the western evening sky, and *Phosphorus* ("Bringer of the Dawn") when it appeared in the eastern morning sky.[65] When translated into Latin, it became known as *Lucifer,* the "Light-bearer."

Ancient astronomers realized from their studies that Venus had a synodic period of roughly 584 days (or more precisely as 583.92 days).[66] What this means is that it took 584 days for Venus to reappear at the same position in the sky, relative to the sun, when observing it from the Earth. The astronomers would record the position of Venus every 584 days at the moment of sunrise. After five consecutive synodic periods from the starting point, Venus would have returned to almost the exact same position in the sky. This process took a period of 2,920 days (584 days x 5 synodic periods), which is exactly eight years (2,920 ÷ 365 = 8).[67]

So what is the significance of this finding? This is probably the origin of the shape of the pentagram and why it appeared so often in the ancient world.

The ancient astronomers discovered that an upright and inverted pentagram
can be traced in the sky by tracking the position of Venus.

When tracking Venus, a straight line can be drawn from the first point and
then to each consecutive point, resulting in the rendering of a pentagram star.
This method of plotting the pentagram points can be accomplished on any
date, as long as Venus is prominently visible and it is done at the same time
each period. Using an astronomy program such as Starry Night™, anyone
can verify this information quickly and easily. Further information regarding
this process, with step-by-step instructions, is detailed in Appendix D.

Another important detail regarding the observation of Venus in the sky
is that there is a one-day slippage every 12.67 synodic periods as the pentagram slowly rotates in a clockwise fashion. The result of this motion is that
approximately every 160 years the pentagram has switched its orientation
and is showing either one or two ascending points as shown here.[68] One
last point of interest regarding the observation of Venus is what's known as
the *Transit of Venus*. A transit occurs when Venus passes directly between
the Earth and the visible disc of the Sun. These transits are considered rare;
on June 8, 2004 the first transit of Venus in 122 years occurred, the last
one being in 1882. It is a "twice-in-a-lifetime event," though, since the next
transit occurs eight years later on June 6, 2012. After the 2012 transit, it will
not happen again until another 122 years, which places it at 2134 CE.[69]

Curiously, the question must be raised as to how much the ancient
Maya people knew regarding Venus, since it was of the utmost importance
to their culture. According to their long-count calendar, which measured
1,872,000 days in length, the end of the current age occurs on December
21, 2012[70]—the same year as the last transit of Venus in this current cycle!
Whether or not there is a direct connection between the two events is not
known. It should be understood, however, that this date is *not* believed to

be the end of the world, as some claim, but rather an end of the current cycle of time recorded by the Maya.

Supporting Evidence

Some skeptical readers may consider the connection between the Pentagrammaton, which is not the official name given in Biblical texts, with the pentagram shape derived from the plotting of Venus, to be unfounded. If it were based solely on these two pieces of data, then I would agree. However, there appears to be a surprising amount of supporting evidence given in both the Old and New Testaments that indicate the pentagram was directly associated with Jesus.

As early as the birth of Jesus, there is a connection to the Eastern Star in the Gospel of Matthew. While there has been much debate regarding exactly what the "star" was that the wise men had seen,[71] it should be noted that these men were astrologers and studied the heavens intensely. As has been demonstrated, probably one of the most important observations in the ancient past was regarding the tracking of Venus in the sky. Is the following passage a definitive reference to Venus? That is unknown, but it is one of the most likely candidates and fits with the remaining evidence.

> Now when Jesus was born in Bethlehem of Judaea in the days of Herod the king, behold, there came wise men from the east to Jerusalem, Saying, "Where is he that is born King of the Jews? for we have seen his star in the east, and are come to worship him"… When they had heard the king, they departed; and, lo, the star, which they saw in the east, went before them, till it came and stood over where the young child was. When they saw the star, they rejoiced with exceeding great joy.
>
> Matthew 2:1–2, 9–10 KJV

The connection between the "star in the east" and the "Eastern Star" is obvious. Reading the text literally, though, does present a slight problem in that it is difficult to determine if the "star" was really a star in the sky, or something completely different. Being astrologers, one would think that the wise men should have been familiar with Venus and therefore nothing was out of the ordinary. This has led many people believe it was a planetary conjunction of some sort, which could place the birth anytime between 7 and 2 BCE.[72]

Some researchers even speculate that the star was actually a UFO guiding the men, particularly since "stars" aren't supposed to move freely through the sky and hover above small children.[73] While this interpretation might sound plausible based on the reading, it seems unlikely at this point in our investigation. A more reasonable conclusion is that the wise men (or gospel authors) recognized the symbolic relationship between Venus and kingship, in addition to the scepter,[74] and were incorporating them into the story. Thus, the awaited divine king was to be associated with the "star."

As explained in a previous chapter, Jesus is connected to the priestly order of *Melchizedek* (מלכיצדק). Melchizedek made his first and only appearance in the Bible when he blessed Abraham, who at that time was called Abram. He is also described as being the high priest of the god El Elyon (אל עליון), the Most High God, and the king of "Salem," which is accepted as the precursor to Jeru*salem*.[75] The pentagram was a symbol for Jerusalem, as shown by the fragment of pottery mentioned earlier. So, if Melchizedek was the high priest of Salem (Jerusalem), and the city's symbol was the pentagram, it is not hard to make a connection that the pentagram would also apply to Jesus since he is directly linked to the same priestly line.

Additionally, Psalm 22 is known as "Aijeleth Shakar," which translates as "Hind of the Dawn," or "Doe of the Dawn" and is a reference to the "morning star." This psalm foreshadows the sacrifice of the messiah figure and provides many of the details that are described later in the gospels. For instance, the song starts "My God, my God, why have you forsaken me?" echoing the same cry from Jesus when on the cross.[76]

Further evidence appears in The Second Letter of Peter, in which he calls for believers to have faith in Christ by writing: "You will do well to be attentive to this as to a lamp shining in a dark place, until the day dawns and the morning star (*phosphorus:* φωσφόρος) rises in your hearts."[77] Similar wording is also used in The Second Letter of Paul to the Corinthians with: "For it is the God who said, 'Let light shine out of darkness,' who has shown in our hearts to give the light of the knowledge of the glory of God…"[78]

Perhaps the most convincing statement is from that of Jesus at the end of Revelation. It is here that Jesus clearly associates his kingship with Venus and the pentagram by saying, "It is I, Jesus, who sent my angel to you with this testimony for the churches. I am the root and the descendant of David, [and] the bright morning star (*aster ho lampros ho proinos:* ἀστήρ ὁ λαμπρός ὁ πρωϊνός)."[79]

Much like the connections between Jesus and the symbol of the penta-gram, the association of Jesus with the figure of Lucifer will at first appear discomforting, if not blasphemous, to readers of a traditional Christian faith. However, a connection between Jesus and Lucifer is in no way im-plied here, only in the *titles* of the two figures. Rather, I will argue that the name or title "Lucifer" has been erroneously applied to the mythology of the supposed first fallen angel.

It was stated before that Lucifer is the Latin term for "Light-bearer" or "Morning Star" and is the planet Venus. The ancients invented a myth to reflect what they saw in the heavens involving the planet and the sun. They observed that this "morning star" would rise before the sun at dawn, but the sun would always eventually overtake it. In telling the story, a parallel myth evolved that described a beautiful angel (Lucifer, or "The Dawn Star") who tried to usurp the authority of the Most High God (the Sun) and fused the two myths together in describing the same astrological knowledge. The reason for the connection is from a single passage in the Bible, which is actually addressing a Babylonian king:

> How you are fallen from heaven, <u>O Day Star, son of Dawn</u>! How you are cut down to the ground, you who laid the nations low! You said in your heart, "<u>I will ascend to heaven</u>; <u>above the stars of God</u>; I will sit on the <u>mount of assembly</u> on the heights of Za-phon; I will ascend to the tops of the clouds, <u>I will make myself like the Most High</u>." But you are brought down to Sheol, to the depths of the Pit.
>
> Isaiah 14:12–15 NRSV

The Hebrew words that were translated as "Day Star, son of Dawn" are *Helel ben Shakar* (הילל בן שחר), meaning both "Morning Star" and also "Shining One of the Dawn." It is commonly understood among scholars that this refer-ence is comparing the Babylonian priest and his pride to that of the infamous legend of a fallen angel's pride. The early Church Fathers taught that Lucifer was not meant to be a proper name of this angel, and rather that it was referring to the angel's previous status when he was still the most beloved of God.[80]

Unfortunately, the Isaiah passage has been lumped together with several other passages in the Bible and erroneous connections have been made. Since Isaiah is referring to a being identified as the "Morning Star" who apparently fell from Heaven, and in the Gospel of Luke, Jesus tells the group of seventy followers[81] that he saw "Satan fall from heaven like a flash of lightning,"[82] many people have drawn a connection between these two passages. Additionally, Paul writes: "...even Satan disguises himself as an <u>angel of light</u>."[83] Finally, the most overt source for these associations occurs in Revelation 12 during the description of the "great red dragon" that "swept down a third of the stars of heaven and threw them to the earth" and is later cast down to the earth with his angels. However, what many do not consider in regard to this passage is that it is describing an event that has not happened yet, and therefore is not the same event as described in Isaiah.

So why have these connections remained unexplored or unaddressed throughout mainstream Biblical scholarship? It seems as though faithful scholars and church leaders have systematically avoided drawing attention to the relationship by enforcing the Lucifer/Satan comparisons and neglecting to mention the "morning star" references that pertain to Jesus even though the connections are clearly discernible. However, because the associations are not in accordance with the dominant ideology endorsed by the Church, these parallels are never emphasized or openly addressed. Despite at least five other Biblical examples that say otherwise, this has resulted in *de facto* evidence based on a misunderstanding of a single verse in Isaiah that is combined with more irrelevant verses. Yet everyone has believed for the last few centuries that the "Fall of Lucifer" is grounded in Biblical fact, even though the Bible offers no such story.

Please understand that it is not my intention to be disrespectful in illuminating these particular connections and associations, and I do not wish to dismiss or oppose traditional concepts of good and evil. I do see evidence that there is some kind of evil being or "dark force" that exerts a powerful influence upon our world—a topic that will be addressed in a later work.[84] However, the name Lucifer and the title, "The Morning Star" have become irrevocably synonymous with the figure commonly known as Satan. These ideas and beliefs are constantly reinforced throughout popular culture and by contemporary religious teachings. Furthermore, these interpretations endure because unfortunately, persons of faith most often subscribe to materials that reinforce these predominantly held views. Finally, as radical as my interpretations might initially seem, I am ultimately advocating that the Bible be read in order to obtain further wisdom, insight, and understanding of not only the text itself, but the mysterious world in which we live. Ironically, in accepting the predominant views, readers are denying the words of the Bible because they refuse to consider any alternative interpretations.

Having analyzed two of the most important *male* names in the Bible, we will now focus on the name of an important *female* who is mentioned numerous times throughout the New Testament. While many other women shared her first name, she is the only one of them to be distinguished by a surname. Could it be that the gospel writers were singling her out to express a specific idea or deeper meaning to their stories? Her name has been made incredibly popular and the source of much controversy, but often for the wrong reasons. This woman is Mary Magdalene.

Mary Magdalene: The Watchtower of God

Perhaps one of the more controversial figures in the New Testament was Mary Magdalene, from whom the Gospels say that Jesus had "cast out seven demons."[85] Erroneously considered by many to be a prostitute for the last several centuries, this female apostle has now acquired an immense amount of attention recently on account of Dan Brown's immensely popular novel, *The Da Vinci Code* (Doubleday, 2003). Was Mary Magdalene really the bride of Jesus and did she possibly carry his child to continue the messianic bloodline? There are so many different books trying to prove and disprove the content and research that it is difficult to answer. However, my own research into these matters has led to significant doubt about such claims.

In the end, many people will simply agree with whatever they'd personally like to believe about the role of Mary Magdalene. Some will consider the idea of her marriage to Jesus as nothing more than a medieval legend that became popularized because of its controversy. Others will see it as a return to seeking the feminine side of God that has been lacking for so long in the male dominated patriarchal religions. And yet others will vehemently use it to "prove" that established religion is not to be trusted.

Whatever your personal belief is regarding this matter, attempting to prove whether or not Mary Magdalene was the "holy grail" or really did have a child with Jesus is not the intention of this book.[86] Instead, we will be looking at meanings and interpretations of Mary Magdalene's name and considering other promising views in relation to the surrounding information. While some of this evidence addresses similarly controversial themes, there is yet another even more provocative interpretation that has yet to be explored.

To begin, the name Mary is shared by many important women in the Gospels. The New Testament records as many as six different women with this name:

1. Mary, the mother of Jesus
2. Mary Magdalene
3. Mary, the sister of Lazarus and Martha
4. Mary of Cleophas, the mother of James the less
5. Mary, the mother of John Mark
6. Mary, a Roman Christian greeted by Paul

Why, in particular, is the name Mary so common throughout the Bible? The sheer amount of repetition indicates that the name itself was considered significant, and probably used as a title. It also makes study of the Gospels quite confusing at times, because it is often believed that Mary, the sister of Lazarus and Martha is actually Mary Magdalene. Other scholars contend that this is not the case. Nevertheless, much of this confusion can be removed if we begin to analyze the name and what it meant to the ancient scribes.

The name in Greek is *Maria* (Μαρία) and means "rebellion." It is derived from the Hebrew name *Miriam* (מרים), which has the same meaning. The name may also have connections with Egypt, which was *Ta Mery*, where *Mery* meant "beloved." It has been passed down through the ages, and is often associated with the salt-water of the ocean. In French, the sea is called *la mer*.

A deliberate variation of the name is occasionally written by the New Testament authors. This variation is closer to the original Hebrew, and is *Mariam* (Μαρίαμ). The reason will become apparent when studying the values using gematria. The sum of the letters in Mariam equals 192—an important number in gematria. It is considered the epitome of the number four, based on the equation: $3 \times 4^3 = 192$. Four was considered a sacred number and represented the material earth, particularly the "four directions," "four corners of the earth," and the triple-four (444) was identified with the "flesh and blood" creatures of earth. The name Mary is also equated with *mother, matter* and *material* in several different languages, and to the Greek word *matrix*. The cube shape was assigned to the element of earth by Plato because even numbers were considered feminine and odd were male.[87] Thus, the cube represented the perfect Earth Mother, and the name Mariam embodied this as the result of 3(4 x 4 x 4).

The name used for the other women, Maria (Μαρία) only has a value of 152. It might be that the gospel authors were trying to connect these women by name to the number 153 (the fish), but they were meant to fall short. However, Mariam (Μαρίαμ) was sometimes used for both the mother of Jesus and also Mary, who was called "the Magdalene." Perhaps the New Testament authors were trying to stress a connection between the mother of Jesus and the one called Magdalene.

Magdalene is derived from the Hebrew and Aramaic root word *Migdal* (מגדל), which means "tower" or "watchtower," or even "elevated." Some researchers such as Margaret Starbid have suggested that this implied Mary Magdalene's status within the gospels was to be raised above the other apostles and that she was perhaps even the bride of Jesus. While this sounds tempting, a different interpretation will be offered shortly. First, we should investigate the traditional explanation.

It is commonly accepted that Mary Magdalene was given the epithet "Magdalene" because it was thought she came from a town called Magdala. However, the small fishing village that's now called Magdala was originally known as Taricheae to the Greeks living at the time of Jesus. Jewish historians recorded that after the town had fallen into ruins, Christians renamed them Magdala because they believed Mary Magdalene was from that particular region, called Magada or Dalmunutha. The original name of the village in Aramaic was thought to be "Migdal Nunayah," which meant "Tower of the Fishermen."[88]

Margaret Starbird's research concerning "the Magdalene" indicates that the "-*ene* (hnh) ending is not a correct or typical one for designating a person from a particular town or region." If this was the intention, the correct ending should be -*ios*. If the authors intended that Mary was indeed from a town called "Magdala," then it should be correctly written as "Magdalaios," (Μαγδαλαιος).[89]

However, the New Testament authors' deliberate "mistakes" signify there is a hidden meaning. "The Magdalene" is written η Μαγδαληνη, with a sum of 153. This is significant, because it means that the authors associated Mary Magdalene with "the fish" and all of the symbolism discussed earlier. This greatly increases the chances of her role as the mystical bride of Jesus and even goddess figure within the New Testament. She is, after all, believed to be the one who performed the anointment ritual that declared Jesus to be the Messiah. It could also indicate that both she and Jesus' mother were portraying different aspects of the Goddess: The Virgin Mary representing the Higher Goddess who gave birth to the Messiah, but who later "falls" into the material world. Then, Mary Magdalene takes on the role as the Fallen Goddess seeking reunion with God.[90] While this comparison may be reading into the text too much, the theme of the fallen and redeemed goddess is prevalent throughout Biblical narratives.

A veiled reference to this type of pagan symbolism is depicted at the crucifixion. The Gospel of John states that there were three different women at the foot of the cross of Jesus. They were "his mother, and his mother's sister, Mary the wife of Clopas, and Mary Magdalene" (19:25). So it indicates that three different women who were all named Mary were standing together. This is possibly an attempt to show the "triple goddess" symbolism of *maiden, mother,* and *crone.*[91]

Since "Jesus Christ" essentially means "The Savior King," it would be sensible to investigate the name "Mary Magdalene." If Mariam means "rebellion" and Magdalene means "tower" or "watchtower," the result appears to be referencing a "rebellious tower." This should instantly make a connection to the Tower of Babel story and the people who rebelled against God. Could it be that Mary Magdalene is not only meant to portray the redeemed Goddess, but also provide a clue as to how the human race can finally reunite with heaven?

> But in <u>the last days</u> it shall come to pass, that <u>the mountain of the house of the LORD shall be established in the top of the mountains,</u> and it shall be exalted above the hills; and people shall flow unto it. And many nations shall come, and say, "Come, and let us go up to the mountain of the LORD, and to the house of the God of Jacob; and he will teach us of his ways, and we will walk in his paths."[92]
> ... And thou, O <u>tower of the flock,</u> the strong hold of the <u>daughter of Zion,</u> unto thee shall it come, even the first dominion; the kingdom shall come to the daughter of Jerusalem. Now why dost thou cry out aloud? is there no king in thee?... Be in pain, and labour to bring forth, O daughter of Zion, like a woman in travail: for now shalt thou go forth out of the city,... and thou shalt go even to <u>Babylon</u>; there shalt thou be delivered.
>
> Micah 4:1–2, 8–10 KJV

This passage seems to be describing a similar holy "mountain" like the Tower of Babel and other ziggurats, except that this time it's created with God's blessing. The term translated as "tower of the flock" is *Migdal-Eder* (מגדלעדר), which refers to a Shepherd's Watchtower. The connection to Mary Magdalene is evident and probably also alludes to a line of "Shepherd Kings," the priestly title that Jesus likely inherited.[93]

The "daughter of Zion" is usually interpreted allegorically as Israel becoming the bride of God, or by Christians as the church becoming the bride of Christ. However, if it is referring to the Fallen Goddess, the Shekinah, awaiting her reunion with God, it is certainly no stretch to think that the New Testament authors were trying to compare the Magdalene to this role as the mystical bride. It is also of particular interest that it tells the "daughter of Zion" to go to Babylon so that she can be rescued. It seems to be speaking of Babylon in a neutral tone, despite the history of how the Jewish people were held captive there for such a long period of time.

Furthermore, there is yet another thread tying Mary Magdalene to a divine gateway and the Watchers. It is commonly understood among scholars who study the Divine Council that the Ugaritic[94] language counterparts of *mrym* (מרום) and *marayima* (מרומים) were used to refer to the "mountainous abode of El."[95] This is quite interesting because it demonstrates that even the vocabulary of other cultures intended a direct link between the name Mary and a divine mountain that led to the home of God.

Other connections between Mary Magdalene and the reunion with heaven can be discovered by building upon the above information and events that occurred much later. Our investigation now leads us to a peculiar location that has received a great deal of attention lately. That place is the village of Rennes-le-Château in southern France.

Rennes-le-Château

Made popular by the best selling book *Holy Blood, Holy Grail,* and later by Dan Brown's *The Da Vinci Code,* the small mountain village and its church have become a popular attraction for tourists. It has a long history, and was built over a sixth century Visigoth church. Later, it was consecrated to Mary Magdalene in 1059 CE.[96]

A legend exists that a group of "heretics" living in this same region, known as the Cathars, were in possession of an important treasure thought to be taken from Solomon's temple in Jerusalem when it was plundered by the Romans in 66 CE. This treasure was thought to "transcend that of 'mere' gold," and could have been the actual Grail chalice, or secret knowledge leading to immense riches. The Cathars were also known as the "Albigensians" and based in the region called Languedoc. They were not overly fond of religious dogma or Roman Catholicism for sure, and this created a great deal of hatred towards them within the ecclesiastical authorities. In 1209 CE, they faced a huge massacre and very few are thought to have survived.[97]

Over many centuries, the church had fallen into disrepair and was appointed with a new parish priest, Bérenger Saunière, on June 1, 1885.[98] Shortly after, Saunière began to restore the broken-down church to its original splendor. It was soon discovered after moving a large altar stone that one of its supporting pillars had been hollowed out. He found two wooden tubes hidden inside, each holding two pieces of parchment. Two of these parchments looked as if they were genealogies dating from 1244 CE and 1644 CE. The other two parchments appeared to be from the 1780s and contained Latin excerpts from the New Testament. One of these parchments, however, did not contain spaces between the words and implemented obvious mistakes such as extra letters, which seemed to indicate that a hidden message was encoded into the text.[99]

Many researchers believe that these hidden messages reveal a long-held secret that Jesus had not died on the cross, but lived on and fathered a bloodline dynasty with Mary Magdalene that culminated in the line eventually known as the Merovingian Kings of France. This secret was passed along by members of a secretive group known as the Priory of Sion, and included such prominent members as Leonardo da Vinci and Isaac Newton.

Saunière is also alleged to have discovered another secret area and possibly hidden treasures. The humble priest suddenly became very wealthy, but the actual source of his funds was never determined with absolute certainty. Some people believe that he had uncovered a secret so deep and dark that the Catholic Church paid Saunière to remain silent.

With seemingly unlimited funds, restorations to the church began once again. Saunière paid to have a road leading to the village paved when a dirt road would have sufficed just fine at the time. Many statues were bought and placed within the church and Saunière had Latin phrases carved into the décor. The most intriguing of all was a tower that he had built honoring Mary Magdalene, called "le Tour Magdala" in French.

On January 17, 1917, Bérenger Saunière suffered a sudden stroke. A priest was called to hear his deathbed confession; but according to some people, after hearing the confession, the priest "never smiled again" and refused to perform the Roman Catholic rite of Extreme Unction. Saunière died on January 22, at the age of sixty-five. Upon the reading of his will, it was found that he was penniless and he had transferred all of his wealth to his housekeeper, Marie Denarnaud.[100]

But is any of this true? How much is fact and how much is legend?

Many of the elements told in the account are apparently fabricated to enhance the genuine facts of the story. For instance, the hollowed out pillar that allegedly contained the secret documents is still available for viewing at the local museum. The problem is that the pillar is not hollowed out and the only hole in it is about the size of a CD case—too small to hold the tubes with the parchments. One can also question the priest's trip to Paris to decipher the documents, since no proof exists to support it.[101]

Apparently, though, Saunière did find some valuable artifacts around the church and made note of these in his journals. He intended to sell them to help raise money and continued excavating other areas of the church and its grounds. The other source of his income was investigated by a local bishop, who accused Saunière of profiting from "trafficking in Masses," which was a common offense for priests of this time. The priests would offer to help a deceased loved one's soul rise from Purgatory to Heaven—as long as the required price was paid. The act itself was not considered wrong by the Church, but it was frowned upon when priests took out large advertisements showing their willingness to perform great masses for the living and the dead, because it was thought to create unfair competition among priests. The situation worsened when many of these priests failed to perform the masses even though they had been properly paid. In 1909 the bishop accusing Saunière asked him to account for himself and his business dealings; Saunière boldly refused and was suspended of his priestly duties and other privileges. But it had little effect, because Saunière appealed to the Vatican and was soon reinstated to Rennes-le-Château.[102]

Making matters worse was that much of the legend involving the grail bloodline associated with Rennes-le-Château appears to be based upon fake documents and information created by Pierre Plantard "de Saint-Clair." Plantard, it turns out, published a magazine during the Second World War titled *Vaincre,* which had anti-Semitic overtones and he was also the leader of a minor occult group known as Alpha Galates.[103] He also enlisted the aid of an artist friend, Philippe de Cherisey, to create the parchments that support the bogus genealogies. Plantard then passed the supposedly authentic parchments and the fictitious story about Saunière's findings to an individual named Gérard de Sède. It is also believed that Plantard invented the entire Priory of Sion story in 1956 and created more fake documents linking the group to Rennes-le-Château. He planted these documents at the National Library in Paris and then later advised the soon-to-be authors of *Holy Blood, Holy Grail* to seek out further information at that particular library.[104]

But for what reason did Pierre Plantard go to all of this trouble to convince everyone about the story involving Rennes-le-Château? It is because he wanted people to think that he was the Grand Master of the Priory and that he was the last living descendant of the Merovingian bloodline. This would therefore give him the title as the rightful king of France and access to the throne, and additionally, he could try to legitimize the claim that he was a blood descendent of Jesus![105] This is important for various reasons, most notably because it largely discredits the legitimacy of the current fascination with Jesus and messianic bloodline.

Nonetheless, the uncovering of these particular deceptions allow us to instead focus upon what (if any) aspects of these stories are indeed true. It cannot be satisfactorily determined what Bérenger Saunière did find at Rennes-le-Château other than some minor artifacts. We may never find out, so we are still left with the mystery of why Saunière suddenly began making so many changes and additions to the church. Some of these changes were considered odd because they did not seem to be related to the character of Mary Magdalene at all—unless Saunière knew something that others did not.

One such modification that has baffled many researchers is a statement that was placed above the porch entrance to the church. It reads: "TERRIBILIS EST LOCUS ISTE," and translates into English as: "THIS PLACE IS TERRIBLE." The writer and researcher of the Grail mysteries, Tracy Twyman, explained in the magazine *Dagobert's Revenge* that:

> …this is a quote from Genesis [28:17], in which Jacob falls asleep on a stone and has a vision of a ladder leading up to heaven, with angels ascending and descending on it. This, of course, is the same Stone of Destiny brought to Scotland by Joseph of Arimathea, and

became the stone upon which British monarchy are crowned, even today. What's noteworthy is that beneath the words "This Place is Terrible" is etched the rest of Jacob's statement in Genesis: "…This is none but the House of God and the Gateway to Heaven," making it not a curse, but a comment upon the dual nature of divinity.[106]

So immediately at the entrance to the church there is a reference to a gateway leading to heaven. While this could simply be nothing more than telling a person that by stepping through the door they are entering the abode of God, it seems peculiar that this particular verse is used, especially in the context of the other evidence that has been presented.

Another oddity is that immediately after entering the church, the person is greeted by a grotesque statue thought to be the demon Asmodeus. This doesn't seem to be what most would expect to encounter upon entering a church. In Judaic tradition, it is said that Asmodeus is in charge of secrets and the guardian of hidden treasure, as well as the chief builder of the Temple of Solomon when the demons were under Solomon's control. Additionally, he was known by the titles of "The Destroyer" and "Rex Mundi," a term meaning "King of the Earth."[107]

Above the head of this devil figure is a scallop shell filled with water that serves as the benitier, or Holy Water stoup. Four angels stand above this, each making a partial gesture of the Sign of the Cross, the act performed by a person after dipping their fingers in the Holy Water. Between the angels and the devil is written the following phrase in French: "PAR CE SIGNE TU LE VAINCRAS," meaning "BY THIS SIGN YE SHALL CONQUER HIM." This is a variation of the familiar Latin phrase: "In hoc signo vinces," meaning "By this sign ye shall conquer" and the "him" is referring to conquering the devil below it.[108]

There is one additional feature of considerable mention that at first seems insignificant and simply just decoration. However, when viewed in context with the rest of the statuary it makes perfect sense. Two salamander creatures feature between the angels and the water stoup. The salamander is a common alchemical symbol for the element of fire, since they were said to be born out of fire. As the author Henry Lincoln notes, what are being represented at this statuary are the four main elements of alchemy. "The Devil (Earth) supports the Water, which in turn supports the salamanders (creatures of Fire), and crowning all are the angels (creatures of Air)."[109]

If the salamanders were not featured as part of this design, it would be easy

The angels (Air) stand over the salamanders (Fire) and the Holy Water stoup, conquering the devil figure, Asmodeus (Earth). *Photo credit: Alan Scott.*

to argue that there is no alchemical significance to it. But of all the different things that could have been incorporated into the design, such as floral patterns or even other animals, salamanders were specifically chosen. This shows that there was more to the design for people who would understand its meaning.

So what did Saunière intend for us to understand? We may never know, since he apparently never told anyone why he chose to incorporate these odd and seemingly symbolic details into the structure of Rennes-le-Château. But when all of these things are combined with the phrase from Genesis about the "Gateway to Heaven," the bizarre Tour Magdala that he built in honor of Mary Magdalene, who also apparently represented a tower that would allow humans to be translated into heaven, and the deliberate alchemical symbolism of the statuary at the entrance, it seems to be converging into a single idea: the human race is meant to transform into something more advanced and ascend to heaven.

The Biblical legends draw our attention to situations when humans were "translated" into heaven, such as Enoch and Elijah, so that they would not taste death. Apocryphal literature elaborates on these strange accounts, such as when Enoch's flesh was dissolved away so that his spirit could be transformed into an angelic being. But what could this mean for the nature of the soul? Ancient cultures had very specific ideas about what happened to a person after their mortal life was extinguished, and it is quite often in stark contrast to what most people choose to believe.

Summary

❖ Names played significant roles in the ancient world and were believed to provide magickal powers to a person in control of a particular "name."

❖ Jewish legends teach that through the use of the Ineffable Name of God, Yahweh (יהוה), the angels and even humans were able to ascend to heaven. Unfortunately, due to secrecy and scribal errors over many centuries, the true meaning and pronunciation of the name has been lost.

❖ Using Gematria, we can gain further insight into the meanings and usages of names and terms by studying their numerical values (e.g. "Yahweh" = 26, "Jesus" = 888, and "the Magdalene" = 153).

❖ The Hebrew name of Jesus, Yehoshua (יהושוע), posed many problems when it was adapted into the Greek language of the New Testament. However, some clever alterations finally resulted in the name Iesous (Ιησους).

❖ The Pentagrammaton was developed during the Renaissance by Christian Cabalists to connect the name of Jesus to the pentagram for use in rituals. Additionally, supporting evidence from the Old and New Testaments, as well as non-biblical sources, indicate that the pentagram was intended to be a positive symbol associated with Jesus.

❖ There are many references throughout the Bible to the "daughter of Zion" in association with the "mountain of God" that will lead people to heaven. Mary Magdalene is distinguished by her name because it means "Rebellious Watchtower," probably referring to the Tower of Babel—the "gate of God" that humans attempted to create so that they could reach heaven.

PART 4

THE REALM OF THE DEAD

Now a word came stealing to me, my ear received the whisper of it.
Amid thoughts from visions of the night, when deep sleep falls on mortals,
dread came upon me, and trembling, which made all my bones shake.
A spirit glided past my face; the hair of my flesh bristled. It stood still,
but I could not discern its appearance. A form was before my eyes; there
was silence, then I heard a voice…

Job 4:12–16 NRSV

OUR INVESTIGATION WILL NOW EXAMINE THE AFTERLIFE, from ancient times to the modern day. We will also look at the methods by which paranormal investigators are capturing and analyzing phenomena attributed to ghosts and spirits. Their findings indicate that science may one day be capable of walking where only mystics have dared to tread. If reliable methods are developed that can detect the souls of the dead, we may ultimately solve one of the greatest enigmas of the universe. More importantly, it may lead to discoveries that explain how the soul can be successfully transformed for the purposes of ascending to the heavens.

The Underworld

The Hebrew term *nephesh* (נֶפֶשׁ) describes the "soul" or "life-force" that animates living creatures. For instance, Adam's body was fully created but not alive until the "breath of life" was given to him (Genesis 2:7). When a person or creature would die, the nephesh separated from the physical body and moved to the spiritual realm.

Throughout much of the ancient world, the people believed that Earth was a flat disc with a semi-circle vault over top that was the heavens. Two seemingly endless planes of water were placed above and below the earth and the vault. These were the chaotic oceans from which everything had emerged. The bottom ocean was part of the underworld, which was cold, dreary, and extremely dark. The original concept of the underworld was greatly different than the relatively new vision of a fiery hell.

The Hebrew term for the realm of the dead was *Sheol* (שְׁאוֹל), and is often translated as "grave," "pit," "hell," and "underworld." However, it is important to understand that Sheol was a place where *all* of the dead were sent, both the righteous and the unrighteous. It was generally not considered a place of punishment, but more like a holding tank for the souls of the deceased until the final judgment.

Many different names were used by the Sumerians for the underworld, among them: *arali, irkalla, kukku, ekur, kigal* and *ganzir,* as well as "earth" or "ground" using the words *ki* ⟨image⟩ or *kur* ⟨image⟩ (Akkadian: *ersetu*). It was also called "the land of no return" and occasionally as "the desert." The word *ganzir* ⟨image⟩ specifically referred to a gate with a stairway that descended into the nether realm through a hole in the ground.[1] Also of importance, the word *kur* meant not only "ground" but also "mountains," and possibly hinted that one way to gain entrance to the underworld was through the mountains.[2] While it could be that the Sumerians were referring to the distant mountains that surrounded the Tigris-Euphrates river valley, recall that their civilization settled in the plains area and that they constructed the ziggurats to serve as artificial mountains. Perhaps the mountains being referred to are not natural mountains at all, but their temples?

As explained above, the underworld was most often described as a cold and dark place, and often employed the use of water imagery.[3] In fact, the gates of the west, associated with both the setting sun and the element of water, are still considered to be the portals to the realm of the dead in modern ceremonial magick. Furthermore, we find within the Old Testament story of Jonah becoming trapped inside the belly of a sea creature that the underworld is compared to chaotic waters (Jonah 2:3–6). Those familiar with Greek mythology may also recall that the dead were required to cross the River Styx in order to reach the underworld.

Additionally, the use of a gate or gateways was also incorporated into the descriptions of the underworld.[4] Throughout Mesopotamian and even Egyptian texts there are references to guardians or gatekeepers who protect these gateways—both to keep the living out and the dead within. These guardians often stood in pairs at the gates, and were sometimes gods and other times depicted as half-human and half-animal.[5] Those who wanted to gain access beyond the gates were required to perform certain rituals or pass the tests required of the gatekeepers. The Greek equivalents would be the ferryman Phlegyas, and the three-headed guard dog Cerberus.[6]

The Sumerians believed that the underworld was the domain of the goddess *Erishkigal* (Akkadian: *Allatu*) and her consort *Nergal*. Within the underworld were various other gods and goddesses as well as demons that were sometimes released to torment humanity on earth. In later Babylonian texts, 600 of the Anunnaki are also imprisoned within the underworld,[7] but the reason for their demise has not yet been determined from any known descriptions. Of course, the Anunnaki's strong resemblance to the Watchers may satisfactorily explain their punishment through comparison to later Jewish texts.

The *Second Letter of Peter* explains how "God did not spare the angels when they sinned, but cast them into hell [Tartarus] and committed them to chains of deepest darkness to be kept until the judgment" (2:4).[8] *Tartarus* (ταρταρώσας) is the Greek term that refers to the deepest region of the netherworld, located as far below Hades as earth is below heaven. It is where the giant Titans were cast after being defeated by the gods.

The dead are called by many names—the most common are *meth* (מֵת) and the plural form *methim* (מֵתִים) in Hebrew. Another related term is *Rephaim* (רְפָאִים), which is derived from an Ugaritic term, and often referred to deceased royalty and slain heroic warriors.[9] Careful readers will remember that the Rephaim were described as being one of the tribes of giants, and counted King Og of Bashan among their numbers.[10]

More terms for the deceased are *'ôb* (אוֹב), meaning "spirits" or "familiar spirits" (particularly those raised by necromancers),[11] and *etemmu* (אֵטִים), a term borrowed from the Akkadian language meaning "ghost." The latter term is probably derived from the Sumerian word *gidim*, which also refers to a person's ghost.[12] The Akkadian *ilu* and *ilim* ("god" and "gods" respectively) were also occasionally used to describe the dead. The equivalent Hebrew term *elohim* (אֱלֹהִים), is used to describe the spirits conjured by the medium of Endor for King Saul (1 Samuel 28:13).

When the Old Testament was translated into the Greek language (the Septuagint LXX version), the word "Hades" was commonly used to refer to Sheol. *Hades* (αδης) was originally the ruler of the netherworld, and the realm was known as the "house of Hades." Later, it was simply referred to as "Hades." It is a place for the dead, but not necessarily a place of eternal torment. Like Sheol, it was believed to be more of a gloomy location where the souls waited helplessly. Sometimes the term is translated as "hell," but this is misleading and not the appropriate term to be used.[13]

Popular culture has long depicted hell as a place of fiery torment for the wicked. However, very little of the predominant and centuries old imagery comes from actual Biblical sources. Of course, it is appealing to think that a person who has committed horrible crimes is swiftly and severely punished after death; but instead, the texts seem to indicate that while some wicked souls may be punished, the great majority go to the same holding tanks as the good people.[14] So, where did the concept of eternal burning and fire and brimstone originate?

Another term used to describe a place of punishment in the afterlife was *Gehenna* (γέεννα). It is referring to the Gehenna Valley (currently "Wadi er-Rababeh," located South of Jerusalem), and derived from the original Aramaic root *gehinnam,* meaning: "Valley of Hinnom." It was a location where large amounts of filth and waste from dead animals were dumped, and children were sacrificed to the Canaanite deities *Molech* (מלך), meaning "king," and *Baal* (בעל), meaning "Lord."[15] This severe form of idolatry consisted of taking the small child and "passing it through the fire" and into the hands of a large statue of the god, thus earning the name "The Valley of Slaughter."[16] One must stop and wonder if perhaps the ancient people were attempting to primitively mimic the passage through the fiery gateways of the gods, but without a proper understanding of the technology.

The horrific practices at Gehenna became symbolic for what awaited those deserving punishment. Other references to a fiery demise are contained in *1 Enoch,* when the Watchers are condemned so that on the Day of Judgment they will be "led off to the abyss of fire" and "to the torment and the prison in which they shall be confined for ever" (10:13).[17] Throughout the New Testament, and especially within the words of Jesus, we also find that reference to the fires of Gehenna are divorced from the original physical location and turned into a more spiritual one.[18] Later, in the book of Revelation, there is a reference to the "second death" in the "lake of fire" where the body and soul are received.[19]

These references to Gehenna in the New Testament also support the idea that it is the final place of punishment for the wicked and that Hades is a completely separate location where the dead currently reside. It is said that Hades will give up its dead for judgment and those without their names written in the "book of life" will face the second death in Gehenna's lake of fire.[20] It is important to note that the texts never state that Satan is the ruler of Gehenna (Hell), which goes against what is commonly believed. Instead, the Bible states that the devil and the fallen angels will be cast into the fire and destroyed.[21]

By now, it should be clear that the ancient concept of the afterlife was not a particularly happy one, and that the souls of the dead are essentially being detained until they are judged. This view varies wildly from other religions and philosophies, but it predates them all. What should now concern us is that if this other realm exists, is there a way to detect it scientifically? In order to answer this question, we must examine the fascinating research and data collected by contemporary paranormal investigators concerning the spirits of the dead.

Investigating the Paranormal

Personal beliefs concerning the afterlife and encounters with spirits have existed since very ancient times and persist through present day. While modern science has definitely changed how the world is perceived by debunking certain widely held superstitious beliefs, the paranormal continues to interest and intrigue present-day society. The popularity of movies such as *Ghostbusters* and television shows like *The X-Files* and *Ghost Hunters* reveal that people are eager to be entertained by the unexplained. But how does real life stack up against Hollywood? At times, alleged encounters with ghosts or spirits are simply the result of a misinterpretation of mundane and explainable events. However, there are times when traditional explanations prove insufficient.

Until recently, the only accepted methods for communication with the other side were through psychics and mediums, or through the use of some kind of tool or object such as a "talking board." While the possibility exists that some people may possess genuine abilities to "speak" with the dead, the vast majority of cases have been found to involve charlatans playing elaborate hoaxes in order to gain profit. Besides, even if fraudulent behavior was not a factor, these situations seem very unreliable for communication with the dearly departed since the medium could easily misinterpret information.

This is one of many drawbacks involving proper investigation of paranormal related phenomena. There are innumerable claims and stories concerning encounters with ghosts or other spiritual beings, yet these encounters remain *subjective* because the ability to properly evaluate such occurrences is limited to our five senses. This does not make the experience any less real to the person involved, only less provable. Scientific investigation on the other hand, relies on *objective* evidence that can be examined and scrutinized by anyone. This has inspired many paranormal investigators to rely much less on the human factor and try to incorporate more tools and equipment capable of capturing viable evidence.

When the subject of a photograph or video came under scrutiny, it was once said that the camera doesn't lie—but people do. In theory, the camera captures only what the camera sees. But ever since the first cameras were invented, people have found clever ways to manipulate the end result (i.e. the film) to make something appear that wasn't originally there. A common trick was double-exposing a photograph so that ghostly images of *living* people (or sometimes even portraits) faintly appeared around other people that were captured on the same film or photographic plate at a different time.[22] Now that more people have become familiar with photographic techniques, though, this is usually quickly identifiable even to those with little photographic knowledge.

Other problems that are associated with photographs are not necessarily caused by trickery, but rather through errors in processing. Traditional film cameras rely on proper chemical mixtures and conditions to develop accurately. If chemicals are mixed incorrectly or extra light is introduced into a dark room, the result might appear as a streak or some type of ghostly fog or human-like form. As long as the original negative image exists and it shows no sign of tampering, it can likely prove that a possible "ghost" image is actually an error that occurred during the development process.

Despite the shortcomings from tampering and possible technical glitches, cameras are still valuable tools for the paranormal investigator when used properly. For starters, they can provide documentation of the location being investigated and show the physical conditions at that time. Also, if something strange does show up at the location, a photograph of it provides much more objective evidence that can be analyzed by a photographic technician rather than simply relying on an eyewitness account.

The advent of digital cameras has offered several advantages to paranormal investigators, especially since the technology has become more affordable in recent years. To begin with, there is no risk of chemical processing errors because digital cameras do not rely on film. Secondly, most models deliver instant results and allow the investigator to review a photo immediately, instead of having to wait for the film to be developed. Finally, digital cameras can provide very high resolutions (although not as high as film yet) and storage capabilities so that hundreds of photos can be saved on memory cards or compact discs. Many digital cameras are also able to capture some of the infrared portion of the light spectrum, which is not visible to the naked eye. Therefore, these cameras can sometimes "see" what we cannot.[23] Unfortunately, digital cameras do not provide an original negative image like film cameras, which is a downside. However, most of these cameras can embed information into the photos (called metadata) that functions as a "digital negative" because it can tell you if the photograph has been altered. In the end, it is really up to the individual investigator as to what type of camera they are most comfortable using in the field. Some people may even choose both types for their work.

It is important for the photographer to reduce the number of potential problems that might lead to a "false positive." For instance, while a flash might be necessary to properly photograph a dark area, one must keep in mind that the flash could reflect off of bright or shiny surfaces and create flares in the picture. A flash can also reflect water vapor present in cold temperatures, rain drops, and even dust, leading to more incorrectly labeled ghost photos. If multiple photographers are present, it is advisable to alert the others by calling, "Flash!" before taking the photo. This will avoid simultaneous

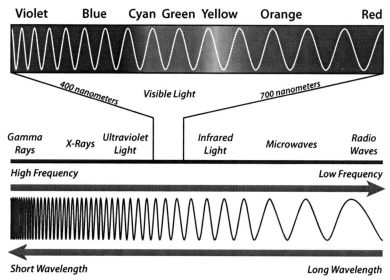

The Electromagnetic Spectrum

flashes in the same area that could lead to undesirable results.[24] Smoking is also prohibited during investigations to avoid wisps of smoke appearing in the photos. Lastly, it is also highly advisable under cold conditions that the photographer holds his or her breath when taking a photo so that they don't accidentally exhale and cause their breath to appear in the photograph.[25]

Common anomalies that appear in modern photos include mists, full or partial apparitions, and mysterious orbs of light. While mists are interesting, we are not going to focus on them here because many of them are too easily explained as reflective water vapor in the air or smoke. More credible paranormal mist photographs have a tendency to capture thicker trails of "smoke" that often appear to be in a state of motion, or interacting with objects in such a manner that they appear to be passing through them.[26]

Apparitions are somewhat like mist photographs, except that they are usually much more defined and a viewer can actually make out details such as limbs, body shape, or facial features. Typically, partial-bodied apparitions (an arm, leg, head, etc.) are much more common than full bodied ones. Of course, this type of photo is forged the most often because it is ultimately what every ghost hunter would like to see: a well-defined form that clearly isn't mist or some other ambiguous element.[27]

Orbs are the strangest yet most common type of paranormal form photographed. Essentially, orbs are tiny balls of light that appear in photos. Sometimes they are faint, while other times they are well-defined and even appear to have depth. Unfortunately, orbs frequently prove to be out-of-focus reflective objects such as dust particles, rain drops, or even small insects flying past the camera.[28]

Too often, people that believe they have captured a genuine orb have unknowingly captured something mundane that was in their environment. Weather conditions and other factors can create perceived anomalies within photographs. This has led to an "orb phenomenon" where many people believe that they have photographed spirits of the dead when in actuality they have not. It is highly advisable that all ghost investigators take plenty of pictures in a variety of locations and weather conditions so that they can learn to differentiate between true orbs and false ones created from everyday objects and conditions.

It is also incorrect to claim that orbs are definitely spirits of the dead—or anything ghost-related for that matter. While they do frequently appear at locations that are believed to be haunted, this does not make them spirits.

They do, on occasion, even appear to show some kind of conscious effort to control their movements when they are captured on video.[29] At this point, however, we simply do not understand the nature of these objects well enough to properly study or explain them.

Because photographs only capture an event for a fraction of a second, they limit how anomalies such as orbs can be studied. Was there a light sprinkling of water from somewhere nearby that reflected in the lens? Or if the orb is moving, how fast was it traveling and what was the direction? These questions are more easily answered when there is more data available, particularly footage like that from a video camera.

Luckily, orbs do also appear on video tape, usually when the camera is set to record in night-vision mode so that it can capture some of the infrared realm. Sometimes the motion of the supposed orb will easily reveal that it is actually an insect flying through a room. Other times, the investigator might see that it is simply dust being blown in from a draft somewhere. If the orb is stationary for the entire video, it is probably a speck of dirt stuck on the camera lens. Still, there are the times when true orbs are captured that cannot be explained by the above scenarios. They might zip across the screen at enormous speed, or even meander along at a slow pace, performing odd maneuvers.[30]

Some of the most interesting examples are when the orbs actually move around and behind objects. To understand what makes this significant, some background about photography and film is needed. When a photographer or camera operator sets up their shot, they want to maximize the appeal of the image by adjusting what is known as the "depth of field." When properly adjusted, the objects in the background or foreground will appear blurred while the subject of the shot will be in focus. The reason that this effect is so desirable is because the photographer knows that the viewer's attention will be drawn to the subject without being distracted by any unnecessary objects or movement in the surrounding areas. You can see this effect frequently in movies and on television.

When orbs are captured on video, there is a chance that they are out of focus, and therefore could be nothing more than a common object that appears blurry. However, if the orb moves around or even behind objects that are in the field of focus, then all of the objects in that area should be in focus—including the orb. So the orb is not actually an out of focus object, but rather it is showing its normal appearance when captured on video and moving within the focused area. Thinking for a moment, consider the movie example mentioned a moment ago. It would not make sense if an actor held an object against their chest and it appeared blurry. We expect to see that object in focus just the same as the person.

Other important equipment used by paranormal investigators include electromagnetic field meters (EMF) and thermometers. EMF meters do exactly what their name implies: they detect the electromagnetic fields given off by electronics and other equipment. All objects, including living creatures such as humans and animals, give off some kind of electromagnetic charge; it is just usually so subtle that it is hard to detect without professional equipment.[31]

EMF meters can serve two primary functions. First, they can be used to detect the electrical fields being emitted by electronic equipment and wiring within buildings. This way, the investigator may be able to rule out paranormal activity if it is determined that the electrical field is coming from a common object. The second function is that it can be used to detect moving "hot spots" of fluctuating electromagnetic activity which might indicate a ghost. It always helps to take a photo or aim a video camera at a particular area if someone is picking up strange readings from an EMF meter. This sometimes leads to an image with an anomaly present, which helps to increase credibility when coupled with the EMF data.

However, investigators should be very careful when using EMF meters so that they do not obtain false readings. It is all too easy to find oneself caught up in the excitement of getting spikes in the readings and not realize that there is an electrical device nearby that is actually the source of the disturbance (it could be behind a wall or even from some of the investigator's own equipment). Properly understanding the wiring of a building and the locations of major electrical devices (both inside and outside of the building) should help reduce these kinds of errors.

A thermometer is another valuable tool for paranormal investigations. Very often, people that report hauntings say they have experienced "cold spots" in areas where ghosts are said to have appeared. Something to consider, however, is that some of these reports are completely subjective and have a more rational explanation. For instance, if a person is nervous or afraid, it is not uncommon for their body temperature to noticeably drop. They may even shiver and feel like ice to the touch. If this is the case, the alleged "cold spot" may be nothing more than the person's physical reaction to what they believe is a frightening situation. If other team members feel okay or cannot find the cold spot, this is probably the cause.[32] For this

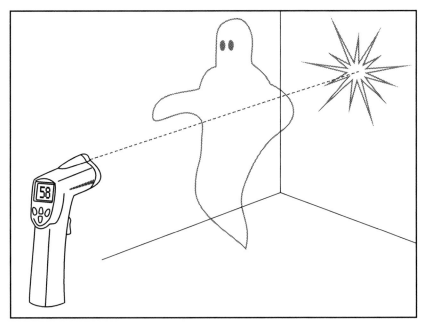

The inherent problem of using a non-contact infrared thermometer for paranormal investigations is that the reading will only be of the reflecting surface, such as the wall.

reason, a standard thermometer is good for placing in a room to record the overall temperature. It should preferably have a large digital display so that you can easily see the reading from several feet away.

Infrared thermometers are another tool often used in investigations because they can read temperatures of distant objects and hard-to-reach areas (sometimes up to hundreds of feet away). These devices often include a laser pointer to show the precise area or surface where the temperature reading is being obtained.[33] They also allow investigators to obtain readings from the corners of a room and can provide feedback to help locate the source of a draft that might actually be causing a supposed cold spot. More advanced models will also record the thermal data so that it can be transferred to a computer for further analysis. Thermal imaging equipment is also something to consider, but it is often very expensive and out of the price range for most amateur paranormal investigators.

However, there is one major problem associated with infrared thermometers often unacknowledged by many paranormal investigators. These devices only read the surface temperatures of objects and not the temperature of the space in-between. Therefore, if someone says they feel a "cold spot" in the center of the room and the investigator points the thermometer at the area, they will actually get the temperature readout of the wall. So, while these thermometers provide no benefit for accurately measuring the temperature of perceived ghosts, they do offer valuable assistance in finding drafts or other sources that could be mistaken as ghostly activity.[34]

Although there are many disadvantages with using cameras, infrared thermometers, and EMF meters, these tools are still essential for paranormal investigations. Even though they do not help to accurately document any paranormal activity, they are extremely useful for documenting the surrounding environment. Every bit of detail that can be gathered may be helpful in determining what causes or influences alleged paranormal activity.

While there is much more equipment that can be used by serious investigators, the last one that we are going to focus on is a device able to record audio. This can be something as simple as a hand-held voice recorder, as well as newer MP3 players that are capable of real time recording, or even personal computers that are set up properly. The purpose of these recordings is to capture "voices" and other sounds that are believed to emanate from the spirit realm, commonly known as Electronic Voice Phenomenon (EVP).

When using an audio cassette recorder, it is essential to get one that uses full size audio cassettes, as opposed to micro-cassettes. Micro-cassettes lack the necessary clarity to hold up against intense scrutiny and therefore should be avoided if possible. Still, even when using a regular cassette tape, it is best to use a brand name and one that is sixty minutes in length (120-minute length tapes tend to break more easily after wear and tear because the tape is actually thinner).[35] It is also best to record using an external microphone to avoid the chance that the tape records the mechanical noises from the device itself. Lastly, it is essential to always use factory sealed tapes for each investigation and to never record over the same portions of a tape again. This negates the skeptical argument that any abnormal sounds are merely garbled versions of normal voices recorded at an earlier time that weren't successfully erased.

Digital recording devices are able to overcome many of the technical limitations associated with regular cassettes. In fact, an exciting new possibility in the area of EVP research is the use of advanced MP3 players with recording functionality. For starters, some of these devices are capable of recording 16-bit 44.1 kHz audio files in stereo format. For those that do not understand this "geek-speak," it means that they can record in full

THE REALM OF THE DEAD

CD-quality sound.[36] Additionally, each recording is also embedded with a time and date stamp, so that you will always know when the audio file was recorded and be able to index anomalous sounds by the time code. This also helps to prevent possible fraud since the file will show whether or not is has been modified from its original form. Also, many players/recorders are now including at least 20 gigabytes of storage space, providing many hours of recording time.[37] Unfortunately, one of the downsides of being on the "cutting-edge" is that these players usually cost a few hundred dollars as opposed to traditional cassette recorders, which cost around $30.

It is the evidence gained from EVPs that will be the focus of our attention in the next section. Despite all of the photographic and video evidence put forth that is believed to show some form of a deceased spirit, there will always be severe doubt surrounding it. This is mostly because even though the event of seeing a ball of light move around a room (sometimes even with seemingly intelligent behavior) rates high on the weirdness scale, we can only say that it is a ball of light until better methods for analysis are created. That does not automatically make it a "ghost." Blurry images and wisps of smoky tendrils can play tricks with our minds and make us "see" things that are really just random patterns, much like images in clouds. However, it is much more difficult to dismiss audio recordings that have the distinctive qualities of human speech—except they are seemingly from people that aren't supposed to have been there.

The Unquiet Dead

The first known technological attempts at EVP stretch back to the early twentieth century. Some telegraph operators reported strange signals from unknown sources that were often blamed on "crossed lines." However, a person by the name of David Wilson became interested in studying this odd behavior in 1913 and two years later, he built a device that was sensitive to electrical fields. Unfortunately, even after all of his attempts and his belief that he did have minor contact with the other side, his work was not enough to attract any mainstream attention.[38]

It will certainly surprise many readers that Thomas Edison, inventor of the phonograph and electric light bulb, also became increasingly interested in communication with the dead. When nearing the end of his life, he stated in the October 30, 1920 edition of *Scientific American* that he was working on a technical device that he believed would allow him to contact the other side. However, details about this device were never publicly disclosed, so it is not known how far along Edison got with his experiments before he passed away in 1931.[39]

In addition to Thomas Edison, another important inventor of the twentieth century, Nikola Tesla, was also attempting to develop equipment to communicate with the spirit world. Tesla even said that he had some success using his device, but he passed away before he had a chance to fully discuss his results with very many people.[40]

The first documented example of EVP occurred in the summer of 1959 and it seems to have happened quite by accident. Friedrich Jürgenson, a Swedish documentary producer and Renaissance Man, was walking along the countryside attempting to record bird songs in their natural surroundings. It was later, when he was listening to the recordings that he noticed there was a strange male voice whispering in Norwegian about the differences between nocturnal and daytime bird songs. The only problem was that nobody else had been around Jürgenson when he was recording.[41]

With his technical background, Jürgenson realized that the voice could perhaps have been electronic interference from broadcasting radio stations. However, upon a thorough examination he determined that none of the radio stations had been broadcasting any shows related to the type of material that he had recorded.[42]

He then made other recordings and noted that the voices sounded different and slightly faster than normal human voices. Eventually, he had amassed a great number of recordings and published a booklet and record combo in 1964, titled *Rosterna fran Rymden ("Voices from Space")*. This book caught the attention of Dr. Konstantin Raudive, who eagerly began to work with Jürgenson. This led to another book in 1967, called *Sprechfunk mit Verstorbenen ("Radio-Link with the Dead")*, and began to draw major attention to EVP work in Europe.[43]

Dr. Konstantin Raudive, a student of Carl Jung and psychologist at Sweden's University of Uppsala, created quite a stir with the release of his book *The Inaudible Becomes Audible* in 1969. It was later expanded and translated for American audiences as *Breakthrough: An Amazing Experiment in Electronic Communication with the Dead*.[44]

Working with many top electronic experts, Dr. Raudive recorded and catalogued over 100,000 EVP samples. He also found that he got better results when he introduced a background element, such as radio static, into the mix.

It was his belief that this noise could be manipulated by the spirits to increase their ability to vocalize. However, and with just cause, many skeptics disagreed with this method and believed that the alleged voices were the result of interference from broadcast radio signals. While this could explain many samples, it did not explain them all—particularly voices that called Raudive by name and even nicknames. He had made such a mark in the field of EVP that some researchers still refer to the anomalous voices as "Raudive voices."[45]

Because of the controversy surrounding the use of "white noise" to capture EVPs, it is generally a good idea to avoid it altogether or use it in ways that eliminate common explanations such as radio static. Some investigators claim that they've experienced no advantage in using noise to capture EVPs. It is up to each investigator to experiment and determine for themselves which methods work best in their investigations.

It is easy to understand how much of the skeptical community believes that EVPs are nothing more than stray radio or electronic signals from broadcasting devices such as CB radios. After all, there are thousands of signals traveling through the air and through our bodies every day. However, if that were really the cause of all EVPs, shouldn't we expect to hear more music and advertisement jingles? For instance, it should be fairly easy to distinguish between "I love Cheesy Poofs!" or "Brought to you by Snacky S'mores,"[46] when compared to a child's voice asking, "Am I dead?" or a gruff male voice threatening, "I'm gonna kill you bastards!" Additionally, even the interception of two-way radios does not explain when EVPs are captured that are reacting directly and in real-time with the investigators (but this is not usually discovered until later when the recordings are analyzed).

Another important distinction with genuine EVP recordings is that for an unknown reason, the voices have a strange oscillation sound to them. This behavior is more noticeable in some recordings than others, but they all seem to have some level of this characteristic present. It is sometimes so noticeable that listeners can clearly tell the difference between the normal voice of the investigator and that of the spirit because it sounds so different. What makes matters even more intriguing is that in some recordings, the voices clearly demonstrate similar acoustical qualities to that of the investigator's surroundings. What this means is that if the investigator is in a large, empty room, the spirit's voice will sound like it was recorded in the same room.

Perhaps some of the more disturbing aspects of EVP are the types of voices recorded. Sadly, a great number of the voices sound like those of children; and they are often asking for help finding their parents. Other times, the voices seem to be threatening the investigators with physical harm, but rarely does anything actually happen. Many of these spirits sound very angry or distraught over their situation and do not like people "invading" *their* space. Luckily, since most investigator's cannot hear the actual voices until later, and actual physical assaults are extremely rare, there does not seem to be any immediate threat to people investigating haunted locations.

The following examples are real EVPs recorded by The Ghost Investigators Society (G.I.S.) of Utah. They have many more available on their website (www.ghostpix.com), but these are some of the best examples that cannot be easily explained by conventional means. The members of the G.I.S. are dedicated to educating people about the reality of EVP and ghostly phenomena, and lending credibility to the paranormal investigation community. They are a non-profit group and take absolutely no payment for their services. In fact, they use their own personal money to purchase equipment and fund investigations. Occasionally, some individuals will donate a piece of equipment for them to use, but no money is ever exchanged. It is highly recommended to check these samples out for yourself and determine what you believe.

While it is often considered bad practice to tell someone what a voice is thought to be saying before they hear it and therefore "taint" their perception, there's really no other way to do this in a book format. However, the majority of these examples are so clear that it is difficult to believe that the voices are saying something else.

Intrigued researchers who would like to conduct their own evaluation of the audio samples should not read ahead for the descriptions of the voices. Skipping to page 209 will allow you to continue reading this chapter without knowing any details concerning the EVP examples. Please visit this book's companion website (www.gatewayofthegods.com) for more information concerning EVPs and other experiments.

EVP GALLERY

Electronic Voice Phenomena Examples Recorded by the
Ghost Investigator's Society of Layton, Utah
(www.ghostpix.com)

Example 1:

The G.I.S. was conducting an investigation at the Gold Hill Hotel in Virginia City, Nevada. Team member Brendan Cook noticed that his EMF meter was fluctuating oddly and commented, "It's acting weird." However, when reviewing the audio, a woman's voice asks, "Are you alone?" a moment before Brendan speaks.[47]

Example 2:

A chilling example involving a child occurred when the G.I.S. was investigating a local residence. After following the lady who lived at the house into one of the bedrooms, Barbara McBeath's recorder captured the voice of a young child who seemed to come to a haunting realization by asking, "Am I dead?"[48]

Example 3:

Perhaps a slightly more positive example of a child's voice occurred when the G.I.S. was investigating the home of a family that believed there was a ghost child staying there and playing with their son. The night before the G.I.S. arrived at the house, the wife had reported that she felt what seemed like a small child rushing up and hugging her. After the investigators arrived, the home owner asked the ghost: "Did you hug her last night?" The voice of a child responds and says, "It's gonna be ok."[49]

Example 4:

This example was recorded at the same location as the previous EVP. What is stunning about this example is how it shows the real-time interaction between the ghost and the person. It is also important to note that no children were present in the house at the time of the investigation. The owners reported that sometimes their six year old son's toys would start up on their own and that on occasion their son would talk to the ghost. The father was instructed to talk to the ghost child like he would to a living person and tells him, "You can go play in Derrick's room, ok?" Amazingly, the child's voice can be heard responding, "Ok." There is a slight pause and the home owner says, "Go ahead and play."[50]

Example 5:

The next example was recorded at Deer Lodge Prison by Brendan Cook. In it, G.I.S. investigator Barry Boris can be heard asking, "Did the guards kill you or did you kill yourself?" There is a slight pause and then a rather depressed male voice laments, "I almost had the key."[51]

Example 6:

In this example, the sound of one of the prison's steel doors can be heard opening. A man's voice says, "Help, I'm in here." This is shortly followed by Barry Boris' voice asking, "Anybody in here?"[52]

Example 7:

Brendan Cook was in the main cell area of the prison when he recorded this example. You can hear him say, "And I'm on the side by myself. If anyone's here, I'd like you to talk to me. We are not here to harm you or disturb you in any way." A creepy sounding voice demands, "Get out of here!" but Brendan's voice shows no indication of having heard or sensed the malevolent presence near to him. He finishes his statement by saying, "We are simply curious about you."[53]

Example 8:

On another outing at a pioneer cemetery, G.I.S. investigator Roger McBeath was in a conversation and said, "...the Knights of the Caribbean." This is repeated by his wife, Barbara. G.I.S. member Jenny found on her recording that it is repeated a *third* time by a spirit with a very gravelly voice. Not only does this voice sound rather sinister, but it also demonstrates some level of intelligent behavior. This means that this particular voice was not an "imprint" or "residual-haunting," which are events that loop over and over again and never demonstrate any interaction with present situations. Also, this raises significant doubt about any radio interceptions. Honestly, what are the chances that just a few seconds after someone says, "Knights of the Caribbean," a radio announcer says the same exact phrase and only that portion of the broadcast is intercepted on one of the investigator's recorders?[54]

Example 9:

This EVP is remarkable because it was captured by two different record-ers—one digital and the other analog. Instances of EVPs being recorded simultaneously on different machines are not unheard of, but fairly rare. The importance is that it demonstrates how this could not be explained by a simple "malfunction." Such a malfunction would require the highly unlikely scenario of two completely different pieces of equipment having the identical failure at the exact same time. The event occurred during the investigation at the Gold Hill Hotel. Investigator Barry Boris can be heard saying, "It wasn't a big one, though," and then the squeal of an opening door can be heard. This is immediately followed by a sinister sounding voice that threatens: "I'm gonna kill ya, right here." The words of this particular voice are somewhat difficult to hear, though, and perhaps the voice is instead say-ing: "I'm okay... prayer." This is one example which demonstrates how EVPs can be interpreted differently based on what a person is hearing.[55]

Example 10:

This particular clip was quite memorable when Brendan Cook described his experience on the late-night radio talk show *Coast to Coast AM* with Art Bell. During October of 2002, the G.I.S. was conducting a preliminary investi-gation of a mortician's home. All of the other G.I.S. members were upstairs while Brendan was in the living room on the main floor. The lights were on and Brendan could see a large mirror on the wall. As he glanced around the room, he asked, "Is anyone here?" When he looked back at the mirror he was astonished to see the reflection of a small boy, from the shoulders up, run across the kitchen that was immediately behind him. However, it was even stranger because the child's head and neck were oddly turned towards him as the child ran past, smiling eerily. On the tape, the child enthusi-astically says either: "I'm Gabe" or "I'm game," and then giggles. While Brendan could not hear the ghost, his reaction from seeing it is apparent when he says, "No way." It's become known as "The Boy Episode" among the members of the G.I.S.[56]

Example 11:

The next example was recorded inside of a mausoleum. Brendan Cook was investigating a section of the building alone when his flashlight went dead. The only other member of the team was at the opposite end of the building and no one else was inside. As Brendan felt around for a light switch, he accidentally fell down the stairs and his recorder hit the ground. There is a loud crash as Brendan falls and he yells, "Dammit!" Immediately after this, the voice of what sounds like a concerned young woman asks, "Are you ok?" This is another example of a real-time interaction between the investigator and the response provided by one of the spirits.[57]

Example 12:

The next example is a very simple one that was recorded at an abandoned mental hospital. Brendan Cook was returning to check on the status of his notebook computer (a.k.a. "laptop") that was being used to record EVPs. A menacing voice says, "I will kill you bastards," just before Brendan enters the room. Brendan, unaware of the voice, says to one of the other members: "Okay, I'll go see how much time is left on the laptop."[58]

Example 13:

This final EVP has been saved for last because of the severely disturbing nature of it. It was also recorded at the abandoned mental hospital. It is very difficult to tell what some of the voices are saying, but parts are clear enough as well as some other sounds to provide some context as to what probably occurred. This EVP is special for a few different reasons. First, it is nearly one minute in length, making it probably one of the longest EVPs ever recorded since most are only a few seconds long. Second, not only does it involve a couple of different voices, but also the sound of *thrashing water*. Third, most EVPs often sound as if they are being played back at slightly faster speeds than normal, but this particular EVP sounds almost as if it has been slowed down.

Brendan Cook explained on *Coast to Coast AM* with Art Bell (aired: Saturday, April 2, 2005), that it was recorded on his notebook computer after he had left the room. After approximately seven minutes of silent audio the sound of a child can be heard saying, "I can't breathe... can't breathe..." A second voice is also heard, which is much deeper and sounds like a male's voice. It is too difficult to tell what he says, though. The child's voice continues to complain about their difficulty breathing as the sound of thrashing water begins. The water noises continue for almost thirty more seconds and then a loud thud is heard just before the water calms.[59]

This EVP presents several interesting problems. First, all of the G.I.S. members were outside at this point, and nobody else had access to the room during the investigation. Second, the building has been abandoned for the past twenty years and so it has no running water at all. So what produced the sounds of the thrashing water? Not only can the water be heard, but it has the acoustics of an empty room. It would seem that this EVP is an example of a residual haunting that was so traumatic that it left an impression in the atmosphere. Perhaps the voices are even the thoughts of the person(s) involved in the event, or the spirits recalling what happened. It is just too difficult to determine and anything more would be pure speculation. But there is no doubt that the sounds should not have been recorded.

A problem with the residual haunting explanation was pointed out by Barbara McBeath, because she has found no indication that the room in question ever had bath tubs or anything with water that could have been used for a drowning like the one recorded. However, over one year later, the owner of the building, LeAnna Reardon, discussed this recording with Brendan Cook on his internet radio show *Contact Beyond*. Reardon said that she had spent the last ten months investigating the history of the building and any possible explanations for the EVP. She learned that several people had drowned in a tunnel located just outside the front of the building, near the room where the EVP was recorded. One woman, in particular, claimed that the voice of the child sounded like her son who had drowned in that tunnel back in 1959. Reardon believes that this might be the prime candidate for explaining the recording, but cautions that she is still investigating other possibilities. For now, the best answer is that it simply remains unexplained and unknown as to exactly who was involved and what happened.[60]

CONTINUE READING HERE IF YOU CHOSE TO SKIP THE EVP DESCRIPTIONS

There are many more examples of high quality EVPs available at the G.I.S. website. There are even thousands more available from other researchers on the web. It is recommended that you take some time to seek out additional examples of EVP and perhaps even begin to try recording your own.

However, many of the examples available on the web are difficult to hear or the results of cross-modulation. Another explanation is Apophenia, a condition where someone "sees" or "hears" something that really isn't there by recognizing some kind of pattern; a Rorschach ink blot test would be a visual example. A common auditory example would be when someone is in the shower and there is enough random "white noise" created by the sound of the running water that someone thinks they hear a doorbell or telephone ring. Their mind has filled in the blanks with the noise pattern and so they are tricked into believing that they heard something that was never there.[61]

While Apophenia might explain some very hard to hear "voices" or single words, it does not satisfactorily explain most of the examples presented here, which are just a small sampling. It is one thing to trick yourself into believing you heard the faint sound of a telephone in the distance, and quite another to record a voice with the distinctive qualities and even personality of human speech. If investigators are careful to record under closed conditions, meaning nobody else is allowed access to the location during that time, then the background noise of someone else talking can be ruled out. This can be taken a step further by removing the investigator from the scene and leaving only the recorder, as long as the location has been secured and is tamper proof.[62] For the extremely cautious ghost hunter, another recommendation is to keep a separate video camera trained on the audio devices or any entrances into the room to document the conditions. If an EVP is recorded, the video will document the conditions and show if anybody snuck inside at the time the voice occurs. Plus, you are increasing the chances of recording an EVP on the audio track of the video as well.

In all likelihood, there will *never* be enough evidence to convince even the most skeptical of people that these voices are those of the deceased or that they originate from another dimension. This is especially true in regard to advances in digital technology and computer software because the digital medium can be easily manipulated. Therefore, critics have every right to be skeptical of such "evidence" because there is always a likely chance that the recordings *might* have been faked. However, the purpose of investigating and documenting Electronic Voice Phenomena is not about convincing other people whether or not it is real. Instead, it should be about the personal experience of recording one yourself. In such a case, you will know that no one else could have tampered with the equipment or digitally manipulated the file because you were involved in every step of the process.

The skeptical community does provide a valuable service, though, because they are encouraging paranormal investigators to acquire and present better scientific evidence. There are some skeptics that readily admit that although they do not believe a majority of the voices are anything paranormal, they cannot fully explain many of the recordings. Eventually, parapsychology may become recognized as a more legitimate field of study, but only if individuals are willing to fairly and objectively approach this subject instead of ignorantly dismissing it or indiscriminately accepting it. Readers that are interested to learn more about an experiment that demonstrates how EVPs might operate may wish to consult Appendix E for more information.

There is still one last valid point brought up by skeptics that needs some explanation. It is concerning why so many "ghost hunters" are capable of recording EVPs with low-tech equipment and yet professionals using high-end equipment almost never report hearing any voices or anomalies in sound recordings. For instance, why aren't more voices picked up during recording sessions for music artists in the studios?[63]

This is a tricky subject to address, especially since the field is still so relatively new and with no established ground rules. Perhaps the most likely explanation is the one also laughed at by skeptics: the investigator's mindset and attitude affect the end result. Considering this for a moment, it does make perfect sense when you take into account that these "ghosts" are supposed to be the spirits of deceased *people*—and people tend to want to be treated with respect. If you are friendly and encourage communication with the ghost, and he or she still shows conscious behavior like they did in life, then why is it so difficult to accept that they might be more likely to "chat" under these conditions?

Another influence might be the attitude of the investigator and that maybe their mind is somehow opening a communication portal with the other side. As ridiculous as this may sound to cynics, the possibility cannot be ruled out. Modern technology has allowed us to intensely study and map the human brain, and yet we know very little about the human mind. This is a great debate that has raged for a very long time, because the mind does seem to be something very separate from the brain, which is the physical organ that interprets and transmits the information provided by the mind. So until we can fully understand the inner-workings of the mind, it certainly seems to be a likely possibility that our attitudes concerning this subject can influence the results.

The attitude of the investigator doesn't explain all of the EVPs, however, since some are recorded in perfectly empty rooms and therefore no mental influence should be available. A reconciliation might be considered, though, if the investigator provided the initial "doorway" to the other side and the spirits were able to manifest through it even after the investigator left the area. More investigation needs to be conducted regarding this before any solid conclusions can be reached, however.

One last and most obvious reason why so many recordings seem to be captured by paranormal investigators is "location, location, location." Most investigators go to specific locations with reported histories of hauntings or other paranormal activity. They do not just go to any random area and expect to get results. So, if someone questions why a recording studio never picks up an EVP, but an allegedly haunted house down the street does, the question must be asked: "Does the studio have a history of paranormal activity?" If not, then we shouldn't consider a recording from the studio with no EVP to be proof that the phenomenon is bogus. You go to someplace like Miami Beach when you want to swim in the ocean, not Kansas.

It is interesting to note some of the key qualities of EVPs and how they relate to the ancient views of the world. Often, but not all of the time, the voices seem distraught about their current situation. Sometimes they say that the place where they are is "dark" or "so cold," which seems to be in keeping with the ancient concepts of Sheol. Many of the messages also seem to be of a threatening nature, but the chance of physical harm seems to be relatively minor (at least currently). Another question that must be raised is that if the spirits of the dead are all around us, then what else might be sharing that space with them? For now, this must remain speculation until further studies can be conducted.

The Science of the Soul

If we return once more to Whitley Strieber's conversation with the stranger in his hotel room, there are a few interesting points concerning these matters that are addressed. During part of the conversation, Whitley asked about the nature of God and whether or not God could be measured by science. The Master of the Key responded, "If you dare."[64]

Perplexed with this answer, Whitley further inquired what he meant. He was told: "If you develop a means that will enable you to communicate with your dead, which, as I have said, is quite possible, you will begin to know in life what you now know only in death."[65] Earlier in the conversation, the Master of the Key also said that other conscious beings and the dead are all around us, and through the use of electromagnetic field and plasma detectors we may discover them. Eventually, we won't even need the use of the equipment to communicate with them.[66] He also insisted that:

> The science of the soul is just another science. There is no super-natural, only physics. But the physics and electronics involved in communicating with living energy is very subtle. Nothing, however, that you are not capable of now. The devices needed to make your beginning are already sold in stores.[67]

Perhaps what we identify as "ghosts" and other spirit beings are actually "leaks" into our world from other dimensions? If so, then someday our scientists might be able to tap into these vibrational frequencies operating at the atomic level, and make definitive contact with the other side. Ultimately, all true science is the pursuit of the unknown so that we may better understand the mysterious workings of the universe. So, to the field of theoretical physics we shall now turn our investigation. Some of the latest findings in the realm of quantum physics are showing that our world may be incredibly stranger than we realize, and might even add credence to the beliefs systems of civilizations from thousands of years ago.

Summary

❖ Contrary to popular and modern beliefs regarding the afterlife, the ancient view was that it was dreary and unpleasant. Most often, the souls of the dead were thought to be stranded in limbo while they awaited their final judgment.

❖ Modern paranormal investigators are attempting to use science and technology to document evidence of supernatural activities. Some of the phenomena that is most frequently captured include: orbs of light, disembodied voices, and apparitions. However, these anomalies do not provide definitive evidence of the afterlife.

❖ Currently, EVPs offer the best evidence that consciousness survives death because they demonstrate human speech patterns and often react to their environment.

❖ Further research and documentation of the paranormal may not only validate the age-old claim that life persists after death, but it may also suggest that we exist in the midst of other external dimensions that are capable of interacting with our own.

THE UNIVERSE NEXT DOOR

My own suspicion is that the universe is not only queerer than we
suppose, but queerer than we can suppose.

—John B.S. Haldane[1]

T HE STUDY OF QUANTUM PHYSICS HAS YIELDED many amazing discoveries concerning the world of sub-atomic particles, and scientists are currently searching for a unified "Theory of Everything" that will explain how our universe operates. The only problem is that in order to fully explain and unify disparate tried-but-true concepts, it seems to require the addition of higher dimensions and even parallel worlds. Could this finally lead to the discovery of additional realms where other beings, such as the Watchers, might exist?

Considering Hyperspace

We have come to know our world instinctively in three spatial dimensions and one temporal dimension known as time. It is so plainly obvious that we can describe objects in three dimensions (length, width, and depth) that we often take it for granted; and this is why the concept of higher dimensions might appear so strange.

The term "hyperspace" is used to describe any space that incorporates more than three spatial dimensions (ignoring time as a fourth temporal space). Unfortunately, it is futile to attempt to visualize higher-dimensional space, as the prominent German physicist Hermann von Helmholtz compared it to how a blind person cannot "see" colors no matter how carefully someone describes them to the blind person.[2]

Since it is nearly impossible for us to truly understand the concept of higher dimensions beyond the ones in which we are currently familiar, we must imagine the concept using lower dimensions. To begin, let's look at an example that's commonly used by physicists to explain the effect of higher dimensions. It's taken from a novel called *Flatland: A Romance of Many Dimensions by A. Square,* written by Edwin Abbot in 1884.

In the world known as "Flatland," everyone is a geometric shape such as a square, triangle, circle or even a straight line. The hero of the piece, Mr. Square, believes just like everyone else in Flatland that the entire world consists of only two dimensions. However, one day a strange figure known as Lord Sphere appears to Mr. Square and completely changes his outlook on the world. Lord Sphere can apparently change his size to be larger or smaller, and he claims he is able to do this because he is from a higher dimensional world, called Spaceland, where all objects are three-dimensional.[3]

Mr. Square, however, does not accept this explanation because the world can only exist in two dimensions. This causes Lord Sphere to peel Mr. Square off of the surface of Flatland and throw him into Spaceland, where he encounters all kinds of enigmatic objects. But since Mr. Square is only a two-dimensional creature, he cannot fully visualize the three-dimensional objects inhabiting Spaceland, and therefore only sees their cross-sections that grow and diminish and even disappear into thin air. Upon his return, he tells everyone about his amazing experience but nobody believes him and the higher authorities charge him with blasphemy for claiming that there is anything more than their familiar two dimensions.[4]

This concept can be illustrated in other ways as well. For instance, if a human being were to stick a finger into the two-dimensional plane of Flatland, all of the creatures in Flatland would see the growing cross-sections of the finger. This would appear even stranger to them if other parts of the hand were also included besides just the finger—especially if it entered at an angle other than directly perpendicular to their surface. Even regular geometric solids such as a cube would appear strange if they entered Flatland in a tumbling motion. The cube's cross-sections would appear to change in a variety of different ways as the object passed through the plane.

However, there is still one slight problem even with this explanation of how a two-dimensional being would perceive its world. Technically, none of the creatures of "Flatland" could look "up" or "down" because that requires a third dimension. Therefore, they could only look forward, backward, and side-to-side. So, this means that Lord Sphere would really appear as a straight line that grows wider or shrinks to a point before disappearing. On the other hand, as three dimensional observers, we would be

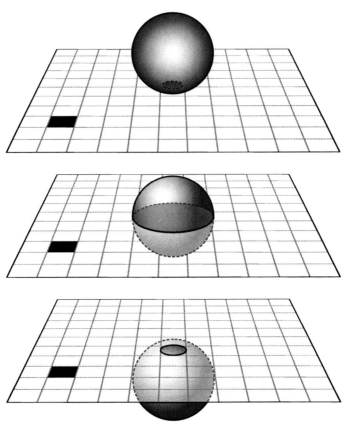

Lord Sphere would only appear as simple cross-sections of varying sizes to all inhabitants of Flatland.

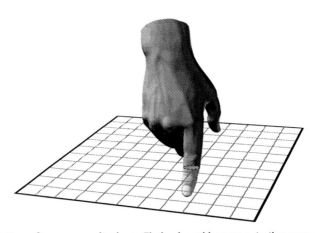

Inserting a finger perpendicular to Flatland would create a similar cross-section.

able to see the entire form of Mr. Sphere as well as recognize his "circles" (or "lines" to Mr. Square) as being his cross-sections.

There is a way to attempt to visualize higher-dimensional objects that was developed by the mathematician, Charles Hinton. After much time, Hinton was able to "see" four-dimensional objects and perfected special hypercubes, also known as Hinton's cubes. He even coined the term "tesseract" to describe an unraveled hypercube. The method involves understanding how the total surface of a cube could be viewed by someone such as a Flatlander. The cube can be unraveled and flattened down to two dimensions, forming six squares arranged in the shape of a cross. If the pieces were joined together again to reform a cube, the Flatlander would only see the individual squares disappear until there was only one remaining.[5]

This, in turn, would apply the same way to a four-dimensional object such as a hypercube. When it is unraveled into three dimensions it would appear as a solid cross-like shape using a series of distinct cubes. If a being that lived in four dimensions decided to reassemble the cube into its proper form, anyone viewing this from three dimensions would simply see the other cubes disappear until only one remained. Hinton's tesseract became so influential that Salvadore Dalí incorporated it into his famous painting *Crucifixion (Corpus Hypercubus),* which showed Christ being crucified on an unraveled hypercube. Two other methods used by Hinton to visualize higher-dimensional objects were to observe the shadow they cast in lower dimensions and to observe their cross-sections and then piece them together in an approximate manner.[6]

But what influences do these higher dimensions have on our world, and why are they necessary? To answer these questions, we must briefly revisit some of the more important discoveries in the realm of physics.

The Dilemma of Gravity

According to the popular story, Isaac Newton was sitting under an apple tree one day in 1665 and saw an apple fall to the ground. This sparked the idea in him that the force pulling the apple down and the force making our planet orbit the sun were the same. He called this unified theory: "Gravity." It quickly revolutionized thinking and yielded such stunning accuracy that his equations are still used to this day—in particular, for the moon landing and for the procedures used to send shuttles and satellites into orbit. However, there was a major problem with Newton's theory of gravity

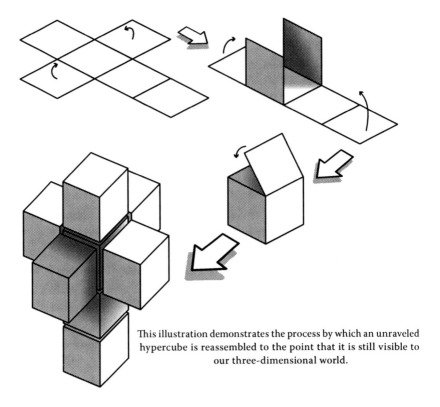

This illustration demonstrates the process by which an unraveled hypercube is reassembled to the point that it is still visible to our three-dimensional world.

that would remain unanswered for centuries: it could calculate the effects of gravity with superb accuracy but did not provide any insight into the actual mechanics of how gravity worked.[7]

Little progress was made towards solving this particular problem until Albert Einstein, a Swiss patent clerk, became interested in the study of light and issued the results of his own experiments. Einstein proposed that the speed of light (670 million miles per hour) was the fastest speed in the universe and that nothing could exceed it. This was supported by studies that showed that contrary to common sense, the speed of light will remain constant regardless of how fast an object attempting to match its speed is traveling. This became known as the *special theory of relativity.*

In other words, if you were to travel at the speed of light, you would not see a motionless light beam (or wave) beside you. Instead, if you measured the speed, you would quickly discover that the light is still exactly 670 million miles ahead of you, as if you weren't moving at all. This bizarre behavior truly shocked Einstein and forced him to come to the only con-

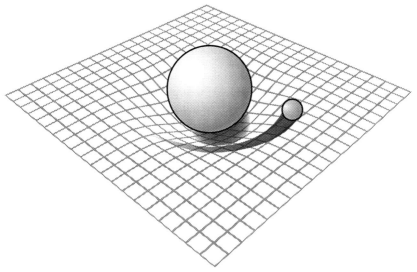

Massive objects distort their surrounding space-time fabric, creating a gravitational field.
Smaller objects are thereby affected by this curvature and orbit the large object.

clusion he could imagine: the light is not speeding up, but instead, *time is slowing down*. The observer would not notice that time has slowed down, because everything in the vicinity around him or her would also be affected; the only indication would be that the light is still being measured as traveling at the same speed as before.[8]

That nothing travels faster than light went against the long held belief of Newton's gravitational theory, which said that gravity acted instantaneously over any distance, and therefore would have been faster than even light. Einstein was in need of a way to explain the speed of light, while still taking into account the effects of Newton's gravity. After about a decade of work, Einstein realized that he could unify both theories by adding the extra dimension of time to the equation.[9] This created a concept of "space-time" fabric that could be warped by gravity. This warping of the fabric would pass along what we "feel" as gravity. Perhaps the best known equation of Einstein, it was called the *general theory of relativity* ($E=mc^2$).

But Einstein had a new problem to overcome. As he studied and marveled at the inner-workings of our world, he saw a grand design behind it and wanted to find the ultimate theory that made it all work. This would require the unification of the two main forces: gravity and electromagnetism (the strong and weak nuclear forces weren't known yet at this time). What made this task so difficult is that when compared to electromagnetism, gravity is extraordinarily weak. In fact, electromagnetism is hundreds of billions of times stronger than gravity.

As an example, let's suppose an object is dropped from the top of a very tall building. If gravity was a strong force, it should cause the object to go crashing through the sidewalk and down towards the planet's core. However, we know that this does not happen. The reason is because everything is made up of tiny atoms, and each atom has negatively charged electrons surrounding it. When the electrons from the falling object come near the electrons of the sidewalk, they repel each other with enough force to overpower the pull of the entire Earth's gravity.[10] Another way of explaining it is when you pick up an object, such as a piece of paper, the muscles in your arm are actually resisting Earth's entire gravitational pull. If gravity were stronger, you would not be able to lift even that simple sheet of paper (not to mention you would probably be flattened to the ground as well).

Gravity likes to work on large objects—and heavier objects have greater gravitational pulls. However, when entering the tiny world of atoms, physicists have found that gravity seems to be irrelevant. All of the cherished beliefs of Einstein's general relativity seem to break down into chaotic disorder when things get very, very tiny. In order to explain the workings of sub-atomic particles, the field of quantum mechanics was developed.

The Quantum World

Sometime around 400 BCE, the Greek philosopher Democritus theorized that everything was made up of tiny particles, called *atomos* (meaning "uncuttable"). For centuries after, atoms were believed to be the smallest objects. Then, in 1897, physicists discovered negatively charged particles orbiting atoms and called them electrons. Since then, more subatomic particles have been identified such as protons and neutrons; and some two hundred other particles which are leptons, quarks, or combinations of quarks have also been found.[11]

In the 1930s, two other forces were discovered working at the atomic level of quantum mechanics. They were the strong and the weak nuclear forces, which were later grouped together with electromagnetism. The *strong force* is actually the most powerful of the four known forces, and its purpose is to bind together the protons and neutrons of atomic nuclei, as well as quarks. The *weak force* is what controls the radioactive decay of elementary particles inside of an atom.

This theory is known as the Standard Model, and unites the three universal forces: strong, weak, and electromagnetism—to precisely describe the subatomic building blocks of our world and how they interact with matter through objects known as point particles. The Standard Model has been experimentally verified and accepted as a valid explanation of how the subatomic universe operates.

However, this tiny world is governed by chaos and seemingly random events where only the probability of an event can be calculated. For instance, in the quantum world you can never truly determine the position of a particle—you can only calculate the chance that it will be in a certain place at a specific time. This defies the general theory of relativity, which explains the force of gravity, and describes the effects of large objects with certainty. In order for the Standard Model to work, it must not take gravity into account. But Einstein's theory cannot explain the sub-atomic universe. It would appear that these are two very different and even contradictory theories at work in our world. They cannot both be correct unless there is a method to unify them. This was the problem that eluded Einstein for the rest of his life and has been a dilemma for other physicists as well.

Enter String Theory

One of the most exciting and controversial theories in physics today involves what is known as superstring theory (or string theory for short). According to the theory, there are even smaller objects inside of atoms than the currently known elementary particles. These objects are tiny, one-dimensional strings of energy that function through unique vibratory patterns. The strings are often visualized as either closed loops, like a rubber band, or open with two ends. It is believed that these strings are only the size of 10^{-33} centimeters and have no width. To put that into perspective, imagine that a single atom was enlarged to the size of our entire solar system—this would make the string only the size of an average tree![12]

String theory is sometimes referred to as a twenty-first century concept of physics that dropped into the lap of the twentieth century by accident. It has been around since the 1960s, and according to the story told by those involved, it was discovered quite by accident. It soon caught on in some physics circles, but would have its ups and downs. Later, when it was revived again, it was thought to only represent strong force nuclear reactions. Upon examination, something else kept appearing—a strange flaw.

The theory was predicting an unknown particle that had zero mass, and any attempt to remove the particle from the equation made it entirely useless. Two physicists, John H. Schwarz and Joël Scherk, made the startling consideration that the massless particle might be a graviton (a particle of gravity predicted by Einstein's theory). String theory was apparently demanding that gravity be included for it to work. Their findings were universally ignored by the scientific community, however, because it required that the strings were so incredibly small that other physicists found it difficult to believe.[13]

Another of the largest stumbling blocks in advancing the theory was attempting to solve the mathematical anomalies it created. Since theories based in physics rely on mathematical equations, the math dictates that they must be free of errors, known as anomalies. If the theory cannot resolve the anomalies, then it is as good as dead. Until the summer of 1984, string theory had many such anomalies. It was then that John H. Schwarz, now working with Michael B. Green, could finally solve the equations and remove all anomalies. The result was that string theory was now capable of explaining all four forces and unifying them together under a single theory.[14]

The benefit of string theory was not only how it could unite all of the previous theories, but also how it could explain them. String theorists often compare the function of strings to that of the strings on a musical instrument, such as a cello. When the strings on the cello are vibrated, they produce sound waves that travel through the air and are heard as musical notes. Superstrings also seem to vibrate on specific frequencies and these different vibrations are what determine the unique properties of particles such as mass and charge.[15]

As with most gifts, though, string theory comes with a price. First, many physicists refuse to accept the theory because even though the math works, the strings are so unimaginably small that there is currently no method to observe or experiment on them to test the theory's validity. This does not mean the theory is wrong, simply that it cannot be proven—yet.

The second perceived problem is that the only way for string theory to work requires that our universe contains either six or seven additional spatial dimensions. This is obviously very difficult for many people to accept. To resolve this, supporters of theory have proposed that these extra dimensions are incredibly small and wrapped up together in such a manner that they are invisible to the naked eye, but their effects on the strings manifest in the three larger dimensions that are familiar to us.[16]

The third problem was that five different versions of string theory soon appeared and without any way of determining which one was most accurate (assuming that only one could be accurate). Skeptics quickly scoffed at the idea of a unifying theory that itself wasn't unified. Despite the major problems associated with string theory, it was about to evolve into something else.

M-Theory

In 1994, Edward Witten and Paul Townsend, both of Cambridge University, determined mathematically that "ten-dimensional string theory was actually an approximation to a higher, mysterious, eleven-dimensional theory of unknown origin." Additionally, this eleven-dimensional theory showed that all five versions of string theory were actually different ways of looking at the same thing—like using five mirrors to create five different reflections of the same object. To top it off, it could even explain another mystery known as supergravity.[17]

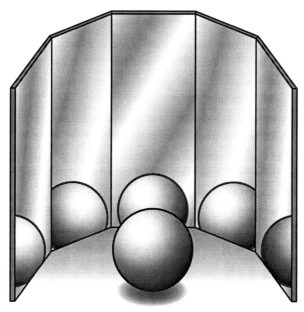

Some physicists suggest that the five versions of string theory are analogous to five mirrors reflecting a single object.

Witten called this new theory "M-theory," although he has never revealed exactly why the letter "M" was chosen. Various suggestions have been made, such as "magic," "mystery," "matrix," and "mother"—but it could also simply be short for "membrane." The concept is that some of these higher dimensions may actually exist on floating membrane surfaces created by the stretching of the strings.

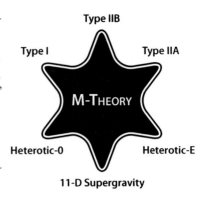

One of the key advantages of M-theory is how it suggests that the higher dimensions might actually be extremely huge in size and therefore observable, as opposed to the tiny dimensions of the superstring theory that cannot be successfully observed in current laboratory settings. One idea of M-theory is that our familiar three-dimensional universe is actually floating on a higher-dimensional membrane in a much larger universe.[18]

The atoms that make up the objects in our three-dimensional world might be limited in their capacity to "jump" to these higher dimensions even though we are floating on the membrane. String theorists like to compare this concept to a loaf of bread. In this example, our universe is stuck to the surface of a slice of bread (the membrane), but there are other slices (parallel universes) to either side of us that make up the rest of the loaf (referred to as "the bulk" by physicists).[19]

This theory even suggests that these parallel universes might only exist as little as one millimeter away from us, but would be invisible to our perceptions. In these other worlds, there might exist other intelligent beings or strange objects we've never seen before that follow completely different laws of physics than what we know.[20]

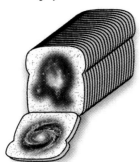

M-theory raises some interesting possibilities in regard to gravity. Recall that there are two basic concepts of strings: closed and open-ended. It is now believed that much of what makes up the objects and energy in our familiar three-dimensional world are composed of open-ended strings, with both ends essentially tied down to these known dimensions. The closed strings, however, are not tied down and therefore can travel freely back and forth between the lower and higher dimensions.[21]

Particles known as gravitons are thought to be made of these closed strings. It has been suggested by physicists that these gravitons can "leak" into higher dimensions. The result is that gravity is not actually weak, but just as strong as the other forces of nature—it only *appears* weak when it disappears into these other dimensions.[22]

Experiments are already under way to test many of these theories and to find the graviton particle. Physicists hope that experiments conducted using very large particle accelerators (also called "atom smashers") will reveal a graviton particle escaping into another dimension. The experiments may not be successfully tested, though, until next-generation particle accelerators are constructed and operational. One such highly anticipated accelerator is the Large Hadron Collider located underneath Switzerland and France, which is scheduled to go online in November of 2007. If the particles suggested by string theory are found, it will provide more circumstantial evidence to support it.[23]

Through the Looking-Glass

It is amazing to consider that the theories proposed by the leading minds of physics are indicating that we live in multi-dimensional worlds that could even have parallel universes inhabited by other creatures.[24] While it is only speculation, this could be pointing towards scientific evidence supporting the existence of realms akin to those of heaven and hell that have been merely discussed by the faithful for millennia. Theoretical physicists, such as Dr. Michio Kaku, have often entertained such ideas in their lectures, articles and books, suggesting that "wormholes" or "gateways" to other worlds could be very similar to Lewis Carroll's classic work, *Through the Looking-Glass, and What Alice Found There* (1871).[25] Kaku writes that just like Alice, "anyone walking through the Looking Glass would be transported instantly into Wonderland, a world where animals talked in riddles and common sense wasn't so common."[26]

If well respected scientists are suggesting that inter-dimensional travel might be possible by creating or manipulating "gateways," the idea of angels and gods coming to Earth from other dimensions does not seem so far-fetched. What is even more exciting is that this concept more closely matches what the ancient texts actually describe, rather than reinterpreting the texts (as authors such as Zecharia Sitchin and Erich von Däniken have done) to argue that these beings came from other planets through space travel. Could it be that modern science is only now confirming something that was understood over five thousand years ago? It is also fascinating to consider that perhaps the disembodied voices that have been recorded and labeled as EVPs are leaking through from these parallel dimensions. Until our technology became advanced enough, we previously had no way to capture such evidence—but that problem may soon be solved.

Another important point for consideration is what the Master of the Key told Whitley Strieber that night in his hotel room. He said, "The understanding of gravity is denied you because of the absence of the child of a murdered Jewish couple. This child would have *unlocked the secret of gravity*" (emphasis mine).[27] If this is to be believed, then quantum physics might only be discovering something that should have been known even sooner. The search for sub-atomic particles that are able to jump between different dimensions, such as gravitons, could reveal part of the secret for mankind to be "translated" into higher dimensions.

But according to the Master of the Key, time may not be on our side. He warned of our planet undergoing catastrophic earth changes, and that we must "square the circle" if we intend to survive. This will now lead us to examine the evidence of severe climate changes in the past, and determine whether or not the next change could already be underway.

Summary

❖ The concept of higher dimensions (or "hyperspace") is difficult to comprehend because we are accustomed to experiencing our world in three spatial dimensions.

❖ A being that existed in hyperspace could appear to have godlike abilities to a being that resided in a lower dimensional plane.

❖ Einstein recognized that he needed to add another dimension (time) to his equations in order to unify his theories about the workings of the universe.

❖ Einstein's General Theory of Relativity accurately describes the effect of gravity and classical physics. However, the Standard Model (which explains the sub-atomic world) is at odds with Einstein's theory and scientists have struggled to discover how the two theories can be unified.

❖ Superstring theory and M-theory are relatively new attempts to bring together the disparate models, but they *require* additional dimensions to make the equations mathematically sound.

❖ If hyperspace is proven to exist, it might be the home to other beings (e.g. "gods," angels, and ghosts), and even the location of places such as heaven and hell.

PART 5

THE COMING STORM

We are now faced with the fact that tomorrow is today. We are confronted with the fierce urgency of now. In this unfolding conundrum of life and history there is such a thing as being too late. Procrastination is still the thief of time. Life often leaves us standing bare, naked and dejected with a lost opportunity. The "tide in the affairs of men" does not remain at the flood; it ebbs. We may cry out desperately for time to pause in her passage, but time is deaf to every plea and rushes on. Over the bleached bones and jumbled residue of numerous civilizations are written the pathetic words: "Too late."

—Dr. Martin Luther King, Jr.[1]

ALTHOUGH THIS SPEECH GIVEN BY DR. KING exactly one year before his assassination was regarding the Vietnam conflict, his words and message could easily apply to the events unfolding before us today. Even if readers find it difficult to accept the evidence and implications presented so far in this book, it would prove disastrous to ignore the warning in the message above. Much of the world, particularly the United States, has been so caught up in the overly politicized debate of whether or not climate change is happening that they do not even realize that it is ominously scratching at the back door. Until recently, the evidence of abrupt climate shifts has been largely ignored by a majority of scientists and world leaders even though well-established data forecasting a severe environmental crisis has been known to many institutions for years. Now, the scientists that have at last awakened to this looming threat are finding themselves in a desperate race to warn the world before time runs out.

The Day After Tomorrow is Now Today

During their conversation together, the Master of the Key revealed a series of events to Whitley Strieber that he found incredibly disconcerting. The scenario was that the planet was about to enter a period of geologic upheaval that would erupt with monstrous superstorms and initiate a devastating loss of life as we are plunged headfirst into a new ice age. At the time, the idea seemed preposterous. Strieber was warned: "The next ice age will begin soon, and this will lead to the extinction of mankind, or to a massive reduction in population, given your inability to expand off the planet. This planet is at present a deathtrap."[2]

Recall that this conversation occurred during the summer of 1998, but *The Key* was not published until 2001. The cause for the delay was that the conversation incited Strieber to begin researching the possibility of abrupt climate change and his findings were published in the book *The Coming Global Superstorm* (Pocket Books, 1999), which he co-authored with friend and late-night talk show host Art Bell. The book became a *New York Times* bestseller, but was largely dismissed and ridiculed by many scientists and members of the mainstream media. The general consensus labeled Strieber and Bell as "irresponsible alarmists attempting to make money by exploiting people's fears," such as when they were interviewed by Matt Lauer on the *Today* show in early 2000.[3] In the preface of a new printing of the book, Strieber explained in his usual straightforward manner: "People don't want to think about the environmental catastrophe that is staring us in the face because they feel helpless, and they are served by a media that reflects this by being indifferent, or even hostile, to discussing these issues."[4]

The essential theory suggested by the Master of the Key and then *Superstorm* is that greenhouse gases trapped in the atmosphere by global warming are causing the polar ice caps to melt and therefore reduce the salinity of the ocean water. This will result in winds that warm the ocean to the point that will shut down or drastically reduce the effect of the North Atlantic Current, which depends on a delicate balance of warm and cold temperature differentials to drive the pump. The shutdown or reduction of this pump has functioned as the triggering mechanism for past ice ages. This time, the crucial difference is that the human race may be expediting the result of this process.[5]

If this nightmare scenario unfolded, our civilization would face the worst environmental crisis in all of human history. Please take a moment and try to imagine yourself in the kind of situation that would inevitably result from it. Some of the world's largest nations, particularly America, have populations that are completely unprepared to handle the type of emergency where they must fend for themselves. We are so accustomed to dining at restaurants, buying food from grocery stores, and having the money to do such things. But if superstorms became the norm, and large sections of the country were devastated, what would we do? The electricity would be gone, causing all of the refrigerated foods in the grocery stores to spoil. We wouldn't be able to perform any electronic transactions to pay for goods, and so you'd be limited to whatever amount of cash that was in your possession before the storm hit. In the best case scenario, people would have to start bartering for goods and hope that they have items that other people want. Otherwise, widespread looting and mobbing would become commonplace as people struggled just to survive. Entire industries would be incapacitated, further pushing society to a breaking point. If these things happened, it would be the beginning of the end of civilization as we know it. As if that is not bad enough, global warming is now believed to be the leading culprit behind several ancient mass extinctions, such as the "Great Dying" that occurred at the close of the Permian period 251 million years ago. At that time, ninety percent of all ocean life and seventy percent of plants and land animals (even insects) were exterminated by the planet.[6]

The Paradox of Global Warming

At first, it is easy to see why so many people could not (or would not) believe the seeming paradox that global warming would cause an ice age (or "Little Ice Age"). After all, at the time of Strieber and Bell's writing there was still much debate about whether or not global warming was even occurring, and if it was, the effects were thought to take hundreds of years to fully manifest. The climate would get a bit warmer and more humid, but mankind would have a chance to adjust and prepare for the rising ocean levels (from the melting ice caps), and develop crops that grow better under the new conditions. However, recent evidence suggests that the actual scenario is far less optimistic.

According to an article from *LiveScience,* three new studies have been published in the journal *Science* indicating that the key arguments used by global warming skeptics are now found to be based on faulty analyses. For many years, these skeptics emphasized that all of the data from satellites and weather balloons showed that climate prediction models were wrong and that global warming was not occurring. In fact, even though surface thermometers demonstrated an increase in temperatures, the satellite and weather balloon data contrarily seemed to show that the atmosphere was cooling. The only possible conclusions were that either the atmosphere was not warming up, or something in the data was incorrect.[7]

As it turns out, the problem was with some of the weather balloons that measure atmospheric temperatures, known as radiosondes. The older instruments that were developed in the 1970s were not as well shielded from sunlight as the more recent ones. This caused the instruments to report incorrect temperature readings that made it appear as though the atmosphere was cooling when these readings were combined with other data.[8]

Satellite data measuring the troposphere (the lowest layer in Earth's atmosphere) was analyzed in 1992 by a team of researchers headed by Roy Spencer at the University of Alabama. There were apparent differences between the satellite data and what surface thermometers reported. When Spencer's team introduced a correction factor that accounted for the drift of the satellites being used to analyze the atmosphere, it showed an apparent cooling effect. Since critics believed that the satellites provided more accurate information, this was their leading reason for dismissing the claims of global warming. However, Carl Mears and Rank Wentz, two California scientists at Remote Sensing Systems, have identified an error in Spencer's analysis. When corrected, the same data now shows that the atmosphere is warming and brings it into agreement with current climate models and theories.[9]

Despite the abundance of new evidence and predictions, certain government officials with key ties to large industries are refusing to accept the reality of global warming. Even as we see a noticeable increase in temperatures and storm activity, politicians regurgitate what the industries want them to say and remind us that it is all *just* a theory. These politicians depend upon the belief common to the public that a "theory" is nothing more than a loose set of speculative ideas—as opposed to what the scientific community considers to be a valid theory (i.e. analysis of facts that are organized into predictions that can be tested and generally hold to be true).

That is why three leading climate scientists are now accusing members of the Republican party of intimidating them with a "witch-hunt" and placing them under exaggerated scrutiny. They are: Michael Mann, the director of the Earth System Science Centre at Pennsylvania State University;

Raymond Bradley, the director of the Climate System Research Centre at the University of Massachusetts; and Malcolm Hughes, the former director of the Laboratory of Tree-Ring Research at the University of Arizona.[10]

The politician who launched this inquiry is Joe Barton, the chairman of the House of Representatives committee on energy and commerce. His demands are for detailed information regarding every source of their funding, their methods, and *every* scientific paper or review they have ever published, regardless of whether it is related to the issue at hand. While this may be extreme, it would not necessarily be a bad thing to ask for detailed background information for scientific claims. However, Mr. Barton is a Texan with very close ties to individuals in the fossil-fuel lobby, and "has spent his 11 years as chairman opposing every piece of legislation designed to combat climate change."[11] This certainly makes it appear as though his goal is to stop or intimidate scientists such as the three mentioned from promoting ideas contrary to his affiliations.

However, recent events are showing that a change may be underway. In February of 2006, George Deutsch, a public relations officer at NASA appointed by the Bush administration, was forced to resign after growing allegations that he was censoring some of the agency's top scientists with views in opposition to those of the White House.[12] NASA's leading climatologist, James E. Hansen, is one of the scientists who feels that he is being unfairly censored. In NASA's defense, it has been up front about the problem and denied any censorship of Hansen. Instead, it says that it is only following company policy by requiring coordination efforts so that a scientist can publicly speak about certain topics while not simultaneously releasing information that contradicts the agency.[13]

There is still another issue even if politicians and the public were to accept that global warming is occurring. The problem is that most scientists are focusing upon very slow changes to the climate and are not predicting how rapid changes would affect our way of life. As Terrance Joyce and Lloyd Keigwin of the Woods Hole Oceanographic Institution point out, this view is fundamentally flawed because "it ignores the well-established fact that Earth's climate has changed rapidly in the past and could change rapidly in the future."[14]

Studies of the past million years reveal that it is very common for the climate to flip-flop between glacial periods and warmer interglacial periods, such as the period we have been experiencing since the dawn of modern

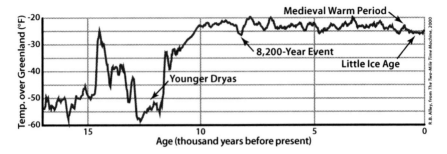

human history. In fact, these shifts may have actually been a major factor in the evolution of our brains.[15] The proof of these abrupt climate shifts has been found in fossil evidence and ice cores taken from Greenland and Antarctica. Geoscientist Richard B. Alley has published his findings in the book: *The Two-Mile Time Machine* (Princeton University Press, 2000).

Analysis of the ice cores demonstrate that the climate can shift violently and rapidly *within a decade*—a mere blip on the scale of time. It is also important to note that the evidence indicates that the situation is not exclusively either abrupt warming or abrupt cooling, but instead a period of abrupt regional cooling that occurs *simultaneously* with a period of gradual global warming.[16]

The scenario involving the salinity of ocean water has been one of the major areas most overlooked by many scientists until now. Presently, leading scientists have only been able to identify one viable method to rapidly induce large, global climate changes: "a swift reorganization of the ocean currents circulating around the earth." These currents are collectively referred to as the Ocean Conveyer.[17]

The Ocean Conveyer has been referred to as the "Achilles' Heel" of our climate system by some scientists. The Gulf Stream is a limb of the Conveyer and carries an enormous amount of warm, salty water up the East Coast of the United States and further northeast towards Europe. This warm water is then released into the atmosphere, particularly during the colder winter months, and significantly tempers the average winter temperatures. But the fossil and ice core evidence show that the Conveyer has slowed down and even completely stopped in the past and therefore did not deliver the necessary heat to the atmosphere, causing drastically reduced regional temperatures. When this happens again, the results could be devastating.[18]

So the question is: what exactly could disrupt the Ocean Conveyor in such a manner? The important factor is that the North Atlantic waters are much more salty than in other parts of the world. Salt water is more

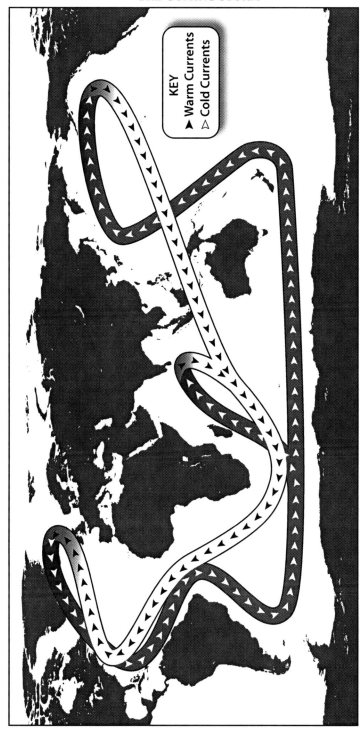

The Ocean Conveyer is the "pump" of our climate system, consisting of warm (fresh water) currents and cold (salt water) currents. If the salinity of the water is reduced by too much fresh water then the Conveyer will slow down or stop, wreaking havoc upon our climate.

dense than fresh water and cold water is likewise more dense than warm water. The result is that when the heat from the salty water is released into the atmosphere, it becomes much cooler and sinks towards the bottom in a process known as "thermohaline circulation," which is derived from the Greek words "thermos" (heat) and "halos" (salt). Recalling that glaciers are composed of frozen fresh water, the result of global warming is that it is causing these glaciers to melt and release vast amounts of fresh water into the ocean. While it is uncertain how much fresh water is required to breach the threshold, it is a critical event that could happen at any time. Once this occurs, it will disrupt the Conveyer and create severe climate change within a decade.[19]

A worrisome account was published in 2002 by *Nature,* showing that the North Atlantic has been freshening continuously over the last forty years. What is even more alarming is that the last decade has seen the speed of this process increase dramatically. Recent data indicates that "since the mid-1960s, the subpolar seas feeding the North Atlantic have steadily and noticeably become less salty to depths of 1,000 to 4,000 meters. *This is the largest and most dramatic oceanic change ever measured in the era of modern instruments.*"[20]

Returning to the message from the Master of the Key, he explained all of this in detail and warned that, "The greater part of human industry and culture, along with the species' most educated populations, will be destroyed in a single season. This will happen suddenly and without warning, or rather, the warning will not be recognized for what it is."[21] When asked what that warning would be, he answered:

First the surface features of the currents will slow down. This will result in violent storms in Europe. At some point, arctic temperatures will rise forty or more points above normal during a spring or summer season. Then the currents themselves will change their routes or stop. Cold air trapped above the arctic will plunge down and collide with the warm tropical air present at the surface. It will create the most powerful storms in ten thousand years, storms unlike any you have seen or imagined. They will bring about the end of the northern civilization and the climate change that follows will lead to the starvation of billions.[22]

The average person is not prepared to deal with the repercussions this would have on life as we know it. Even leading scientists who are concerned with the impact of the outlined global warming scenario say that while they are referring to "rapid" change, that it is in geologic terms, which is slower than what most people consider to be rapid. This is a valid point worth considering because there is no sense in growing alarmed about waking up to find your house buried in snow and ice if it isn't likely to happen. These scientists must walk a fine line between responsibility to the data, and the responsibility not to create widespread panic.

However, consider that many of the same people who initially dismissed these claims about global warming and climate change scenarios back in 1999 are now seeing how they were wrong. What is even worse is that it is happening at a faster rate than scientists could have imagined. They readily admit that they need more funding and do not have the necessary equipment to properly monitor and analyze the situation. If they were wrong before, how can they be sure that they won't be wrong about this impending situation? This is not an attack upon their knowledge or expertise, but rather a recognition that human beings make mistakes and that we presently know very little about how to properly forecast scenarios such as the one described here.

Both *Superstorm* and *The Key* appear to have been published *before* there were any mainstream articles or books projecting the dire consequences of global warming. Undoubtedly, climate scientists had written about such topics within their scientific journals and other related papers for years, but such data is typically not brought to the public's attention. While Whitley Strieber never considered the books to be psychic predictions, he does believe they serve as both a warning and a forecast of things to come. Science is based on observing data and then making predictions. If the predictions turn out to be true, then it is generally considered that the hypothesis is reliable. Anyone observing our current weather patterns should take heed of these predictions.

It is often said about gambling that "the House *always* wins." Well, we shouldn't forget that we're in a betting game in which we don't know all the rules and the Earth is our House. Who do you think is going to win? The longer that we wait to solve the problem, the bigger a gamble we take with our lives and those of future generations.

Dark Skies on the Horizon

A shocking announcement from the World Meteorological Organization (WMO) in 2003 warned that the world's weather was about to enter a phase of extreme unpredictability over the next several years. What made this warning so serious was that the WMO is typically viewed as a conservative group that is highly respected and not prone to exaggeration. According to the reports of the WMO, supercomputer climate prediction models showed that warmer atmospheres not only make the climate hotter, but also more unstable. "Recent scientific assessments indicate that, as the global temperatures continue to warm due to climate change, the number and intensity of extreme events might increase," the WMO warned, and cited these examples from the same year:[23]

- Record temperatures in southern France during the month of June.
- The hottest June in Switzerland in at least 250 years.
- In the US, a record number of 562 tornadoes during the month of May that caused 41 deaths. The previous record was 399 in June 1992.
- India faced a record heatwave that killed 1,400 people.
- Sri Lanka had heavy rainfall from a tropical cyclone that killed 300 people in flooding and landslides.
- The hottest June for England and Wales since 1976.[24]

The situation worsened for Europe in July and August of 2003, when it faced a heat wave considered to be "the worst weather disaster to hit the region in centuries." With temperatures reaching into the triple digits, between twenty and twenty-five thousand people died from the intense heat. France lost over fourteen thousand people alone, most of them were elderly and without air conditioners or fans to help keep cool.[25]

During 2004, the Atlantic region saw an increase in hurricane activity that was well above normal for most seasons. The final total amounted to fifteen named storms with nine turning into hurricanes (six of which were major hurricanes).[26] The above average season was yet another indication that the weather was about to become drastically worse over the next several years. All of the scientific forecasts for the following season, however, proved to be regrettably underestimated.

The 2005 Atlantic Hurricane season exceeded even the worst meteorological expectations. It started with a few tropical storms: Arlene and Bret. In early July, the first declared hurricane was Cindy (formerly designated as a Tropical Storm).[27] Immediately following Cindy was Dennis, a powerful Category 4 storm at one point, which caused considerable damage to Cuba and part of the Florida panhandle. Next was Emily, another Category 4 when its forces were at their strongest. Emily brought strong winds and damage to areas such as Cozumel and the Yucatan peninsula of Mexico. It made final landfall on July 20, about 75 miles south of Texas in Northeastern Mexico.[28] Another hurricane, Irene, formed in mid-August but never made landfall. However, most people soon forgot about Dennis, Emily and Irene—and for a good reason.

On August 29, 2005, Hurricane Katrina decimated New Orleans. Quickly becoming inundated with water, the levees could not hold and were breached, causing over eighty-percent of the city to disappear underwater. Without electricity or safe drinking water, the city was placed under a total evacuation order.[29] But poor planning and response to the situation intensified an already terrible situation and people became outraged. Total anarchy erupted as riots and widespread looting broke out. Bodies floated in the toxic water while others died waiting for help and much needed food and supplies. The death toll reached just over 1,000 people in Louisiana alone, but was substantially less than what officials had at first feared. More than 22,000 people were without permanent housing. Damages have been estimated to be in the billions of dollars and rebuilding efforts will be a long and arduous process. Katrina quickly went down in the records as one of the most devastating storms to ever hit the United States.

Despite the horrific outcome, the situation could have been much worse. Katrina was a Category 5 monster, packing 175 mile-per-hour winds, but was downgraded to a Category 4 just before it made landfall with sustained winds of about 135 miles-per-hour. At the last moment, its path veered slightly to the right and reduced the damage that a direct hit could have caused the Big Easy and spared it from a total doomsday scenario. Of course, anyone who lived through the event will surely tell you that it was a tragedy worse than they could ever have imagined.

While most of the media attention was focused on New Orleans, we should not forget that many other areas were also affected by Katrina. The hurricane ripped through over 270 miles of coastline and destroyed areas of Mississippi and Alabama. People's homes were lost and their lives were devastated. Rescue workers scrambled to provide aid to those in need, but little could be done since the damage was so widespread.

The destruction of Katrina occurred before the most active time of a hurricane season, which is usually in autumn. Experts soon warned that even more devastating storms could appear.[30] The entire season runs from the beginning of June through the end of November. Gerry Bell, the lead meteorologist for the National Oceanic and Atmospheric Administration (NOAA) Atlantic Hurricane Season Outlook, cautioned that, "Although we have already seen a record-setting seven tropical storms during June and July, much of the season's activity is still to come." NOAA was forced to revise its 2005 forecast to accommodate for a more active season. The new forecast estimated a total of "18 to 21 tropical storms, with nine to 11 becoming hurricanes, including five to seven major hurricanes." Compare this to the normal forecast, which has "10 named storms in which six become hurricanes, including two major hurricanes with winds of at least 111 mph."[31]

The cause for the increase in both strength and occurrence in hurricane activity is warmer than normal surface temperatures of waters in the Gulf Coast region. "This may well be one of the most active Atlantic hurricane seasons on record, and will be the ninth above-normal Atlantic hurricane season in the last eleven years," warned Brigadier General David L. Johnson, USAF (Ret.), director of the NOAA National Weather Service.[32]

It certainly appears worrisome that nine out of eleven seasons are showing increased activity. While NOAA recognizes that this may be in part due to a multi-decadal cycle that began in 1995 and lasts 20-30 years (or longer),[33] it is difficult to predict how much worse this cycle will be when combined with the effects of global warming. It could prove to be absolutely catastrophic.

After Katrina, the Atlantic region generated Hurricanes Maria, Nate, Ophelia, Philippe, and then Rita; the last being yet another killer storm to hit the United States in less than a month after Katrina. It made landfall between the border of Texas and Louisiana on September 24, as a deadly Category 3 hurricane, packing winds of 120 mph. Just 48 hours earlier, it had peaked as a Category 5 storm, with winds measured at 175 mph. The central pressure of the hurricane fell to 897 millibars, making it the third lowest on record in the Atlantic Basin region and displaced Katrina to position five (902 millibars). Damage was widespread and caused severe storm surge flooding and wind damage in areas of southwestern Louisiana, including areas affected by Katrina, as well as places in the extreme southeastern regions of Texas.[34]

Hurricane Rita was followed by Stan and then Vince (which quickly weakened to a tropical storm and became the first ever recorded to hit Spain). But it was Hurricane Wilma that broke the record books yet again. On October 19, 2005, Wilma rapidly increased from a Category 2 storm to a Category 5. In fact, it became the most powerful hurricane ever recorded, with maximum sustained winds of 175 mph, and even higher gusts. Data from dropsondes (instruments dropped into the storm by Hurricane Hunter planes) reported that Wilma's central pressure was estimated at 882 millibars. "This [was] the lowest pressure on record for a hurricane in the Atlantic basin," according to scientists.[35]

Wilma made landfall twice. The first time was in Mexico's Yucatan Peninsula on October 22. The final landfall occurred over the Florida Keys as a Category 3 storm on October 24, but affected the entire state and caused extensive damage that was worse than anticipated. After leaving Florida, Wilma continued traveling up the Atlantic Coastline, but it was not over just yet. Some weather forecasters projected that Wilma would eventually combine with cold fronts from the north, and even began using the term "Super Storm."[36] As expected, the spinning action of Wilma's strong winds pulled down much colder air from Canada and mixed it with its own subtropical moisture, creating an intense "nor'easter" storm. Early for the season, the storm blasted some regions in the Northeast U.S. with as much as twenty inches of wet snow and ice. Dozens of schools had to be closed and conditions grew increasingly dangerous, causing several traffic-related deaths. Thousands were without electricity after snow-covered tree branches snapped under the heavy weight, pulling down power lines.[37]

Shortly after Wilma, the formation of Tropical Storm Alpha was immediately immortalized in meteorological history books. The unprecedented event forced scientists to begin using the Greek alphabet after they had exhausted the list of standard names.[38] Next was Tropical Storm Beta, the twenty-third named storm of the season. Beta strengthened to Category 3 status by the end of October, but quickly weakened to a Category 2 by the time it made landfall on the Central East Coast of Nicaragua.[39] The close of the extended hurricane season witnessed three more tropical storms (Gamma, Delta, Zeta), and one last hurricane (Epsilon) that set yet another record by lasting for five days during the month of December.[40]

After the close of the 2005 season, NOAA released their disturbing analysis. They warned that 2005 had shattered all previous records and expected things to grow worse over the next several seasons. The report showed that 2005 was the first season to have:

- 27 named storms
- 15 hurricanes
- Three Category 5 hurricanes
- Four major hurricanes hit the U.S. (plus two less powerful storms)[41]

But it is not only hurricanes that threaten our future. Other storms are also likely to become stronger and more frequent, perhaps even becoming the speculated "superstorms." However frightening, try to imagine freakish tornados, floods and tsunamis of Biblical proportions, (and I *really* should resist quoting this, but…) "forty years of darkness, earthquakes, volcanoes… the dead rising from the grave… human sacrifice, *dogs and cats living together*—MASS HYSTERIA!"[42]

A Global Warning

In December of 2004, an article was released by Ohio State University that described how Lonnie Thompson, a professor of geologic sciences at the university and a researcher with the Byrd Polar Research Center, discovered evidence for an extremely rapid change in the weather that occurred over 5,000 years ago. Contained in an ice core that was drilled from an enormous glacier in the Peruvian Andes were perfectly preserved plants that were carbon-dated to approximately 5,200 years ago. The cellular structure of the plants were so astonishingly preserved that it suggests they were flash-frozen in perhaps a matter of only minutes, or as long as a few hours. Either way, it was incredibly fast.[43]

Readers may also remember how in 1991 some hikers discovered an ancient man that had been trapped in an Alpine glacier. Subsequent tests on the man, called Oetzi, revealed that he died and was frozen in the glacier during an event that occurred approximately 5,200 years ago. Among other evidence pointed out by Thompson, he also notes how the Sahara Desert was once very habitable region but something occurred at around that same time to turn it into the barren desert we are familiar with today. He believes part of what may have triggered this event is tied to sunspot activity, citing more recent examples when two periods of decreased activity seemed to coincide with the Little Ice Age that lasted from 1450 to 1850 CE.[44]

Continuing with more strange weather, on July 29 of 2005, the BBC reported a story concerning a rare F2 tornado that tore through Birmingham with winds of 130 miles-per-hour. Twenty people were injured, three of which very badly, with much destruction caused to buildings and cars. The roofs of houses were torn off and trees were uprooted. Tornados of this kind are not common in the UK, especially near cities, because the tall buildings prevent their formation from occurring. A Met Office spokesperson said, "We have an average of 33 reports of tornadoes in the UK each year but these are especially rare in built-up areas and there has not been one of this strength in many years."[45]

Tornados also damaged parts of Brazil, which so rarely sees a tornado that it does not even have the equipment to detect and track them. Two twisters touched down in the same afternoon in the town of Criciúma, with winds estimated at 100 kilometers-per-hour. Over 250 homes were badly damaged and numerous people were injured with two found dead.[46]

At Sequoia National Park, a tornado formed at an elevation of 12,000 feet, making it the first to ever be observed at such a high elevation in the United States. This event was strange because a tornado normally requires the dense, humid air of the lower atmosphere to form. Such abnormal behavior may be an indication that new weather patterns are beginning to emerge.[47]

Photos of the first recorded tornado to form at 12,000 feet in Sequoia National Park. *Photo Credit: Scott Newton (2004).*

In April of 2004, a freak hailstorm eerily reminiscent of a scene in the film *The Day After Tomorrow* pummeled parts of China with hail up to thirteen centimeters (5.12 inches) in diameter. When it was over, eighteen people were dead and twenty-five were injured, with damages totaling 140 million yuan ($17 million U.S.) and over 27,800 houses and crop areas were destroyed. Many considered it to be the worst hailstorm in China for at least twenty years.[48]

The Japanese also became very frightened by the sudden changes in weather during the 2004 season. The season produced seventeen typhoons and numerous earthquakes. Perhaps the strangest event of all occurred at 11:29 a.m. on December 5, when Tokyo's temperature rose to 77 degrees Fahrenheit from 38 degrees in only a matter of *minutes*. This broke a previous record of a sudden temperature change that was set back in 1923. Earlier that same morning, 90 mile-per-hour gale winds were recorded, forcing drivers off roadways and causing massive power outages.[49]

Not only is storm activity expected to increase, but other natural disasters as well. Current trends and side effects suggest that there will be more forest fires, earthquakes and flooding. For instance, few people will forget when a magnitude 9.3 earthquake fractured the sea floor off the northwest coast of Sumatra on December 26, 2004. This set in motion a devastating sequence of events as it pushed a massive wave thousands of kilometers across the Indian Ocean. The tsunami came with almost no warning and killed over 200,000 people (perhaps closer to 300,000) in countries spreading from Indonesia, the Maldives, Sri Lanka and Somalia.[50] Several months later, scientists were astonished to discover that the quake had created a "dead sea." Now, four kilometers beneath the ocean surface is an "eerie emptiness" that it is completely devoid of life.[51]

Another devastating quake struck Sumatra the following March—just one more in a series that continued to pummel the planet. Large parts of Pakistan and Kashmir were leveled by a massive 7.6 quake in October that ended the lives of over 80,000 people. The harsh winter claimed even more lives due to the lack of reasonable shelter or even thermal blankets for people who had lost their homes.[52]

Shortly after the 2004 tsunami, the international community implemented a regional tsunami-alert system for the Indian Ocean to provide better warning about future killer waves. However, the system proved to be insufficient on July 17, 2006. An undersea quake registering a 7.7 magnitude generated *another* tsunami that crashed into a 177 kilometer stretch of Java's

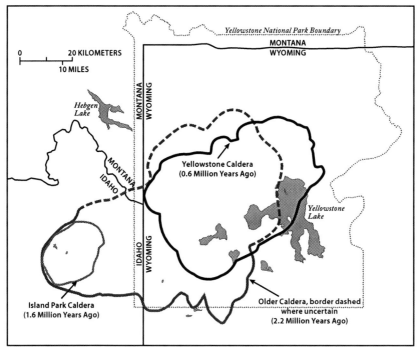

Illustration of the massive Yellowstone caldera and markings of prior eruptions.

shores. The two-meter waves came "without warning," and tore through people's houses. After it was finished, approximately 700 were dead, almost 1,000 badly injured, and over 20,000 families were homeless.[53]

One more ominous fact concerning large-scale catastrophes is that many people are not even aware that one of the most active volcanoes in the world resides at Yellowstone National Park—and the hot magma under the earth's crust is what powers over 10,000 vents, geysers, and hot springs at the tourist attraction. It is known as a supervolcano. What many tourists seem to forget is that when they are in certain areas of the park, they are actually walking *inside* the caldera of the volcano, and an eruption would prove to be one of the most devastating calamities to affect not only the United States, but the entire world.

In a recent report by geologists studying supervolcanoes, they claim that "A super-eruption is also five to 10 times more likely to happen than an asteroid impact." It's estimated that asteroid impacts occur roughly every 400–500 thousand years, but that super-eruptions occur every 100,000 years, or possibly even more frequently. Eruptions large enough would create "volcanic winters" by blocking out sunlight, causing tremendous devastation to plants and wildlife as well as civilization. Yellowstone is North America's largest volcanic system, and the caldera from the last eruption is large enough to fit Tokyo, the world's biggest city, inside of it. There have been at least three super-eruptions at Yellowstone in the past, usually occurring every 600,000 years. The last one occurred 640,000 years ago, making it overdue for another.[54]

During May of 2005, the U.S. Geological Survey reported that the Yellowstone caldera was classified as a high threat for possible volcanic eruption. Reasons cited in the report are "recurring earthquake swarms, swelling and falling ground, and changes in hydrothermal features."[55] According to sonar data mapped by scientist Lisa Morgan, she has identified a newly formed "massive bulging dome the size of seven football fields." The only other underwater dome was the site of an explosion 13,800 years ago that shot boiling water, steam and rocks up to five miles from the source. While scientists aren't eager to shy people away from the park, they admit that they know very little about the activity of the volcano and it must be carefully observed. Besides the bulging dome, another ominous sign soon appeared. The trail near the Norris Geyser has been closed since the summer of 2003 because the ground became so hot that it was melting people's shoes![56]

There are numerous other examples of increased storm activity and other natural disasters—too many to list here. However, some readers will probably still not be convinced, or wonder why this should be taken seriously. After all, the Bush administration says that global warming is *only* a theory and not a priority. Unfortunately, the administration has also been criticized by scientists for falsifying reports, manipulating data and using "pseudoscience" to promote the agendas of major oil companies and other businesses behind it.[57] Months before the 2004 election, the media became aware of a secret email being sent to Republican congressmen advising how to deny reports of global warming and climate change. Instead, they were encouraged to say that everything is only getting better.[58]

Now, even people appointed by the administration are growing concerned about the problems. When the Bush administration backed Rajendra Pachauri to the post of the U.N.'s IPCC (Intergovernmental Panel on Climate Change) chairman, they assumed he would be more "friendly" towards their policies. This was after Exxon Mobil complained that the last chairman, Robert Watson, was far too hard on them. Surprisingly, Pachauri is now warning that the world has reached a critical tipping point and if humanity is to survive, then CO_2 emissions need to be reduced dramatically. He says climate change "is for real" and "there is not a moment to lose."[59]

There is perhaps something even more startling. While the White House continues to deny that there is a growing threat from global warming, the Pentagon has been secretly strategizing how to handle future "climate wars." Mark Townsend and Paul Harris wrote in *The Observer* about a shocking report commissioned by Pentagon defense adviser Andrew Marshall and compiled by CIA consultants Peter Schwartz and Doug Randall of the Global Business Network.[60] The report created enough attention that it was the subject of several news stories, including a major article in *Fortune* magazine.[61]

While the authors of the report claim it is only a "worst case scenario," and that it is uncertain how likely the climate change scenario may be, they warned, "the risk of abrupt climate change… should be elevated beyond a scientific debate to a U.S. national security concern."[62] The report suggests that global warming will lead to more severe weather, rising seas will flood major European cities, Britain will have a "Siberian" climate by 2020, and the struggles for dwindling resources and food will lead to nuclear conflicts among nations.

So how much time do we have? Unfortunately, we do not know. What is worse is that observing the events as they unfold, it seems we have already begun a downward spiral toward disaster. Ice cores indicate that there was a large spike in the amount of methane gas in the atmosphere before the onset of extreme warming 15,000 years ago. Methane gas is twenty times better at holding heat in the lower atmosphere than carbon dioxide. In August of 2005, climatologists' worst fears began coming true when the Siberian permafrost started melting much faster than anticipated. A warning from U.S. climatologist Larry Smith stated that the Siberian peat bog could release seventy billion tons of methane, which is one-fourth of all the methane stored in the ground worldwide. If the methane continues to be released over the next few summers, the heat trapped in the atmosphere would intensify greatly and accelerate the effects to terrifying new levels. If that occurs, we will have already breached the tipping point.[63]

The beginning of 2006 saw a vast arctic cold front sweep down from Norway to Siberia to Japan. Moscow urged its citizens (especially the homeless) to stay out of the cold when temperatures began plummeting to minus-35° Fahrenheit. The same system piled over a foot of snow onto the roofs of Japan, causing many of them to collapse under the tremendous weight. As it continued across the Pacific Ocean, it even brought rare *blizzard* conditions to the slopes of the Mount Mauna Kea volcano in Hawaii! Tourists were nearly stranded when the sudden change in weather began. Park rangers said that while snow was common on the volcano, the conditions necessary to create blizzards are rare.[64]

In February of 2006, satellite imagery revealed that Greenland's ice cap was melting at *twice the rate it was five years ago!* Yet again, we see evidence that the process is accelerating much faster than anticipated by most scientists. Jim Hansen (the NASA climate scientist gagged by the Bush administration) warned that the "implications for rising sea levels—and climate change—could be dramatic."[65] Adding to the problem is that many species, such as polar bears, are quickly moving towards extinction as the caps melt and the climate changes.[66]

Additionally, it is widely known that the Sun and space weather play a major part in influencing our weather systems.[67] The problem is that even though our star is supposed to be at a solar minimum of an 11-year cycle, it has been behaving as if it is in a solar maximum. Incredibly powerful solar flares have bombarded the Earth (including an unprecedented X-class 40 in November 2003—for comparison, an X-17 is considered tremendously high), causing disruptions to electrical signals and satellites.[68]

According to scientists at the National Center for Atmospheric Research (NCAR), the next sunspot cycle will begin in late 2007 or 2008 (a year later than normal) with a 30–50% increase in intensity that will peak during 2012. The increase in solar storms has the potential to wreak havoc upon our modern electronics and other technology by crippling communications and causing widespread power blackouts.[69] Then, scientists at NASA predict that the following cycle will result in a period of extremely weak solar activity.[70]

The fluctuation between the increase and decrease in solar activity might then trigger another "Little Ice Age" similar to the one that coincided with the decrease in solar activity during the "Maunder Minimum" of approximately 1645–1715 CE.[71] Past data and research indicate that this kind of activity may be greatly contributing to the growing warmth of the planet and a future of more unstable weather. It certainly should make you stop and wonder exactly what the Maya knew about our Sun, especially since their calendar ends on December 21, 2012.

Arctic perennial sea ice has been decreasing at a rate of 9% per decade. The top image shows the minimum sea ice concentration for the year 1979, and the bottom image shows the minimum sea ice concentration in 2003. Images based on data collected by Defense Meteorological Satellite Program (DMSP) Special Sensor Microwave Imager (SSMI). *Credit: NASA*

Nevertheless, there is still time for us. There are some things that everyone can do to help reduce or delay the effects of global warming. Whitley Strieber has created a section on his website (www.unknowncountry.com) to track data, called the Superstorm Quickwatch, which roughly attempts to indicate the likelihood of severe storms resulting from an abrupt climate shift. For the last few years, he has also been encouraging everyone to follow the "Canada Challenge," first proposed by the Canadian Prime Minister. These small changes in lifestyle would greatly help to reduce the annual CO_2 emissions and cost virtually nothing to people or even businesses. The following table indicates approximately how much CO_2 emissions could be reduced by simply performing the following tasks:

Conservational Procedure	CO_2 Reductions (pounds/year)
Get an energy efficient fridge	3,000
Discard one less 30 gallon bag of garbage a week	300
Leave the car at home two days per week	1,590
Recycle	850
Switch two light bulbs to fluorescents	1,000
Get a low-flow shower head	2,000
Turn the thermostat down 2° in winter and up 2° during summer	300
Cut vehicle fuel use by 10 gallons	200
Switch to cold water for laundry	600
Clean or replace dirty filters on your furnace or air conditioner	350
Wrap your water heater in an insulation blanket	1,000

While doing the above may only contribute a small part to the solution, to ignore it and do nothing would be far worse. Even if you cannot do everything right now, start with just a few and work towards the rest. Encourage other people to do the same. Over time it *will* make a difference.

Heaven Help Us

Anyone spending time studying ancient myths of cultures from around the globe will undoubtedly begin to notice patterns emerging. Astute readers may have already noticed that the rapid climate change event that contributed to the death of Oetzi occurred approximately 5,200 years ago—placing it near the vicinity of the emerging Sumerian civilization. Their stories and myths recall great natural disasters, just like many other cultures. One of the most prevalent myths involves the destruction of all life in the world—sometimes even multiple times.

For example, Native American and Mesoamerican cultures recall how the world was destroyed four previous times and we are currently living in the fifth age, which will also come to an end. Typically, the destruction is said to have been because human beings grew decadent or became corrupted and the gods decided to destroy everything and start anew. Compare this to the Biblical story, which claims that humanity was so wicked that God sent the flood. However, we also now understand another reason for the flood myth, and that it was probably intended to explain why the Watchers were punished for their reckless behavior.

A brief survey of the flood myth shows that the Biblical account was certainly not the only one. For instance, the Sumerian account of a man named Ziusudra who built a boat to escape a flood is found in the *Eridu Genesis* and also a mention of *the* flood can be found in the *Sumerian King List*. The Babylonian *Epic of Gilgamesh* relates how the hero seeks out Utnapishtim, a man who was advised by the god Ea (Sumerian: Enki) to build a vessel that would protect him from the deluge. He was then turned into an immortal by the gods. The Greek counterpart says that Zeus destroyed the world with a flood, but the Titan Prometheus warned a man called Deucalion to build a chest to save himself and his wife. All other men perished except for some who escaped to the mountains. Additionally, India and China also relate tales of a devastating flood that wiped out all living things except for a few.[72]

There are many books that go into much greater detail about comparisons between these ancient stories that are worth looking into, so we will not do that here. Interested readers may refer to *Parallel Myths* by J.F. Bierlein (Ballantine Books, 1994), *Hamlet's Mill* by Giorgio De Santillana and Hertha Von Dechend, and the extensive studies by the master of myths, the late Joseph Campbell.

The most common thread connecting these so-called myths involve severe storms and a globally devastating flood that nearly wipes out all life on Earth. Even if some of these stories are truly nothing but myths—or real events that have been greatly exaggerated—then we are still left with a problem. There is a possibility that somewhere in mankind's distant past, there was an event so horrific that its fearful memory still remains in our psyche.

There is yet another common theme that is not always brought to attention. It concerns how some of the gods came to humanity's rescue and saved them from these disasters. After the world was destroyed, the gods taught humans how to rebuild society and passed along important knowledge. For instance, the Aztecs said that the gods had civilized their peoples and taught them how to build their immense temples. The Hopi offer accounts of how the wise kachina spirits rescued them and taught them to respect nature and the Creator. The first "dragon kings" of China that brought the empire to power were said to have come from the heavens. This has been one of the major problems for scholars and scientists studying many ancient cultures. They do not want to delve into the realm of myth to explain how these societies developed, and yet the ancients themselves said that they did not achieve these enormous feats alone.

For instance, let's look at the civilization of Sumer. They referred to themselves as "the black-headed people" (*sag-gi-ga*) and the land in which they lived was *ki-en-gir,* meaning "the place of the civilized lords." It is believed that they were invaders or migrants from another region, but archaeology has so far been unable to tell us the place of their origin. Among various theories, one speculation is that they were from what is now the bed of the Persian Gulf after it was flooded during the end of the last ice age. Interestingly enough, their language is considered to be isolated in linguistics because it apparently doesn't belong to any known family of languages. Scholars have tried for decades to find the origin of the language, but without success.[73]

Besides language, the people of Sumer are also accredited with many historical firsts, such as the first writing system, the wheel and potter's wheel, as well as the first civilized society and set of laws. They also were the first astronomers and conceptualized dividing the hour into sixty minutes and dividing a minute into sixty seconds. Probably the most important breakthrough was their development of agriculture and irrigation so that they could transform desolate lands into suitable places for living.[74]

After the Ice Age, these are the people who suddenly sprang up out of nowhere and had a fully developed society at a time when our ancestors were all still supposed to be milling about in the Stone Age. Until solid evidence surfaces and indicates precisely how the Sumerians were able to achieve these feats virtually overnight, is it so far-fetched to consider taking their word that they had help from an outside source?

However, this does present another problem.

If we are about to face another global climate catastrophe, we may need the help of the gods once again. But that means that some of these gods became involved in unsavory behavior and therefore the gateways were closed. Even if we are able to determine that there are extra dimensions with living beings in them, will we be able to access them? And if so, how do we know that our first attempt won't be our last if we essentially open the gate to Hell? Yes, it may sound like a cliché storyline from a sci-fi movie or video game, but it is a serious question worth asking. This is why we must be absolutely certain of what we are doing. To do nothing may initiate the eradication of nearly all life on Earth on account of severe climate shifts. But choosing what's behind door number two may unleash unspeakable horrors "from beyond" that are straight out of some twisted Lovecraftian vision of *The Price is Right*.

However, there are some promising experiments that may hold the key to our future. For centuries, many great minds have been preoccupied with alchemy and the dream of turning lead into gold. Now, one man may have finally rediscovered some of the forgotten knowledge of alchemy and how the properties of gold may finally unlock the secrets of hyper-dimensional physics.

Summary

❖ The world's leading climatologists are concerned that global warming is a major threat to the future of our planet and the survival of the human race.

❖ Computer models used by climatologists predict that as the atmosphere becomes warmer, the climate systems that regulate our weather will become dangerously unstable and unleash violent storms. Additionally, other geological disasters also appear to be increasing in both frequency and in intensity.

❖ Glacial melting is rapidly releasing large amounts of fresh water into the ocean, causing the Ocean Conveyer to falter. If the Conveyer stops completely, the climate may change rapidly and trigger a new ice age.

❖ Our current society will be stretched to a breaking point as severe climate changes affect all facets of life such as agriculture, habitation, the economy, and the threat of new diseases (especially insect-born diseases). We have already seen precursory examples of such calamities from the tsunami of 2004 and Hurricane Katrina in 2005.

❖ Each person can help to lessen the effects of these earth changes by making small adjustments to their daily routines that will reduce carbon dioxide and other greenhouse gas emissions.

❖ According to ancient legends, the human race was able to survive catastrophes like the "Great Flood" with the help of celestial intervention. However, we may not be able to enlist such help unless we discover how to recreate the gateways through which these beings were believed to have traveled.

FOLLOW THE YELLOW BRICK ROAD

A discovery is said to be an accident meeting a prepared mind.
—Albert Szent-Györgyi[1]

WE ARE ABOUT TO DELVE INTO SOME FINDINGS that, if true, are simply extraordinary. This is a key chapter for scientists seeking physical materials and methods of experimentation to determine the validity of hyper-dimensional physics. Please understand that some of the descriptions of scientific tools and experiments do seem to be at odds with conventional scientific teaching. However, this is partially the reason why this alternative research has gained so much attention and why it could be revolutionary.

Additionally, I do not have any experienced professional background in geology, metallurgy, or high-end electronics. I have tried to understand and explain the following concepts to the best of my abilities, but I do not pretend to understand all of the details completely. This means that there may be errors or misunderstandings in the descriptions of the data that are my fault, and not necessarily those of the people or institutions mentioned. It will be up to people experienced in these types of fields to fully explore and examine the claims to determine if they are authentic.

Also, please note that much of the information provided within this chapter is condensed and paraphrased from lectures delivered by David Hudson as well as the research of the British author Laurence Gardner. Gardner was one of the first people to bring the work of David Hudson and the possibilities of monatomic gold to the public's attention. There are many websites and resources devoted to the subject, but with varying levels of credibility. For this reason, I am relying mostly upon Mr. Gardner's published works for reference material, although there may be other sources available.

For the Love of Gold

There has been a fascination with gold since the beginning of recorded history—so much so that it continues to hold great importance to this day. But why is gold so important? There are certainly rarer and more precious metals, but gold has always held a strong appeal for many people. Perhaps one of the reasons is because of the *perceived* value it has been given by society. If enough people are told that it is highly important and of significant value then they are likely to eventually accept it.[2]

However, what if there is something more to it? After all, many of the ancient empires such as Sumer, Babylon, Persia, Egypt, Rome, Greece and the Inca all claimed that gold was important to the gods and to heavenly matters. They collected as much gold as they could and used it to create decorative items and furnishings. It was used for sacred temples, doors, walls, floors, statuettes, mirrors, and much more. Think back to all of the golden treasures that were discovered in the tomb of the boy-king Tutankhamen. Our ancestors apparently held a highly spiritual connection to gold at a time when their religions and sciences functioned as one.

The Inca believed that gold was the "sweat of the Sun," so nearly every inch of the walls within the Temple of the Sun were covered in gold. The goldsmiths had developed many wonderful techniques for creating gold alloys and gold plating as well. The legends of vast amounts of gold in the New World drove explorers on quests across great oceans. Such was the case in 1519 CE, when the Spanish conquistador Hernándo Cortés invaded the cities of the Aztecs to plunder their gold. Later, in 1531, Francisco Pizarro captured nearly eight tons of gold from the Inca in Peru. They looted so much gold that the only way to ship it back to Spain was to have all of the artifacts melted down.[3]

According to the World Gold Council, just over 125,000 tons of gold has been mined over the last six-thousand years. However, it is estimated that barely 10,000 tons of gold had been mined since ancient times until the beginning of the California gold rush in 1848. By this calculation, more than 90% of the world's gold has only been excavated during the last 157 years![4]

Today, gold is still in very high demand, not just for jewelry but also for use in electronics. Everything from wires to computer circuit boards, telephones, wristwatches, and other equipment rely on gold for its outstanding properties. Some of the most cutting-edge science is also harnessing the power of gold for use in emerging fields such as nanotechnology.

The Phoenix Rises

The city of Phoenix, Arizona was a fitting location for a discovery made in 1976 by a wealthy, third-generation cotton farmer named David Hudson. Self-described as "Mr. Material Man," Hudson farmed approximately 70,000 acres of land in the Yuma Valley, complete with a 15,000 square-foot home, forty employees, and a $4 million line of credit at the bank.[5]

Farming in Arizona faces a natural difficulty because "the soil suffers from a high sodium content, which causes the surface to be crunchy, black, and impenetrable by water." David Hudson dealt with this problem regularly and employed the use of tanker-trucks loaded with highly concentrated (93%) sulfuric acid, which was injected into the soil at thirty tons per acre. Irrigation trucks would then spray water (with calcium carbonate as a buffer for the acid to help preserve trace nutrients and not diminish crop growth) onto the acid, causing it to break down the alkaline crust into something more manageable. This process was part of a two-year program designed to make the soil suitable for planting crops.[6]

However, some of the elements in the soil were not dissolved by the sulfuric acid. Hudson found one material, a black precipitant, to be very peculiar. He then left the black precipitant out to dry in the hot Arizona sun (about 115° Fahrenheit at 5% humidity). Because he did not have a drying furnace or drying oven, he used a large porcelain funnel with filter paper on it to dry the black substance. However, when the material dried, it would flare into a great blaze of white light "like fifty thousand flash bulbs" and totally vanish from sight.[7]

Extremely intrigued by what had happened, Hudson set up a small experiment. Taking another sample of the material and once again putting it into the funnel, he took a brand new unsharpened pencil and stood it up next to the funnel. Once again, the material made a tremendous flash when it had fully dried, but amazingly, the pencil was still standing up (although slightly burned). This indicated that the flash was not an explosion or an implosion, but something else entirely.[8]

Tests were then performed to discover more about the mystery material. After being slowly dried away from the sun, it was melted down and mixed in a crucible with lead. This process, called "crucible reduction," determined that the substance was a very dense metal (like gold or silver) because it settled at the bottom of the lead instead of floating out of it.[9] According to Hudson, the mining community refers to this as "ghost gold," an unknown form of gold that is non-assayable (meaning it cannot be properly analyzed).[10] Another strange factor was that it would shatter like glass when hit with a hammer instead of being malleable like gold or silver, which can be hammered into very thin sheets.[11]

Analysis at a commercial laboratory showed that it was composed of iron, silica, and aluminum. However, all three will dissolve in sulfuric acid, nitric acid, or hydrochloric acid, but this material would not. An unnamed Ph.D. at Cornell University specializing in precious elements was hired and recommended that Hudson should have the material tested by a machine at the university that was capable of analysis down to 3-5 parts per billion.[12] The first set of tests once again revealed that it was made of iron, silica, and aluminum, but this time detected some very small impurities that had to be removed because they were affecting the analysis. After removing these impurities, 98% of the original sample remained. The second set of tests stunned everyone at the lab with what happened next. Even though the technicians could clearly see a glowing white bead in front of them, their machine was reporting that there was absolutely nothing there![13]

The results led to the hiring of an expert trained at West Germany's Institute for Spectroscopy, and who was working at a spectroscopic equipment manufacturer in Los Angeles as its senior technician.[14] In his book, Laurence Gardner explained the process used by the technician to test the sample:

> Arc Emission Spectroscopy involves placing a sample in a carbon electrode cup and another electrode is brought down above it to strike an arc. As the current flows, the elements in the sample ionize, giving off their individually specific light frequencies, which are then read to determine the analysis. After about 15 seconds at 5,500° centigrade [nearly the surface temperature of the sun], the carbon electrode burns away, so laboratories have to limit their tests to this burn time.[15]

The spectroscopist found that fifteen seconds of burn time was simply not enough to bring the material to its boiling temperature and so the results were limited and unsatisfactory.[16]

Yet another sample went to Harwell Laboratories of AEA Technology in Oxfordshire, England. This time, the sample would go for neutron activation analysis (NAA) as an alternative method to try to discover anything more about it.[17] NAA is a highly sensitive procedure for multi-element analysis of major, minor, and trace elements in samples from nearly all imaginable fields of interest for scientists and technicians. Because it is incredibly accurate and reliable, NAA is considered to be the "referee method of choice" during the development of new procedures or when conflicting results from other fields appear.[18] Unfortunately, not even Harwell Laboratories could obtain a suitable reading of the sample.[19]

Still undaunted, Hudson continued his research and found an answer from the Soviet Academy of Sciences. They explained that a spectroscopic burn-time of 300 seconds would be necessary—not 15 seconds. However, recall that the carbon electrode burns away after 15 seconds of such extreme temperatures. The Soviet Academy's solution was to sheathe the electrode with an inert gas, such as helium (He) or argon (Ar), to keep all of the oxygen away from the DC arc. This prevents the carbon electrode from oxidizing and falling apart.[20] Hudson finally had a viable method to test the sample once he had acquired the necessary equipment.

Using a new sample, the test was performed again and the first 15 seconds were as expected, reading: iron (Fe), silica (Si), and aluminum (Al), but also with small traces of calcium (Ca), sodium (He), and a hint of titanium (Ti). Also just like the Cornell University results from before, once the materials were boiled away and only the 98% sample remained, the machine registered it as "pure nothing"—but now the test could continue for much longer. For the next 75 seconds it still registered as nothing, until something amazing occurred at the 90-second mark. Suddenly, the material began registering "real" again as the element palladium (Pd). After 20 more seconds, it was platinum (Pt), and after each successive boiling temperature was reached (a process called "fractional vaporization") it became: ruthenium (Ru), rhodium (Rh), iridium (Ir), and osmium (Os) by 220 seconds. Ultimately, the tiny white bead that was previously "nothing," proved to be composed of platinum group metals.[21]

Further tests and experiments were conducted over the next two and a half years, headed by the German spectroscopist. The conclusion was that the samples consisted of noble metals, but in a form totally unrecognized by science at that time. To make matters even more interesting, it was determined that the soil from David Hudson's farmland contained up to an astounding 2,400 ounces per ton of absolutely pure platinum metals![22] Compare this to the richest known platinum group deposits located a half mile underground at the Bushveld Igneous Complex in South Africa. These deposits produce only one-third of one ounce per ton of ore of the precious metals.[23]

The breakdown for Hudson's soil samples for one ton of ore were: 6–8 ounces of palladium, 12–13 ounces of platinum, 150 ounces of osmium, 250 ounces of ruthenium, 600 ounces of iridium, and 1200 ounces of rhodium.[24] Traditionally, platinum group metals sell for extremely high prices. For example, Rhodium (which was the most plentiful in Hudson's soil), can sell at about $3,000 per ounce. However, Hudson's Rhodium was not in its normally recognizable metallic state.[25]

A Ph.D. from the U.S. Department of Energy's metallurgical school at Iowa State University, who also functioned as a consultant for Motorola and Sperry's wastewater problems in Arizona, was contacted. Over the next three years, he conducted his own tests that confirmed Hudson's findings. More research continued from 1983 through 1989 and included the full-time work of four master chemists and two technicians. Their work included cluster chemistry and the breaking of elemental bonding using very sophisticated computer equipment from Dow Chemical.[26] Unfortunately, none of the individuals involved are named in any of the documents or transcripts that I have managed to obtain.

Interestingly enough, David Hudson soon caught word that scientists at General Electric were conducting advanced research into fuel-cell technology using iridium and rhodium that bore some similarities to his own research. After Hudson made contact with the senior catalytic chemist and his team in Massachusetts, they affirmed that they had also witnessed the "white-light explosions." They were also having some difficulties with their analyses, and so Hudson was able to offer his expertise, eventually leading to a tentative deal between both parties. During this time, Hudson filed twenty-two worldwide patents for his discoveries, which he referred to as Orbitally Rearranged Monatomic Elements (ORMEs).[27]

In order to successfully file these patents, however, David Hudson was asked by the patent offices for more specific data relating to weights and measures. This required Hudson to obtain a machine used for thermogravimetric analysis, which would control all atmospheric conditions while simultaneously weighing the samples during the procedure. What they found during the tests was remarkable.[28]

The sample would be heated by 1.2° C per minute, and then cooled at 2° C per minute repeatedly. Metallurgists refer to this process as "annealing."

They found that oxidation of the sample (causing a loss of electrons) made it rise to 102% of its starting weight. Its weight was 103% after hydro-reduction (gain of electrons). This was expected, however.[29]

The situation did not become radically strange until the material was weighed after being transformed from its normal dull color into the white powder form through continued annealing. As the powder, it weighed only 56% of its starting weight and the remaining 44% seemingly vanished![30] They put the sample on a silica test boat and it still registered as only 56% of the starting weight. But if the material was heated to the point that it turned to a blackened glass, it returned to 100%. This meant that all of the original material was still there during the entire process, but for some reason it couldn't be weighed any more.[31] Repeated experiments revealed that the inexplicable results were not by a fluke or accident.

Next, the sample was repeatedly heated and cooled under inert gases (such as helium or argon) to measure the differences in weight. When it was cooled, it weighed between 300–400% of its beginning weight. Contrastingly, the heating process actually made the material weigh *less* than nothing! If that wasn't amazing enough, it transferred its apparent weightlessness to its surroundings by affecting the weight of the measuring pan. Removal of the substance would cause the weight of the pan to return to normal.[32]

Perplexed by these results, the scientists wanted to cancel out any magnetic fields that might be affecting the readouts. The wiring used by the heating element was bifilar-wound, meaning that the wires wrapped around in alternating directions to cancel out any magnetic fields created by electricity. To help further tests, they implemented a special material that becomes magnetic after reaching 300° and then loses its magnetism after reaching temperatures above 900°. When this magnetic material was run through with the sample, there was absolutely no response or weight change during the time that magnetism was gained or lost. But every time the sample was in its white powder form, it would once again read as 56% of its starting weight (and remain that weight even after the machine was turned off), less than nothing when heated, or up to 400% when cooled.[33]

Thinking that there might be a malfunction with the machine, Hudson contacted technicians who determined it to be in fine working order.[34] The only exception was when they used the white powder. After reviewing the notes provided by Hudson, they speculated that the white powder might be superconducting, but only if the weight loss occurred during the cooling process (which it was not). However, they were apparently unaware that in 1986 two scientists working at an IBM Research Laboratory in Zurich, Switzerland discovered that high-temperature superconductors were possible, instead of ones that needed stability by using liquid helium to provide very low temperatures.[35] However, it should be noted that these "high-temperature" superconductors still operate at very cold temperatures ($\leq$ -140° Celsius).

Normally, noble metals such as gold and silver are not supposed to have superconductive properties. However, Hudson explained his own research into superconductors and that they can apparently have a single frequency of light within them, but the light flows (like "liquid light") at the slower speed of sound. There is also a null magnetic field that is capable of repelling both North and South magnetic poles, but it is also able to produce more light by absorbing high magnetic energy. The magnetic field generated by the Earth is even enough to cause a superconductor to defy gravity and levitate. Hudson believed that the sample's "missing" weight was caused by this levitation. He also determined that the white powder was so incredibly white because it was excluding all external magnetic fields.[36] If it had been absorbing the fields, it would appear black.

Unlike standard conductivity, the concept behind a superconductor is that there is "a complete absence of electrical resistance and the damping of the interior magnetic field (the Meissner effect)."[37] When two external electrons are both tuned to the same frequency as that of the light contained in the superconductor, they can be conducted. Better yet, light is unique in that it can be perceived by our senses, but it does not reside in any physical space. In fact, an unlimited amount of light can occupy the same area of space and the result will be that it just keeps getting brighter and brighter. Superconductors then, have the ability to hold limitless amounts of energy that can be transferred across any distance by a quantum wave, and there is never any loss in energy.[38] As Hudson stated in one of his lectures:

> You literally start the superconductor flowing by applying a magnetic field. It responds to this by flowing light inside and building a bigger Meissner Field around it. You can put your magnet down and walk away. Come back a hundred years later and it is still flowing exactly as when you left. It will never slow down. There is absolutely no resistance; it is perpetual motion and will run for ever.[39]

Of course, these ideas could revolutionize all kinds of industry and energy use. If superconductive fuel-cells were perfected, it would solve many problems associated with our finite natural resources. However, it is only to be expected that many big companies, particularly those involved in the oil industry, do not want this to happen unless they can profit from it. Additionally, it would be a tremendous undertaking to convert all of our current technology in order to utilize something as radically different as a superconductive fuel-cell.

By 1989, David Hudson intended to build a far-reaching plant and enterprise focused on the potential of ORMEs. However, people with certain interests did not want to let this happen. All of Hudson's team members had signed confidentially agreements, but certain information was made known to the Department of Defense because his work involving superconductivity was "of strategic importance to this country." At this time, a mysterious sponsor contacted Hudson and was aware of specific details that no person outside of the team or DOD should have known. A private detective was hired and uncovered that this man was actually "a military official operating out of Langley Air Force Base, Virginia," whose job was to invest government money from a Swiss bank account into select partnerships that the DOD found promising. Upon learning this, Hudson declined the offer, but was then informed that his promising future into superconductivity would never move forward![40]

With millions of dollars already on the line, Hudson pushed ahead but began running into obstacles that were supposed to have already been worked out. For example, the company that had formally green lit the entire process thus far, the Legal & General Assurance Group, decided that they needed more research and documentation (including information that was protected by confidentially agreements). "At the same time, David was informed from government sources that the neutron diffraction studies (required to prove the superconductivity of his samples) would be tactically delayed for up to three years!" Not knowing who to trust (investors could have been secret government agents trying to steal secrets), David Hudson decided to fund the project himself and began giving a series of recorded lectures, therefore openly discussing and publishing certain information so that it would not be suppressed.[41]

New Insights and Challenges

A new face entered the scene at this point in Hudson's venture. It was Dr. Harold E. Puthoff, Director of the Institute for Advanced Studies in Austin, Texas. More commonly known as Dr. Hal Puthoff, he is a theoretical and experimental physicist that specializes in fundamental electrodynamics. "A graduate of Stanford University in 1967, he has published over thirty technical papers in the areas of electron-beam devices, lasers, and quantum zero-point energy effects."[42] Dr. Puthoff was also involved with the development of the Remote Viewing program, a joint endeavor between the Stanford Research Institute (which has been formally separated from the university since 1970) and the CIA, which ran from 1972 until 1995.

Hudson's work was able to confirm Puthoff's studies concerning zero-point energy and gravity. Puthoff's theoretical predictions stated that "when matter begins to react in two dimensions... it should theoretically lose around four-ninths of its gravitational weight." This was the precise amount of weight that the white powder was losing during the tests. This led Puthoff to believe that since gravity determines space-time, then the "missing" weight of the powder was actually resonating in a different dimension! Puthoff further theorized that when such a material is in this other dimension, that it should become invisible.[43]

To determine if this was indeed the case, the researchers attempted to move and scoop the substance with spatulas during the time that it seemed to disappear (recall the bright flashes of light in the desert). The idea was that if it were truly "invisible," the spatula would still be able to move it around the pan. However, when the material finally became visible again, it was in the *exact* same position and shape as it had last been seen. This seemed to confirm that the substance had been temporarily shifted into another dimension. Dr. Puthoff compared this to a hypothetical example of a stealth aircraft that doesn't show up on radar versus one that actually phases into and out of another dimension.[44]

Unexpectedly, the early 1990s began to show considerable interest into "stealth atoms" and superconductivity that were suspiciously similar to David Hudson's research. "The Niels Bohr Institute, University of Copenhagen, the USA Department of Energy's Argonne National Laboratories, Chicago, and their Oak Ridge National Laboratory in Tennessee all confirmed that the elements which had been filed in the Hudson patents existed in the monatomic high spin state." Except, instead of being referred to as Orbitally Rearranged Monatomic Elements, the scientific terminology for this phenomenon was "Asymmetrical Deformed High-spin Nuclei." Because these high-spin atoms are able to transfer energy between each other with no measurable net loss of energy, they are classified as superconductors.[45]

Articles in scientific journals such as *Classical and Quantum Gravity*[46] and *American Scientist*[47] were published that dealt with the manipulation of space-time. Scientists were now openly stating that "exotic matter" would allow the local expansion and contraction of space around a spacecraft to allow faster than light speed travel, effectively making the science fiction "warp drive" a reality. This does not violate Einstein's theory concerning faster than light travel, because the warping of space-time would create enormous theoretical acceleration speeds, but the craft would actually be stationary the whole time.[48]

Returning again to Hudson's work with high-spin gold, Argonne National Laboratories was brought in to "prove the procedure by making the white powder from a starting base of pure yellow-gold material," which also required a signed affidavit by the Patent Office. Argonne's head of ceramics and superconductivity directed David to a metallurgical chemist [Mike McNallen] that then produced the white powder from pure gold by following Hudson's specifications. Analysis showed the material to be composed of iron, silica, and aluminum, just like before. "When signing the required affidavit, the chemist made specific mention of the fact that (despite any further tests that might be conducted), he positively guaranteed the material to be 100% gold" from his own laboratory.[49]

Hudson was then asked to completely reverse the process and convert the powder back into solid gold. The task was likened to "asking someone to remake an apple from a pan of apple sauce." The early attempts were unsuccessful and many very expensive tungsten electrodes, which are supposed to last several minutes, were "burning away in less than a second." Matters grew even worse, though, when "short wavelength gamma radiation was produced," fragmenting laboratory equipment and causing bubbles to appear within glass beakers, even causing them fall apart when touched. However, by late 1995, David Hudson had successfully reformed a solid ingot from the white powder that registered as pure gold.[50]

By 1995, Hudson had spent approximately $8.7 million of his own money to pursue the ORMEs investigations. In order to build the processing plant, he established ORMEs L.L.C., and raised money through

Science of the Spirit Foundation *Newsletter* subscriptions detailing the progress and research of the project.[51]

A building site was soon acquired, all necessary construction permissions granted, and $2.5 million raised through the subscriptions to pay for the project. Everything was moving forward smoothly, and in November 1996, ORMEs L.L.C. even announced that it would also include research and work into metal catalysts, metalo-ceramics, as well as supply precious metals developed for commercial applications.[52]

However, problems seemed to begin appearing, but not because of "Murphy's Law." Even though the plant's electrical power had been formally approved, the county inspector cited a "zoning" problem that was expected to take many months to fully resolve. A notice was received claiming that the plant could not be finished until it fit under an existing classification, stating: "No one is doing anything similar to what this plant will be doing, and it will not fit into any of the Government categories."[53] Hudson did not want to classify his work as either "drugs" or "fuels" and chose to wait out the remaining months using an independently installed generator until he could finally be connected to the power grid.[54]

Tragically, in June of 1998, an accident caused 4,500 gallons of nitric acid to leak into a secondary containment facility. "When the emergency services team arrived, they sprayed foam onto the acid instead of simply diluting it with water, as a result of which a red gas cloud lit up the sky." The Department of Environmental Quality (DEQ), the Occupational Safety and Health Administration (OSHA) and the Environmental Protection Agency (EPA) all soon arrived to investigate the mess. The DEQ tests determined that there was no toxic residue, and the spillage was completely internal and contained, so it should not have been a major problem.[55]

However, the EPA soon ordered all chemical equipment to be disassembled and removed immediately from the property. When Hudson said that their demand was extensive and would take a few months for him to fully comply, they dropped their offer and promptly fined Hudson $103,800. They also threatened that if he did not pay the fine, it would immediately jump to $250,000 and cost even more money in a long courtroom battle. Additionally, Hudson was in poor health at this time after suffering a heart attack, which necessitated major bypass surgery. More stress in his life was not a good thing. Another major problem was that even though his building had been approved a few years earlier, the residential area was allowed to grow considerably and many homes were located in close proximity to the ORMEs plant. Hudson wrote that he felt the best option, and practically only one remaining, was to sell the land (which was now worth more because of the developed residential area). He offered to use this money to reimburse donations from subscribers that wanted their money back. By November 2000, the project was over and Hudson considered himself to be "regulated out of existence."[56]

If all of the claims are true, then this is indeed very disappointing to know that such a pioneering effort was quashed. However, this is where the scientific community can help. Certainly, some scientists should have the required knowledge and expertise to test the claims of David Hudson and determine the validity of his experiments. Reporters and other investigators should look into the details of these events to help substantiate them (or disprove them). If enough people know about this technology and make a concerted effort to study it, there is no way it can quietly disappear or be monopolized by larger corporate interests. It is a technology that is meant for everyone, not just a few. These experiments may hold the key to unlocking anti-gravity and levitation, manipulation of the space-time fabric, and even access to previously unknown dimensions.

There are still some pieces left to the puzzle, though. If David Hudson's monatomic gold is related to the "Philosophers' Stone" of alchemy lore, we must study it from that angle for a better understanding. Alchemists often communicated through symbolism to shield their secrets from the eyes of the uninitiated. But since the history of alchemy has existed for thousands of years, many of these symbols have been concealed in places that most people never thought to look. We must now decode the meaning of how to "Square the Circle."

Summary

❖ Far from being only economically valuable, gold was held in a nearly mystical reverence by cultures throughout the ancient world. It was their most precious element and they believed that it was closely associated with the gods and heaven.

❖ In 1976, a wealthy Arizona farmer by the name of David Hudson accidentally discovered a substance in his soil that possessed unusual properties, such as vanishing in a bright flash of light when left out to dry under the hot sun.

❖ The substance from Hudson's soil was determined to be composed primarily of platinum group metals, but it was in a "high-spin" state that made it unrecognizable. Hudson referred to these new substances as Orbitally Rearranged Monatomic Elements (ORME).

❖ Further tests that were performed on the ORME revealed that it had the ability to disappear and to levitate by "losing" some of its mass. This "missing" weight suggested that the substance might actually be shifting into another dimension.

❖ After suffering many setbacks, Hudson was forced to discontinue his research into monatomic elements. However, some scientists and laboratories may be able to pick up where he left off and continue his work so that we can harness the powers of this mysterious substance.

SQUARING THE CIRCLE

After this I looked, and there in heaven a door stood open! And the first voice, which I had heard speaking to me like a trumpet, said, "Come up here, and I will show you what must take place after this." At once I was in the Spirit...

Revelation 4:1–2 NRSV

WE HAVE ALMOST REACHED THE CONCLUSION of our investigation. After assessing the amazing properties of gold particles and how this might relate to future explorations in quantum physics, it will prove beneficial to return once more to ancient legends concerning the true purpose of alchemy. The symbolism associated with the alchemical process has been prevalent throughout ancient myths and religious texts for thousands of years. Most of these symbols, however, have gone largely unnoticed because they are not unlike the pieces of a puzzle—the image only becomes complete when every piece is placed in its proper location. Many people have attempted to understand these pieces on their own—and some have come admirably close to realizing the ultimate goal—however, without having viewed these pieces in their proper context, the ideas have become distorted or missed their mark.

The Philosophers' Stone[1]

Most of the ancient "sciences" centered around astrology and alchemy. The term "alchemy" is derived from the native name for Egypt, *Khem,* plus the Arabic reference to the country: *al-khame* (the blackness). Clues and hidden references were embedded in many of the legends and myths that were passed down by those few people still versed in the lost arts, but the meanings have become obscured with time. There was a revival of interest in the alchemical arts during the Middle Ages, but this was also a time of

271

great misunderstanding. Practically no idea was too foolish as numerous individuals sought to discover the elusive method of transmuting lead into precious gold. Meanwhile, this created an atmosphere that allowed many gullible people to be preyed upon by money-hungry charlatans. This dangerous combination led to a great deal of faulty and contradictory information that was spread throughout Europe.[2]

The Paradise Stone was also known as the Philosophers' Stone, and it was believed to be the missing link that could activate the transformation process of alchemy. As might be expected, however, the exact details of what the real Philosophers' Stone was have remained undiscovered. Over the centuries, many philosophers have suggested that the legend of the *Golden Fleece* (sought after by Jason and the Argonauts) offered clues concerning how the Philosophers' Stone might be obtained. Some of the notable researchers that came to this conclusion were the 16th century German philosopher Salomon Trismosian, the French philosopher Fulcanelli, and more recently, the Swiss psychiatrist Carl Gustav Jung in his book *Psychology and Alchemy*.[3]

The alchemist unites the duality of male and female principles by squaring the circle.
M. Maier, *Atalanta*, 1618.

The seventeenth-century British alchemist Eirenaeus Philalethes, a man revered highly by other fellow alchemists such as Isaac Newton, Robert Boyle, and Elias Ashmole (to name just a few), proposed an intriguing possibility concerning the nature of the Philosophers' Stone. In 1668, Philalethes stated: "Our Stone is nothing but gold digested to the highest degree of purity and subtle fixation… it is fixed and incombustible like a stone, but its appearance is that of a very fine powder."[4]

The above description would seem to indicate a connection to the powder of monatomic gold that was rediscovered by David Hudson in the 1970s. But we still need more evidence to reach a convincing conclusion that monatomic gold is what the ancient sages referred to in their writings.

A Discovery in the Desert[5]

In March of 1904, the British archaeologist Sir W.M. Flinders Petrie and his team were on an expedition in the Sinai desert peninsula to survey old copper and turquoise mining regions in that area. Part of their expedition involved what was believed to be the Mount of Moses, which ascends over 2,600 feet over the Plain of Paran. After the team had climbed to the top of the mountain, they were astonished to discover the ruins of an old Egyptian temple on the sandstone plateau, approximately 230 feet in length that extended from a great man-made cave. Inscriptions at the site gave an approximate date of 2600 BCE, during the reign of the 4th-dynasty pharaoh, Sneferu.[6]

The items discovered by Petrie's team were removed from the site and taken to museums while others found their way into personal collections. Unfortunately, many of the items from the excavation were hidden away and remained unavailable to the public. The suggested reason for Petrie's secrecy was because the Egypt Exploration Fund (now known as the Egypt Exploration Society) was funding his expedition and he knew that the find violated their policies. The group stated in their 1891 *Memorandum and Articles of Association* that their objective was the "promotion of surveys and excavations for the purpose of elucidating or illustrating the Old Testament narrative."[7]

Within the cave, which was dedicated to the goddess Hathor, the team members found many statues and stelae dedicated to various pharaohs that had reigned throughout the time that the temple was in operation. The flat inner walls were cut deep into the natural cave rock and then carefully smoothed. In the outside temple courts and halls were found many round tables, trays, alabaster vases and cups, glazed plaques, cartouches, scarab ornaments, baskets and some conical stones. Probably the most enigmatic of items discovered here were a metallurgist's crucible as well as a "considerable amount of pure white powder concealed beneath carefully laid flagstones."[8]

At this point in history, Petrie and his team did not know what this mysterious white powder was or what its purpose might have been. Unfortunately, we cannot test the material because it was apparently blown away by the wind after Petrie's men had uncovered it. However, based on some other clues, we can speculate that this powder may have been the monatomic white powder gold.

Laurence Gardner has explained in his books, *Genesis of the Grail Kings* and *Lost Secrets of the Sacred Ark,* that Egyptologists debated over why crucibles were needed at what was thought to be a religious temple. The likely answer is that the temple was probably not only used for religious ceremonies, but also functioned as a workshop for important rituals. The Egyptologists were also attempting to understand references to a mysterious substance identified as *mfkzt* (thought to be pronounced "muf-kuzt"). According to Gardner, Petrie had discovered numerous references to this substance in wall inscriptions and stelae.[9]

It was eventually determined that *mfkzt* was not any typical stone or metal such as turquoise, malachite, or copper. Yet references to it indicate that it was an extremely valuable "stone" of some sort, although it was considered to be somewhat unstable in nature. Additionally, there were numerous references in the temple inscriptions to "bread" as well as the traditional hieroglyph for "light" ⊙.[10]

The best clues for describing *mfkzt* derive from what are known as the *Pyramid Texts*—sacred texts dating back to the 5th-dynasty, which decorated the tomb walls of King Unas at Saqqara. These texts were meant to provide a detailed account of how the King could be resurrected into the Afterlife. Within the texts, it is said that the pharaoh will be resurrected in order to join the gods at a place identified as the *Field of Mfkzt.* This "field" is believed to pertain to some kind of heavenly dimension.[11]

Gardner once again directs our attention to a pair of important round-topped stelae that were found at the temple. They are apparently from the 18th-dynasty reigns of Tuthmosis III and Amenhotep III. The first depicts the pharaoh Tuthmosis presenting what appears to be a conical loaf to the patron god Amun-re, and is inscribed: "The presenting of a white bread that he may be given life." The other stele portrays the pharaoh Amenhotep offering a similar loaf to the god Sopdu, with the inscription: "He gave the gold of reward; the mouths rejoiced." Based upon these examples and many other similar images depicting the presentation of conical objects, it is reasonable to assume that the Egyptians believed this substance provided a life force and was made from gold.[12]

In what is commonly known as the *Egyptian Book of the Dead* (or more accurately, the *Book of Going Forth by Light/Day*),[13] the deceased must answer a series of questions at each stop along their journey in the afterlife. As we read the following passage, we can see a reference to heavenly food in relation to a mysterious gateway:

> I arrive at the Island of the Horizon-dwellers, I go out from the holy gate. *What is it?* It is the Field of Reeds [Paradise], which produced the provisions [food] for the gods who are round about the shrine. As for that holy gate, it is the gate of the Supports of Shu [the god who separated the earth from the sky]. *Otherwise said:* It is the gate of the Duat [underworld]. *Otherwise said:* It is the door through which my father Atum passed when he proceeded to the eastern horizon of the sky.
>
> Chapter 17: Plate 8
Dr. Raymond Faulkner Translation[14]

Could this reference to the food "for the gods" be the same as the "bread of life" mentioned above? The passage indicates that this special food originated in the "Field of Reeds," which scholars identify as "Paradise" or "heaven." Additionally, the phrase "What is it?" is asked many times throughout the journey. This question reveals a very important parallel to a significant Old Testament figure.

As many readers will recall, Moses was said to have been raised as royalty in the kingdom of Egypt. He would have grown up learning the arts and crafts of Egypt, and there are obvious allusions to Moses' Egyptian upbringing expressed throughout the Old Testament. While the actual historical account seems doubtful, the figure of Moses was probably based closely upon, or at least associated with, the Pharaoh Akhenaton. This is supported by evidence presented in books by such authors as Ahmed Osman, Ralph Ellis, and even Sigmund Freud. However, the identification of this Biblical patriarch is not our concern here—rather, it is the influence of Egyptian culture on the Hebrew texts and the underlying message within it.

After fleeing from Egypt, the book of Exodus states that Moses was instructed to tell the wandering people that God would perform a miracle and rain "bread from heaven" for them to eat (16:4). After the layer of morning dew lifted the next day, the people found a very fine and flaky substance covering the ground that was like frost. Having no idea what this mystery substance was, they asked, "What is it?" (16:14–15). The Hebrew term for "what is it?" is *manna* (מן). Further description compares it to a "coriander seed" and says that it was "white" and tasted "like wafers made with honey" (16:31).

There is another curious incident that occurs later in Chapter 32 of the book of Exodus that goes largely unnoticed. While Moses was on the mountain with God, the Israelites grew restless and collected all of their gold items in order to construct the infamous golden calf.[15] On the surface, this seems to be a story specifically addressing God's disapproval of idolatry, but careful examination reveals that the story yields a much deeper meaning. Upon coming down from the mountain and witnessing the reveling, Moses smashes the original tablets given to him by God and then he "took the calf that they had made, <u>burned it with fire</u>, <u>ground it to powder</u>, <u>scattered it on the water</u>, and <u>made the Israelites drink it</u>" (32:19–20).

Scholars that have noticed this passage have often found it to be incredibly troubling. Why does it say that Moses burned the gold with fire and turned it into a powder? Applying extreme heat should produce molten gold—not powder. This becomes increasingly bizarre when we are told that the Israelites were forced to drink it. When put into context with the properties of the white monatomic gold powder, however, this passage appears to make a great deal more sense.

There are only a few minor references to manna throughout the rest of the Bible. In Numbers 11:17, the manna's color is compared to an unknown substance called *bdellium*. The exact nature of this material is unclear. Some scholars believe it is a gum resin while others think it pertains to some precious stone. There is only one other mention of bdellium in the Bible, and it currently seems to favor the precious stone concept. This other reference to bdellium connects it to the land of Havilah, a part of Eden. The association of gold to manna, and manna to bdellium, can be found in the passage stating that in Havilah, "there is gold; and the gold of that land is good; bdellium and onyx stone are there" (Genesis 2:11–12).

What does gold have to do with a white-powder called "manna?" Furthermore, what does manna have to do with "precious stones" and the

Garden of Eden? Why are the ancient scribes trying to guide us back to such obscure passages? None of this seems to make any sense—unless they are clues for solving a much larger puzzle.

Symbols of Heaven

For centuries, Biblical scholars have debated about the precise location of the mysterious "Garden of Eden." The problem is that everyone has attempted to use the written description as a literal "map" of Eden's features and general location. However, it is soon discovered that several of the named geographic features do not make sense, and are sometimes counterintuitive. For example, Eden is described as being "in the east," yet there is no reference point provided to determine where to begin the search. It is also supposed to contain a single river that splits into four branches as it leaves the garden—a feature that is most unusual. Additionally, two of the rivers named are the Pishon and the Gihon, but there are no records of these rivers in *any* of the ancient chronicles. The third river named is Hiddekel (a.k.a. "Tigris"), but it is incorrectly described as flowing "east" of Assyria (it actually runs through the *middle* of ancient Assyria). Finally, there is no further description for the fourth river other than naming it the Euphrates. All of these problems can be solved, however, if we analyze the names and features of Eden using symbolism.

We shall begin with the description of the garden itself. Genesis states that the garden housing the Tree of Life and the Tree of Knowledge was located on the eastern side of Eden (2:8–9). A river flows into this garden and then splits into four branches. The numerical symbolism of four is often used to denote something of the earth or the earth itself. For example, the "four corners" of the earth implies the four cardinal directions and is a way of saying "all of the earth." This is also why the square and the equilateral cross are considered to be symbols for the Earth, since they emphasize the "fixed" state of the physical realm.[16]

Genesis 2:11 identifies the first branch of the river as *Pishon,* which flows around the land of Havilah that was discussed above. *Havilah* (חוילה) is of interest not just because of its association with gold, but because it means "circle." The circle is often used as a symbol for the heavenly realm and the spirit because a circle has no straight sides and neither a beginning nor an end. Therefore, the heavens are thought to be limitless.[17] So far, we have the symbols of a cross and/or square, a circle, and gold all found together.

The next river branch is called *Gihon* and it flows around the land of Cush, which is now known as Ethiopia (Genesis 2:13). Like Egypt, the country of Ethiopia has had a long history with the Jewish people, such as the tales concerning King Solomon, for example. The name *Cush* (כוש) means "blackness" and has significant alchemical meaning. As discussed earlier, because alchemy is thought to have been born in Egypt (Khem), this lost science was referred to in the Arabic language as *al-khame,* meaning "the blackness." It was reasoned that the blackness was something to overcome by gaining the knowledge of supreme enlightenment.[18] Since there are other words in Hebrew that also mean "black" or "blackness," one is left to ponder if Cush was specifically chosen *to hide the clue within the name of a geographic location.*

The third river is named *Hiddekel,* but is more commonly known as the Tigris, and we are told that it flows east of Assyria.[19] The significance of *Assyria* (אששור) is that it means "a step," and this could be referring to climbing the stairs of the ziggurats, which were believed to lead to the heavens. This is further supported because the fourth river is named the *Euphrates* (פרת) in Genesis 2:14, meaning "fruitfulness," and might be pertaining to the fruits of the trees in the Garden of Eden. It would seem that the authors of Genesis were encoding the description of Eden with alchemical symbols that point to the region between the Tigris and Euphrates Rivers. This is now part of present day Iraq of course, but was once home to Babylon.

Additional descriptive details of the Garden of Eden may also contain veiled references to alchemy and ascension. The starting location in Mesopotamia is associated with the "steps" or ladder that rises to heaven. By overcoming "the blackness" one is able to successfully merge the "circle" of heaven with the earthly "square" that ultimately leads to the Tree of Life in the Garden of Eden.

Further symbolism may be embedded within the names of various locations appearing throughout the New Testament. We are told that Jesus was born in Bethlehem of Judea so as to fulfill prophecy (Matthew 2:1). However, Biblical scholars have engaged in seemingly endless debates over the details associated with Jesus' birth. Much of this debate is fueled by inaccuracies and even contradictions within the Biblical texts themselves. However, many of these issues can be resolved if the story is interpreted symbolically rather than literally.

In earlier chapters, we have already examined the symbolism of the eastern star and its association with Venus and the pentagram, as well as the role of

Virgo (the virgin) and its opposing position to Pisces (the fish) on the zodiac wheel. An additional symbol becomes of interest when we examine the name *Bethlehem* (Hebrew: בית לחם and Greek: Βηθλέεμ), which means "House of Bread." It is quite possible, if not probable, that given all of the symbolism embedded within the ancient texts, that setting the location of Jesus' birth at Bethlehem was no accident. It isn't even necessarily for the purpose of fulfilling prophecy as many have long believed. The symbolism of Bethlehem directly connects Jesus to the "heavenly bread," or sacred manna.

Evidence of this can be found in the Gospel of John. After the story of the feeding of the five-thousand, the people go looking for Jesus and he tells them not to search for normal bread like they had eaten the day before, but to seek the "true bread of heaven" that "gives life to the world" (6:25–34). If there is any doubt, he then directly states: "I am the bread of life," and continues with an allegory of how belief in him is the true manna of immortality and that the faithful will be "raised" on the "last day" (6:35–40).[20]

However, many Christians will be surprised to find that what they have been taught to believe in regard to the resurrection and the rapture might not be in accordance with the messages embedded within Biblical texts.

The Rapture: Let's Not Get Carried Away

Christians around the world currently believe in an idea referred to as the "rapture"—a time when God's most faithful believers will ascend to heaven and join Jesus Christ, leaving everyone else behind on the (doomed) planet Earth. Christians look forward to this event with enthusiasm because they believe that they are truly God's chosen people. Furthermore, they believe that they will be spared from the suffering and torment that will occur during the Great Tribulation, the point at which the Antichrist obtains power over the world.

Unfortunately, many Christians that believe in the rapture are going to be sorely disappointed and some will be viciously opposed to the information which I am about to present. It is not my intention to be disrespectful or dismissive of anyone's beliefs, nor do I wish to foster any animosity between people. I simply wish to present factual and unbiased information that I have discovered in the process of my research. Readers are encouraged to make up their own minds after evaluating *all* of the evidence presented in this book (as well as the research presented by others) in an objective and fair manner. Some readers may still disagree with my views regarding this matter, but that is okay. However, if that is the case, I must ask whether the disagreement is because of a fault with my analysis, or because it is not what they *want* to believe? Shortly, I shall address specific Biblical passages that are used to support the idea of the rapture, but first, it is important to examine how this belief became predominant in contemporary society.

The general popularization of the rapture began with the teachings of the British evangelist Joseph Nelson Darby (1800–1882). Prior to the nineteenth-century, the concept of the rapture was unknown to Christians. However, there is some speculation that Darby is not the one who originated the idea. Instead, some researchers argue that the modern concept of the rapture is based upon the alleged vision of a fifteen-year-old Scottish girl named Margaret MacDonald.[21]

Margaret claimed that God granted her a vision of faithful believers ascending into the sky and meeting Jesus in the clouds, which she promptly wrote down and sent in a letter to the London preacher Edward Irving. Shortly after, Irving's church released the first known public acknowledgement of the rapture in an article written for the September 1830 issue of their periodical, *The Morning Watch*. The ideas were then picked up by Darby and incorporated into his sermons. Miss MacDonald also claimed that she received additional information from God, but apparently the messages must not have come through too clearly since she incorrectly predicted that the nineteenth-century socialist Robert Owen was none other than the Antichrist.[22]

Over a century later, Hal Lindsey's mega-bestseller *The Late Great Planet Earth* (Zondervan, 1970) exploded onto the scene to the delight of Biblical prophecy enthusiasts everywhere. Lindsey pointed to so-called "predictions" that Israel would be reborn and that wars would rage throughout the Middle East. As well, he warned of the reemergence of Satanism and witchcraft and prophesized the approach of the rapture.[23]

Shortly after the publication of Lindsey's book, many Christian audiences became engrossed with the 1972 film, *A Thief in the Night,* which frightened many people and led them back to church. It borrowed several ideas directly from Lindsey's book as well as those of cartoonist and Christian fundamentalist Jack Chick. The film was followed by three sequels: *A Distant Thunder* (1978), *Image of the Beast* (1980), and finally *The Prodigal Planet* (1983). The films take place as the Book of Revelation unfolds, chronicling the lives of those "left behind" in a world ruled by the Antichrist. The films had quite an effect upon many people, and the third film, *Image of the*

Beast, is considered the best and perhaps most terrifying to those who have seen it. However, the films are quite dated, with some rather stilted acting and obviously much lower budgets when compared to most modern films.

On the heels of Lindsey's book appeared Edgar C. Whisenant's *88 Reasons Why the Rapture is in 1988,* which predicted that the rapture would occur sometime during the Jewish New Year of Rosh-Hashanah, beginning at sunset on September 11 until the 13. When that didn't happen, he revised his calculations to 10:55 a.m. on September 15 of that same year. After that date passed, he revised again for the new date of October 3. When asked by *Christianity Today* why the rapture had not yet occurred, he responded: "The evidence is all over the place that it is going to be in a few weeks anyway." And still after a few more weeks had passed and nothing happened he claimed to have made an error in calculation due to the Gregorian calendar, and so he revised yet again and published *The Final Shout – Rapture Report 1989.* Then it became *The Final Shout – Rapture Report 1990…* then *1991, 1992, 1993* and on and on.[24]

We're all still here.

Millions of believers grew anxious and upset that their expected rapture wasn't happening and interest in the subject began to wane. Then in 1995, the first in a series of books exploded onto bestseller lists: *Left Behind* by Tim LaHaye and Jerry B. Jenkins (Tyndale House Publishers). The *Left Behind* books emerged just at the right time for everyone to be "caught up" in yet another sensational frenzy; and this time, LaHaye and Jenkins had the tremendous marketing power of the mass media, which enabled their products to reach an even broader demographic.

The *Left Behind* series received a great deal of media coverage and exposure. As of this writing, the series has spawned twelve books and three prequels (with a final novel in the original series still on the way); a similar series geared towards children, graphic novels, music CDs, video games, and audio dramatizations for Christian radio have also been produced. There have even been other miscellaneous items spun off from the series, such as bumper stickers that read: "In case of the Rapture, this car will be unmanned." Additionally, the first two books have been made into motion pictures (with limited theatrical release) but fell somewhat short of what many fans were expecting.

Now, over ten years later, we are still hearing about how wonderful the rapture is going to be and that it is just around the corner. Thousands of websites, such as *Rapture Ready* (www.raptureme.com), provide information and updates about the approach of the rapture and what people should expect. There are even online letter services designed to explain to all non-believers via email why millions of their friends and family around the world have suddenly vanished after the rapture has occurred![25] As a result of the *Left Behind* series' success, this idea has remained fresh in people's minds—not to mention because other influential Evangelical figures such as Pat Robertson, Jack Van Impe, Hal Lindsey, Grant Jeffrey, and Thomas Ice have all endorsed the possibility of an impending rapture. According to these men, the rapture is an established Biblical doctrine that cannot be refuted. However, closer inspection of Biblical texts suggests otherwise.

The general concept of the rapture primarily derives from Paul's First Letter to the Thessalonians:

> For the Lord himself, with a cry of command, with the archangel's call and with the sound of God's trumpet, will descend from heaven, and <u>the dead in Christ will rise first. Then we who are alive, who are left, will be caught up in the clouds</u>[26] <u>together with them to meet the Lord in the air</u>; and so we will be with the Lord forever.
>
> 1 Thessalonians 4:16–17 NRSV

The phrase "caught up" in the above verses is the Greek term *harpazo* (ἁρπάζω), which was translated into Latin as "rapere," to later become "rapture." The actual meaning of the word is to "seize, grab, or snatch away." However, the above verses complicate contemporary notions of the rapture.

These issues are tackled by John Noe, Ph.D., who argues that the original meaning of harpazo did not infer "up," but rather "taken away." Now, the verse does say "in the clouds," which certainly would seem to indicate that a person would ascend into the sky. However, the key problem is in the language used. In Greek, there are two different words that mean "air." The first is the word *ouranos* (οὐρανός), which is meant to describe very high elevations and higher atmospheres such as where birds fly. It is also used to describe the heavens and the universe. But that is not the word used in the above verse. It is the other Greek term *aer* (ἀήρ), pronounced, ah-air, which refers to the air in the lowest part of the atmosphere. It is the air that we breathe every day and Paul even refers to it when he mentions that he does not box "as though beating the <u>air</u>" (1 Corinthians 9:26), meaning that he is not in battle against an imagined adversary.[27]

Perhaps the most detrimental flaw in regard to the rapture is the idea of immanency. For example, many believers claim that the rapture is *imminent,* meaning that it could happen at any given moment. Therefore, they encourage people to prepare in advance for the event by "getting right with God" so that they won't be "left behind." Unfortunately, there are some people that capitalize upon the uncertainty of the rapture in order to manipulate and persuade others to adopt their own system of beliefs.

For an event to be considered imminent, every sequence of events before it must have already occurred—only the next item in the list can be considered "imminent." To explain this in everyday terms, imagine that you are boiling a pot of water. The events would consist of:

1. Pouring water into the pot
2. Placing the pot on the stove
3. Turning the heat setting of the stove to high
4. The water will begin to boil when it reaches 212° F (100° C)[28]

You cannot expect the water to boil if the requirements of the first three steps have not been met. If the water is in the pot, but sitting next to the hot stove, the water will not boil. It is only after the first three steps have occurred that the boiling of the water can be considered imminent. During the last step, you may not know the exact second that it will reach the boiling point (unless you have more data about specific influences factored into calculations), but you can reasonably estimate when it will occur.

So what is the reason for this comparison? It is because the New Testament writers stated that the resurrection event was imminent *at the time of their writing*. So if they expected it to occur then, it means that the event has been imminent for almost 2000 years! That is certainly a long time to wait for something that is supposed to be *next* on the prophetic calendar. Just try to imagine waiting over 1900 years for a working clock to finally change from 11:59 p.m. to 12:00 a.m!

Also, consider how key supporters of the rapture doctrine, like Thomas Ice, often omit specific verses from their sermons, such when Jesus proclaimed, "Truly I tell you, there are some standing here who will not taste death before they see the Son of Man coming in his kingdom" (Matthew 16:28). Or consider when Paul writes to his fellow Christians: "We will not all die," (1 Corinthians 15:51) or "For this we declare to you by the word of

the Lord, that <u>we who are alive, who are left until the coming of the Lord</u>…,"
and "Then we <u>who are alive, who are left</u>, will be caught up in the clouds
together…" (1 Thessalonians 4:15, 17).

These statements were addressed to audiences alive during Biblical times,
not readers two-thousand years removed in the future. Certainly, the people
to whom Paul was preaching have passed away, however, it is safe to say that
they did not experience their promised rapture. When modern supporters
actually use these verses without omitting sections of the texts, they often
twist the meanings in such a manner that their followers are led to believe
that the verses were written exclusively for those living today.

The purpose in debunking mainstream views of the rapture is not to
upset or insult anyone, but rather to illustrate how the concept has been
distorted in such a manner that encourages otherwise compassionate and
thinking individuals to deny their responsibilities as human beings. Simply
believing in Jesus and awaiting the rapture does not help to solve the problems
that we are currently facing as a society, nor will it enable us to collectively
combat the impending challenges of the future. Yet unfortunately, many
people do not believe that they should worry about potentially catastrophic
issues such as abrupt climate change or the annihilation of our civil liberties
because they expect to be raptured away at any moment. To further complicate matters, these same events are ironically interpreted by the faithful
as indisputable evidence of Jesus' imminent return, therefore they neglect
to take responsibility in rationally addressing these conflicts! But remember,
that return has been "imminent" for over 1900 years and counting.

Whatever the case, faithful supporters may have legitimate reasons to
believe in something akin to the rapture. The Bible *does* allude to some
kind of transformation event that will affect all of humanity. In fact, this
is not limited to the Bible alone, for it is one of the "myths" common to
cultures all around the world. The idea of the dying and rising god who
is transformed into something superior and more powerful is at the heart
of most mystery school teachings.

Would it be so strange to consider that *maybe,* just maybe, a rapture-like
event cannot happen until we *make* it happen? What if all of these myths
and symbols were intended to convey an important message—but one that
could only be understood *after* we had acquired the necessary skills and
knowledge to figure out the clues that had been left for us?

Reuniting Heaven and Earth

Readers will recall that ancient Sumerian legends concerning the creation of the universe (*an-ki:* ✳⟨⬦⟩) described how heaven and earth were once united, until they were separated by the gods (e.g. Enlil) before humankind appeared on the cosmic scene. Close examination of similar legends worldwide reveal parallel accounts and unanimously indicate that it is up to humans to once again reunite Heaven and Earth.

This is what I believe is ultimately meant by the phrase, "squaring the circle." It is not intended to be a mathematical or geometric problem—such exercises are designed to occupy people and perhaps distract them from discerning another layer of important symbolism. If we recognize that it is a riddle, we can finally unveil the true meaning that has remained obscured for millennia.

As a mathematical stumbling block, it should be interpreted as a symbol for overcoming problems by making the *impossible* once again possible. Additionally, we have seen that the square represents "earth," the circle is "heaven," and the triangle conveys "transformation" through fire, light and understanding. Therefore, the task of equating the square with the circle was intended to portray the reunion of Earth and Heaven. This is why the alchemists sought the elusive Philosophers' Stone—they recognized that the ultimate goal of The Great Work was to transform a regular human (base lead) into a divine god-like being (pure gold).

The ancient Egyptians, Sumerians, and Aztecs (to name just a few) all built sacred temples and large pyramids (conveying the triangle and fire symbolism) where they claimed the gods would manifest. They consistently described these gods as having human-like features, but with distinct differences such as white skin and hair (indicating a possible lack of genetic inheritance) as well as possessing supernatural capabilities. If these gods were indeed from another dimension ("Heaven") and they were able to come to the earth through the ancient gateways by "translating" their spirits into physical form, then it is imperative that we discover how to once again operate these gates. Our planet's climate is entering a phase of extreme unpredictability that could generate storms so severe that the human race is wiped out. While many animals would also be affected and possibly go extinct, they have a much better chance of survival because they know how to live off of the land. The human race, on the other hand, has grown too dependant upon technology and has taken for granted how stable our climate has been for the last few thousand years. Nevertheless, we do have one major advantage, and that is our ability to use our minds and work together to find a solution. Sooner or later, the Earth simply will not be able to support our ever-growing population. If the gateway legends are true, then we might have a viable way out of this problem.

Exactly how these gateways functioned is unknown at this time. Appendix B offers a potential idea, but my theories in that regard do not rise above pure speculation. More studies and further exploration will be necessary before we can begin to comprehend how these gates operated, if they even existed at all. However, the most important clue that has saturated all of the ancient myths and alchemical texts is the significance placed upon the properties of gold. All signs indicate that gold is one of the necessary elements for accessing the hyper-dimensional realms.

Now, after the (re)discovery of monatomic gold by David Hudson, we may have uncovered one of the most important clues as to how these gateways operated. If gold in its monatomic state has the capacity to be transferred into another dimension, then consider this question:

Would monatomic gold that is flowing through the bloodstream of a human being (or attached at a molecular level) allow that person to be translated into another dimension of reality?[29]

If the monatomic gold is within a person's body, there may not necessarily be any noticeable difference in their appearance. However, when that person enters one of the gateways or a device with a similar function, the latent potential of the monatomic gold can be utilized and the gateway technology will be activated. Returning once again to the Bible, we find that there are other clues mentioned that relate to the transformation of humans into something divine. In the New Testament, Paul writes about one of the "mystery" teachings:

…flesh and blood cannot inherit the kingdom of God, nor does the perishable inherit the imperishable. Listen, I will tell you a mystery! We will not all die, but we will all be changed in a moment, in the twinkling of an eye, at the last trumpet. For the trumpet will sound, and the dead will be raised imperishable, and we will be changed.

1 Corinthians 15:50–53 NRSV

These words are from the oldest known New Testament writings and therefore the earliest description of the expected resurrection. Obviously, Paul believed that the resurrection would occur within his lifetime, which it did not. What is important here is that it establishes the belief that the early Christians were expecting their bodies to be physically changed before they could enter heaven. Paul clearly indicates this belief and emphasizes that "flesh and blood cannot inherit the kingdom of God." This is significantly more than a mere metaphor encouraging good behavior or promising devout followers that their souls will rise to heaven upon their death, because Paul emphatically states that peoples' physical bodies would be transformed.

What Paul writes concerning the dead is also problematic on the surface. One of the long held beliefs among Christians is that when the resurrection takes place, it will consist of transformed physical bodies, including those of the deceased. This is why it was customary during Medieval times that if a person lost a limb in battle or an accident, it should be collected and placed alongside their bodies in the grave. This assured that their bodies would be fully intact at the time of the resurrection. Incidentally, this belief is also the reason why some warlords would dismember a body and scatter the pieces in various locations throughout the land. Not only did it send a terrible message to their enemies, but they also thought that if the person's entire body couldn't be gathered together, they could not be resurrected.

But what about the bodies that have completely decayed and there is nothing left to resurrect? This is certainly a logical dilemma that eventually surfaces, but if we consider the new way of thinking about the resurrection and the gateways, then the problem is potentially solved. The physical remains do not have to exist for the dead to be raised because they are already in spirit form. New bodies could be constructed for them much like bodies were constructed for the angels. If the souls of the dead are really in Sheol, these spirits could be translated into the new realm and into their new bodies.

Reading the Biblical texts reveals yet another important detail concerning the belief of resurrection. Something that is rarely mentioned is that if humans are transformed and given divine status, they will not only be like the gods/angels, they will surpass them! In Hebrews 2:7, it states that God made human beings "for a little while lower than the angels," and compares them to Jesus, who was also temporarily "lower than the angels" (2:9).[30] The author also claims that Jesus has "become as much superior to angels as the <u>name</u> he has inherited is more excellent than theirs" (1:4).

Rabbinic lore teaches that not only was Enoch translated into heaven, but also that he was transformed into the angel Metatron, the highest angel. Additionally, the prophet Elijah is similarly taken to heaven and believed to be transformed into the angel Sandalphon. The Angel of Death is not pleased with a human being escaping his jurisdiction so he challenges Sandalphon to a battle. But the Angel of Death is no match for him and is nearly destroyed.[31]

Earlier in our investigation, it was noted that Elijah was in the region known as Gilgal prior to his ascension (see Chapter 6). Recall that Gilgal refers to a "rolling wheel," "circle," or even "whirlwind." We must begin to wonder if the New Testament authors were creating an intentional connection between the disappearance/ascension of Elijah and the death/ascension of Jesus by naming Golgotha as the location of the crucifixion. Typically, *Golgotha* (Γολγοθα) means "place of the skull"—a name quite suitable given that it is the location of death. The Hebrew variation was *Gulgoleth* (גֻלְגֹלֶת), meaning "head," "skull" or even "poll" (as in a "headcount"). We may have another ancient wordplay operating here since the primitive root of Gulgoleth is *galal* (גלל), meaning, "to roll." It is related to the Aramaic root *galgal* (גלגל), also meaning, "roll" or "wheel." If this wordplay was intentional, it means that we should be associating the crucifixion of Jesus with the ascension and transformation of Elijah (as well as Enoch) into angels.

We now also have another important clue that addresses a mystery described in many of the ancient stories and legends. Most people know the story concerning the fall of Satan on account of his sinful pride. In fact, on account of John Milton's epic poem *Paradise Lost,* more people are familiar with this version of the "fallen angel" legend than the one concerning the Watchers, although the latter is more Biblically authentic. However, the story regarding the fall of Satan is closely associated with Persian and Arabic lore regarding the fallen angel Iblis (or Eblis). It is said that when God created Adam and commanded all of the angels to bow down and worship him, Iblis refused. He could not understand why an angel should bow down to such an "inferior" being. What Iblis failed to comprehend was that this lowly human would actually have the capability to become more powerful than any of the angels. Careful reading of many ancient tales shows the real reason why so many of the fallen angels despised and harmed humans: they were afraid that we might become beings more powerful than themselves.

There are even early Cabalistic ideas found within Biblical texts that indicate Mystery teachings about the role of humanity. For instance, everyone knows that Jesus was crucified on a cross. However, while reading the Acts of the Apostles it is mentioned by Peter and the others that Jesus was "hanged from a tree" (5:30; 10:39 KJV). The removal of Jesus from a tree is described shortly later (13:29). It is also repeated by Paul in his letter to the Galatians that Jesus became cursed when he was hanged "on a tree" (3:13).[32] The First Letter of Peter also asserts that Jesus was placed on a tree (2:24).

This may seem trivial, especially since someone could argue that the cross was made of wood that obviously came from a tree, but it is important. If the writers had meant for everyone to read "cross," then they should have used the Greek term *stauros* (σταυρός), which they *did* use elsewhere throughout the New Testament.[33] Instead, they specifically chose to use *xulon* (ξύλον), which is most often translated as "tree."[34] It is because many of the other Mystery schools incorporated similar ideas of a dying and rising god-man that was hung on a tree, such as the cult of Attis, whose effigy was tied to a pine tree[35]—or Adonis, who was referred to as "He on the tree."[36] The intentional usage of the word "tree" suggests that at least *some* of the writers were attempting to inject similar Mystery teachings into the New Testament.

Trees have played an extremely important role in the ancient mythology of other cultures as well. Norse legends of the Scandinavian people describe the giant "World Tree," known as *Yggdrasil* that connects the nine different realms of their cosmology and is believed to play an important role in the end of the world, known as Ragnarok. The name Yggdrasil is thought to mean "Odin's Steed" and the poem of the Hávamál describes Odin's self-sacrifice upon the tree:

> I hung on that windy tree for nine nights wounded by my own spear.
> I hung to that tree, and no one knows where it is rooted.
> None gave me food. None gave me drink. Into the abyss I stared
> until I spied the runes. I seized them up, and, howling, fell.[37]

Notice once again that we have the symbolism of a god-man hanging on a tree. Not only that, many people have noticed that it also mentions that Odin has been pierced by a spear, just like what is described in Jesus' crucifixion. We also discover that through this sacrifice of Odin upon the tree, he was able to attain some kind of spiritual knowledge by taking the mystical runes.

Yggdrasil is also described as having an eagle named Vidofnir perched at the very top in the realm of Asgard, the home of the gods. The roots are

A Mesopotamian depiction of a stylized "tree of life" and purification ritual for the king.

in the lower realm of Niflheim and are gnawed at by a great dragon called Nidhogg.[38] In some sources, the dragon is said to be offering immortality. Curiously, there have been ancient carvings recently discovered in China that similarly depict a bird on the top of a tree and a dragon at the bottom.[39] As many people know, the dragon is highly important in Chinese mythology and represents immortality. Additionally, the first royal emperors were identified as "Sons of Heaven" as well as "Dragon Kings."

There is also a highly enigmatic depiction of a "stylized" or "sacred" tree found numerous times throughout Mesopotamian artwork and literature. The exact nature of the tree is unknown to Mesopotamian scholars, but they realize that it played a highly significant role in the ancient world. Many have even tried to connect it to the "Tree of Life" in Genesis. Artwork showing the tree usually has it placed in a prominent location and flanked by gods, kings, semi-human genies, and other supernatural creatures. It is not known exactly what ritual is being depicted, but scholars believe it is some kind of "purification ritual." Careful study of the drawing shows the king (twice) reaching for the sacred tree and the solar rays of the god Šamaš being cast down on him. Behind the king are the guardian spirits or genies, each holding a bucket (*banduddû*) and what is believed to be a pine cone (*mullilu*, meaning "purifier"). It is highly significant that these supernatural beings are aiming the cone at the head of the king, perhaps to symbolize some form of enlightenment.[40]

To Cabalists, however, there is an entirely different tree that plays a role in this story. It is called the "Tree of Life," but is not a physical tree like the one that is supposed to be planted in the Garden of Eden. Instead, it consists of a specific arrangement of ten Sephiroth or spheres, which are individually called Sephira. The Sephiroth are divided into three columns that represent Judgment (Left), Mildness (Center), and Mercy (Right). The spheres are connected by twenty-two lines known as "Paths," which represent the letters of the Hebrew alphabet. Together with the Sephiroth, they are counted as the Thirty-Two Paths of Wisdom. There are many books that provide further details about Cabalistic teachings and the Tree of Life, however, it is beyond the scope of this study to fully explore all of the secrets connected with the Tree, so we shall only touch upon what pertains to our investigation.

Followers of the Cabala believe that the Tree of Life, or *Etz Hayim*, represents a symbolic journey to know God. The lowest Sephira is *Malkuth*, representing the earthly realm and material foundation of the Kingdom. The topmost sphere is *Kether*, the destined goal of the practitioner where the Crown of God is located. Looking at the Tree (p. 292), a person can see that there are essentially three paths to reach Kether. There is the Left Hand Path, which is not necessarily something evil, but it is considered to be "severe" and so it is invested with a negative influence. On the Right is the Path of Mercy, consisting of positive influences but not without its own inherent problems. Therefore, the Middle Pillar is meant to represent a balance between the two forces and a straight course for reaching the Divine. However, as you can see, there appears to be a missing sphere between Tiphareth and the goal of Kether.

A modern way of looking at this problem would be like playing a video game. The player's character can jump from one platform of the Sephiroth to another and the course taken is marked by each of the twenty-two paths in the tree as he or she progresses. Unfortunately, the character can only jump a limited distance and Kether is too far away. Jumping across the chasm would cause the player's character to plummet into the abyss. So, the player must make a choice. They can either jump to one of the Left or Right Paths, or discover the secret Sephira of "knowledge" called *Daath*, which would allow them to continue successfully along the Middle Path.

Daath is meant to house the secret knowledge necessary to reach God and so it is the "invisible" sphere of the Tree. It is the vital link between the seven lower Sephiroth and the upper three. Also of particular interest

The Cabalistic Tree of Life

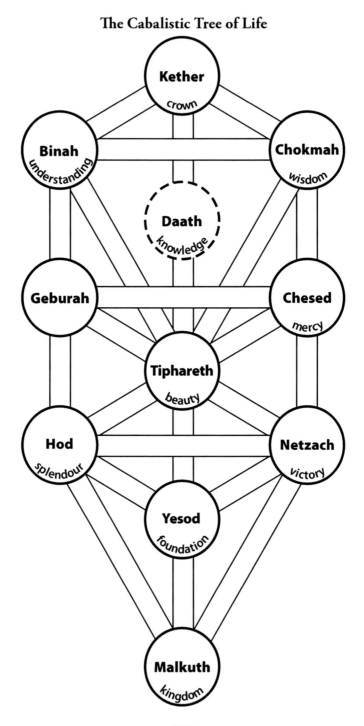

is that once Daath is added to the Tree, there are now thirty-three Paths total. Recall the symbolism of Jesus dying at the age of thirty-three and the raising of the serpent of knowledge through a person's thirty-three vertebrae. Jesus said that he taught through parables and that he would "proclaim what has been <u>hidden from the foundation of the world</u>" (Matthew 13:35). The phrase "foundation of the world" suggests that it is a reference to the lowest Sephira, Malkuth (the "foundation" of the "Kingdom"). The connection to other New Testament passages will soon become clear.

The heavenly body linked with the sphere of Tiphareth (Beauty) is the Sun. It is a symbol often used for Jesus, who said, "I am the light of the world. Whoever follows me will never walk in darkness but will have the light of life" (John 8:12).[41] The three images that are associated with Tiphareth are the majestic king, a child, and a sacrificed god, all of which have connections to Jesus. It is also believed by Christian Cabalists that Jesus hints of the hidden knowledge of Daath when he tells Thomas: "I am the way, and the truth, and the life. No one comes to the Father except through me" (John 14:6). Therefore, Tiphareth is designated as a symbol of the Messiah, who is leading the way up the Middle Path towards enlightenment and God.[42]

So what is the secret knowledge that leads to God? A surface level reading would seem that all that is required is a belief in Jesus. However, after analyzing so many of the references and symbols used throughout the texts, it all seems to come back to the reactivation of the gateways.

After teaching the parable of the Weeds among the Wheat and proclaiming that he is revealing the hidden secrets of heaven, Jesus explains the deeper meaning of the parable to his disciples. He warns them that the Weeds are people who follow the devil and evil ways, while the Wheat symbolizes the "children of the kingdom." He continues:

> Just as the <u>weeds</u> are collected and <u>burned up with fire</u>, so will it be at the end of the age. The <u>Son of Man</u> will send his angels, and they will collect out of his kingdom all causes of sin and all <u>evildoers</u>, and they will throw them into the <u>furnace of fire</u>, where there will be weeping and gnashing of teeth. Then <u>the righteous will shine like the sun</u> in the kingdom of their Father. <u>Let anyone with ears listen</u>!
>
> Matthew 13:40–43 NRSV[43]

Mesoamerican drawing of Quetzalcoatl. Notice the recurring theme of the serpent-footed appearance.

The command for people "with ears" to "listen" is another indication that we should dig further into the words than just the surface level. On one hand, it seems to be indicating a sequence of events that are supposed to happen at the "end of the age." On the other hand, the clues reside in the phrases such as "the furnace of fire" and how the "righteous will shine like the sun." First, the furnace reminds us of the "fiery furnace" used by Nebuchadnezzar.[44] But the reading of this certainly declares that it is not the desirable fate of people who are "evildoers." This furnace could still be the same, though. Remember, the duality of most things that have the power to create also have the power to destroy. Therefore, if the furnace or "gateway" can translate spirit into matter, or create matter to house spirit, it is within reason that it would also have the capability to annihilate such things as well. The shining of the righteous also links humanity's role to evolve into the "Shining Ones" as described in the ancient texts. Revelation says that after the transformation, humans will "reign on earth," but it is a new earth that is *united* with heaven (5:10).

Also in Revelation, John provides a description of Jesus' appearance that is extremely reminiscent of the Watchers:

> Then I turned to see whose voice it was that spoke to me, and on turning I saw <u>seven golden lampstands</u>, and in the midst of the lampstands I saw <u>one like the Son of Man</u>, clothed with a long robe and with a golden sash across his chest. <u>His head and his hair were white as white wool, white as snow; his eyes were like a flame of fire, his feet were like burnished bronze</u>, refined as in a furnace, and his voice was like the sound of many waters. In his right hand <u>he held seven stars</u>, and from his mouth came a sharp, two-edged sword, and <u>his face was like the sun</u> shining with full force.
>
> Revelation 1:12-16

As you may recall from earlier in our investigation, we are supplied with the same familiar phrases such as hair like "white wool" and "white as snow," eyes of "fire," and a shining face "like the sun," as well as the serpent imagery because of the bronze wordplay (see Chapter 5). The stars are said to represent the seven angels who reside over the seven churches (represented by the lampstands). Cabalistic teachings indicate that the seven stars may also be referring to the lower seven spheres of the Sephiroth. Another possibility, although it is unlikely, is that seven refers to the seventh level of a ziggurat where the gateway to heaven was located. Then again, perhaps it was meant to be associated with the *Book of Enoch's* reference to seven burning mountains that would be the final prison for the fallen Watchers.[45]

As we read further into Revelation, we are introduced to some very enigmatic concepts in the context of the seven angels and seven churches of Asia (properly Asia Minor). However, now that we have laid all of the groundwork concerning the Watchers, the gateways, and the alchemical transformation of humans into gods, we are much better prepared to understand these (formerly) puzzling statements.

The Mystery of the Seven Churches

The first church to be addressed is Ephesus. While at first glance, it seems as though the message to the church is one of both praise and criticism, our focus is on the closing of the message and the information it conveys. Jesus says, "<u>Let anyone who has an ear to hear listen</u> to what the Spirit is saying to the churches. To everyone who conquers, <u>I will give permission to eat from the tree of life</u> that is in the paradise of God."[46]

Recalling what is depicted in Genesis, mankind was not only exiled from the Garden for disobedience, but also because God (or the being that thinks it is God)[47] feared that humans might eventually eat from the Tree of Life and become as powerful as the gods.[48] Now, we find that Jesus is essentially overturning the forbidden action so that people can become *like* the gods.

The second church is Smyrna. Once again, it is the end of the message that contains the important distinction. The end of every message to each of the seven churches has Jesus reiterating the saying about having "an ear to listen." This is the clue necessary for understanding the veiled meanings of these passages. Jesus says that he will give the faithful "<u>the crown of life</u>," and that: "Whoever conquers [the test] <u>will not be harmed by the second death</u>."[49]

The "crown of life" that is described may not only be symbolic of kingship, but also the top Sephira of Kether on the Cabalistic Tree of Life. In fact, "crown" is the exact definition of *Kether* (כתר) in Hebrew. Additionally, the Sumerian word for heaven, *An* (✳), can also mean "crown" as pertaining to the *top of a tree!* Could this be a direct reference that Jesus is granting access to the *real* "Tree of Life" through this specialized knowledge of the Cabalistic Tree? The reference to the "second death" is also not precisely understood, but we can reasonably assume that it might have something to do with transitioning through the gateways. If a person is meant to pass through the gate, then they will be translated unharmed and therefore not face the "second death." Unfortunately, those people who are not prepared may end up being destroyed in the process.

Pergamum is the third church addressed by Jesus in Revelation. He states: "To everyone who conquers I will give some of the hidden manna, and I will give a white stone, and on the white stone is written a new name that no one knows except the one who receives it."[50] This is perhaps the most interesting of all the passages because it seems to be referring directly to the alchemical process and the Philosophers' Stone. We have already seen the descriptions of the manna that was fed to the Israelites, although it was not supposed to be as powerful as the manna described here. Notice that it also mentions the "white stone" and recall that the true gold of the alchemists was also said to be a "white stone." It is not a stretch of the imagination to consider that this may be referring to the white powder substance of monatomic gold. Additionally, Jesus stated that there will be a "new name" that is known only to the person that receives it. This is significant because careful study of the ancient legends revealed that "names" were meant to have a certain power and perhaps influence the activation of these gateways. The leader of the Watchers was Shemyaza ("the strong name") and Jewish legends claim that he was in charge of the Ineffable Name that allowed transition between heaven and earth.

The next church is Thyatira. Jesus proclaims that he will give authority to rule over nations to the chosen people.[51] This was previously a position held by the original angelic "sons of God,"[52] but mankind will be more powerful than them at this point. He then continues by saying that just as he had received authority from the Father, he would also give people "the morning star." Once again, we find the association of the morning star with Jesus and it is not to be interpreted as something devilish or ominous.

The rest of the churches emphasize the same important details as those listed above. The fifth church that is addressed is Sardis, and Jesus says that the elect will be clothed in "white robes" and that he "will not blot your name out of the book of life."⁵³ To the church of Philadelphia, he promises to write "the <u>name of my God</u>, and the name of the city of my God, the <u>new Jerusalem</u> that comes down from my God out of heaven, and <u>my new name</u>."⁵⁴

Finally, Jesus challenges the seventh church of Laodicea to purchase "<u>gold refined by fire</u>," "<u>white robes</u>," and "salve" to anoint the eyes so that people may "see" properly. He also promises that people who have earned the proper status will become co-rulers on the new heaven and new earth and sit on his throne.⁵⁵ Further analysis forces us to ponder if the "gold refined in fire" is another reference to alchemy, particularly when combined with the purity symbol of the white robes and the salve for seeing things properly. The robes also bring us to another connection that is likely to be overlooked. Not only do robes function as a symbol of purity, but they symbolize the newly resurrected bodies that everyone is meant to receive at the appointed time. We find the following passage in the writings of Paul:

> For we know that if our earthly house of this tabernacle were dissolved, we have a building of God, an house not made with hands, eternal in the heavens. For in this we groan, earnestly desiring to be <u>clothed upon with our house which is from heaven</u>: If so be that being clothed we shall not be found naked.
>
> 2 Corinthians 5:1–3 KJV

Notice that it mentions the desire to be "clothed upon" with a "house" from heaven. The term used for "clothed upon" is *ependoumai* (ἐπενδύομαι), which refers to putting one piece of clothing over top of what is presently worn. The word translated as "house" after it is the very interesting term: *oiketerion* (οἰκητήριον) which is pronounced "oy-kay-tay-ree-on." It means a dwelling place or habitation, but in this context it has the meaning of a container for a heavenly spirit. There is only one other place where this specific word is used in the Bible:

> And the <u>angels which kept not their first estate</u>, but left their own <u>habitation</u>, he hath reserved in everlasting chains under darkness unto the judgment of the great day.
>
> Jude 6 KJV

Once again, we are led back to the infamous incident in Genesis when the Watchers came to the earthly realm. Obviously, this passage is speaking of how the angels disobeyed and did not stay in "their first estate," the *arche* (ἀρχή), or heavenly realm. Oiketerion is translated as "habitation" in this passage, and is referring to the angels' state of being. Essentially, the angels "disrobed" from their heavenly forms to gain physical bodies, but humans are meant to ascend and claim these very same "robes" as our own.[56] It is possible that this is the same as the *melam* cloak of the gods in the written accounts of the Sumerians.

Jude continues to make further comparisons in the next few passages and even solidifies the connection to the *Book of Enoch*. He mentions the events which transpired at Sodom and Gomorrah, but understands that the "sin" was not quite the homosexual practices as they are commonly believed, but rather that the people lusted after "strange flesh" (Jude 7 KJV). This "strange flesh" is referring to the two angels that visited Lot.[57] After the incident of Genesis 6, the union between humans and angels was considered extremely taboo and therefore the people were once again guilty of trying to engage in sexual relations with the angels. This also supports the idea that the angels may have appeared as men, but they clearly had strange physical qualities that distinguished them from humans but rendered them identifiable to the townspeople. Jude goes on to say that people that do not comprehend the meanings of these texts, but still choose to reject them, are slandering the angels (Jude 8). He then quotes from the *Book of Enoch* by exclaiming, "See, the Lord is coming with ten thousands of his holy ones, to execute judgment on all..." (Jude 14–15).[58]

So, it appears as though the *Book of Enoch* had an unmistakable influence upon the writers of the New Testament, and there is a much greater connection between the fall of the Watchers and the Bible than what has been previously believed. As a result of the systematic suppression of *Enoch* on account of its "unorthodox" depictions of angels becoming flesh and blood and reproducing with mortals, several important details have remained unacknowledged and ignored for centuries. Unfortunately, this has meant that many scholars and theologians have lacked the proper context to understand the bizarre phrases that may be pivotal to the ascension of the human race. All of the prophets and writers of the Biblical texts return to this idea as being essential to future events.

The idea of humans being transformed into immortal gods is also supported by a puzzling passage from the gospels. In John 3:1–11, we read that the Pharisee Nicodemus approached Jesus and was told that unless a "man be born again, he cannot see the kingdom of God." Perplexed by this response, he asks if it means a man must reenter his mother's womb to be reborn. Jesus responded by telling him that a person must be reborn of both "water and Spirit." The reference to water is obviously understood as pertaining to baptism, but what about the Spirit? Many "born-again Christians" believe that this means that they must be reborn spiritually through their strong conviction in Christ and that it has nothing to do with the physical body. However, in light of this new evidence, it would seem that many people have largely misunderstood the meaning of being "born again." If the gateways do function as translation devices, this is almost certainly the method by which a fully-grown human could be "reborn."

The New Testament authors even painstakingly describe the attributes of the resurrected body. When Jesus returns from the dead, Mary Magdalene does not recognize him until a short time later.[59] He then tells her not to touch him because he has not yet "ascended to the Father" (John 20:14–17-).[60] Later, he miraculously demonstrates hyperspace abilities by passing through walls when he appears to the other disciples (Luke 24:36–37; John 20:19, 26). He reveals to them that he is made of physical flesh and blood and is not a ghost or hallucination (Luke 24:38–39). Jesus also appeases the doubts of Thomas by encouraging him to place his finger into his wounds to prove that he is a corporeal being (John 20:24–29). He even eats a piece of broiled fish with them (Luke 24:41–43). Obviously, the New Testament authors were trying to emphasize that they expected the resurrected body to be physical, but with the addition of spiritual powers.

When questioned by the Pharisees about the resurrection, Jesus directly states that after it occurs human beings no longer "marry, nor are given in marriage, but are like the angels in heaven" (Matthew 22:30).[61] Not only is Jesus stating that humans will become angels, he uses the phrase "marry, nor are given in marriage," to contrast with the events recorded in Genesis 6 and the *Book of Enoch* when the "daughters of men" were given to the "sons of God" in marriage (1–2).[62] Some theologians have even used this statement to discount the story of the Watchers because they misinterpret the meaning to infer that angels are sexless.[63] This is clearly not the case and requires a person to ignore reputable texts that say otherwise. The passage can simply be interpreted as a reference to the events of the distant past, which further emphasizes that the notion of angels and humans intermarrying had been forbidden by heaven.

The frequent statements concerning the time marking Jesus' return also remind us of the events involving the Watchers. Jesus warns that the situation on earth will be "as the <u>days of Noah</u> were," and that people were "eating and drinking, <u>marrying and giving in marriage</u>, until the day Noah entered the ark," (Matthew 24:36–39).[64] You should be familiar by now with the "hidden" story behind the story of Noah and the flood, and once again, the use of the phrase pertaining to marriage should confirm this. Jesus even continues to describe the rapture-like event and how some people will be taken and others left behind. It is also interesting that Jesus emphasizes how a person should be "awake" or "watchful" regarding the end times (40–44). Perhaps this is another veiled clue to the Watchers. If there is still any doubt in your mind that Jesus is referring to situations involving gateways and angelic beings—even after all of the evidence presented thus far—I'll direct your attention to a statement made by Jesus in John's Gospel:

> Very truly, I tell you, you will see <u>heaven opened</u> and the <u>angels of God ascending and descending upon the Son of Man</u>.
>
> John 1:51 NRSV

The description of an opening in heaven and angels "ascending and descending" conjures the image of a portal and is an obvious reference to Jacob's vision of the stairway to heaven (Genesis 28:11–19).

There is yet another veiled reference to the gateways within the New Testament that is of interest to our investigation. After the apostle Simon declares Jesus to be the Messiah, Jesus renames him Peter and says:

> ...you are <u>Peter</u>, and on this <u>rock</u> I will build my church, and the <u>gates of Hades</u> will not prevail against it. I will give you the <u>keys of the kingdom of heaven</u>, and whatever you bind on earth will be bound in heaven, and whatever you loose on earth will be loosed in heaven.
>
> Matthew 16:18–19 NRSV

After having received the "keys of the kingdom of heaven," Saint Peter became known as the "gatekeeper." Today, many people are familiar with the popularized version of Peter in comedies, cartoons, and other works, where he is depicted as an elderly man standing outside the pearly gates of heaven, acting as heaven's doorman or bouncer.

But if all of this information has been so easily overlooked for many centuries, what else have we been missing?

Hidden in Plain Sight

It should be abundantly clear by this time that the Bible and other ancient texts have contained a secret about the purpose of the human race: We are expected to take the next evolutionary step to become something more than human. This has been the teaching of the mystery schools and hidden behind symbolism and mythology for ages. But this is not something that will happen unless we make it happen, for our destinies are within our own hands.

To my knowledge, this is the first time that anyone has connected the dots between the various topics discussed in this book in such a manner. Other authors have come exceptionally close to the theory put forth in this book, but usually have steered away on some other tangent. Yet, it seems that the knowledge of our destiny has somehow been with us all along, whether we've realized it or not.

For instance, let us consider the most well-known and perhaps most misunderstood secret society: the Freemasons. While the fraternal organization itself probably dates back no later than the late seventeenth century, their philosophies contain numerous principles that have been passed down for many centuries prior to its creation. An example would be the emphasis the society places upon its members being known as "masons" or "craftsmen." It is no accident that the members are referred to by these terms, since many of the ancient mystery schools referred to their members using the same terminology.[65]

Most people believe that Jesus was the son of a carpenter, but this is not entirely accurate. The Greek term used in the gospels is *tekton* (τέκτων), which *can* mean carpenter, but generally refers to *any* craftsman or mason (e.g. an architect). Therefore, it could equally refer to a title of recognition and not an actual trade, therefore Jesus was to be regarded as a "Master Craftsman."

Also, the Scottish Rite of Freemasonry contains thirty-three degrees for a member to attain. This may be due to the significance that Jesus was believed to have been crucified at the age of thirty-three, but also remember that it is the same number of vertebrae in the human spine and the climbing serpent symbolized the attainment of knowledge. However, it should be understood that anything after the third degree is generally not considered to be higher by the Freemasons. The additional degrees numbering from four through thirty-three are thus considered to be lateral in nature and only for members wishing to further their understanding and involvement in the group. There are other rites associated with the Masons, such as the York Rite, and these have varying additional degrees, so it should be noted that not all groups place emphasis on just thirty-three degrees.[66]

The Freemasons also recognize important symbolism pertaining to a cube. The cube is a three-dimensional representation of the square and is also associated with the element of earth. In Freemasonic teachings, the cube is frequently used as a symbol for the "hewn stone" (the "journeyman" lodge brother). The significance is that the "rough stone" symbolizes the apprentice or initiate who is then fashioned into the final result of a perfect cube as they work towards the goals of "moral self-education; the harmonic form itself," and "the necessary observance of moral standards."[67]

The Kaaba (literally "cube," and also the origin of the word) is located within the Mosque at Mecca and is considered to be the holiest place for people of the Muslim faith. It is the cubic shrine housing the sacred "black stone," which is presumed to be a meteorite fragment. Every able-bodied and faithful Muslim is expected to make the pilgrimage of Hajj to visit the Kaaba at least once in their lifetime. According to Islamic traditions, the first Kaaba was built by Adam after Allah had instructed him to create an earthly place of worship that reflected the house of heaven known as *Bait ul Ma'amoor*. The Qur'an says that the Kaaba was built by the prophet Ibrahim (Abraham) and his son Ismail (Ishmael).[68]

It is rarely acknowledged that within the Bible, the description of the "New Jerusalem" is that of a perfect cube. The Book of Revelation describes how the city descends from the heavens onto the newly formed earth. All of its physical dimensions are measured by an angel with a golden rod to be 12,000 stadia (1,500 miles), a number that relies on a perfect base number of twelve (21:15–16). Twelve different types of precious jewels decorate the outside walls, and there are twelve gates that are made of pearl, but everything else in the city and the street is said to be made of "pure gold" that is "clear as glass" (21:18–21). It is also said to emit such a brilliance of light that the sun and moon are no longer necessary (21:22–26).[69]

So, how do all of these seemingly disparate elements relate to one another? The symbolism of the cube represents the heavenly city manifested on earth, where mankind as an ascended race is expected to live. It is the

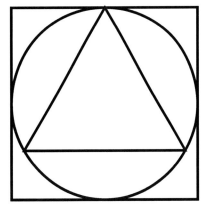

Graphic symbol of the Royal Arch Plate in accordance with the *Aldersgate Ritual*.	Graphic symbol of the Philosophers' Stone as in the *Rosarium Philosophorum* (1550).

idea of taking the two-dimensional square and projecting it further into another dimension of space, resulting in a physical object. This cube is also used by the Freemasons to symbolize the alchemical process of turning a regular person into a better one. Of course, someone could argue that this is only meant to be interpreted as leading a good life and doing what is right so that you can be a good pillar of society. However, this view may also be downplaying something quite extraordinary.

Returning once again to the research of Laurence Gardener, we must examine his description of the Royal Arch ritual of the Freemasons. The ritual is said to make particular reference to an engraved "plate of gold" that was thought to have been found on a marble pedestal. The description of this "plate of gold" says that it was engraved with the "Ineffable Name of God" (the Tetragrammaton), and two geometric shapes: "an equilateral triangle within a circle." He then notes how the graphical depiction in the Royal Arch documents show it "as a pair of concentric shapes in the surround of a square – essentially three shapes in all: a circle, a square, and a triangle."[70]

The ritual then quotes a Biblical passage to reveal the meaning behind this symbol as being a secret of wisdom "more precious than jewels, and nothing you desire can compare with her. Long life is in her right hand; in her left hand are riches and honor. Her ways are ways of pleasantness, and all her paths are peace. She is a <u>tree of life</u> to those who lay hold of her..." (Proverbs 3:15–18).[71]

We now have a Freemasonic ritual involving a gold plate, the Tetragrammaton, a circle, square and triangle, and clue that it has something to do with secret wisdom leading to the Tree of Life. It certainly would appear that there is a definite interest within the society of the Freemasons to square the circle. This is not just some obscure reference, but something that penetrates to the core of Freemasonry.

Most people have seen the identifying logo of the Freemasons at one point or another in their lives, but perhaps did not recognize it. It consists of a carpenter's square, overlaid with a drawing compass, and usually with the letter "G" (for "God," "Great Architect," and/or "Geometry") or a Blazing Star (pentagram) in the center. The symbols function on multiple levels of interpretation, but let's break them down to their simplest forms.

The carpenter's square is used to measure and make right angles, and the most obvious geometric object associated with it is a square: the symbol of earth. The drawing compass is used to mark a center point and draw a perfect circle around that point, symbolizing heaven. The letter "G" or the Blazing Star then also symbolizes light and the important knowledge that is gained from the initiate's transformation. When combined with the appearance of the compass, it reminds us of a triangle. Thus, the Freemason logo contains all three elements that are key symbols of squaring the circle.

This secret code has permeated our world to such an extent that we see signs of it everywhere and yet we fail to recognize its powerful message concerning our ultimate destiny. We lost touch with this ancient treasury of knowledge, and therefore we forgot our purpose and lost our way. The blind cannot continue to lead the blind—we must learn how to "see" again. Perhaps these symbols and clues keep resurfacing in one form or another as suggested by Jung's concept of the "Collective Unconscious"—thereby acting as a subtle reminder that we not only have a purpose far greater than we imagined, but also a responsibility to complete the task that has been given to us.

The next logical step is that we need to develop methods to test the theories outlined throughout this book. The process may take years, but we need to do *something* before time runs out for our planet. Inevitably, some people will be opposed to such experiments, particularly since the underlying concepts are so intimately connected to religion. In many cases, their opposition will be based on fear that their personal beliefs, whether religious or not, could be undermined. Therefore, it is to their benefit to prevent the ideas and experiments from taking place by dismissing them as being a "waste of time" and "impossible."

But nothing is impossible, only improbable—and we base that improbability on our own limited understanding of how things are supposed to work. We are the ones that determine the limits of our scientific knowledge. The problem is that we do not know everything. Just because something might *seem* to be impossible doesn't mean that it is. We only know the human "laws" of the universe, which are incomplete, but there are certainly still many more laws of Nature just waiting to be discovered.

If some extraordinary event appears to violate one of our perceived laws of physics, it must still be within the laws of Nature or else it could not have happened. The only laws that were broken were those of man, and so revisions to the laws would need to accommodate the new findings. The British physicist and chemist, Michael Faraday (1791–1867), proved this when he responded to the ridicule of his scientific peers who did not believe he could generate an electric current by passing a magnet through a coil of wire: "Nothing is too wonderful to be true if it be consistent with the laws of nature."[72]

Summary

❖ The alchemical arts were widespread throughout the ancient world, especially within the land of Egypt (referred to as "Al-khame" in the Arabic language). Over time, however, the ancient secrets became obscured and forgotten.

❖ Alchemists claimed that the true Philosophers' Stone was not a stone at all, but instead a very fine white powder. If so, it closely matches the descriptions found throughout ancient Egyptian writings and the Jewish legends of "manna" that fell from heaven.

❖ The true purpose of alchemy was to transform a mortal human (lead) into a god-like being (gold). This concept is prevalent throughout numerous ancient texts, especially the Biblical accounts of Enoch and Elijah, as well as many New Testament references.

❖ Bible researchers have forever been at a loss to locate the mysterious Garden of Eden because they have assumed that the description was of a literal location. However, the Genesis account contains many alchemical clues that offer a symbolic "guide" to the elusive garden that cannot be found on any map.

❖ The Cabalistic Tree of Life offers clues as to how we can attain the hidden knowledge that will reunite Heaven and Earth and transform the human race into immortal beings. Jesus also says that it will require a "white stone" with a "new name" that is to be used in conjunction with the "hidden manna."

❖ The message of "Squaring the Circle" is prevalent throughout history and has been passed down by various traditions. The most widespread version of it in modern time is concealed within the emblem of the Freemasons.

EPILOGUE

THE RIDDLE OF SQUARING THE CIRCLE is something that has been with us for a very, very long time. It has been hiding in plain sight and yet has eluded us because it was thought to represent an impossible task. The concept is so elegantly simple and yet the ramifications incredibly complex. After stripping away the surface covering and decoding the esoteric symbolism, we find buried within the myths and legends of the ancient world the secret destiny of the human race.

Not everything will be a wonderful utopian vision, though, and a rough road awaits those who dare to travel it. Anything that has the ability to grant a person the types of power and knowledge hinted at in these legends can be manipulated to cause great harm. There certainly exist selfish people who will stop at nothing to seek out the final clues to solve this riddle and then seize the power for themselves. History has shown that these people have come dangerously close to achieving their goals.

For instance, it is not necessarily common knowledge how much influence the occult had upon Adolf Hitler and the Nazi party. It is an ominous fact that is only briefly acknowledged in history books or omitted altogether. But it is wrong to ignore these details because whether or not you choose to believe that there was any legitimate basis for the occult practices, Hitler and his followers *believed* in it. That belief was immensely strong and terribly destructive. The Nazis and other eugenic supporters of the time, some in our own country, believed in genetic racism and sought to destroy everything that was deemed inferior. And what was the ultimate goal behind the Nazi eugenics agenda? It was to create a race of super humans—"demigods," if you will—of the Aryan race. Hitler wrote: "It may be that today gold has become the exclusive ruler of life, but the time will come when man will again bow down to a higher god."[1]

Thankfully, the Nazis were unable to accomplish their distorted vision of this super race. They recognized the traits of these beings, such as white skin, white/blonde hair and such, but had not yet made the proper connections to the legends of the past. They were convinced that their genetic line was superior, but they did not realize that *everyone* has the potential to ascend. It is not because one person's skin or hair color is "purer" than that of another person. This is why the Nazis failed. But just imagine if they had found a way to do this. It is certainly a very frightening thought and a lesson should be learned from it.

I must say with great trepidation that my ongoing investigation into such matters has led me to believe that there *are* powerful people working towards this goal right now. What they desire is a one-world system of power—a "New World Order," as some call it—with the general population as their slaves. My next work will explore this topic in depth and connect it to the research presented within this book. However, if you think you've heard the same old tired conspiracy theories about the NWO and expect it to be another similar venture, think again.

We are entering uncharted waters, but we need only to look to the stars for guidance. They illuminate the vast ocean of opportunity that extends beyond the horizon and keep us on our path. We now have a choice to make: Do we bravely continue our journey and follow the path that may lead to the next great discovery? Or do we blindfold ourselves and hope that the ship will steer itself out of harm's way? The entire concept of "squaring the circle" is about making the impossible possible—but it is meaningless if we refuse to recognize that *we* are the vehicle of change. We can make tremendous breakthroughs in science and expand our understanding of the universe; or we can completely obliterate ourselves and open the proverbial gateway to hell. The choice is in our hands, as it has been all along. This is our test—our opportunity to fulfill our destiny. I can think of no better time than now to recall the final words of the prophetic message left to us by the Hopi Elders: "We are the ones we have been waiting for."

APPENDICES

ADDRESSING PROBLEMS WITH THE THEORY

I T IS MY SINCEREST HOPE THAT YOU HAVE FOUND the evidence and ideas that I have presented throughout this book to be compelling. However, they are not without their faults. For this reason, I feel it is only fair to recognize some of these issues, as well as areas that demand further study and exploration.

The Reliance on Mythology

Naturally, a great many of the concepts outlined in this book have their origins in mythology and legends. The use of these myths and legends does not automatically mean that I endorse them as being literal events. As I have explained earlier in this book, a lot of these stories are best understood as lessons concerning astronomy, agriculture, and other more "down-to-earth" concepts (See Chapter 2).

The very attempt of incorporating mythology into a theoretical framework creates a host of problems all on its own. Which myths get used, and which ones discarded? What if there are several variations of the same myth, particularly within the same culture? Which one is correct? Are *any* correct? The preponderance of variations among these myths is a prime reason why skeptical minds might find it difficult to attribute any validity to them. One could argue that it is simply a matter of finding the right myth to justify your idea. I know this because I have seen many examples of evidence that have been slanted or misused to serve particular agendas.

However, after studying so many of these myths and legends, I'm reminded of the saying that within every legend is a kernel of truth. This itself is a completely subjective view, and might mean absolutely nothing to you. Or perhaps I've provided enough material to make my case. Whatever you choose to take away from this study, these stories concerning a race of otherworldly beings interacting with our ancient ancestors are some of the most prevalent accounts to have survived several millennia. I genuinely believe that you'd be hard-pressed to find a single ancient culture that did not speak or write of such extraordinary encounters.

It is certainly not an exaggeration to acknowledge that modern people readily subscribe to a number of bizarre ideas or beliefs; therefore, it comes without surprise that skeptics would argue that our ancestors were just overly superstitious. I would agree, but only to a point. Almost daily, archaeologists are uncovering additional artifacts from the time of our ancient ancestors. These discoveries are providing valuable insight into the formation of early societies and their systems of belief. However, they are also raising many questions, and challenging many of the long-standing beliefs about these civilizations.

Admittedly, myths by themselves do not have any credibility unless there is something to back them up. However, in a somewhat ironic twist, these very same myths are what provide the necessary support to lend credibility to the theory. There is a co-dependant relationship forged because the myths cannot be verified without the scientific experiments. Likewise, we may never have known to develop such types of experiments without the clues within the myths.

The Lack of Physical Evidence for Angels and Giants

A common trait attributed to the giants was an extra digit on their hands and feet. The medical terminology for this condition is hexadactyly. It is the most common form of polydactyly (which encompasses any number of extra digits). Hexadactyly is a relatively common congenital malformation that is reported in about two children per every thousand, and is usually treatable at birth. Treatment typically involves a physician tying a suture tightly around the base of the extra digit, eventually causing it to fall off. The remaining tissue heals quickly and all that usually remains is a very tiny scar.[1]

The possibility exists that the "giants" suffered from birth defects such as hexadactyly not from interspecies breeding, but as a side effect of their environment. For instance, cases of children being born with extra digits are more common in areas that are geographically isolated, such as islands. This is explained by the evolutionary phenomenon known as the "founder effect." The founder effect occurs when a small population inhabits an isolated region and then multiplies quickly. This results in a sharp decrease in genetic variation when compared to the parent population, often causing distinctly different genetic characteristics among the offspring.[2]

However, the founder effect is not strictly limited to geographical isolationism; it can be created through cultural isolationism as well. For example, the Amish community exhibits greater occurrences of polydactylism than other populations in the United States because they do not allow many newcomers into their society and often marry within the same community.[3]

Being mindful of this, it is reasonable to believe that reports of numerous beings with extra fingers and toes might have been the result of nomadic tribes settling in new areas that resulted in the founder effect. The people may have become frightened by these abnormalities and considered the afflicted persons to be monsters. Over time, these stories may become exaggerated, eventually forming the basis of the giant myths that are now familiar to us.

However, this does not satisfactorily explain everything about these beings. For instance, the giants were often described with multiple physical deformities (such as the addition of an extra row of teeth, or oddly shaped skulls), not just a single extra finger or toe. Also, they were clearly described as being very powerful and mighty warriors. As I have already pointed out in Chapter 5, these combined traits are at odds with the reality that people suffering from Gigantism or other ailments face.

This still leaves us wanting an explanation for the size of these giants. It is not enough to assume that people just exaggerated their size. Words can have different meanings depending upon their context. Clearly, there is a difference between describing someone as "huge" in a non-physical way as opposed to a physical characteristic. For example, fans of a rock group or movie star will say that they are "huge," usually meaning that they are very popular. This is quite different than describing someone as "huge" because they are over seven feet tall.

Conclusive evidence such as actual fossilized remains will be needed to settle this debate once and for all. Unfortunately, I am not aware of any authentic "giant fossils" in existence. The only fossils I can recommend worthy of further examination are the oddly shaped skulls in Peru and the Malta Skull (See Chapter 5).

Political and societal factors also greatly influence our ability to validate or refute claims of giant beings in the past. For instance, legends abound all across the globe about these giant humans, especially in Middle Eastern countries, such as Syria. However, the native people closely guard many of the sites believed to be the graves of giants. Scientists are forbidden to desecrate the graves by digging them up or disturbing them in any way.[4] Other less invasive techniques will have to be used or developed to find out if these graves are authentic.

Another probable reason accounting for the lack of evidence is that the giants might have had different burial customs. It is already very difficult for human remains to become fossilized. Typically, only the hardest bones such as skull fragments and teeth are what remain. This is further compounded if the giants were cremated in funeral pyres, a method often used in the ancient world. Other methods may have employed sealed sarcophagi that would eventually decompose the body into a foul smelling slime.[5]

Besides a lack of available fossil evidence, the other major problem is the widespread number of hoaxes and/or use of deliberately misleading "evidence." These hoaxes range from manipulated photographs to even molded replicas of "authentic" bones.

In July of 2004, emails began circulating throughout the internet claiming that the skeletal remains of a giant human were discovered in the Arabian Desert. The email went something like this, and even included a photo attachment for proof:

```
Subject: [Fwd: Interesting discovery]

FYI. Just got this Email, only God knows better about this
story, but check it out:

Recent gas exploration activity in the south east region of
the Arabian desert uncovered a skeletal remains of a hu-
man of phenomenal size. This region of the Arabian desert
is called the Empty Quarter, or in Arabic, 'Rab-Ul-Khalee'.
The discovery was made by the Aramco Exploration team.
As God states in the Quran that He had created people of
phenomenal size the like of which He has not created since.
These were the people of Aad where Prophet Hud was sent.
They were very tall, big, and very powerful, such that they
could put their arms around a tree trunk and uproot it.
Later these people, who were given all the power, turned
```

314

against God and the Prophet and transgressed beyond all boundaries set by God. As a result they were destroyed.

Ulema's of Saudi Arabia believe these to be the remains of the people of Aad. Saudi Military has secured the whole area and no one is allowed to enter except the ARAMCO personnel. It has been kept in secrecy, but a military helicopter took some pictures from the air and one of the pictures leaked out into the internet in Saudi Arabia. See the attachment and note the size of the two men standing in the picture in comparison to the size of the skeleton !![6]

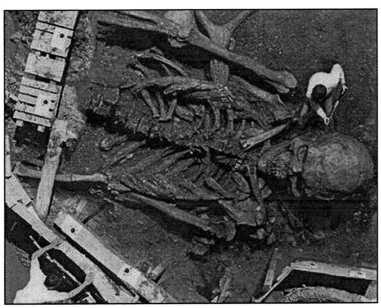

The image of the alleged giant skeleton that was attached to the email.
Artist credit: "IronKite."

Investigations into the email revealed it to be a hoax. To be fair, the photograph was not originally intended to be part of this hoax. It was created for a contest hosted by Worth1000.com, entitled: "Archaeological Anomalies." The purpose of the contest was for people to create a picture "of an archaeological discovery that looks so real, had it not appeared at Worth1000, people might have done a double take." Contestants were only given forty-eight hours to

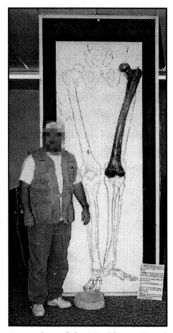

A member of the Mt. Blanco Fossil Museum research team stands next to the giant human femur exhibit.

submit their entries. Several submissions featured giant skeletons, but the one shown on the previous page was awarded Third Place and created by the artist "IronKite." After the contest, someone must have gotten the bright idea to circulate it throughout the internet accompanied by a fictitious story. The source image was obtained from the Cornell University website regarding an archaeological dig for a mastodon skeleton discovered near Hyde Park, New York.[7]

But altering a photograph and sending out an email with a story is more of a prank than a deception. There are people, however, that want you to believe what they do so very much that they are willing to *create* the evidence to support their claims.

The most deceptive piece of "evidence" to appear in recent years is the alleged "Giant Human Femur." It is most often displayed at museums that support the "Creation Science" views held by many fundamentalist Christians. Particularly, it is featured at the "Creation Museum" of Dinosaur Adventure Land[8] (operated by Dr. Kent Hovind, aka: "Dr. Dino"— whose Ph.D. isn't in paleontology, but in Christian Education from an unaccredited university), and the Mt. Blanco Fossil Museum.[9] When displayed in museums such as these, the bone is often shown next to a partial "life-size" drawing of a giant skeleton to visually illustrate how large it was believed to have been in real life.

The reason why this particular "artifact" should be considered so misleading is because there is not a single shred of credible evidence to support it; and the evidence that is used is either highly circumstantial or downright fraudulent. Christians that believe this so-called "bone" has any credibility should investigate the matter thoroughly and hold those that declare it to be "scientific evidence" accountable for making such claims.

Kent Hovind prominently displays the bone in his *Creation Seminar Series* as a background decoration in his office.[10] In fact, during Part 7 of the series, he actually points to the bone as if it is undeniable proof and says:

…like this thigh bone here over my head which is from a human which would have been nearly thirteen feet tall. […] That would have been a thirteen foot human. Well, if just a fragment of that bone was found nobody would dream it came from a human—if they believed in evolution.[11]

Earlier, in Part 2 of the series, a slide shows Hovind using the femur as a prop with a small child standing next to it for effect. The slide also says that it was from a "giant skeleton found in Egypt."[12] However, his claim that the bone is from Egypt is an important detail that contradicts the original story of this bone, as you will learn in a moment.

The first major problem is that this is not real bone at all, but a replica.[13] "Well," you say, "that's alright. In fact, it is customary for museums to display replicas of fossils so that the real ones do not become damaged or stolen." However, this is not the replica of any authentic skeleton, thigh bone, or even bone fragment. Instead, Joe Taylor (director and curator of Mt. Blanco Fossil Museum) tells us that he sculpted the giant femur at the request of Mr. Jack Wagner. Wagner sent him an article containing a letter from an *unnamed* person, claiming that very large skeletons were found during road construction in *Turkey* (remember that Kent Hovind said it was from Egypt). However, no actual bones or physical evidence were ever presented to support the claims in the letter, which reads:

Dear Christian Friends, I was born and lived in the Middle East from 1938 to 1968. I was Ain-Tell and Euphrates water works Engineer and was very interested in archaeology and history and had some very interesting findings, some of which may sound unbelievable. I have brought with me a few silex arrow heads, etc., from the very battle-field where King Nebuchadnezzar and Pharo-Necho's armies fought. And what about the giants mentioned in Genesis? In south-east Turkey in the Euphrates Valley and in Homs and at Uran-Zohra, tombs of about four meters long once existed, but now roads and other construction work has destroyed the spots. At two places, when unearthed because of construction work, the leg bones were measured about 120 cms. It sounds unbelievable. I have lived with my family at Ain-Tell for more than 14 years at the very spot where King Nebuchadnezzar had his headquarters after the battle of Charcamish, where I dug the graves of kings' officers and found their skeletons like sponge, and when you touch them they become like white ash, with spears and silex and obsidian tools and ammunition laying by.[14]

Nevertheless, Taylor decided to sculpt the enlarged femur despite not having any physical bone as evidence to support the article. On his website, he tells us that he used the femur of one of the "Malachite Man *females*" (emphasis added) as his model.[15] However, there are slight differences between the bones of a male and female, so it would be incorrect to view the sculpted femur as an accurate representation of one that belonged to a male giant.

Additionally, the skeptical researcher Carl Marychurch has pointed out on his website that Taylor apparently ignored the laws of basic anatomical proportions when sculpting his work. Specifically, Taylor was violating what is known as the Square-cube Law, which states that when the size of an animal is doubled, the mass of the animal will be eight times greater.[16] To explain this better, let's look at the following examples:

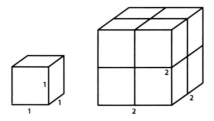

We'll begin with a cube that is 1 cm. To find the surface area of the cube, we multiply the number of sides (6) by the area of each square, making the equation: $6 \times (1 \times 1) = 6 \text{ cm}^2$. The volume is found by multiplying the length, width, and height: $(1 \times 1 \times 1) = 1 \text{ cm}^3$. If the cube is then doubled in size, the surface area will be: $6 \times (2 \times 2) = 24 \text{ cm}^2$, while the volume would be: $(2 \times 2 \times 2) = 8 \text{ cm}^3$. This shows that the doubling of the cube results in a surface area *four* times greater than the original, but the volume that it holds is now *eight* times greater.[17]

The next image demonstrates this effect, also. Although not realistically portrayed, imagine that the bone of a mouse is half the size of a human's bone, and that an elephant's bone is twice the size of the human bone. If these bones were then scaled non-proportionally so that all of their lengths were equal, we can see considerable differences between their widths.[18]

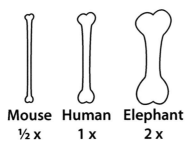

Mouse   Human   Elephant
½ x   1 x   2 x

This presents problems with the idea of simply scaling something up or down in proportion. Essentially, a very tiny human could not have the same proportions as a normal sized human or else they would not be able to move their limbs—not to mention that their metabolism and muscle strength, among other things, would be drastically increased. On the other hand, if a human was proportionately scaled to the size of twenty feet tall, their bone structure would not be able to support them. In fact, it is believed that a much larger "human" would not be human looking at all.[19] This is interesting, especially since the ancient texts seem to describe the giants with monstrous appearances.

Returning once again to Joe Taylor's "giant femur," we realize that since he merely increased the scale of the bone, it would not provide the strength necessary to support a being that was thirteen feet in height. Instead, the cross-section of the bone should have been increased by eight times the original capacity to provide the required strength. Additionally, this means that all of the other bones in Taylor's "life-size" drawing are also out of proportion for a being of these dimensions.[20] I must state with all fairness to Taylor, however, that when I contacted him via e-mail, he stressed that the femur is a "sculpture based on what we believe is an accurate report."[21] Nevertheless, it seems incredibly dubious to feature a replica of a bone that is not only anatomically incorrect, but also based on an *unverified rumor from a letter* as evidence of giant humans. It seems as though such a grievous error would be quite damaging to the reputation of Mr. Taylor, who has been studying fossils for most of his life. Perhaps he did not know that the Square-cube Law can also relate to biological creatures, but that would also not bode well for his reputation.

These critiques are simply intended to show supporters of such beliefs that not everything is as truthful or accurate as you may have been led to believe. Outspoken "Creationists" are frequently heard bashing the ideas and theories of scientists that support evolution, yet their own evidence (such as that described above) does not hold any weight (pun intended). It is extremely hypocritical to cry foul over hoaxes used in the past to support evolution concepts, but then create and/or use unsubstantiated "evidence" of your own to support the beliefs of Creationism. Even if Hovind wasn't aware of Joe Taylor's mistakes, it still does not explain why he purposefully changed the location of the "giant skeleton" to Egypt instead of Turkey as the letter stated. Wouldn't he want to report this phenomenal "discovery" accurately? After all, Hovind frequently states during his debates how much he hates lies and the people who spread them.[22]

The Circular Argument about Physical Structures

Yet another potential problem for my proposed theories is the lack of any complete physical structures from the ancient world, such as the pyramids and other temples. Certainly, we have the remains of these massive buildings, but none of them have been entirely preserved and their functions are shrouded in mystery.

For example, the only surviving pieces of the Ancient Mesopotamian ziggurats are the base foundations. Additionally, the Great Pyramid is missing most of its limestone casing, as well as the capstone and anything else that was once stored inside of it. Then, there are the jungles of South America that have grown over many of the stepped-pyramids and temples, helping to somewhat preserve them better than their counterparts. However, we still do not have any living persons that completely understand the functions of these buildings or who know if anything is missing from them.

Skeptics always demand physical evidence to support extraordinary claims. The best physical evidence I can direct anyone to for further studies are these structures themselves and the related ancient texts. If we believe the ancient people, they almost unanimously tell us that these buildings were used as gateways or portals to heaven; but of course, they're not working now. This becomes a bigger problem because it leads to a frustratingly circular argument:

1. If you want physical evidence, refer to the buildings.
2. Since the buildings are so old and deteriorated, we must rely on written accounts by the people alive at that time.
3. However, the ancient descriptions make amazing claims, therefore requiring physical evidence (see #1).

These deteriorated remains of a once mighty ziggurat.

You are probably starting to get the picture now. This would be like having actual crash wreckage from an alien spacecraft but the scientists won't believe you until they see the rest of the wreckage. However, when you take them to the location, you discover that the craft is missing and there are no traces of the wreckage! The scientists will not believe you unless they see the craft for themselves, but the only physical piece of evidence now remaining to back up your story is what you are holding in your hand.

Are the Global Warming Scenarios Too Far-Fetched?

I realize that not everyone will agree with my suggestion that global warming will lead to worldwide superstorms of a magnitude that has been unprecedented throughout all of human history. But there is another important reason why I am stressing a "worst case" scenario. It is because even though scientists are working towards effective solutions for these problems, I think we need to formulate a "Plan B" just in case the situation grows beyond our control.

Earth is the only home we have ever known and if it cannot support us anymore, we are essentially out of options. Some scientists are concerned that we could reach a tipping point in as little as thirty years (some scientists say ten years) that will lead to large-scale crop failures, massive starvation, the spreading of deadly diseases, and the forced-relocation of millions of people—just to name a few things. Even the world-renowned British astrophysicist, Stephen Hawking, warns that our planet is facing a dangerous future and that the "survival of the human race" will depend upon our ability to find another planet to call home. Hawking suggests that within twenty years we could have a permanent base on the moon, and even a settlement on Mars in another twenty years.[23] However, without trying to sound too pessimistic, I simply do not see how there is any feasible way to transport large populations into space and colonize other planets in the timeframe that we are facing with our current technology. In the best case scenario, Hawking's idea would only have a *small* population on Mars by 2050, and that means that the rest of the people of Earth would be at the mercy of whatever disaster was at hand. But if my interpretations of the ancient stories about the gateways are correct, we *do* have another option that could be used to relocate the population of the entire world.

I am certainly not advocating that my theory is the only answer to this problem—especially since it is incredibly hypothetical. I think that there are many things that we as individuals can do to help lessen the effects of global warming. I have outlined a few of those items in Chapter 10, but there are still many more that we can do, depending on our lifestyles. If you are concerned about what you can do to help the situation, please visit the website for this book (www.gatewayofthegods.com). Once you are there, you will find links to other important websites that are devoted to combating against global warming and severe climate change.

I refer to my theory as a "Plan B" because I think that we need to listen to what responsible scientists and environmentalists are recommending. I could compare it to the following type of situation. Suppose that you are sitting in a movie theater. Unbeknownst to you, an employee in a different room notices that a small fire has started. Quickly thinking, the employee enacts "Plan A" and grabs the nearest fire extinguisher. Luckily, they are able to put out the fire before it does any further damage. If that employee had not become aware of the fire, the whole building could have burned down, along with the people inside. However, if they had not noticed the fire and it grew out of control, the situation becomes much more desperate and everyone must evacuate the building. That is where "Plan B" comes into action. The employee can pull the fire alarm and alert everyone that there is an emergency so that they can safely exit the building. Having a "Plan B" is mandatory for situations just like this one. While this simplified example is obviously on a much smaller scale, the same principle still applies to more complicated scenarios. However, the dilemma we face is that currently we cannot exit the movie theater (Earth).

Have I Fallen for Monatomic Fool's Gold?

Most of the problems revolving around the research into monatomic gold have already been explained throughout Chapter 11. However, it might be beneficial to address some other thoughts and concerns here.

My biggest problem with the subject is that very few people have the money or resources to recreate the experiments of David Hudson, and so virtually all of the research comes from him. Most of the consulting scientists or laboratories are not named by Hudson, apparently at the request of the individuals, making it much more difficult to verify any information.

It would be helpful to finally hear some genuine thoughts from the scientific community regarding this topic after they have read the chapter and related materials. Perhaps some scientists will even be bold enough to conduct some of the experiments on their own. If there are major problems with the research or the experiments I am certain that it would be brought to our attention. After reviewing the transcriptions from David Hudson's lectures and comparing them to other material relating to metallurgy, superconductors, and hyper-dimensional physics, it appears to me that much of it is compatible. Admittedly, I am not trained in any of those fields, so my knowledge is extremely limited.

One other researcher that has been experimenting with monatomic elements is Barry Carter. Details involving his experiments are on his website (http://www.subtleenergies.com/ormus/). Some people may find his research and documentation useful; others may not. There is a great deal of material, however, and I have barely had a chance to evaluate most of it. I usually do not like to mention or recommend websites that I haven't examined thoroughly, but it appears to be a potentially reliable source since Carter is actually conducting his own original experiments rather than merely repeating Hudson's material.

There is one last issue of concern regarding monatomic gold. At this present time, it seems that monatomic gold is the best prospect for unveiling the secrets of alchemy, especially on account of the references to powdered gold substances in ancient texts. However, if Hudson's work is found to be false, or that monatomic gold does not live up to the hype, it does not mean that the rest of my theories are invalid. Gold definitely played a major role in the ancient world—that is a fact. If the answer is not monatomic gold, then it will simply force us to start over and find a new candidate for the mysterious Philosophers' Stone.

The Use of Symbolism

The ideas I have presented in this book greatly depend upon interpretations of symbolism used throughout ancient myths and legends. The problem is that symbols, by their very nature, can be interpreted in a variety of ways depending on how someone wants to "spin" their point of view to an audience. This is both a blessing and a curse.

For instance, I've come across many "Christian" researchers who argue that "occult" influences have infiltrated nearly every facet of our society, in order to prove various conspiracy theories claiming that Satan rules the world and he's coming to take everyone straight to hell. They present photographic "evidence" of things such as "pentagram" stars on the sides of U.S. military aircraft in order to suggest that the military is actually full of diabolical devil worshippers. Or they will present pictures of Bill Clinton flashing the signal for "I Love You" in sign language, or George W. Bush doing the Texas Longhorn's salute and then compare these innocent gestures to the "El Diablo" sign used by Satanists. These hand gestures serve as concrete evidence, of course, that the presidency bows to Beelzebub.[24] Please don't think for a moment that I'm actually defending either of those guys—but it frustrates me to see things taken out of context and intentionally misappropriated.

But what about the well-intentioned uses of symbols? We see and use them all the time, such as when we read a map, or need to find a restroom, or use computer software. Symbols allow people to easily identify something through a kind of universal language. Someone who doesn't understand English can still figure out where the restroom is located and whether or not it is designated for men or for women. Symbols help us to communicate more effectively in situations where there might otherwise be a barrier.

My ideas concerning symbolism in the ancient world are somewhat bold because I'm suggesting that they might actually have been developed by extraterrestrials as a method of communicating with our modern world. Some people may find this absurd, but I think that it is a simple and worthy concept. These beings (the Watchers) probably recognized that the languages spoken at the time they were here would eventually become obsolete, or "dead." If they wanted to send a message thousands of years into the future when technology had advanced enough for humans to traverse the heavens, then what better way of preserving their message than to use symbols embedded in religious concepts?[25]

Another benefit of symbols is that they can represent a plurality of ideas. For example, let's consider a very simple shape such as a circle. It is composed of a single curved line, yet it can tell us so much more. Since it is comprised of only one line that closes in on itself, it has neither a beginning nor an end. A circle also contains the mathematical formula for Pi (π), showing how it offers unlimited potential. These traits suggest that a circle is the perfect symbol to express the ideas of heaven.

Now the square is just the opposite and a good representation of the earthly plane. It has four fixed sides and we can easily calculate its measurements both inside and out. The square provides a solid foundation to build upon and also signifies our limited understanding.

The triangle is a fusion of the other two symbols. It has a solid foundation like the square, but its sides converge at a single point—like the single point that creates a circle. This also allows it to work effectively as a guide by pointing us in a single direction; that's why most directional arrows incorporate a triangular shape in some form or another. Just imagine trying to decipher which direction to go if a circle was used instead.

So perhaps the idea that this symbolic language is of extraterrestrial origin is too far out for some people to accept. But is this really so different than when the Pioneer 10 and 11 probes were launched into space, both of which included plaques utilizing symbols and mathematical data, in anticipation that an extraterrestrial race might discover them? Whatever the case, discovering symbolism that has been encoded into religious myths ultimately does not substantiate my claims for the existence of an advanced extraterrestrial presence, thus much of what I have written remains subjective.

Whitley Strieber's Influence

Clearly, some of Whitley Strieber's work has influenced my own research. However, I am also aware of the many arguments against him raised by skeptical investigators. I must admit that this section has proven difficult for me to write because I am forced to adopt an objective and detached point of view in regard to an individual that I have come to respect on a personal level.

I cannot possibly address all of the critiques that have been directed toward Strieber or his claims, for they have been covered thoroughly by skeptics and readily available for anyone interested in such details. Besides, I think that Strieber's name has been dragged through the mud enough in the past already and neither he nor his family deserve any additional stress in their lives. For those of you that think that I'm turning a blind eye to some of Strieber's flaws, I assure you that I am not. I am well aware of the problems with many of his beliefs and proposals and I have taken them into consideration. However, I have listened to his radio program for years now and I am wholeheartedly convinced that Strieber is a genuine, sincere, and caring individual. What is most admirable about Mr. Strieber is that even after facing a barrage of both professional and personal attacks from critics and the media, he remains focused upon his research and has refused to compromise his principles.

Above all, for a man reputed to be so disconnected from reality, Mr. Strieber is an extremely personable and charismatic host and writer. When you listen to him speak, or read his writings, Strieber addresses his audience in a such a candid and thoughtful manner that it is as though he is engaging in a conversation with long-time friends. His demeanor is that of a gentlemen, as opposed to a fanatic with a theoretical or dogmatic axe to grind. However subjective or quaint my opinions of Mr. Strieber might seem to skeptics, I feel that his contributions to the field of paranormal studies and alternative scientific research ultimately stem from a genuine and humble desire to benefit the world in which he lives. As I would with any individual, I carefully assess the claims that Mr. Strieber makes and I evaluate them based upon my own knowledge, experience, and intuition in order to reach my own conclusions. But more often than not, I find myself more inclined to agree with Mr. Strieber, or at least interested in what he might have to say, simply because of the way in which he so tactfully and humbly presents his arguments. This particular quality has become increasingly more difficult to detect in other leading figures within academia, the media, and the world at large.

All that said, I will play devil's advocate and hopefully demonstrate that despite my admiration for Whitley Strieber, I can still approach his work objectively and without bias. Probably the largest problem with Strieber's material is that he has stated numerous times in his books and online journals that sometimes he has great difficulty discerning between "real" paranormal events and his imagination. He still questions to this day whether or not his conversation with "The Master of the Key" genuinely occurred or if he's just convinced himself that it has. For now, he hopes that someday people will either be able to validate what the Master has said or to assist him in relocating the man.[26]

My aim is neither to condemn Strieber nor to vindicate him. As I have been so quick to point out mistakes or fraudulent claims in the work of others, why am I reserving that treatment when it comes to Mr. Strieber? To begin with, I can say that he provided the *inspiration* for my work. Knowing that his work is so controversial, I never actually use him as a source of evidence. If you look back, you will find that none of my data comes directly from him. All of the important facets of my ideas are supported by legitimate articles, papers, definitions, and other independent sources. When I do incorporate his work, it is merely to encourage thought.

Also, it is difficult for me to put into words, but there does seem to be *something* about *The Key* that resonates with me. I know that very few people have actually read it, and that even if only a thousand people picked it up, I am probably the only one that has ever had any kind of "Eureka!" moment (especially after only reading three little words) and felt compelled to write an entire book about it. The instant that I saw the words "square the circle" on the page, my head practically exploded with information and I suddenly knew everything that I had to do. I know that it sounds crazy and absurd, but that is just the way it was. If I told you anything else then I would be lying.

While I was putting the finishing touches on this book, I found it was very intriguing to consider exactly how much *The Key* had been an influence. To my knowledge, my book is the first of its kind to tie together so many different subjects, such as fallen angels, EVP, climate change, quantum physics, and Biblical symbolism into such a unified concept. But after looking back at *The Key,* it is plainly evident that the framework had already been shaped in a very short but powerful conversation. I could see patterns emerging and topics discussed that had been left open-ended in Strieber's book that now make much more sense in the context of my own research. It was almost as if what I had written was a perfect companion piece, but with the research to back it up. I had never intended it to be such a thing, but that is how it looks to me in hindsight.

Whitley Strieber wrote in one of his online journal entries concerning *The Key* that, "there will come a day when its value is realized, and then perhaps … [the Master of the Key's] message will enter the world in a new way, and have the impact that it deserves to have. I look forward to that day with all my heart and soul." I will be looking forward to that day as well. I hope that perhaps, in some small way, my own work has contributed to this possibility.

THEORETICAL GATEWAY PHYSICS 101

A FTER A GREAT DEAL OF INTERNALIZED DEBATE, I have decided to proceed with a section that formally speculates how the ancient gateway technology might have operated. Initially, I felt that it would be best to leave the idea alone and let experts in the proper scientific fields tackle this problem. Inevitably, my own curiosity got the best of me, so I have decided to present some different possibilities concerning how inter-dimensional beings might have traveled to our realm. Particularly, I wanted to develop an idea that I thought many scientific minded people would find appealing and a few steps closer to scientific fact, as opposed to science fiction.

After several weeks of studying both current and emerging technologies, I managed to develop an idea that seemed plausible. However, it is by no means my opinion that this concept is "the answer" to how the gateway technology operated—it is only a *single* idea. Other theoretical models providing far better solutions to this problem might eventually be developed by people much brighter than myself. With any luck, a sufficient number of people will take my theories seriously enough to begin having open and cross-disciplinary discussions to address such possibilities.

To my pleasant surprise, I found a very similar description of my idea while skimming through *Parallel Worlds* (Doubleday, 2005) by Dr. Michio Kaku, a theoretical physics professor at the City University of New York. Near the end of his book, Dr. Kaku describes several methods that a technologically advanced civilization might use to "escape" the destruction of their universe. The method that bore a striking resemblance to my own idea was called "The Last Hope."[1] While my intent is certainly not to infer that Dr. Kaku would support my theories, observing that I share a similar line of thinking with a respected expert was certainly a refreshing validation that my own ideas might have merit.

Phase I: Establishing the Link

For the sake of comprehension and clarity, let me begin by presenting a few presumptions concerning my theory. First, let's suppose that the Watchers and other angels are actually biological entities instead of merely non-physical spirit beings as most people think. This would also mean that the realm they inhabit is a physical world as well. Now, let's suppose that they have existed for millions of years and their technology is sufficiently advanced beyond our own. Additionally, their science has proven the existence of the multiverse,[2] and that they co-exist in a vast expanse of parallel worlds.

The Watchers take an interest in the little realm we know as Earth, but are faced with the problem of how to get there. Spacecraft are out of the question for two major reasons. First, the earthly realm is not located at some far-off planet in a distant galaxy, it is less than a millimeter away from them—practically right under their noses (supposing they have noses, of course). Second, even if it was located in a galaxy far, far away, it seems impractical to use large clunky ships that will take such a long time to reach their destination, not to mention the trouble of transporting crew, supplies, food, fuel of some sort, and anything else necessary to endure such a long journey.

They realize that they could attempt to create "wormholes" to traverse the dimensions, but there is still another problem. The amount of energy required to open up a sufficiently sized wormhole for the necessary duration of time is too demanding and impractical. Another obstacle is that the other end of the wormhole might not be stable enough to work properly due to the unknowns of the destination realm. There is, however, a different way of approaching this problem while still using the wormholes.

If the civilization is advanced enough to be creating wormholes, they have also probably made amazing breakthroughs in the field of nanoscience. Nanoscience involves the study and application of things that are extremely small—specifically, objects smaller than 100 nanometers (0.00001 cm). To put that into perspective, a typical human hair is approximately 70,000 to 80,000 nanometers thick. The application of this science to create or modify the size and shape of objects at such a tiny scale is referred to as nanotechnology.

Nanotechnology has actually been studied and theorized by scientists since the 1950s. It has only been in recent times, though, that our equipment and knowledge has advanced enough to put it to any kind of practical usage. With apparently unlimited potential, nanotechnology boldly promises a future of "everything from the mundane (better paints, self-cleaning windows) to the bizarre (tiny submarines that will glide through our veins destroying bacteria)."[3] Despite some far-fetched and impractical ideas involving the use of nanotechnology, the incredible possibilities that it offers have captured the attention of governments, militaries, and major

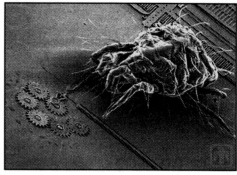

Nano-sized gears compared to the size of a mite. *Courtesy of Sandia National Laboratories, SUMMiTTM Technologies, www.mems.sandia.gov*

industries that are all investing in the nanotech "revolution."

What many people find surprising, though, is that nanotechnology is nothing new. In fact, "the most complex and highly functional nanoscale materials and machines have already been invented—by nature."[4] Therefore, every one of the chemical interactions, spinning atoms, and molecular structures surrounding you are examples of natural nanotechnology in action. So if the advanced race identified as the Watchers knew how to use advanced nanotechnology, it probably would have appeared to our ancient ancestors as "magic" to their eyes. But what does this have to do with the wormholes and moving between dimensions?

My suggestion is that the Watchers could have opened a very tiny wormhole that connected their realm to ours. But the purpose of this initial wormhole is to send tiny nano-robots (often referred to as "nanobots") to the other side. These nanobots could be programmed to gather raw materials by extracting single atoms from various sources and then recombining them to create new materials necessary to replicate themselves. Next, the increased team of nanobots could begin to manufacture the equipment designed by the Watchers that would create a stable "mouth" for the wormhole on this end.

There is also another issue that needs to be addressed. Throughout the texts, there are countless examples of how "mountains" played an important role in these gateways. Even the ziggurats and pyramids were created to represent the primeval "first" mountain. But why were mountains important or even necessary?

I gave this question some thought and there is only one possibility that seems to make sense. Perhaps the mountains were the most remote locations available and therefore the most convenient to establish gateways. Most of the people and their settlements would have been on much lower ground near water bodies and fertile soil. If the Watchers had tried to open gateways in such places they would increase their risk of colliding with foreign bodies (e.g. people, animals, and structures). The nanobots would probably become trapped if the gateway opened right into the middle of a stone wall. Even a person or animal that just happened to be passing through that exact spot could pose considerable risk to the project (not to mention it might kill them). Therefore, the remote locations of the mountains were probably the safest place to set up shop.

But what about the suggestion that there were gateways located within some of the ziggurats and pyramids found throughout the world? These were probably built later, after the Watchers were established in our world. It is interesting to note that many of the pyramid structures have been rebuilt or modified many times, but they always remained at the same locations. For instance, archaeologists have found that the core of the ancient ziggurat known as Etemenanki ("Foundation of Heaven and Earth") actually contained the remains of previous ziggurats. At one time it was simply a mound, and then the Mesopotamians continued to modify it until the final tower was built. This may indicate that the device for the gateways was set up here and then elevated each time the structure was built higher. Additionally, European folklore provides accounts regarding faeries and how they used mounds and hills as portals to the Faery realm.

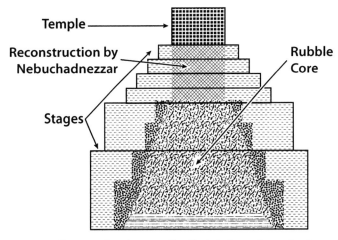

Temple

Reconstruction by Nebuchadnezzar

Rubble Core

Stages

Cross-section view revealing the interior makeup of a ziggurat.

At this point, the first phase of the gateway is now complete.

Phase II: The Ghost in the Shell

There is still a small problem involving the limitations of using a wormhole. As I already mentioned, the wormhole will probably be extremely small (it might be invisible to the naked eye) because the energy required to create one that is larger and yet remain stable would most likely be enormous. So, the Watchers are still faced with a problem of not being able to transport large items across dimensions. However, they do know that they can transport information, just like how a computer transfers information by creating electrical signals that are converted into digital codes and interpreted by software: think of it as an inter-dimensional super internet.

The next step would be that the Watchers would need to create a suitable "shell" to receive the information—in this case it would be a body. Once again, the nanobots could gather the necessary materials and assemble the body according to a standardized blueprint of the human genome. As discussed in Chapter 5, this body wouldn't have any "inherited" genetics from a mother or father such as skin or hair color. Therefore, the body's skin and hair would probably be a very pale or whitish color, just like the ancient texts describe. They would also probably be sensitive to the sunlight, again supported by the ancient stories.

Once the body is complete, the consciousness of the Watcher is converted into information, sent through the gateway, and downloaded into the body. Or, perhaps it is actually the "soul" of the Watcher that is being transferred into the body. I have often entertained the idea that perhaps what we consider the "soul" or "mind" is really hyper-dimensional in nature. If so, it would explain how it is still able to manipulate objects within the physical world and yet be something that our science cannot currently weigh or measure.

In regard to the gateways, we now have a newly formed body that awakens once the information has been downloaded. The Watcher now has the ability to directly interact with the physical world and everything in it. Their tweaked genetics may even give them special abilities beyond mere mortals, and might also be the cause for the genetic deformities of their offspring from their unions with humans.

Phase III: Making a Round Trip

After the Watchers make it to the earthly realm and get adjusted to their new bodies, another problem emerges: how do they return home? It is possible that they could have constructed similar devices used in their home realm (a.k.a. "heaven"), and simply repeat the process of uploading their information into the system and sending it back to a waiting body (perhaps even their original body, if it could be preserved). Additionally, there is also another issue raised by the ancient tales: how do humans (such as Enoch) get transported to the heavenly realm without being killed?

Once again, I suppose it is possible that the Watchers could apply the same process to a human that they did to themselves. After all, Enoch was apparently still human when he was first "translated" into heaven. Perhaps his body could be transferred, too, instead of only his mind. However, the texts seem to indicate that something was done to Enoch so that he could become like one of the angels. Recall that Richard Laurence's translation of the *Book of Enoch* says that all of Enoch's "flesh was dissolved."[5] Perhaps this was describing the process whereby he acquired a new body. Or maybe something such as the nanobots disassembled his molecules, modified them, and then reassembled him into the angel Metatron. For now, it is far too difficult to determine one way or another from the old tale.

If Enoch was capable of being transported in his original body, then maybe the Watchers had perfected the technology for opening a stable wormhole of suitable size so that they could simply walk through it. It might be that Enoch needed to ingest a substance such as the monatomic gold into his bloodstream to allow his transfer, though. If the monatomic gold works according to David Hudson's claims, then perhaps the hyperdimensional shifting abilities would transfer to Enoch. If he didn't ingest the substance, he might be destroyed by the gateway, such as when Nebuchadnezzar's men were incinerated by the furnace but the three priests remained unharmed.[6] But once again, I must stress that this is all speculation at this point in time.

Conclusion

While the theory proposed here is not without its complications or limitations, it does seem to offer potential answers to many questions. It resolves how the first gateways could have been developed, how the Watchers could transfer themselves between dimensions, and how they created bodies for themselves. It is certainly not intended to be the definitive answer concerning how the gateways were developed and how they operated; we still know far too little about these subjects. However, I've included this appendix for any scientifically minded people who might initially dismiss my "babble" about hyper-dimensional angels moving through gateways as complete nonsense. It is my hope that it will make them pause for a moment and reevaluate their opinions about the topics explored in this book. Perhaps they won't think the idea is so crazy after all.

HOLEY(ER) THAN THOU

I WAS FACED WITH A TOUGH DECISION regarding whether or not I should take this appendix out. But if I am going to make enemies, I'd much rather be hated for making terrible puns than for writing heavy-handed critiques of fellow researchers. This section is not intended to ridicule, libel, or attack the authors discussed herein, but rather, I hope to encourage discerning readers to evaluate the writings of these individuals much more carefully. I cannot in good conscience look the other way, so to speak, when confronted with research that presents misleading information or when encountering "scholars" that make crucial errors when translating important texts. Furthermore, one must not necessarily be an ancient language expert or advanced mathematician to notice these major (and oftentimes deliberate) oversights. Therefore, I believe that it is necessary to discuss two specific writers (but there are certainly others) whose work I have found to be particularly problematic.

Does this mean that I think my own work is flawless? Hardly. I know that it is only a matter of time before someone objects to something that I have written. I have no desire to spread erroneous information, but I do feel that I have an obligation to teach others what I've learned. If I have made any major mistakes, you should expect to see them corrected or acknowledged in future editions of this work. Making mistakes and reevaluating our work are crucial parts of the learning process. Ultimately, I encourage my readers to search far and wide and to diligently verify the information for themselves.

How to Make an Ancient Astronaut of Yourself

According to the biographical blurb included with his publications, Zecharia Sitchin is described as an eminent Biblical scholar "distinguished by his ability to translate ancient Sumerian and other ancient texts." However, despite numerous requests, Mr. Sitchin has *never* produced any credentials proving that he is qualified to comprehend and translate such languages. Many other reputable language scholars dismiss Sitchin's work and claim that his translations are incorrect and even fraudulent. While they are correct in their evaluations, this has also created an unfortunate side effect. Now, some scholars automatically dismiss any alternative theories and ideas that bear even a slight resemblance to Sitchin's material, simply because they assume that Sitchin was a source. Therefore, they might be missing important information because they don't want to waste their time on another idea that probably came from one of Sitchin's books.

I realize that some readers are going to be displeased with the information I am about to present, however I hope that those interested in these subjects will take the time to investigate these matters on their own. When I first began my research, I too was enamored with Sitchin's work and I believe that he is the avenue through which many people may find their way to this area of study. My intention is not to attack Mr. Sitchin, but to instead illustrate to those that fervently revere his work that there are many inconsistencies and errors which unfortunately render his scholarship quite suspect. In order to demonstrate Sitchin's errors, Dr. Michael S. Heiser, Ph.D., has kindly permitted me to adapt a portion of one of his papers that presents undeniable proof that Sitchin's work is riddled with inaccuracies.[1]

While I could spend a great deal of time pointing to the numerous errors and mistranslations that Sitchin has made in order to support his theories concerning "ancient astronauts," I need only provide one specific example that will prove to be devastating to Sitchin's work. In the book, *The Stairway to Heaven*, Sitchin recounts the ancient legend concerning the strange birth of Noah and his father's fear that the newborn was a child of the Watchers:

> Behold, I thought in my heart that the conception was from one of the *Watchers*, one of the Holy Ones, and (that the child really belonged to) the *Giants*.[2]

Sitchin remarks on the above fragment as follows:

> But as we examine the Hebrew original we find that it does not say "Watchers"; it says Nefilim—the very term used in Genesis 6.
> Thus do all the ancient texts and all the ancient tales confirm each other: The days before the Deluge were the days when "The

336

Nefilim were upon the Earth—the Mighty Ones, the people of the Rocketships."[3]

What Sitchin is trying to do is equate the Watchers and the Nephilim as being one and the same so that he can say the Nephilim are really space aliens ("those who came down," i.e. "fallen") from another planet. In the above passage, he is providing his own translation of Genesis 6:4, rather than any official translation. Additionally, notice that he says the Nefilim are "the people of the Rocketships." But we've already explored how the actual word is *shem* (שם), meaning "name" in Hebrew (see Chapters 6 and 7). This is just one of many other examples where Sitchin substitutes *his* (mis)-translation of a word to make it say what he wants. To further prove his point—just in case you doubt him—Sitchin reproduces the lines of the scroll fragment and underlines the word for "Nefilim" (Note: only the first line of the scroll as it appeared in Sitchin's book is reproduced here):

[4]הא באדין חשבת בלבי די מן עירין הריאנתא ומן קדישין הן]א ולנפילין

Unfortunately for Sitchin, he commits three serious blunders that are actually quite amusing. First, he mistakenly refers to the scroll fragment quoted above as a "Hebrew original"—but it's not written in Hebrew—it's written in *Aramaic!* Anyone trained to read these ancient languages could clearly tell this fact by noticing the "-in" (ין-) endings for masculine plural words in Aramaic, as opposed to the "-im" (ים-) endings used in Hebrew. So the correct rendering of the word from this text isn't Nephil<u>im</u> (נפילים), it is Nephil<u>in</u> (נפילין). This kind of mistake is absolutely inexcusable for someone who is supposed to be a trained "expert" in Semitic languages.

Secondly, he is using the wrong word to emphasize his point. If you recall, the Hebrew and Aramaic languages are written from right to left. Now, look again at the English translation of the scroll fragment. Sitchin is trying to tell you that the word in the *middle* of the line is incorrectly translated as "Watchers," and that it should be "Nefilim," but he underlines the *last* word in the sentence. The underlined word is indeed "Nefilin," but if you compare it to the English translation you can clearly see that it's correctly rendered as the *last* word: "Giants." This is yet another mistake revealing his poor understanding of *basic* grammatical rules of the Hebrew and Aramaic languages.

Finally, Sitchin completely shoots himself in the foot by using this particular verse to prove his point. Remember that he tells us that the line does not say "Watchers," but rather "Nefilim?" Well, he misses the word for "Watchers" IN THE LINE just a few words prior to "Nephilin!" Let's look at the line again and notice this time that the enlarged word is "Watchers" written in Aramaic:

⁵הָא בֵּאדַיִן חָשְׁבֵת בְּלִבִּי דִּי מִן עִירִין הָרִיאָנְתָא וּמִן קַדִּישִׁין הֲוֹ֯א וְלִנְפִילִין

Clearly, Sitchin is mistaken here and the entire point he was attempting to make ironically refutes his own work. Unfortunately for him, the translations and meanings of words that he tries so hard to dismiss are indeed the correct ones and his theories begin to fall apart from here. If you are a Sitchin supporter, please try to let the enormity of these blunders sink in for a moment. Zecharia Sitchin has been telling his audience for years that he is qualified to decipher several ancient languages. Additionally, his skills are supposed to be so great that he can freely *invent* his own translations when it suits his needs because he alone possesses the "correct" understanding of the texts. But he clearly does not possess such skills. In fact, his very own work deceives him. Because his theories depend upon *his* interpretations of words—and not those of qualified scholars—all of his theories fall apart once his skills are discredited. Furthermore, since the debut of *The 12ᵗʰ Planet* in 1976, Sitchin's unwillingness to present his credentials to critics or to acknowledge flaws with his work suggest that he has deliberately kept his followers in the dark about his misguided theories.

So where do I get off being so critical of Sitchin when I do not possess any such degrees, either? It's simple: I never claimed to have such skills and was completely honest about it from the beginning. Instead, I pulled all of my definitions and translations from reputable scholarly sources to support my theories. If you look up the meaning of the word "shem" in *any* standard Hebrew or Aramaic lexicon, you will see that it means "name"—*not* "rocketship." The most important difference is that my theories are supported by the accepted scholarly definitions of the words, whereas Sitchin's are not. Sitchin must invent his meanings to support his theories—he has no other choice.

There is an additional problem that I have with some of Sitchin's work, however this issue has more to do with the fans than with the work itself. After completing the six volumes of *The Earth Chronicles* series, plus two

338

additional follow-up works, Sitchin released a book titled, *The Lost Book of Enki* (Bear and Company, 2002). The problem is that even though it is clearly labeled as a work of *fiction,* the book is written in a similar style of Sitchin's previous books and professes to be a "lost book" which tells the "true" story of the Anunnaki. While I have no problem with Zecharia Sitchin writing a piece of fiction dealing with this material, I do feel that it was presented in a manner too similar to his other works. I immediately recognized the danger in this because I knew that there would be many loyal fans out there who simply wouldn't realize that it was a complete work of fiction. Unfortunately, the damage has already been done.

A case in point, on an episode of *Coast to Coast AM,* airing July 6, 2005, Marshall Klarfield was invited to discuss his new book: *Adam, the Missing Link.* During the interview, Mr. Klarfield directly acknowledges Sitchin as an important source informing his research and theories. Even though I was aware of Sitchin's errors, this did not bother me greatly because many other authors refer to Sitchin's material and I didn't want to specifically hold this against Klarfield. However, Mr. Klarfield soon began quoting from some supposedly ancient Sumerian text that sounded vaguely familiar. I thought to myself, *It sounds like he's quoting from* The Lost Book of Enki. *Doesn't he realize that it's fiction?* Apparently not, because Klarfield confirmed that his source was indeed from Sitchin's fictional work. He continued to make references to *The Lost Book of Enki,* holding it in high regard. I can laugh about this incident in retrospect, but at the time I found myself repeatedly shaking my head and yelling at the radio in frustration, "It's fiction—look at the book jacket!"

If readers doubt my estimations of Sitchin's work, I wholeheartedly encourage them to revisit his material and compare his translations with more reliable and informed sources. Be wary of anyone promoting Sitchin as an "eminent scholar" or "expert" in ancient languages, for they obviously have not attempted to verify the accuracy of his work.

Apocalypse... wow
(A Red "Heron" is Discovered at the Great Pyramid)

As I mentioned in Chapter 6, some researchers believe that the dimensions of the Great Pyramid demonstrate how to solve the riddle of "squaring the circle." One such person that has been championing this idea is Patrick Heron, particularly in his book, *The Nephilim and the Pyramid of the Apocalypse* (Xulon Press, 2004). I became aware of Heron's work in January of 2005. Naturally, I was eager to investigate Heron's book since it appeared to overlap with my own research, for his study discussed the riddle of how to "square the circle" in context with the Nephilim and ancient prophecies.

When I first picked up the book, I was automatically skeptical of the claim that it was the "first in-depth book to throw light on a mysterious race known as the NEPHILIM." Above all, I was amused by its overly dramatic: "WARNING: THIS BOOK IS NOT FICTION" emblazoned in bold text across the back cover. I wondered if perhaps Heron was unaware of the *numerous* other fiction and non-fiction books, not to mention movies and television shows, which explored the subject of the Nephilim and the Watchers.

Upon opening the book, the first thing that I noticed was that the so-called "evidence" and other data presented in the first few pages quickly fell apart. This is because Heron's initial theories require some manipulation of numbers and measurements in order for his solution to work. For instance, it must be assumed that the base unit of measurement is the "Hebrew cubit" equaling 25.025 inches, but this measurement is not authentic (not to mention we should be dealing with Egyptian units, such as the Royal Cubit of 20.65 inches).[6] Unfortunately for Heron, he uses these "facts" as the foundation for the rest of his theories to undeniably prove primitive humans couldn't have constructed the pyramids and it must have been "evil" fallen angels.

Using this 25.025 inch unit of measurement, Heron states that the length of each side of the pyramid's base equals 365.2422 cubits—which is intriguing because it matches the number of days in one year, including the extra quarter day that accommodates for a "leap day." Then Heron claims that the rising sides of the pyramid apparently converge at a height of 232.52 cubits. Next, he multiplies the length of each side of the base by two and then divides this figure by the pyramid's height to get the following formula: $(365.242 \times 2) \div 232.52 = 3.14159$. This is meant to suggest that the numerical value of Pi had been incorporated into the pyramid's design. He then explains how the perimeter of the base ($365.242 \times 4 = 1,460.968$)

equals the circumference of a circle with a diameter that is twice the height of the pyramid (232.52 x 2 x 3.1416 = 1,460.968).[7]

This seems almost too good to be true. However, the key to successfully solving the equations depends solely upon using the measurements he lists in conjunction with the 25.025 inch "cubit," which is a fabrication and a clever tactic to make the numerical values seem to have significance. If the reader were to review the measurements of the pyramid provided by reputable Egyptologists, and compare them with the measurements in "Hebrew cubits," discrepancies quickly appear. For reference, I have repeated the measurements of the pyramid on the following page.[8]

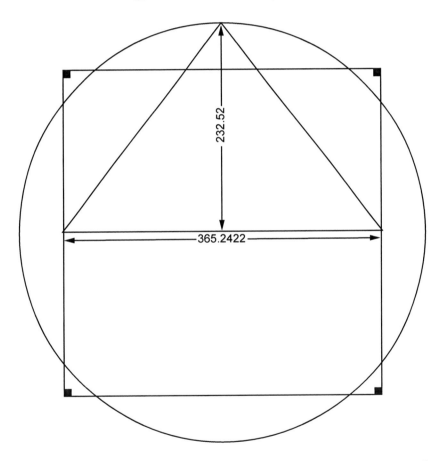

The illustration provided by Heron to "prove" that the dimensions of the Great Pyramid contain the solution to "Squaring the Circle."

- The pyramid was nearly 481 feet (146.59 m) high upon completion.
- Erosion and the loss of the capstone now make the pyramid 455.21 feet (138.75 m) high.
- Each side of the base was approximately 755.8 feet (230.37 m) across after the limestone coverings were placed.
- The pyramid's sides now measure approximately 746.4 feet (227.5 m) across after the limestone casings have been removed.

Now, we can compare the mathematical formulas and determine whether or not they match the figures suggested by Heron. Interestingly, Heron tells us that his measurements and observations concerning the Great Pyramid are from the "esteemed architect and eschatologist [a person who studies the 'End Times'] Clarence Larkin." Larkin, however, more than likely obtained his data from the Astronomer Royal of Scotland, Charles Piazzi Smyth (January 3, 1819–February 21, 1900) who wrote the book, *Our Inheritance in the Great Pyramid* (published in 1864). Additionally, Smyth was building upon the ideas put forth by the Victorian newspaper editor, John Taylor (1781–1864). Taylor appears to have invented the 25.025 inch unit to help explain his theories about Pi and the pyramid proposed in his book, *The Great Pyramid* (published in 1859). Prior to this time, there are no references to this particular "Hebrew cubit," and there is no evidence substantiating the claim that any of the ancient cultures used it as one of their units of measurement. Using the dimensions of the pyramid that I have found, we can attempt to verify the work of Heron and his predecessors.

If the side of the pyramid was 755.8 feet across, we first need to convert both measurements to a common unit, in this case inches: (365.2422 cu x 25.025 in/cu = 9140.186 in) and (755.8 ft x 12 in/ft = 9069.6 in). Next, we find the difference between the values and convert back to feet: (9140.186 in − 9069.6 in = 70.586 in), then (70.586 in ÷ 12 in/ft = 5.88 ft).

As you can see, if we accept Patrick Heron's measurement of 365.2422 Hebrew cubits, it means that the Great Pyramid must have been 5.88 feet *greater* on each side than what has been calculated by archaeologists and Egyptologists—and that measurement is only valid if we use the "full" dimensions of the pyramid that included the limestone casings! Even if we assume that the Egyptologists have miscalculated, and we work only with the current measurements of the pyramid (i.e. without the casing stones), the difference becomes greater (15.28 feet on each side). Since Heron's number does not match the actual dimensions of the pyramid, it seems that the value is presented solely for the purpose of making it appear as though the number of days in a solar year were intentionally figured into the construction of the pyramid. However, the proof is in the numbers, and Heron's suggestion turns out to be incorrect.

But what about the pyramid's height? Once again, we can compare Heron's value with that of other measurements. First, it is necessary to covert the supplied measurements from cubits and feet to the common unit of inches: (232.52 cu x 25.025 in/cu = 5818.813 in) and (481 ft x 12 in/ft = 5772 in). This results in a difference of nearly four feet greater than the accepted height (5818.813 in – 5772 in = 46.813 inches or 3.9 feet). So not only is the height incorrect, but the measurement Heron provides is what he uses to derive the value of Pi that is used for the rest of the equations ((365.242 cu x 2) ÷ 232.52 cu = 3.14159 cu). This shows that Heron's end results cannot be trusted because he is using his earlier (and flawed) calculations to construct his final formulas that supposedly prove his ability to "square the circle."

Probably the most negligent error occurs *twice* on the same page and is in his final calculation result of "14609.68" because the decimal place should be moved one more place to the left.[9] Normally, I'd be willing to let a decimal mistake slide, but not when it occurs twice on the same page and the equations are plainly listed for anyone to verify. Certainly, *somebody* should have double-checked the math before the book went to press and caught such an error, especially because these equations are being used as evidence to support Heron's claims that the pyramid is the key to successfully squaring the circle.

Other problems occur with the math when Heron rounds numbers to make them appear exactly equal. He states that the perimeter of the square base (365.242 x 4 = 1460.968) and the circumference of the circle (232.52 x 2 x 3.1416 = 1460.968) are "exactly equal" even though his equations clearly show that they are not. Careful attention to the second equation shows that he rounded the original number 3.14159 up to 3.1416 and plugs it in to get "1,460.968" (please note that I have corrected all of the occurrences of the decimal point mistake here for the purposes of this demonstration) which is yet *another* rounded number (from 1,460.969).[10] If the numbers are said to be "exact" then they should be just that. Instead, they are conveniently adjusted and shown matching in the book to make it seem as if they offer a solution. This behavior is just plain deceptive because it clearly reveals that Heron intentionally padded the numbers.

My complaints might appear rather harsh, but I believe that authors should be held accountable for their work, and be responsible with the information that they present to their audience. Heron boldly claims that he can successfully "square the circle" using inaccurate mathematical equations associated with the Great Pyramid—a claim that is demonstrably false.

Remember, it is mathematically *impossible* to "square the circle" because it uses Pi (π), for which we only know an *approximate* value. Any other attempt using math requires the deceitful use of numbers to successfully balance the equations. Second, the idea of "squaring the circle" is that the *area* of a circle equals the *area* of the square, but authors such as Heron try to equate the *circumference* of a circle with the *perimeter* of a square. The phrase "square the circle" directly implies that the answer involves the areas of the shapes, and not their outside perimeters. *It's what's inside that counts.* This is an unacceptable method of pushing alternative ideas regarding how and why the pyramids were built and using "pseudo mathematics" for no other purpose than to make such false claims appear credible to audiences.

Although there are numerous other issues that I have with the quality of Heron's work, there is one other particular issue of his that I would like to address. Heron makes some very basic mistakes with ancient languages that even laypeople such as myself (who are without the ingenious translation abilities of Zecharia Sitchin) could easily identify. A primary instance occurs in Heron's interpretation of the origin of Lucifer, whom he (like so many others) mistakenly identifies as the leader of the fallen angels. During his overview of the Book of Isaiah (14:12–14) Heron inserts a comment that infers the phrase "O Morning Star" is derived from the original *Hebrew* word "Lucifer."[11] The problem is that "Lucifer" is a *Latin* word, not Hebrew! The correct Hebraic term would have been *Helel ben Shakar* (הילל בן שחר). Now, I'm willing to give the benefit of the doubt that this could just be a typographical error and Heron meant to say that the word is Latin, but it should still be addressed. Minor mistakes such as this are the kind that can easily place one's credibility into question.

The last topic that I wish to address in regard to Patrick Heron concerns what he believes to be the purpose of the Great Pyramid. Heron's interpretation of Biblical texts argues that all of the various pyramids found throughout the world, particularly the Great Pyramid, are counterfeit decep-tions created by Satan to mimic the Holy City of God described in Chapter 21 of Revelation.[12] I obviously disagree with his interpretation. There are numerous differences between the descriptions of the Holy City and the Great Pyramid if anyone wishes to compare them. Furthermore, I believe that my own explanation of the symbolism found throughout Biblical texts relies more closely upon the exact meanings and definitions of the original words. Most notably, the majority of Biblical scholars would tend to agree that Revelation describes the Holy City with the dimensions of a perfect cube, further supporting my theories.

While Heron briefly mentions the cube description, he suggests that it should really be a pyramid since it can fit inside of a cube.[13] This might be a satisfactory answer for some readers, but not for me. Having a background in 3D computer graphics and multimedia, I know that this is a rather simplistic and inaccurate suggestion on Heron's part, which ultimately substantiates nothing of any significance. For example, when creating three-dimensional geometry on a computer, the models can become quite complex. To help speed up how quickly the computer processor can "draw" the image, the artist can adjust settings so that approximations of the objects are visible. These are typically known as "bounding boxes" because *any* object can fit within a cube or rectangular box of the proper dimensions. So, it seems pointless to argue that it must be a pyramid because a pyramid can fit within a cube—so can anything else.

But wait, isn't he referring to a pyramid of equal length, width, and depth? Actually, yes, he *is* referring to such a pyramid. Unfortunately, Heron

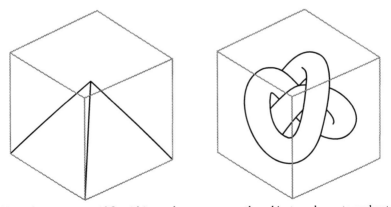

Not only can a pyramid fit within a cube, so can any other object, such as a torus knot.

cannot justify his argument that a pyramid is the only other geometric shape that's capable of satisfying the dimensions of a cube. For instance, a sphere is equal in all of its dimensions as well (or else it would not be a sphere) and would fit quite nicely within the cube. Since John describes very specific details about the heavenly city in Revelation, I think that if he wanted to say it was shaped like a pyramid then he could have easily done so. Instead, he describes it as a cube. Heron then creates ambiguity about this description and considers it proof that supports his belief.

Again, you might be wondering why I am so critical of Heron's opinion that Satan designed the Great Pyramid to deceive mankind—that is his opinion, so why can't I just leave it alone? Simply put, it is because it does not withstand closer scrutiny and I believe readers are being misled by his theory. The entire reason Heron is saying that Satan and similar demonic spawn are the architects of *all* pyramids worldwide is because he is trying to convince you that no human being could ever achieve such precision, thus proving by default that the architects *must* have been supernatural. But I've already demonstrated that Heron's data concerning the pyramid is erroneous. Once this supposed precision is removed, there is no reason to believe that it was supernatural in origin (but even if the precision had been correct, it doesn't dismiss the likelihood of highly innovative *human* architects).

To be fair, I have taken the same equations used by Heron but replaced his supplied measurements with my own. I have included the results below for you to see. Amazingly, my numbers come much closer to matching and require less rounding than Heron's work, but they are still not exact matches. Aside from a coincidence, it *is* possible that the architects of the pyramid were trying to incorporate mathematical information into the structure, such as an *approximate* answer of how to square the circle.

Formulas for this Example:

Heron's method to get approximate value of Pi (π) = 2s ÷ h
(Please note that Heron is using an incorrect formula to get his contrived Pi. The actual value of Pi is obtained by taking a circle's circumference and dividing it by the circle's diameter.)

Perimeter of a square = 4s

Circumference of a circle = $2\pi r$ *(or)* πd

Measurements:

Pyramid's Side (s) = 230.37 meters

Pyramid's Height (h) = 146.59 meters (this value is doubled in order to obtain the circle's diameter)

Test:

(2 x 230.37) ÷ 146.59 = 3.143052 meters

4 x 230.37 = 921.48 meters

3.143052 x (146.59 x 2) = 921.47998 meters

As you can see, the calculation for the perimeter of the pyramid's base (921.48 m) is almost exactly the same as the circumference of a circle that is twice the height of the pyramid (921.47998 m). However, as I've stated before, the idea of squaring the circle is not about the outside, it is about the inside. Let's test the Great Pyramid's measurements using surface formulas.

Formulas for this Example:

Heron's method to get approximate value of Pi (π) = 2s ÷ h

(Once again, please remember that the actual value of Pi is obtained by taking a circle's circumference and dividing it by the circle's diameter and that Heron's method is incorrect.)

Area of a square = s^2

Area of a circle = πr^2

Measurements:

Pyramid's Side (s) = 230.37 meters

Pyramid's Height (h *and* r) = 146.59 meters (this is the circle's radius)

Test:

(2 x 230.37) ÷ 146.59 = 3.143052 meters

230.37^2 = 53,070.3369 sq. meters

3.143052 x 146.59^2 = 67,539.8755 sq. meters

Now, we can clearly see that the areas of the square (53,070.3369) and the circle (67,539.8755) are not even remotely close. The result is a difference of about 14,469.5386 square feet!

I will admit that the Great Pyramid and similar structures are stunning achievements that have withstood the test of time. Many of them display qualities that are unmatched by today's advanced architectural achievements and still inspire a sense of awe and mystery when trying to assess how these monuments were constructed. I will even go so far as to say that I cannot rule out the possibility that in order to build such monuments, mankind was guided or aided by supernatural intelligences. However, what I am primarily concerned with is the actual mechanics of the gateway technology, which I do believe was developed by non-human intelligences. The buildings only seemed to have been houses for these devices, but with the additional purpose of encoding other important information such as mathematical formulae or calendar systems (such as the Temple of Kukulcán).

The first several pages of *The Nephilim and the Pyramid of the Apocalypse* are available for previewing via Amazon (www.amazon.com) or you can preview the first three chapters at Heron's website (www.nephilimapocalypse. com). You can see for yourself the errors in which I am writing about to know that I'm not making them up or exaggerating them. Normally, I would not have made such a big deal about this issue, but I have watched the sales of this particular book jump quite high. Furthermore, Heron's theories have inspired a television and DVD documentary, entitled, *The Apocalypse and the End Times,* by Grizzly Adams Productions. I believe that people have a right to know about these mistakes and I hope to do my part in preventing any further misinformation from being accepted as the truth.

TRACKING THE MOVEMENTS OF VENUS

T HE OBSERVATION OF THE PLANET VENUS played a significant role in the studies of ancient astronomers. It was known as both the "Morning Star" and "Evening Star," depending on when it appeared in the sky. It was also called the "Eastern Star" and "Lucifer," or "the Light-bearer." The watchful eyes of the astronomers saw that a five-pointed star shape could be derived by plotting the points of Venus at sunrise. Today, anyone can replicate this study by using computer software.

The program used for this tutorial is Starry Night™ Pro Plus 6.0 by Imaginova™. Several other versions of this software designed and priced for amateurs and hobbyists are available, as well as comparable programs by other companies. The Starry Night™ product line, however, is the most highly recommended by astronomy enthusiasts and professionals. I have provided some sample files on the website for use with Starry Night if readers want to proceed through this tutorial more quickly. Otherwise, you may simply follow along with the steps outline below, or use them as a guide if you are using a different astronomy program.

For clarification, some technical terms related to astronomy will be defined here:

- **Sidereal year:** the time for a planet or object to return to the same position in respect to the stars as seen from the surface of Earth.

- **Synodic period:** for planets, the mean interval of time between successive conjunctions of a pair of planets, as observed from the Sun. The synodic period for conjunctions between Earth and Venus is 583.92 days.

Some of the information in this tutorial is based on the data and example provided by Trevor W. McKeown and Dr. Leigh Hunt Palmer,[1] with some slight modifications made by myself. To begin, start with a new session.

Tutorial 1: Tracking Venus in Ancient Babylon

1) Change your observation point to **Baghdad, Iraq** (Lat. 33° 20' N, Long. 44° 24 ' E), by going to the toolbar and clicking on **Other...** to open the Viewing Location dialog box and find the listing for Baghdad. Press the **Set Location** button to close the dialog and move to your new location. *(Note: it is not mandatory that the location be Baghdad. This will work for any location where Venus is prominent in the sky at sunrise.)*

2) Next, manually adjust the date to **March 23, 716 BCE** in the toolbar.

3) Press the **Sunrise** button below the time and date to automatically adjust the time to the moment of sunrise; in this case: 7:13:31 a.m.

4) Click on the **Find** tab to open the listing of observable objects. Right-click on Venus (Cmd-click on a Mac) and select the **Centre** option from the menu. The software should now adjust itself to bring Venus into prominent view. If needed, the **Label** checkbox beside Venus can also be activated to identify the planet more easily.

5) *This is a very important step, so please do not skip it.* After centering Venus on your screen, you will need to **disable** this feature to continue with the tutorial. If you do not disable this option, it will keep Venus centered all of the time and *you will lose the ability to properly track its movements.* The easiest way to disable the Centre option is to simply move your cursor into the viewing area and click your mouse button. There might be a very subtle perspective shift of your viewing area when this is done, but it will not affect our results. If you are still unsure if the Centre option has been disabled, go back into the Find tab and right-click (Cmd-click on a Mac) to verify that Centre is no longer checked.

6) Click on the **Find** tab again to close the panel and increase your viewing area.

7) Now, go to the toolbar and adjust the **Time Flow** to **584 days** (the synodic period of Venus), or for more precision, click on it and open the **Edit...** dialog box.

8) *(Note: if your software does not support more precise measurements, you may skip this step and leave the setting at 584 days.)* Inside the **Time Units** box, click on the + button to add a new unit. You may name this unit whatever you like, but for this example we will use "Venus synodic period (precise)." Enter **583.92** as the **unit duration** and change it to "**days.**" Press the "OK" buttons for both the Add Time Unit and Time Unit boxes to return to the main window.

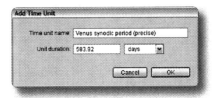

9) If it is not automatically selected, change the **Time Flow** to match your new time unit (583.92 days or 584 days, depending on your software).

10) Make a note of the location of Venus in the sky at sunrise.

11) Using the VCR-like controls, press the **Step Forward** 🖸 button to advance ahead one unit. *(Note: this is not the Play button.)*

12) Press the **Sunrise** button to adjust the time, and make another note of the new location of Venus in the sky.

13) Repeat Steps 11 and 12 **four** more times (for a total of six points plotted in the sky), until Venus returns to approximately the same starting position. *(Your finish date should be March 21, 708 BCE at 7:16:17 a.m.)*

14) If a line is drawn from one point to the next, it will form a pentagram shape in the sky. This is a construct based on these plot points, and not the actual path of Venus as it moves through the sky. If the actual path of Venus were tracked, it would result in a strange pattern (opposite page).

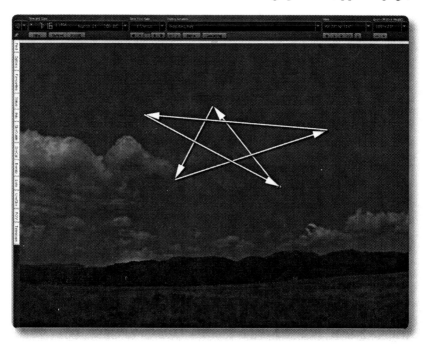

An easy method to create the pentagram star on your own is to use the images from Starry Night™ in a graphics program such as Adobe® Photoshop®. Simply save an image using the **Export as Image** command from the **File** menu, or alternatively, you can do a screen capture by pressing the **Print Screen** key on your keyboard to copy the entire screen into memory. Then, create a new document in Photoshop and **Paste** the image(s) onto a new layer one at a time. However you choose to do this, you can then

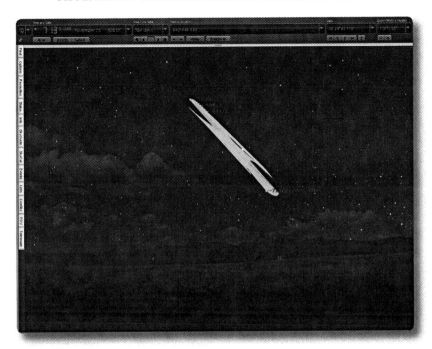

adjust the transparency of each layer to see the difference between the others, or make certain layers visible or invisible like frames in an animation. An animated example of the final result is available for viewing at www.gatewayofthegods.com.

As you can see, tracing the points in proper order makes a pentagram but it is not a perfect geometrical figure. Unfortunately, there is no location on the earth that will result in plotting a perfect pentagram in the sky. Observing near the equator results in the irregular shaped pentagram whereas viewing locations farther north will elongate the shape. However, **Tutorial 3** will explain how to plot a nearly perfect pentagram observable from outer space. For now, we shall move onto the next lesson.

Tutorial 2: Inverting the Pentagram

Ancient astronomers realized that there was a slight slippage (measured at 0.0789 every 584 days) in the movement of the planet Venus. This results in approximately a one day slippage (0.9996) during every 12.67 synodic periods. Therefore, the pentagram will rotate clockwise inside of an oval. Eventually, after approximately 160 years, the pentagram will appear inverted with either one or two points upward.

You may start a new session or continue from the last one. In either case, reset the starting date once again to **March 23, 716 BCE.** in Baghdad, Iraq and set the time to the moment of sunrise.

1) In the toolbar, adjust the **Time Flow** to **160 years** and press the **Step Forward** ⏭ button to advance. The date should now be February 11, 556 BCE.

2) Press the **Sunrise** button to adjust the time to 8:00:18 a.m.

3) Return to the **Time Flow** input and reselect the custom time unit created in Tutorial 1 (583.92 days), or manually enter 584 days in the increment.

4) Make note of the position of Venus in the sky and repeat steps 11–13 in Tutorial 1 to chart the new movement of Venus. It will now appear inverted with two points upward.

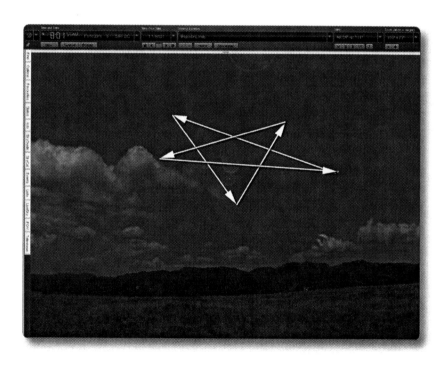

Tutorial 3: Tracking Venus from Space

It is possible to trace a nearly perfect pentagram from an overhead view in outer space. In this demonstration, you will notice that the final position of Venus is in *almost* the exact same place. However, this slightly different position does not affect the geometric appearance of the final pentagram in any significant way.

1) Go to the toolbar and click on the **Viewing Location** to select **Other...** and bring up the dialog box.

2) In the Viewing Location dialog box, set the options to View from "**the surface of**" "**Sun.**"

3) Click the **Latitude/Longitude** tab and change the latitude to **90° N**. Press the **Set Location** button and the software will change your position to the north pole of the Sun.

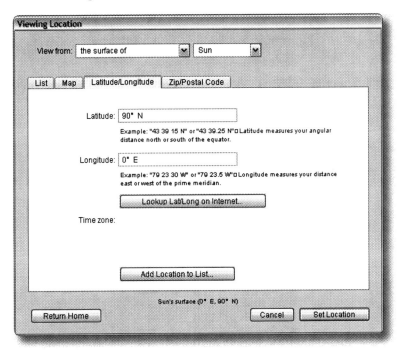

4) Use the **Increase Elevation** button to raise your view until you are approximately **2.25 au** (astronomical units) from the Sun.

5) Right-click on the **Sun** (Cmd-click on a Mac) and from the menu choose to **Centre** it on your screen.

6) Click on the **Options** tab to open the panel and expand the **Solar System** options. Activate the "**Labels**" box next to the **Planets/Moons** options. The names of the planets and sun should now appear on your screen.

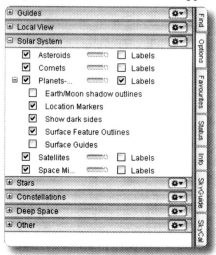

7) Click on the **Find** tab to switch to that panel. Activate the boxes next to "**Mercury**," "**Venus**," "**Earth**," and "**Mars**" to enable the viewing of their respective orbits. When done, click once again on the **Find** tab to close it.

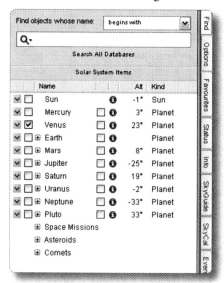

8) Now, it is time to adjust for the conjunction between Earth and Venus when the Transit of Venus last occurred. The date should be **June 8, 2004 A.D. (C.E.)** and set the time to **5:00:00 Universal Time** (the time of Greenwich, England). You will now see that a straight line can be drawn from the Earth to the Sun that passes through Venus. You can even use the **Angular Separation** tool ▨ to accomplish this.

9) Adjust the **Time Flow Rate** to be **584 days**.

10) Press the **Step Forward** ▣ button to advance and note the new positions of Venus and Earth. They are still aligned.

11) Repeat the **Step Forward** action **four** more times (for a total of six plotted points), noting the position of Venus and the Earth each time. The final position is eight years later, when the next Transit of Venus occurs on June 6, 2012.

12) Using the technique described at the end of the first tutorial, it is now possible to draw a line from each consecutive point to yield a nearly perfect geometric pentagram.

357

THE RADIO EXPERIMENT

MANY PEOPLE WANT TO KNOW "how" Electronic Voice Phenomena (EVP) works. Unfortunately, there is no simple answer, so we do not know. For many years, paranormal investigators suggested that the voices were directly imprinted on electromagnetically-sensitive tape, such as a typical audio cassette, especially since the investigators believed that "ghosts" were electro-magnetic manifestations. However, when digital recorders were introduced and EVP and other anomalies were similarly being recorded in a digital format, the investigators were forced to revise their thinking. The following is an explanation and demonstration put forth by Joshua P. Warren and his paranormal research team, L.E.M.U.R. (the League of Energy Materialization and Unexplained phenomena Research).[1]

The human ear is capable of distinguishing sounds ranging from 20–20,000 hertz, although this varies among some people and can be significantly affected by a person's age. Some audio equipment is capable of recording a wider range of frequencies, but most of the devices used by paranormal researchers are limited to about the same range as the human ear. The most distinctive characteristic of EVP is that it is not perceptible to the naked ear at the time it is being recorded. It is only when the investigator goes back to review the audio that the voices or sounds can be heard. Some people find this troubling to think that their equipment can "hear" the voice, but they cannot.

However, a simple demonstration may help to explain how ghostly sounds are recorded without being audible. Instead of thinking that ghosts are directly imprinting their voices onto tapes, we should consider the possibility that they are generating electromagnetic oscillations that are imperceptible to the human ear, but captured quite easily by electronic equipment like microphones.[2] We are surrounded by various electro-magnetic frequencies, such as radio waves, all of the time that we cannot hear without the proper electronic equipment that can receive these frequencies. The only major difference between those kinds of signals and EVP is that scientists understand and can explain how the other frequencies operate.

What You Will Need

The following is a list of supplies and equipment that you will need to conduct the experiment. Except for the copper wire spool, most of the other items are inexpensive. Please note that you may need different connections and plugs than listed here, depending upon your setup. Here is what you will need:

- Large Spool of Copper Wire (e.g. 500 feet)
- AM/FM Radio (with Line-out or Headphones feature)
- 1/8" Plug to RCA Plug Cable (e.g. #15-2473 in Radio Shack catalog)
- Connecting Wire with Mini Alligator Clips on both ends
- Digital or Cassette Audio Recorder
- Audio Cassette (not necessary if using digital)
- External Unidirectional Microphone (preferably one that is battery operated and includes a cable for easy connection to the recorder)

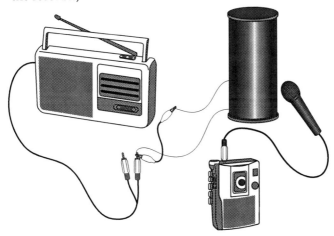

Set-up and Recording

1. Power on the radio and set the tuner to your favorite station. Make sure the signal is coming through loud and clear.
2. Plug the 1/8" end of your cable into the Headphone or Line-out of your radio. If this is done correctly, you should not hear any audio from the radio even though it is still turned on.

3. Connect one of the Alligator Clips to one of the RCA plugs.
4. Connect one end of the copper wire to the Alligator Clip/RCA Plug.
5. Connect the other end of the copper wire to the other Alligator Clip.
6. Turn the radio's volume to its maximum setting.

Note that you will not hear any more sound coming from the radio, even though it is broadcasting the radio station very loudly. The reason is because the electrical signal from the radio is traveling through the copper wire, but the wire does not output the sound like a speaker. Now that the radio and copper wire are set up, you will prepare the audio recorder and microphone:

7. Connect the microphone to the audio recorder's Line-in jack.
8. Place or hold the microphone very close to the copper wire spool.
9. Begin recording using your audio device.

After you are finished, listen to the recording and you will find that the radio station was recorded even though you were not able to hear it. The reason is because the sound was carried through the copper wire as an electrical signal and then transferred electromagnetically to the microphone. The microphone then interpreted this electrical signal as "sound" that could be recorded by your analog or digital recording device. Since the human ear depends on "hearing" sound waves, you were never able to hear the radio station because there were not any sound waves resonating throughout the air (which is how a speaker operates). However, an electrical signal was present that could be picked up by other electromagnetic equipment like the microphone. The strength of the radio signal can also be increased by using larger sized coils of wire. You can even experiment with different microphones and vary their positions and distances from the coil to see how it affects the results.[3]

If ghosts are operating on the electromagnetic spectrum, like many researchers believe, the above experiment may be a clue as to how EVPs are recorded. The prospect of real-time communication may even be possible if paranormal investigators are able to set up multiple microphones and constantly monitor the audio signals through headphones or other equipment. However, most EVPs are relatively quiet and therefore go unnoticed by investigators until a later time when they are able to analyze the audio. For more information concerning EVP experiments and paranormal investigation equipment, please visit the website (www.gatewayofthegods.com).

NOTES AND REFERENCES

INTRODUCTION

1 Northrop Frye, *The Educated Imagination* (paperback edition) (Bloomington, Indiana: Indiana University Press, 1964), p. 14.

2 Of course, the answer to the "Ultimate Question" is "42." If you got that joke, feel free to raise your towel.

3 For example, there are numerous Greek and Hebrew lexicons available that readers can use to look up and verify the usage and definitions of words that I will be covering throughout this book. Many of these lexicons are also freely available on the internet with other Bible study tools, such as at Crosswalk. com (see: http://bible.crosswalk.com/Lexicons/). It is slightly more difficult to locate dependable resources for other ancient languages, such as Sumerian, outside of specialized universities and expensive textbooks. However, interested readers may still be able to freely review and verify my information by checking such online resources as the University of Pennsylvania's Sumerian Dictionary Project (http://psd.museum.upenn.edu/epsd/index.html).

4 For instance, I have chosen to use the free online encyclopedia *Wikipedia* (www.wikipedia.org) for general background information. The nature of Wikipedia is a double-edged sword, though, and I'm well aware of the criticism and reputation it has among many academic circles. On one hand, there are articles on just about any topic imaginable, and often with much more specific information than what some other encyclopedias offer. Additionally, it is free and anyone with access to the internet can look up the information and verify its accuracy. On the other hand, the fact that anyone can post articles and/or edit existing information on the website means that the potential for biased or incorrect information exists. There are some built-in protections, however. For instance, the website keeps track of all changes and stores all previous versions of the article as well as records specific information regarding who

has made those changes. If other users feel that information is incorrect or biased, they can notify the administrator and notices will be placed at the top of the article to alert readers. The incorrect information can then be changed if necessary, through this process of peer-review. In situations where I have used Wikipedia articles, I have tried to validate much of the information myself and consider it to be trustworthy (at least at the time and date that I have listed in my sources). One of the main reasons I have decided to use it as a reference for my work is so that my readers may be able to freely research on their own, without needing special access to rare books or software. Use your own discretion, however, with anything you find on the internet.

5   The words *Sumerian* and *Sumer* are more accurately pronounced: "Shoo-marian" and "Shoo-mer," respectively. The term "Sumerian" is actually an *exonym* (a name given to them by another people—in this case the Akkadians). Also of interest, is that the Sumerian language is unique because no one has been able to successfully connect it to other known ancient languages. It is as if the language and writing system just "appeared" out of thin air.

CHAPTER 1: A SMALL, QUIET VOICE

1   Cyril Connolly, *The Enemies of Promise* (London: George Routledge and Sons, 1938).

2   For anyone interested in pursuing a career in game design, I'd recommend looking into the schools now. Many of the problems from back then have been resolved, and the schools have greatly improved their courses. Also, many game developers are working directly with the schools by offering advice on how the courses should be taught so that the students are learning relevant information. The tuition for these courses is still rather high, though, so the option might be out of the range for many people. One other reason why I feel more confident about recommending these schools now is that the software and other related technology have dramatically increased in the last few years so there is a very steep learning curve. I was able to learn as the technology grew since I started so early, but for people just entering the field it might be a little overwhelming without someone there to teach you. It seems to be that every twelve to eighteen months a new version of important software is released and it can be a full time job just trying to keep your knowledge of the products up to date.

3   "Hypnogogia," *Wikipedia* (January 5, 2006), <http://en.wikipedia.org/wiki/Hypnagogia>. See also: "Sleep Paralysis," *Wikipedia* (January 16, 2006),

<http://en.wikipedia.org/wiki/Sleep_paralysis>; *Sleep Paralysis Page*, <http://www.arts.uwaterloo.ca/~acheyne/S_P.html>; *The True Night-Mare: SP in Myth and Legend*, <http://watarts.uwaterloo.ca/~acheyne/night_mare.html>; *The Intruder*, <http://watarts.uwaterloo.ca/~acheyne/intruder.html>.

4   I'm sure that many skeptics will find this a convenient excuse, but it's the truth. As more time passes it seems as if it was all just imagined, but I believe that my passion for solving this demonstrates the impact it has had on me.

5   Please understand that even though *The Key* is described as a nonfiction book, I am aware of some problems regarding Whitley Strieber's work that have been raised by many skeptics. Please see Appendix A for more information.

6   In his online journal, Strieber first described the man as being noticeably short, "maybe four and a half feet tall," but in *The Key* just described him as "short." My mention of this is not to nit-pick, but to point out any potential discrepancies between the stories. See: Whitley Strieber, "Encounter of June 6, 1998," *Whitley's Journal* (July 20, 1998), *Unknown Country.com*, <http://www.unknowncountry.com/journal/?id=8>. Cf., Whitley Strieber, *The Key: A Conversation About The Nature and Future of Man* (San Antonio, TX: Walker & Collier, Inc., 2001), pp. 3, 4.

7   Strieber, *The Key*, pp. 3–5.

8   Ibid., pp. 12–15.

9   Ibid., p. 34.

10   Ibid., pp. 49, 50.

11   Ibid., pp. 68–9.

12   Ibid., p. 69.

13   Strieber has wrestled often with the details regarding his experience with the "Master of the Key." At times, he wonders if he had imagined the whole thing, if it was simply a dream, or if a mysterious stranger really did walk into his room that fateful night. Obviously, I can relate to this experience and the maddening effects it can have on a person's psyche. One thing is certain—and I agree with him on this—that whatever the case, he has a tendency to be "pathologically honest" about his experiences. Even to this day, he still finds himself struggling with whether or not it was real or a complete product of his imagination. This waffling pattern creates a real problem not only for Strieber, but for anyone reading his work, too. Unfortunately, such behavior is a common characteristic of his material and something that he's been forthright about for many years now. In all efforts of fairness, though, I must point this out and I encourage my readers to learn about my own thoughts

regarding Strieber's work and how it relates to my research by reviewing Appendix A. For more information regarding his detailing of the experience, please see: Whitley Strieber, "Encounter of June 6, 1998," *Whitley's Journal* (July 20, 1998), *Unknown Country.com*, <http://www.unknowncountry.com/ journal/?id=8>; Whitley Strieber, "Encounter of June 6, 1998 Pt II," *Whitley's Journal* (July 20, 1998), *Unknown Country.com*, <http://www.unknowncountry. com/journal/?id=9>; Whitley Strieber, "The June 6, 1998 Experience: Update," *Whitley's Journal* (November 1, 1998), *Unknown Country.com*, <http://www. unknowncountry.com/journal/?id=11>; Whitley Strieber, "The Majesty of the Key," *Whitley's Journal* (September 20, 2005), *Unknown Country.com*, <http:// www.unknowncountry.com/journal/?id=194>. Please note that in the last entry given, Whitley mistakenly mentions that the event happened in 1999, instead of 1998.

CHAPTER 2: EVALUATING THE EVIDENCE

1   Elbert Hubbard, *Philosophy of Elbert Hubbard* (East Aurora, NY: Roycroft Press, 1930), p. 14.

2   Joe Nickell, *Entities: Angels, Spirits, Demons, and Other Alien Beings* (Amherst, NY: Prometheus Books, 1995), p. 11.

3   Ralph Ellis, *Jesus: Last of the Pharaohs*, 1999, 2d ed. (Kempton, Illinois: Adventures Unlimited, 2001), p. 69, quoting from: *The Epic of Gilgamesh (Penguin Classics),* (Penguin Books), p. 66.

4   Ibid.

5   Stephanie Dalley, *Myths from Mesopotamia: Creation, The Flood, Gilgamesh, and Others,* 1989, trans. by Stephanie Dalley, revised edition (New York: Oxford University Press, Inc., 2000), p. 53.

6   Ellis, *Jesus,* quoting from: *Gilgamesh* (Penguin Classics), p. 75.

7   Ibid., p. 70, quoting from: *Gilgamesh* (Penguin Classics), pp. 81–3.

8   Ibid., p. 71, quoting from: *Gilgamesh* (Penguin Classics), p. 88, both references.

CHAPTER 3: THE NATURE OF ANGELS

1   Rumi, as he is sometimes known, was a thirteenth-century Persian poet, theologian, and teacher of Sufism (a mystic tradition of Islam).

2   Joe Nickell, *Entities: Angels, Spirits, Demons, and Other Alien Beings* (Amherst, NY: Prometheus Books, 1995), p. 152.

3 Ibid.

4 Billy Graham, *Angels: God's Secret Agents* (Garden City, NY: Doubleday, 1975), p. ix.

5 Nickell, *Entities*, pp. 154–5. Cf., Graham, *Angels*, p. ix and Margaret Ronan, *Strange Unsolved Mysteries* (New York: Scholastic Book Services, 1974), pp. 99–101.

6 Ibid., p. 155, quoting: Rosemary Ellen Guiley, "A Radiance of Angels," *Fate* (December 1993), p. 66.

7 Ibid., pp. 155–6, quoting: Guiley "Radiance," p. 66.

8 Ibid., p. 156.

9 Ibid., quoting: Guiley, "Radiance," p. 65.

10 Ibid.

11 Rosemary Ellen Guiley, *The Encyclopedia of Angels, 2d ed.* (New York, USA: Checkmark Books, 2004), s.v. "angels," p. 36.

12 e.g., Zecharia 14:5. *Author's note:* Some Bible translations use "Saints" in place of "Holy Ones," presumably to mask some of the polytheistic overtones associated with the term.

13 e.g., Deuteronomy 17:3; 1 Kings 22:19.

14 e.g., Genesis 6:4. *Author's note:* An alternate rendering of the phrase is "sons of the gods."

15 e.g., Genesis 18:1-8. *Author's note:* Some theologians believed and taught that angels could not eat or drink (as in *The Testament of Abraham*, for example). They even explained that the angels only *appeared* to eat, and that they were actually manifesting an *illusion* of consuming food. While there are certainly times when the angels refused to partake in meals, I tend to disagree with this view. I will admit that perhaps they did not *need* to eat, but I see no reason why they could not eat—especially if they had physical bodies of flesh-and-blood.

16 Genesis 32: 24–30.

17 Genesis 6: 2, 4.

18 Justin Martyr – (c. 100/114–162/168 CE); Irenaeus – (c. 130–202 CE); Athenagoras – (c. 133–190 CE); Origen – (c. 182–251 CE); Clement of Alexandria – (c. 150–211/216 CE); Tertullian – (c. 155–230 CE).

19 All translations of this text, unless otherwise noted, are from *The Book of Enoch: I Enoch*, trans. R.H. Charles (Oxford: Clarendon Press, 1912), pp. 7–8.

20 Contrary to popular belief, there is actually no record found within the Bible that details the story of Satan leading a rebellion against God. This is an example of a doctrine created by fusing several different concepts together

from different sources (both Old and New Testaments) and then molding it into the belief system. Usually, the story goes that Satan was banished from heaven either shortly before or after the creation of Adam. Therefore, the "serpent" in the Garden of Eden that tempts Eve is thought to be Satan, but nowhere does Scripture specifically state this. Later, a passage in Isaiah refers to a heavenly being (Lucifer) that wanted to claim the throne of God but was cast out of heaven. However, this passage is actually an old astrological myth concerning the planet Venus and its context informs us that it was meant to compare a certain king to this mythological being. This view is then coupled with a passage from Revelation (12:7–9) in the New Testament that describes the expulsion of Satan and his angels from heaven—but this is something that is supposed to be *post*-Flood. Obviously, this could not be true if Satan had already been banished from heaven at the beginning of the Genesis account. Despite what is actually presented in the Bible, the "common knowledge" role of Satan has been greatly exaggerated and unduly emphasized. Most of the ideas concerning Satan's supposed war against God and his diabolical influence upon events in the Garden of Eden can be traced back to the publication of John Milton's epic poem, *Paradise Lost,* in the late seventeenth-century.

21 Sadly, it seems that this is the same tactic used by the media and government as well as some conspiracy theorists. For instance, news reports and government agencies constantly warn the public of the threat of terrorism, but present it in such a way that it is a faceless entity nearly impossible to fight. It's not actually battling against specific people—it's battling against an "idea." Similarly, some conspiracy theorists depend upon finger pointing at vast networks of global corporations, secret societies and "shadow governments" to explain their ideas. While I certainly agree that there are misguided or even immoral people trying to push their agendas and wishes upon the world, I do not subscribe to any of these ideas completely. For now, the point that I am trying to stress is that both situations utilize the "faceless enemy" tactic to gain psychological control over masses of people.

22 Elizabeth Clare Prophet, *Fallen Angels and the Origins of Evil* (USA: Summit University Press, 2000), p. 9, referring to: Filastrius, *Liber de Haeresibus,* no. 108.

23 Ibid., pp. 9, 66–7, referring to: Franz Delitzsch, *A New Commentary on Genesis,* trans. Sophia Taylor, 2 vols. (Edinburgh: T. & T. Clark, 1888), p. 223.

24 Ibid., p. 61, quoting: Jean Chrysostom, "Homelies sur la Genèse," *Saint Jean Chrysostome Ouevres Complètes,* trans. M. Jeannin and ed. L. Guerin (Paris,

1865), 5:136–7.

25 Ibid., pp. 61–2, referring to: Bernard Jacob Bamberger, *Fallen Angels* (Philadelphia: Jewish Publication Society of America, 1962), p. 80.

26 Justification for claiming that Seth's line was "godly" and "righteous" is usually done by citing Genesis 4:26, which says that after Seth's son is born "people began to invoke the name of the Lord" (NRSV).

27 Cf., 2 Peter 2:4–10; Jude 5–7.

28 Andrew Collins, *From the Ashes of Angels: The Forbidden Legacy of a Fallen Race* (Rochester, Vermont: Bear & Company, 2001), p. 16, referring to: James Bruce, *Travels to Discover the Source of the Nile,* abridged edition, ed. C. F. Beckingham, (Edinburgh University Press, 1964), p. 14, quoting Fanny Burney, who described him as "the tallest man you ever saw in your life."

29 Ibid.

30 Ibid., p. 19, quoting from: Bruce, *Travels,* vol. 2, p. 422 (Unabridged edition only).

31 Ibid., p. 20.

32 Ibid., p. 21.

33 Ibid.

34 Ibid., p. 22.

CHAPTER 4: THE FALLEN ONES

1 Juvenal was a Roman poet of the late 1st century and early 2nd century. The familiar rhetorical question used for the opening quote is also translated as "who guards the guardians?" and originated in his satire *On Women,* pertaining to the usefulness of having eunuchs stand guard over women.

2 For example, Psalm 82 refers to the angels in the divine council of heaven as "gods," "children of the Most High," and "princes" (or more accurately as "shining ones").

3 It is also important to note that the Hebrew word for God, *Elohim,* is plural and can mean god, goddess and gods (with a small "g"). By itself, the word is actually morphologically plural in nature, but the grammar of the sentence determines if it should be read as a singular form or plural. A few comparative words in the English language are: deer, sheep, and swine. The reader can only understand if these words are meant to be singular or plural when they are used within a sentence. For example, compare: *He saw a deer grazing in the field* (singular), to *He saw deer grazing in the field* (plural).

4   While I am not aware of any passages that specifically state that the Watchers engaged in homosexual acts, the idea can definitely be inferred from the story of Sodom and Gomorrah (Genesis 19:1–13). The text states that the angels appeared as very attractive men that caught the attention of the local male residents. This has caused a great deal of confusion regarding a proper understanding of this story since the residents were not technically engaging in homosexual behavior with other men, but they did want to "know" the angels. However, the absence of details in this story does allow for speculation that the fallen angels from Genesis 6 did perform sexual acts with both men and women, which inspired additional reasons for the church fathers to reject Apocryphal texts such as *Enoch* and to further promote the taboo against human/angel unions.

5   Raven Grimassi, *The Wiccan Mysteries: Ancient Origins & Teachings* (St. Paul, Minnesota: Llewellyn Publications, 2001), p. 107.

6   Michael S. Heiser, "The Meaning of the Word Nephilim: Fact vs. Fantasy," <http://www.michaelsheiser.com/nephilim.pdf>.

7   I have used the definitions associated with the Hebrew version of *nephal* (נפל) because there is more information readily available about it than its Aramaic counterpart.

8   While "the fallen" is a common euphemism for the dead, it does not appear that it is to be understood this way in the context of the passages. However, if it were intended to refer to dead beings, the Hebrew word used would be *nophelim* (נפלים), such as in Jeremiah 6:15, which states: "...they shall *fall* among those who *fall*."

9   Cf., Jude 6; 1 Enoch 12:4.

10   Cf., *The Book of Jubilees* 4:15; 5:1–10

11   Heiser, "The Meaning of the Word Nephilim," <http://www.michaelsheiser.com/nephilim.pdf>. While I may disagree with Michael Heiser's opinion, he has presented the most scholarly evidence concerning the reality of fallen angels in relation to ancient texts. See also: <http://www.sitchiniswrong.com>.

12   Since some of these beings were involved in misdeeds, the scribes were able to expand this title to also include those who were "spiritually fallen."

13   Genesis 32:28.

14   Cf., Numbers 13:33.

15   Genesis 6:9. The word used to describe Noah as "perfect" is *tamyim* (תמים), which means perfect or without blemish. Some researchers, such as Chuck Missler, believe this could be referring to his genetic heritage.

16   Some people may consider it harsh of me to say that God conducted an

exercise in "futility" by flooding the world, but it is true. If the purpose was to destroy the Nephilim, the Bible clearly states that they were back again later. Additionally, we must not forget that God sent a destroying angel to kill all of the Egyptian's firstborn (Exodus 12:29–32) as the Tenth Plague. If God had the capability of selectively targeting only the firstborn children of Egypt, why would it not be reasonable to target only the Nephilim and those in league with them? Why would animals have to be destroyed, too? It is more likely that the Flood myth is based on an ancient memory of devastating climactic changes. This topic is further explored in Chapter 10.

17 Cf., *The Book of Jubilees* 4:15.

18 *The Book of Enoch: I Enoch,* trans. R.H. Charles (Oxford: Clarendon Press, 1912), p. 20.

19 Cf., *The Book of Jubilees* 4:15.

20 It is particularly interesting to see the resemblance between the name of this angel, Kokabel, who taught humans about the constellations, and the Akkadian word for star (usually pertaining to constellations) is: *kakkabu(m)* 𒀭. The same sign in the Sumerian language is *mul* 𒀯. There is no doubt about the Mesopotamian influence on the name of this particular angel.

21 Cf., *I Enoch* 69:1–13 in Charles' translation: pp. 136–9; Gustav Davidson, *A Dictionary of Angels Including the Fallen Angels* (New York: The Free Press, 1971) s.v. "The Watchers," p. 349.

22 I note that in this instance, the descriptions of what the angels "revealed" to humans do not seem terrible. However, much later in the *Book of Enoch* (69:1-13), more angels and "sins" are described, such as: Gâdreêl (which is possibly another name for Azâzêl), who taught all "blows of death" and "weapons of death" to humans; Kâsdejâ, who taught "all the wicked smitings of spirits and demons, and the smitings of the embryo in the womb, that it may pass away." Additionally, the angel Pênêmûe "instructed mankind in writing with ink and paper, and thereby many sinned from eternity to eternity and until this day. For men were not created for such a purpose."

23 The reference to "root-cuttings" is interpreted here as agriculture and herbalism. It is also generally thought by some researchers to be referring to harmful drug use, although it is difficult to determine precisely what is meant. I have chosen to refer to agriculture and herbalism for medicinal purposes because Shemyaza seems to have been genuinely concerned about the ramifications if he pursued further misdeeds and also that most cultures throughout the world indicate that the leader of the gods taught them agricultural skills. However,

given the context of the story, it is not unreasonable that the knowledge was intended for misuse at the hands of the angels.

24 The spelling "magick" is used here to distinguish between the occult art and the sleight of hand tricks of stage magicians, which is spelled "magic."

25 It would certainly seem reasonable to believe that the actual amount of food consumed by Shemyaza's children (not to mention the particulars of their diet) is being exaggerated in the mystical texts.

26 Rosemary Ellen Guiley, *The Encyclopedia of Angels, 2d ed.* (New York, USA: Checkmark Books, 2004) s.v. "Semyaza," pp. 324–5. See also: Louis Ginzberg, *The Legends of the Jews: Volume I – From the Creation to Jacob,* 1909–1938, trans. Henrietta Szold (Baltimore, MD: Johns Hopkins University Press, 1998), pp. 149–150.

27 L. Zalcman, "Orion," in *Dictionary of Deities and Demons in the Bible DDD (2nd Extensively Rev. Ed.),* ed. Karel van der Toorn, Bob Becking & Pieter W. van der Horst (Grand Rapids, MI: Brill; Eerdmans: Leiden, 1999), pp. 648–9.

28 Christopher Knight and Robert Lomas, *Uriel's Machine: Uncovering the Secrets of Stonehenge, Noah's Flood, and the Dawn of Civilization* (Gloucester, MA: Fair Winds Press, 1999), pp. 103–4.

29 L. Zalcman, "Orion," pp. 648–9.

30 Interestingly, there also appears to be a reference in the New Testament: 1 Corinthians 11:10. It instructs women to cover themselves so as not to tempt the angels. This is the original reason why many women in the Middle East are required to veil themselves. Now, the modern belief is that a woman must wear a veil so that men passing her on the street do not become tempted and rape her.

31 Davidson, *A Dictionary of Angels,* s.v. "Azazel," p. 63.

32 Ibid., s.v. "Azza" and "Azzael," p. 65.

33 Numbers 13:28

34 Silver RavenWolf, *Angels: Companions in Magick* (St. Paul, Minnesota: Llewellyn Publications, 2000), p. 8.

35 The word for "god" in the Sumerian language is *dingir* ✳ pronounced "din-gee" with a hard "g" sound and a silent "r." When it is used as *dingir-e,* meaning "by god," then it is pronounced "din-geer." The plural form for "gods" is *dingir-dingir* and/or *dingir.meš.* In the Akkadian language, *il* meant "god, deity" and *iltu* was the feminine version for "goddess."

36 The Sumerian word *An* ✳ not only means "god" and "heaven," but also "upper" and "crown (of a tree)." The last definition will create an interesting association by the end of our investigation. The Akkadian equivalent is the word *šamû.*

37 Samuel Noah Kramer, *Sumerian Mythology: A Study of Spiritual and Literary Achievement in the Third Millennium B.C.* (Philadelphia: University of Pennsylvania Press, 1972), p. 41.

38 Stephanie Dalley, *Myths from Mesopotamia: Creation, The Flood, Gilgamesh, and Others,* trans. Stephanie Dalley, rev. ed., 1989 (New York: Oxford University Press, Inc., 2000), p. 326.

39 Kramer, *Sumerian Mythology,* p. 52.

40 Jeremy Black and Anthony Green, *Gods, Demons and Symbols of Ancient Mesopotamia,* 1992 (Great Britain: University of Texas Press, Austin, 2003), s.v. "Anuna (Anunnakkū)," p. 34.

41 Dalley, *Myths from Mesopotamia,* p. 318.

42 Ibid., p. 323.

43 R.A. Boulay, *Flying Serpents and Dragons: The Story of Mankind's Reptilian Past* (Escondido, California: The Book Tree, 1999), p. 80. *Author's Note:* I have been unable to verify Boulay's definition for the Igigi as being "those who observe" or "the Watchers" in any scholarly resources. However, I have found some cuneiform signs associated with the term that relate to "eyes" and even "gateways." Therefore, I can only suggest that the meaning is implied by the ancient texts until I have located a scholarly reference to either support or refute this claim. I would encourage my readers, particularly those with a reputable background in ancient languages like Sumerian and Akkadian, to look into this matter and contact me through this book's website (www.gatewayofthegods.com) regarding their findings.

44 John Heise, 1996 (April 19, 2004), <http://www.sron.nl/~jheise/akkadian/Welcome_mesopotamia.html>.

45 e.g., Robert Todd Carroll, *The Skeptics Dictionary,* s.v. "ancient astronauts and Erich von Däniken's Chariots of the Gods?," (June 15, 2004), <http://skepdic.com/vondanik.html>. The particular incident that I am referring to is when the investigators for the *Nova* public-television science program discovered the person who made the pottery for von Däniken. This completely destroyed his claims that these were evidence of ancient pots depicting UFOs. The investigators confronted von Däniken and he responded that he could justify his deception because people would not believe him unless he had photographic evidence.

46 Michael Heiser has gone to great lengths to demonstrate Sitchin's language blunders and contrived "facts." Many of Sitchin's errors are extremely damaging, and at times, quite comical, especially when Sitchin's mistakes are illuminated by Heiser. For more information, I recommend going to: <http://

www.michaelsheiser.com>, <http://www.sitchiniswrong.com> and <http://www.thedivinecouncil.com> as well as reviewing Appendix C.

47   Ronald S. Hendel, "When the Sons of God Cavorted with the Daughters of Men," *Understanding the Dead Sea Scrolls,* ed. Hershel Shanks (New York, NY: Vintage Books, 1993) p. 172.

48   Black, *Gods, Demons and Symbols of Ancient Mesopotamia,* s.v. "Egyptian gods and symbols," p. 74.

49   Hilary Wilson, *Understanding Hieroglyphics* (New York: Barnes & Noble Books, Inc., 2003), p. 68.

50   John Michael Greer, *The New Encyclopedia of the Occult* (St. Paul, Minnesota: Llewellyn Publications, 2003), s.v. "Alchemy," p. 14.

51   Richard Parkinson, *Pocket Guide to Ancient Egyptian Hieroglyphs: How to Read and Write Ancient Egyptian* (New York: Barnes & Noble, Inc., 2004), p. 20.

52   It was very difficult for me to track down a book that defined *neter* as "guardian" or "watcher" since most authors simply translate it as "god." I did eventually find one, though, and it was independent of the work done by Zecharia Sitchin. Unfortunately, I do not recall the title of the book in which I verified this definition. Since the Hebrew language shares many common root words with that of Egypt, I have decided to include a reference to the Hebrew word *natsar* (נצר), pronounced "naw-tsar," which is similar sounding. Natsar refers to someone who guards, watches, or observes something. It should also be noted that according to Graham Hancock in his book *Fingerprints of the Gods,* the Egyptians referred to a group of neteru who were intermediaries between the gods and humans as the *Urshu,* which meant "Watchers." I have not been able to properly verify this information in more academic sources yet.

53   Moustafa Gadalla, *Egyptian Divinities: The All Who Are THE ONE* (Egypt: Tehuti Research Foundation, 2001), p. 39.

54   Ibid., p. 11.

55   Grimassi, *The Wiccan Mysteries,* p. 100.

56   See Deuteronomy 32: 8–9.

57   James R. Lewis and Evelyn Dorothy Oliver, *Angels A to Z,* ed. Kelle S. Sisung (Canton, MI: Visible Ink Press, 2002), s.v. "Jinn," pp. 230–1.

58   Carol K. Mack and Dinah Mack, "Djinn," *A Field Guide to Demons, Fairies, Fallen Angels, and Other Subversive Spirits* (New York: Henry Holt and Company, 1999), p. 147.

59   Davidson, *A Dictionary of Angels,* s.v. "Jinn," p. 159.

60   Mack, "Iblis," *A Field Guide to Demons,* p. 146.

61 Guiley, *The Encyclopedia of Angels*, s.v. "Seraphim," p. 325.

62 Daniel 4:13, 17 and 23.

63 *The Book of Enoch: I Enoch*, pp. 44–5.

64 Guiley, *The Encyclopedia of Angels*, s.v. "The Watchers," pp. 366–7.

65 *The Complete Dead Sea Scrolls in English*, ed. & trans. Geza Vermes (New York: Penguin Books, 1998), pp. 128–9.

66 *Strega* is the Italian word for a female witch, while *Stregone* (pronounced "stray-go-nay") is for a male witch. Witchcraft in general is called *Stregheria* (pronounced "stray-gah-ree-ah") under Raven Grimassi's tradition. In addition, the word strega is similar to the word "strigoi" which means "undead spirit" or "vampire" in Romanian.

67 Raven Grimassi, *Italian Witchcraft: The Old Religion of Southern Europe* (St. Paul, Minnesota: Llewellyn Publications, 2000), p. xv.

68 For simplicity's sake, the term Celtic is being applied in this book since that is how most people identify this group of people. However, the term is derived from the Greco-Roman *keltoi* or *celtae*, which was simply used to refer to "strangers" of any sort. The tribes had names for themselves, such as the "Britons" and the "Gauls"; obviously, it would not make sense if they called themselves Celts ("strangers"). For more information, see: "Celt," Wikipedia, (May 26, 2006), <http://en.wikipedia.org/wiki/Celt> and: Laurence Gardner, *Realm of the Ring Lords: The Myth and Magic of the Grail Quest* (Gloucester, MA: Fair Winds Press, 2002), p. 109.

69 Cassandra Eason, *A Complete Guide to Faeries & Magical Beings* (Canada: Weiser Books, 2002), p. 3.

70 Ibid., p. 3.

71 Ibid., p. 28.

72 Ibid., p. 27.

73 Ibid., p. 163.

74 Ibid., p. 30.

75 Ibid., p. 31–2.

76 This is an obvious reference to the universal symbol known as the Ouroboros.

77 It is also interesting to note that the gods were called the Aesir. This is extremely similar to the name of the chief Egyptian deity, which can be rendered into English as *Aesir,* but is usually given in the Greek form as Osiris.

78 Neil Philip, *Illustrated Book of Myths* (New York, NY: DK Publishing, Inc., 1995), pp. 64–7.

79 See: "Asura," Wikipedia, (September 1, 2006), <http://en.wikipedia.org/

wiki/Asura>; "Asura (Buddhism)," Wikipedia, (August 10, 2006), <http://
en.wikipedia.org/wiki/Asura_(Buddhism)>; "Ahura," Wikipedia, (August 29,
2006), <http://en.wikipedia.org/wiki/Ahura>; "Mount Meru (Mythology),"
Wikipedia, (September 3, 2006), <http://en.wikipedia.org/wiki/Mount_
Meru_(Mythology)>; "Sumeru," Wikipedia, (September 3, 2006), <http://
en.wikipedia.org/wiki/Sumeru>.

80 Guiley, *The Encyclopedia of Angels*, s.v. "Devas," pp. 99–101.

81 Frank Waters, *Book of the Hopi* (New York, NY: Penguin Books, 1977), pp.
67-8.

82 The mysterious Red City of the South has never been located, but is important
in Hopi beliefs.

83 This mountain is the San Francisco Mountain, located near Flagstaff, Arizona.

84 A *paho* is a prayer feather or stick used to communicate with the spirits.

85 Ibid., p. 71.

86 Ibid., p. 31.

CHAPTER 5: ANGELIC BLOODLINES

1 *The Book of Enoch: I Enoch,* translated by R.H. Charles (Oxford: Clarendon
Press, 1912), p. 18. See: 1 Enoch 7:2–6.

2 Jane Ellen Harrison, *Themis: A Study of the Social Origins of the Greek Religion*
(London: Cambridge University Press, 1912), p. 17. *Author's note:* The complete
text of this book is available online through the University of Chicago
Library <http://www.lib.uchicago.edu/cgi-bin/eos/eos_title.pl?callnum=BL781.
H32>.

3 See: 1 Samuel 17.

4 See: Numbers 13:28–33, Deuteronomy 1:28; 2:10; 9:2, Joshua 11:21,22;
14:12,15; 15:13,14; Judges 1:20.

5 See: Genesis 14:5; 15:20; Deuteronomy 2:11, 20; 3:11,13; Joshua 12:4;
13:12; 17:15. These giants were also known as the *Zamzummim* (זמזמים) in
Deuteronomy 2:20, 21.

6 See: Genesis 14:5; Deuteronomy 2:10,11.

7 See: 2 Samuel 21:15–22; 1 Chronicles 20:4–8.

8 Deuteronomy 3:11.

9 Ibid.

10 Gregorio del Olmo Lete, "Bashan," in *Dictionary of Deities and Demons in the
Bible DDD (2nd Extensively Rev. Ed.),* ed. Karel van der Toorn, Bob Becking

& Pieter W. van der Horst (Grand Rapids, MI: Brill; Eerdmans: Leiden, 1999), pp. 161–3.

11 "Weights and Measures," Jewish Encyclopedia.com, 2002, (February 11, 2005), <http://www.jewishencyclopedia.com/view.jsp?artid=81&letter=W#213>.

12 "Gigantism," Wikipedia, (January 16, 2005), <http://en.wikipedia.org/wiki/Gigantism>.

13 "Robert Pershing Wadlow," Wikipedia, (January 31, 2005), <http://en.wikipedia.org/wiki/Robert_Wadlow>.

14 Patrick Howard and Barbara Haberman, "The Official Site of Andre the Giant: Biography," (February 18, 2005), <http://www.andrethegiant.com/bio.html>.

15 Buffalo Bill (William Frederick Cody), "An Autobiography of Buffalo Bill," Project Gutenberg, (June 25, 2004) <http://www.gutenberg.org/etext/12740>. Please note that this reference is from a freely available online version of the text through the Project Gutenberg website. For a printed source, please see: Colonel William F. Cody, *Buffalo Bill's Life Story – An Autobiography*, (New York: Farrar & Rinehart, Inc., 1920), p. 114.

16 Cf., "Giants with Double Rowed Teeth," Moundbuilders.org, (2004), <http://www.moundbuilders.org/allegewi-giants/allegewi-giants-gazetteer/double-rowed-teeth-giants.htm>.

17 Cf., I Chronicles 20:6.

18 *Author's Note:* I have tried to find this location (Lompock Rancho, CA) on a map but without success. This leads me to consider three possibilities regarding the story: 1) It is bogus and everything was made up, including the location as a tip off for people who knew that no such place existed; 2) The name of the town has changed since 1833 and so therefore it cannot be verified on any map; or 3) I simply overlooked it on the map.

19 Quoted from: Stephen Quayle, *Genesis 6 Giants: Master Builders of Prehistoric and Ancient Civilizations* (Bozeman, MT: End Time Thunder Publishers, 2002), p. 191 referring to: David Hatcher Childress, *Lost Cities of North America* (Stelle, IL: Adventures Unlimited Press, 1992), p. 509.

20 Ibid.

21 Paraphrased from: Quayle, *Genesis 6 Giants,* p. 192, referring to: *Historical Collections of Ohio in Two Volumes,* (Noble County, OH), pp. 350–1.

22 Paraphrased from: Quayle, *Genesis 6 Giants,* p. 192, referring to: Childress, *North America,* p. 468.

23 The island of Shemya is only found on U.S. Military Charts, according to author of the FATE magazine article. Its location is described as being near

the volcanic island called Attu, near the western end of the Aleutian Islands
in the Pacific Ocean. It is possible that this is a fictitious island invented by
the author of the article.

24 Paraphrased from: Harold T. Wilkins, "The Giants in the Earth," in *Out of
Time and Place,* ed. Terry O'Neill (St. Paul, Minnesota: Llewellyn Publications,
1999), p. 66. This article originally appeared in the January, 1952 issue of FATE
magazine.

25 Ibid., *Author's Note:* There appears to be a discrepancy in the article when the
informant tells the reporter that the smallest of the giants was "twenty-four
feet" high (p. 66), and yet later says one was measured as being eighteen feet,
six inches in height (p. 68). Either this was an error in the recalling of the
story by the informant, or perhaps there was some hoaxing involved.

26 Ibid., pp. 67–8.

27 "Out of Place Artifacts & Ancient High Technology—Giants in Those Days,"
(February 21, 2005), <http://www.s8int.com/giants2.html>.

28 Ibid.

29 Cf., 2 Samuel 21:10; I Chronicles 20:6.

30 Some of these cranial deformities resulted from the fact that mothers would
often carry their children around with them on a flat board strapped to their
backs. Over time, this flat board would eventually flatten and elongate part of
the infant's skull. What must be distinguished here, however, are the instances
in which this was done on purpose in order to achieve this look, rather than
the side-effect of a parent carrying their child with them. In regard to the
"neck-stretching" of Burmese Paduang women, the procedure is intended to
honor the tribe's mythical dragon kings, or *naga.* This is yet another example
deliberate body modification that is intended to mimic or honor the physical
appearances of gods that are thought to be only myths. The actual stretching
of the neck is apparently only an illusion, however, because the rings are really
pushing the collar bone down over time, making the neck appear longer.

31 Adriano Forgione, "The Mystery of Malta's Long-Headed Skulls," *Atlantis
Rising #43* (Livingston, MT), January/February 2004, pp. 23, 59.

32 Ibid.

33 "Anatomy of the Newborn Skull," Lucile Packard Children's Hospital,
(February 21, 2005), <http://www.lpch.org/DiseaseHealthInfo/HealthLibrary/
craniofacial/skullanat.html>.

34 Forgione, "Mystery of Malta's Long-Headed Skulls," p. 60.

35 Ibid., p. 61.

36 Most likely, the good angel that is described as the leader of the "Sons of Light" is Melchizedek, while the evil angel that rules over the "Sons of Darkness" is named Melkiresha' and is probably also known as Belial.

37 *The Complete Dead Sea Scrolls in English,* ed. & trans. Geza Vermes (New York: Penguin Books, 1998), p. 535.

38 Louis Ginzberg, *The Legends of the Jews: Volume I – From the Creation to Jacob,* 1909–1938, translated by Henrietta Szold (Baltimore, MD: Johns Hopkins University Press, 1998), pp. 71–2, 77.

39 Ibid., pp. 105–7.

40 *The Book of Enoch: I Enoch,* pp. 264–5.

41 "The Lord of Righteousness" is generally believed to be a reference to the high priest Melchizedek.

42 Enoch is reported to have been "translated" into heaven and became the holy angel Metatron.

43 1 Enoch 71:1.

44 1 Enoch 71:10.

45 Jeremy Black and Anthony Green, *Gods, Demons and Symbols of Ancient Mesopotamia,* 1992 (Great Britain: University of Texas Press, Austin, 2003), pp. 130–1.

46 Exodus 34:29–35.

47 Matthew 17:1–3. See also: Mark 9:2–4; Luke 9:28–31. It should also be noted that Elijah is another character in the Bible who was reportedly translated into heaven like Enoch.

48 Matthew 28:1–3. See also: Mark 16:1–5; Luke 24:1–5.

49 Cf., Numbers 21:9 and John 3:14.

50 Cf., Genesis 3:1-2, 4, 13-14; Numbers 21:9; Daniel 2:32, 35, 39, 45; Daniel 4:15, 23 (the latter verse is also included in the context of the only chapter in the Bible that directly mentions a Watcher); Daniel 5:4, 23; Daniel 7:19.

51 See: Hebrews 5: 6; Hebrews 6: 20; Hebrews 7.

52 Cf. Psalm 110:4.

53 See: Revelation 1:14.

54 "Human," Wikipedia, (October 8, 2005), <http://en.wikipedia.org/wiki/Human>.

55 "Human Skin Color," Answers.com, (February 16, 2005), <http://www.answers.com/skin%20color>.

56 "Hair Color," Wikipedia, (February 17, 2005), <http://en.wikipedia.org/wiki/Hair_color>.

57 "Albinism," Wikipedia, (February 17, 2005), <http://en.wikipedia.org/wiki/Albinism>.

58 Genesis 32:22–32.

59 "Hybrid," Wikipedia, (February 5, 2005), <http://en.wikipedia.org/wiki/Hybrid>.

60 Trey Parker, Matt Stone, and Brian Graden, Executive Producers, Episode 105: "An Elephant Makes Love to a Pig," in *South Park*, DVD (Comedy Partners/Paramount Pictures, 2004), originally aired: Wednesday, September 10, 1997 on Comedy Central.

61 Maryann Mott, "Animal-Human Hybrids Spark Controversy," National Geographic News, (January 25, 2005), <http://news.nationalgeographic.com/news/2005/01/0125_050125_chimeras.html>.

62 *The Book of Enoch: I Enoch,* pp. 187–8.

63 Even though the earlier account claims that Shemyaza was the first to fall, this portion of the text is clearly referring to Azazel and not Shemyaza because the "star" is later punished in the same manner as Azazel. Besides, the earlier text essentially removes the blame from Shemyaza and places it fully on Azazel. See: 1 Enoch 88:1 in ibid., p. 189.

64 1 Enoch 88:1–3 in ibid., p. 189.

65 1 Enoch 89:1-9 in ibid., pp. 190–1.

66 "Sumerian King List," Answers.com, (February 21, 2005), <http://www.answers.com/sumerian%20king%20list>.

67 Ibid.

68 Ibid.

69 Since Enoch is noted to have lived for 365 years before being taken to Heaven, this number is probably significant because it is trying to link him to a solar deity, basing his life span on the 365 days in a year.

70 "Methuselah," Wikipedia, (February 15, 2005), <http://en.wikipedia.org/wiki/Methuselah>.

71 Neil Philip, *Illustrated Book of Myths* (New York, NY: DK Publishing, Inc., 1995), pp. 140–3.

72 Moctezuma is also commonly known as Montezuma. Cortés was also fortunate in that he arrived on one of the years that the Aztec calendar marked for the possible return of the tribe's beloved god.

73 "Hernan Cortes," Wikipedia, (February 20, 2005), <http://en.wikipedia.org/wiki/Hernan_Cortes>.

CHAPTER 6: THE GATEWAYS OF THE GODS

1 Arthur C. Clarke, *Profiles of the Future: An Inquiry into the Limits of the Possible,* revised edition (New York, NY: Henry Holt and Company, 1984).

2 Lorna Oakes and Lucia Gahlin, *Ancient Egypt* (Barnes & Noble, Inc., 2003), p. 66. *Author's note:* This book was previously published as *The Mysteries of Ancient Egypt* by Anness Publishing Limited.

3 Rainer Stadelmann, "The Pyramids of the Fourth Dynasty," in *Treasures of the Pyramids,* ed. Dr. Zahi Hawass (New York: Barnes & Noble, Inc., 2003), p. 122; and also: "Great Pyramid of Giza," Wikipedia, (March 24, 2005), <http://en.wikipedia.org/wiki/Great_Pyramid_of_Giza>. It should be noted that there are apparent discrepancies regarding the exact measurements of the Great Pyramid. When consulting several different reference materials, each one may have slightly different measurements, or at the very least different units that need to be converted to verify accuracy. This is not helped by the fact that sometimes authors will not explain that they are providing measurements based on the original size (including the outer-casing and capstone), while other times they are referring to the current dimensions.

4 Dr. Zahi Hawass, "The Pyramids," in *Treasures of the Pyramids,* p. 14. Cf., John DeSalvo, Ph.D, *The Complete Pyramid Sourcebook* (Authorhouse, 2003), p. 2.

5 *Author's note:* Other Egyptologists state that the angle of the pyramid's slope is 51° 50' 40". I have decided to use the other dimensions in the text for demonstration purposes related to the argument for "squaring the circle." Cf., Rainer Stadelmann, "Fourth Dynasty," in *Treasures of the Pyramids,* p. 122.

6 DeSalvo, *Complete Pyramid,* p. 2.

7 Christopher Dunn, *The Giza Power Plant: Technologies of Ancient Egypt* (Santa Fe, NM: Bear & Company, Inc, 1998), p. 59.

8 According to a new theory suggested by Egyptologists, the large blocks used in the construction of the pyramids could have been moved on sledges if a team of workers first lubricated the ground with water. However, this still is not an "easy" task and it does not explain how the some of the largest blocks were raised to such heights.

9 Max Toth, *Pyramid Prophecies,* p. 81, quoted in: Dunn, *Giza Power Plant,* p. 61. *Author's Note:* Recently, some Egyptologists believe they have discovered ancient depictions of how the large blocks were moved across the sand by having several workers pour water onto the ground in front of the rollers, allowing the blocks to be more easily moved.

10 Paraphrased from: Dunn, *Giza Power Plant,* p. 62, and containing quote from:

Mark Lehner, *The Complete Pyramids*, p. 209.

11 DeSalvo, *Pyramid Sourcebook*, p. 15.

12 Dr. Zahi Hawass, "The Pyramids," in *Ancient Egypt*, ed. David P. Silverman (New York, NY: Oxford University Press, Inc., 2003), p. 170.

13 Ibid., pp. 170–171.

14 Ibid., p. 171.

15 Stephen S. Mehler, *The Land of Osiris: An Introduction to Khemitology* (Adventures Unlimited Press, 2001), pp. 49–50.

16 Herbie Brennan, *The Secret History of Ancient Egypt* (New York, NY: Berkley Books, 2001), p. 29.

17 Quoted from: Lehner, *Complete Pyramids*, p. 34, in Mehler, *Land of Osiris*, p. 50.

18 Mehler, *Land of Osiris*, p. 48.

19 Dr. Robert K. Ritner, "The Cult of the Dead," in *Ancient Egypt*, ed. Silverman, p. 136.

20 Dr. William J. Murnane, "Three Kingdoms and Thirty-Four Dynasties," in ibid, p. 24.

21 Dr. James P. Allen, "The Celestial Realm," in ibid, p. 116.

22 Genesis 11:1–9.

23 Jeremy Black and Anthony Green, *Gods, Demons and Symbols of Ancient Mesopotamia*, 1992 (Great Britain: University of Texas Press, Austin, 2003), s.v. "ziggurats," pp. 187–9.

24 Emil Soleyman-Zomalan, *Assyrian History: Observations of Mesopotamian and Elamite Ziggurats*, (2003), <http://www.nishra.com/assyrians/ziggurats/>.

25 Ibid. *Author's Note:* It is important to point out that even though the source of this material has been indicated, I have changed the arrangement and meaning of the colors for this book because I believe they were described incorrectly on the web page. The author of the web page states that the uppermost stage was colored red and therefore would have represented the sky. I have changed this so that the second stage is red, and represents the earth, while the third stage is white (the sky). Red is typically associated as a color for the earthly realm because red dirt or clay is most often described as the substance that was used to create mankind. It is also the color of blood, another reason it is associated with earth. There does not seem to be very specific information regarding this readily available to verify for accuracy. If the changes I have made to the colors of the stages are in error, it is completely my own.

26 Black, *Gods, Demons and Symbols*, s.v. "Temples and Temple Architecture," p. 175.

27 Ibid., s.v. "Sacred Marriage," pp. 157–8.

28 "Ziggurat," Wikipedia, (March 18, 2005), <http://en.wikipedia.org/wiki/Ziggurat>.

29 Black, *Gods, Demons and Symbols,* s.v. "E-kur," p. 74.

30 Ibid., s.v. "Cosmology," p. 53.

31 Joan Oates, *Babylon: Revised Edition,* 1979 (New York, NY: Thames and Hudson, 2000), p. 60.

32 Zecharia Sitchin, *The Twelfth Planet,* The Earth Chronicles, vol. 1 (New York, NY: Avon Books, 1978), pp. 149–150, 171.

33 Technically, the instruction was given specifically to Adam since Eve had not yet been formed in this second version of the Creation story. However, since Eve was created from Adam, it was understood that she should already know about it or that Adam would have told her not to eat from that particular tree.

34 Genesis 3:4–5. Please note that I have substituted the alternate translation "gods" for "God" in this verse. The original Hebrew word is *elohim* (אלהים), which can be translated as either singular or plural based on the grammar of the sentence. It is perfectly acceptable to use "gods" for this verse, although it is usually downplayed to avoid the polytheistic overtones in a belief system that is generally considered to be monotheistic.

35 "The Secret Book of John," in *The Secret Teachings of Jesus: Four Gnostic Gospels,* trans. Marvin W. Meyer (New York: Vintage Books, 1986), pp. 65–6.

36 Michael Heiser has written that the verse in Genesis 35:7 that recounts the original incident when God appeared to Jacob atop the shrine should actually be understood in the plural sense. Not only did Yahweh appear to Jacob, but so did the other gods that made up the Divine Council.

37 While this is pure speculation, it is worth considering that perhaps these "Seven Great Rulers" are identical to "The Seven" gods/demons called the *sebittu* (Akkadian) or *iminbi* (Sumerian) in the Middle East. There were also the "Seven Sages" known as the *apkallū,* who were often depicted as men dressed in fish suits or as winged figures with the faces of birds. See: Black, *Gods, Demons and Symbols,* s.v. "Seven (demons)," p. 162; ibid., s.v. "Seven (gods)," p. 162; ibid., s.v. "Seven Sages," pp. 163–4.

38 "Chichen Itza," Wikipedia, (July 22, 2005), <http://en.wikipedia.org/wiki/Chichen_itza>.

39 Quoted in: Adrian G. Gilbert and Maurice M. Cotterell, *The Mayan Prophecies: Unlocking the Secrets of a Lost Civilization* (New York: Barnes & Noble, Inc., 1996), p. 204.

40 The actual wording used to describe this divine being is *bar elahin* (אלהין
לבר), the singular form of the Aramaic equivalent to *bene elohim* (אלהים
בני), "son of (the) god(s)."

41 John Michael Greer, *The New Encyclopedia of the Occult* (St. Paul, Minnesota: Llewellyn Publications, 2003), s.v. "Fire, Element of," p. 174.

42 Ibid., s.v. "Triangle of Manifestation," p. 492.

43 Black, *Gods, Demons and Symbols*, s.v. "Du-ku," p. 72.

44 Exodus 34.

45 Special thanks to Michael Heiser for pointing out this connection between Eden and the "mountain of God."

46 *The Complete Dead Sea Scrolls in English*, ed. & trans. Geza Vermes (New York: Penguin Books, 1998), p. 329.

47 See: 1 Enoch 6:6 in *The Book of Enoch: I Enoch*, trans. R.H. Charles (Oxford: Clarendon Press, 1912), pp. 15–16.

48 1 Enoch 18:6, 8–9, in ibid., pp. 40–1.

49 Ibid., p. 42.

50 Another acceptable variation of the word for "tongues" is "vibrations" in Richard Laurence's translation.

51 *The Book of Enoch: I Enoch*, trans. Charles, p. 33.

52 This is meant to explain the origin of demonic spirits that take possession of people. The slaying of a giant merely kills the physical body; the spirit that is half-watcher, however, is released. Due to the nature of this hybrid spirit, though, it is bound to the earthly plane and cannot do anything of apparent significance. Resenting this newfound impotence, these demonic spirits must now force their way into the human hosts in a futile attempt to take on flesh-and-blood bodies once again.

53 1 Enoch 14:15–25 and 1 Enoch 15 in ibid., pp. 34–7.

54 1 Enoch 16:3–4 in ibid., pp. 37–8.

55 1 Enoch 17:1–2 in ibid., p. 38.

56 1 Enoch 22 in ibid., pp. 46–51.

57 Ibid., pp. 53–4.

58 "Translated" can also be understood as "hidden" or "concealed."

59 *The Book of Enoch: I Enoch*, trans. Charles, pp. 142–4.

60 Please note that the version of Richard Laurence's translation that I have used for this verse is numbered slightly differently than that of Charles. Laurence's verse is marked as: 1 Enoch 70:13.

61 Elizabeth Clare Prophet, *Fallen Angels and the Origins of Evil* (USA: Summit University Press, 2000), p. 21.

62 *The Book of Enoch: I Enoch,* trans. Charles, pp. 144–5.

63 Rosemary Ellen Guiley, *The Encyclopedia of Angels,* 2d ed. (New York, USA: Checkmark Books, 2004), s.v. "Enoch," pp. 116–7.

64 Ibid., p. 118.

65 Ibid. Other names for 3 Enoch are: the "Hebrew Apocalypse of Enoch," the "Sefer Hekalot" (the Book of the Palaces), and the "Chapters of Rabbi Ishmael."

66 Ibid., s.v. "Metatron," pp. 240–1.

67 Ibid., p. 240.

68 2 Kings 2:1.

69 Guiley, *The Encyclopedia of Angels,* s.v. "Elijah," p. 112.

70 Cf., Psalm 8:4–6.

CHAPTER 7: WHAT'S IN A NAME?

1 "Akhenaton," Wikipedia.com, (February 23, 2005), <http://en.wikipedia.org/wiki/Akhenaton>.

2 Rosemary Ellen Guiley, *The Encyclopedia of Angels,* 2d ed. (New York, USA: Checkmark Books, 2004), s.v. "names," pp. 273–4.

3 Louis Ginzberg, *The Legends of the Jews: Volume I - From the Creation to Jacob,* 1909–1938, translated by Henrietta Szold (Baltimore, MD: Johns Hopkins University Press, 1998), p. 146.

4 Ibid., p. 149.

5 John Michael Greer, *The New Encyclopedia of the Occult* (St. Paul, Minnesota: Llewellyn Publications, 2003), s.v. "Tetragrammaton," p. 477.

6 Donald Tyson, *Tetragrammaton: The Secret to Evoking Angelic Powers and the Key to the Apocalypse* (St. Paul, Minnesota: Llewellyn Publications, 1998), pp. 1–2. *Author's Note:* This book has since been republished in 2004 under the new title: *The Power of the Word: The Secret Code of Creation,* by Llewellyn.

7 Greer, *The New Encyclopedia,* s.v. "Tetragrammaton," p. 477; also: Tyson, *Tetragrammaton,* p. 1.

8 Tyson, *Tetragrammaton,* pp. 3–4.

9 Ibid., p. 3.

10 The name Jupiter is from the Latin *Jovis Pater* meaning "Father Jove."

11 Greer, *The New Encyclopedia,* s.v. "Tetragrammaton," p. 477.

12 Several other variations for the spelling of Cabala are Kabbalah, Kabala, and

Qabala. Sometimes, certain practitioners wish to differentiate between belief systems by using Kabala to refer to the original Jewish form, Cabala for the Christian form, and Qabala for those using the Hermetic form. I have decided to use what is considered the oldest known form, Cabala.

13 *Sepher Yetzirah,* trans. William Wynn Westcott (New York: Weiser, 1980), p. 17, quoted in: Tyson, *Tetragrammaton,* pp. 7–8.

14 Greer, *The New Encyclopedia,* s.v. "Tetractys," p. 477.

15 Tyson, *Tetragrammaton,* pp. 10, 16.

16 Ibid., pp. 11–12.

17 Ibid., pp. 23–24.

18 Greer, *The New Encyclopedia,* s.v. "Gematria," p. 191.

19 Aramaic was one of the most commonly spoken languages during the first century.

20 See: Timothy Freke and Peter Gandy, *Jesus and the Lost Goddess: The Secret Teachings of the Original Christians* (New York, NY: Harmony Books, 2001), pp. 14–15 for a convincing argument that the story of Jesus is a clever retelling of Moses' and Joshua's stories. Careful examination of the Exodus story and the Gospels reveal many similarities: Moses is saved from the evil Pharaoh's mass infanticide by being floated in a basket and then raised in Egypt. Likewise, Jesus must be saved from the child slayings of King Herod and flees safely to Egypt. Later, the Israelites are "baptized" by Moses when they crossed the Red Sea, which began their "purification process" of conquering their fears and doubts while spending forty years in the desert. This is paralleled by Jesus spending forty days in the wilderness and being tempted by Satan after he was baptized by John. The next step in the process involved the "death of the old self" when Moses dies before his people can enter the land promised to them by God. The obvious parallel in the New Testament is the crucifixion and death of Jesus. The final step is the "realization of Gnosis" or "Wisdom," when Joshua takes command and leads the Israelites into the Promised Land, echoed in the New Testament by the resurrection and heavenly ascension of Jesus.

21 Migene González-Wippler, *Keys to the Kingdom: Jesus and the Mystic Kabbalah* (St. Paul, Minnesota: Llewellyn Publications, 2004), p. 112.

22 Daniel Gleason, "The Evolution of the Name Jesus," *The Sacred Geometry Mysteries of Jesus Christ,* (1998–2003), <http://www.jesus8880.com/chapters/gematria/yehoshua.htm>.

23 Ibid., "The Alpha-Numeric Greek Alphabet," <http://www.jesus8880.com/chapters/gematria/greek alphabet.htm>.

24 Margaret Starbird, *Magdalene's Lost Legacy: Symbolic Numbers and the Sacred Union in Christianity* (Rochester, VT: Bear & Company, 2003), p. 40.

25 Timothy Freke and Peter Gandy, *The Jesus Mysteries: Was the "Original Jesus" a Pagan God?* (New York, NY: Harmony Books, 2000), p. 116. See also: David Shulenberg, *Treatise on Intervals: With a Review of Fractions and Decimals and Recipes for Some Keyboard Temperment.* (Wagner College: One Campus Road, Staten Island, New York 10301, 2004) <http://www.wagner.edu/faculty/dschulenberg/tunetemp.html> and "Pythagorean Tuning," Wikipedia, (February 23, 2006), <http://en.wikipedia.org/wiki/Pythagorean_tuning>.

26 While most Bible authorities contend that the "number of the beast" is the widely recognized 666, some other ancient manuscripts have been discovered that list 616 or 665 as the authentic numbers.

27 See: Mark 4:9; Matthew 13:9; Luke 8:8.

28 See: Matthew 13:10–17; Mark 4:10–12; Luke 8:9–10.

29 John 21:1–14.

30 Freke, *Jesus Mysteries,* pp. 39–40.

31 Starbird, *Magdalene's,* pp. 112–113.

32 The wobbling of Earth's axis causes the signs of the Zodiac to move backwards (known as "precession") through the wheel very slowly over a 25,800-year cycle.

33 See note 20 for additional information.

34 Ibid., pp. 49, 139–140.

35 Laurence Gardner, *Genesis of the Grail Kings* (Gloucester, MA: Fair Winds Press, 2002), p. 155.

36 Jeremy Black and Anthony Green, *Gods, Demons and Symbols of Ancient Mesopotamia,* 1992 (Great Britain: University of Texas Press, Austin, 2003) s.v. "Dragons," p. 71

37 Ibid., s.v. "Snake-dragon," p. 166.

38 It should also be noted that *nachash* (נחש), not only means serpent, but is also used to refer to someone who is a healer and practices divination and can also mean "Shining One."

39 The Gospel of John records three Passover events (2:13, 6:4, and 13:1) and there is also an unnamed feast that is thought to be another Passover (5:1), which would make the period last three years.

40 Gardner, *Genesis,* pp. 161, 164.

41 Tyson, *Tetragrammaton,* p. 47.

42 Greer, *The New Encyclopedia,* s.v. "Pentagrammaton," p. 369.

43 Tyson, *Tetragrammaton,* pp. 47–48.

44 Ibid., p. 50.
45 Cf. Mark 16:17; Mark 9: 38–41; Luke 9: 49–50.
46 Tyson, *Tetragrammaton*, pp. 148–149.
47 Greer, *The New Encyclopedia*, s.v. "Pentagram," p. 367.
48 Symbols.com, "Group 27:21," 1997–1999, <http://www.symbols.com/encyclopedia/27/2721.html>.
49 Ibid.
50 Rod Thorn, "The Pentagram and the Templars," <http://www.thornr.demon.co.uk/kchrist/pent.html>.
51 Herbert B. Huffmon, "Shalem," in *Dictionary of Deities and Demons in the Bible DDD (2nd Extensively Rev. Ed.),* ed. Karel van der Toorn, Bob Becking & Pieter W. van der Horst (Grand Rapids, MI: Brill; Eerdmans: Leiden, 1999), pp. 755-77.
52 In Greece, the pentagram was commonly known as the pentalpha.
53 Greer, *The New Encyclopedia*, s.v. "Pentagram," p. 367.
54 Symbols.com, "Group 27:21," <http://www.symbols.com/encyclopedia/27/2721.html>.
55 Greer, *The New Encyclopedia*, s.v. "Pentagram," p. 367.
56 In the poem, the pentagram is referred to as a pentangle and also as the Endless Knot, both of which were common for this time in history.
57 Ibid.
58 Ibid.
59 Greer, *The New Encyclopedia*, s.v. "Lévi, Eliphas," p. 271. As a side note, the magickal pseudonym used by Lévi was actually his legal name, Alphonse Louis Constant, translated into Hebrew.
60 Greer, *The New Encyclopedia*, s.v. "Pentagram," p. 368.
61 Ibid.
62 "Venus (Planet)," Wikipedia, (July 23 2004), <http://en.wikipedia.org/wiki/Planet_Venus>.
63 "Ishtar," Wikipedia, (July 19 2004), <http://en.wikipedia.org/wiki/Ishtar>.
64 The goddess Ishtar's name is where we derive the name *Esther* or *Ester,* which means "star" in Hebrew, as well as the name for the holiday *Easter*. It is also the basis for the root word *aster,* which means "star" and is applied to objects like *asteroids,* situations known as *disasters* ("bad stars"), and disciplines such as *astronomy*.
65 "Venus (Planet)," Wikipedia, <http://en.wikipedia.org/wiki/Planet_Venus>. Also of interest, in the fourth century BCE, it was proposed by Heraclides Ponticus that the both Mercury and Venus revolved around the Sun, rather than Earth.

66 Ibid.

67 These numbers are accurate, however, they are based on whole numbers and do not figure in "leap days" caused by the more precise ¼ of a day addition to each year. This formula would be: 583.92 x 5 = 2919.6 days, and then calculated as: 2919.6 ÷ 365.25 = 7.99 years.

68 Trevor W. McKeown and Dr. Leigh Hunt Palmer, "Venus and the Pentagram," (March 16, 2004), <http://freemasonry.bcy.ca/anti-masonry/venus.html>.

69 Robert Roy Britt, "Transit Headquarters: Venus Crosses the Sun June 8," Space.com, (May 18, 2004), <http://www.space.com/scienceastronomy/venus_transit_2004.html>.

70 "Maya Calendar," Wikipedia (July 14, 2004), <http://en.wikipedia.org/wiki/Mayan_calendar>. Another variation of the date given is December 23, 2012.

71 The range of explanations has covered a variety of ideas, but the ones given most credence are: a planet conjunction, a passing comet, or even a nova explosion.

72 Joe Rao, "Star of Bethlehem: Going Back in Time to Examine Its Origins," Space.com (December 20, 2002), <http://www.space.com/spacewatch/star_bethlehem_021220.html>.

73 Barry Downing, *The Bible and Flying Saucers,* 1968 (New York, NY: Marlowe and Company, 1997), p. 134.

74 See: Numbers 24:17.

75 See: Genesis 14:18–20.

76 Cf. Matthew 27:46; Mark 15:34.

77 2 Peter 1.19.

78 2 Corinthians 4:6.

79 Revelation 22:16. Of course, some people will argue that it is David who is identified as the "morning star," not Jesus. However, this argument is not reliable because the rendering of the verse varies between different translations of the Bible. Ultimately, it does not matter if it is meant to refer to David, because Jesus is still being identified under the same lineage and symbolism as David.

80 "Lucifer," Wikipedia, (August 2, 2004), <http://en.wikipedia.org/wiki/Lucifer>.

81 Interestingly, even though most Bibles state there are seventy people, some ancient authorities state the number is seventy-two. This is significant because according to legend, there are seventy-two holy names of God, and this group of people has been sent to cast out demons in the name of God. Perhaps there is a connection here.

82 Luke 10:18.

83 2 Corinthians 11:14

84 At this point in my research, I am still investigating the details surrounding the being commonly referred to as the Antichrist. Most people are familiar with the enigmatic number 666 described by John: "This calls for wisdom: let anyone with understanding calculate the number of the beast, for it is the number of a person. Its number is six hundred sixty-six" (Revelation 13:18 NRSV). For centuries scholars and theologians have tried to decipher the "name" that equals 666, but often without success. However, the second-century bishop, Irenaeus, may have solved the riddle. In his work, *Against Heresies* (Book V, Chapter 30), he noticed that an alternate form of spelling Titan (τιταν) is Teitan (τειταν). This alternative spelling yields the equation: 300 + 5 + 10 + 300 + 1 + 50 = 666. Considering what we now know about the gateways and the angels mating with humans, it is possible that if an Antichrist figure ever emerged, he/it would be a hybrid being—half human and half angel (i.e. a Nephil). This theory is still subjective and I must do more research into it, but I feel that it is worth mentioning now. My views on this may change, however, by the time I have concluded my research.

85 Mark 16:9; Luke 8:2. While there is no direct basis for this, it is interesting to speculate if the mention of these "seven demons" might be referring to the Akkadian *sebittu* or Sumerian *iminbi,* a group of seven demons, referred to simply enough as "The Seven." The same words were apparently also used to refer to a group of "seven gods" who were benevolent and called upon to battle the demons.

86 Personally, my own research has caused me to greatly doubt claims of the holy bloodline and similar legends. However, there *does* seem to be a potentially sinister agenda involving certain individuals pushing for the holy bloodline theory, and this will be addressed in an upcoming book.

87 Starbird, *Magdalene's,* p. 123.

88 Ibid., pp. 128–129.

89 Ibid., 128.

90 This is echoed in certain Jewish beliefs that the "Holy of Holies" inside the Temple of Jerusalem represented the sacred marriage chamber between Yahweh and the Shekinah, which was the feminine counterpart of God. When the Temple was destroyed, Yahweh returned to heaven and ruled alone, while his beloved bride was left to roam the earth, longing to be reunited. The creation of the New Jerusalem and heaven on earth symbolizes the goal of this event. The bride of God is also portrayed in the "Song of Songs" or the "Song of Solomon."

91 Freke, *Jesus Mysteries,* p. 58.

92 Cf., Isaiah 2:2–4.

93 See: Ralph Ellis, *Jesus: Last of the Pharaohs,* 1999, 2d ed. (Kempton, Illinois: Adventures Unlimited, 2001) for a very interesting, although quite technical, revision to history that is quite believable and involves the Hyksos Pharaohs who invaded Egypt and were called "The Shepherd Kings."

94 The Ugaritic language was an ancient Semitic language that used cuneiform symbols that were later developed into an alphabet. This difference separated it from many other Semitic languages, which instead used the symbols as a syllabary, but it is closely related to that of the Canaanite culture. The Ugaritic language was "lost" for thousands of years until it was discovered in 1928 by French archeologists investigating the ancient city of Ugarit in Syria. The key benefits of its discovery has allowed scholars of the Old Testament to better understand ancient Hebrew texts and how Judaism incorporated many common phrases, idioms, and expressions from surrounding pagan cultures.

95 Michael S. Heiser, "The Divine Council in the Dead Sea Scrolls: An Introductory Survey," <http://www.thedivinecouncil.com/>, p. 7.

96 Martin Lunn, *Da Vinci Code Decoded* (New York, NY: The Disinformation Company Ltd., 2004), p. 68.

97 Ibid., pp. 27–8.

98 Marilyn Hopkins, Graham Simmans, and Tim Wallace-Murphy, *Rex Deus: The True Mystery of Rennes-le-Château and the Dynasty of Jesus* (Boston, MA: Element Books, Inc., 2000), p. 7, citing: Gérard de Sède, *Rennes-le-Château, Les Impostures, Les Phantasmes, Les Hypothèses* (Robert Lafont, 1988) p. 19.

99 Lunn, *Da Vinci Code Decoded,* p. 68.

100 Ibid., pp. 73–4.

101 Massimo Polidoro, "The Secrets of Rennes-le-Château," *Skeptical Inquirer* 28, no. 6 November/December 2004: Notes on a Strange World <http://www.csicop.org/si/2004-11/strange-world.html>.

102 Ibid., and also: Lunn, *Da Vinci Code Decoded,* p. 73.

103 Ibid., and also: Lunn, *Da Vinci Code Decoded,* pp. 43–4. It should also be noted that in Lunn's book he argues that Plantard claimed his magazine, *Vaincre,* only contained anti-Semitic statements because it was subject to approval by those pushing Nazi propaganda, and that it was really intended as a resistance magazine with secret messages for other resistance members.

104 Ibid.

105 Ibid.

106 Quoted in: Lunn, *Da Vinci Code Decoded*, p. 71.

107 Ibid.

108 Henry Lincoln, *The Holy Place: Saunière and the Decoding of the Mystery of Rennes-le-Château* (New York: Arcade Publishing, Inc., 1991), pp. 34–5.

109 Ibid., p. 36.

CHAPTER 8: THE REALM OF THE DEAD

1 Jeremy Black and Anthony Green, *Gods, Demons and Symbols of Ancient Mesopotamia*, 1992 (Great Britain: University of Texas Press, Austin, 2003), s.v. "underworld," p. 180.

2 Ibid., s.v. "kur," p. 114.

3 An important distinction is that in Mesopotamian beliefs, the underworld was located underneath the watery deep *abzu*, but the place was extremely dry and dusty, and the dead were tormented by thirst.

4 See: Psalms 9:13; 107:18; Job 38:17; Isaiah 38:10; Matthew 16:18.

5 Black, *Gods, Demons, and Symbols*, s.v., "gatekeepers," p. 86.

6 In modern times, most people attribute Charon to be the ferryman who helps the dead to cross the River Styx. However, the original Greek and Roman sources, as well as Dante, place Charon as the ferryman for the River Acheron (another of the main rivers in Hades).

7 Black, *Gods, Demons, and Symbols*, s.v., "underworld," p. 180.

8 Cf., Jude 6–7.

9 Theodore J. Lewis, "Dead," in *Dictionary of Deities and Demons in the Bible DDD (2nd Extensively Rev. Ed.)*, ed. Karel van der Toorn, Bob Becking & Pieter W. van der Horst (Grand Rapids, MI: Brill; Eerdmans: Leiden, 1999), pp. 223–31.

10 See: Deuteronomy 3:11, 13; Joshua 12:4; 13:12.

11 Joseph Tropper, "Spirit of the Dead," in *Dictionary of Deities and Demons in the Bible DDD*, pp. 806–09.

12 Tzvi Abusch, "Etemmu," in ibid, pp. 309–12.

13 Michael S. Heiser, "Ancient Ghosts, Spirits, Demons, and the Departed Dead: An Overview of the Underworld in Ancient Texts," (December 1, 2004), p. 13. <http://www.michaelsheiser.com>.

14 Even though the dead all seem to go to the same place, it does appear that there is some kind of division according to the degree of the sins committed and whether or not the person was punished in their lifetime or not. See *1 Enoch* 22

for further description concerning the "four hollow places" that hold the dead shown to Enoch during his journey through heaven.

15 Ibid., p. 15.

16 See: Jeremiah 7:31–32; 32:35.

17 See also: 2 Peter 2:4; Jude 7.

18 See: Matthew 5:22, 29–30; 10:28; 23:15, 33; Mark 9:43, 45, 47; Luke 12:5.

19 See: Revelation 19:20; 20:10, 13–14; 21:8.

20 Revelation 20:13–14.

21 See: Matthew 25:41; Revelation 20:10.

22 Joe Nickell, *Entities: Angels, Spirits, Demons, and Other Alien Beings* (Amherst, NY: Prometheus Books, 1995), pp. 31–2.

23 Unfortunately, some camera manufacturers are actually fixing this "bug" so that their cameras will no longer capture infrared light. Interestingly, this means that apparently a large portion of people are capturing anomalies from the infrared realm, but perhaps do not understand what these could potentially be and therefore think they are glitches with the camera. Then again, they might just be glitches.

24 Another benefit of calling the flash is that if another investigator is videotaping the location, there is a vocal cue that a flash is going to appear and this can be used with the video to determine if any anomalies were created from the flash reflecting off some other surface.

25 Joshua P. Warren, *How to Hunt Ghosts: A Practical Guide* (New York, NY: Fireside, 2003), pp. 154–5.

26 Ibid., pp. 157–9.

27 Ibid., p. 159.

28 Ibid., pp. 155–6.

29 Ibid., p. 157.

30 Ibid., pp. 155–6.

31 Ibid., pp. 143–7.

32 Ibid., pp. 171–2.

33 Ibid., p. 173.

34 Frederick Sineath, "Cold Spots, or Cold Shoulders — Infrared Thermo Detection Re-Evaluated," *Ghost! Magazine,* Issue 4: Tools of the Trade (2005), pp. 14–16. Website: <http://www.ghostmag.com>.

35 Richard Southall, *How to Be a Ghost Hunter* (St. Paul, Minnesota: Llewellyn Publications, 2003), p. 66.

36 More advanced digital audio recorders are able to capture better than CD-

quality, such as 24-bit 96 kHz uncompressed audio. However, devices offering this level of professional quality are often very expensive.

37 A standard 20 gigabyte hard drive would hold hundreds of hours of high quality audio files. The recording time available doubles if the files are reduced from stereo to mono. A stereo file is actually unnecessary since the recording input is coming from a microphone source that is only capable of providing a single channel.

38 Konstantinos, *Speak with the Dead: Seven Methods for Spirit Communication* (St. Paul, Minnesota: Llewellyn Publications, 2004), pp. 54–6. *Author's Note:* This book was formerly titled: *Contact the Other Side: 7 Methods for Afterlife Communication,* published in 2001 by Llewellyn.

39 Ibid., p. 53–4.

40 Southall, *Ghost Hunter,* p. 61.

41 Ibid., and also Konstantinos, *Speak with the Dead,* p. 58.

42 Konstantinos, *Speak with the Dead,* p. 58.

43 Ibid., p. 59. See also: Robert Todd Carroll, "Electronic Voice Phenomena (EVP)," *The Skeptic's Dictionary* (June 30, 2005), <http://www.skepdic.com/evp.html>.

44 Ibid., p. 61. Cf., Carroll, "Electronic Voice Phenomena," <http://www.skepdic.com/evp.html>.

45 Ibid., pp. 60–1. Cf., Carroll, "Electronic Voice Phenomena," <http://www.skepdic.com/evp.html>.

46 Acknowledgments to Trey Parker and Matt Stone.

47 G.I.S., "Are you alone?," *EVP Gallery 12,* <http://www.ghostpix.com/showevpjune/evpg12.html>.

48 G.I.S., "Am I dead?," *EVP Gallery 7,* <http://www.ghostpix.com/gis/evpg7.html>.

49 G.I.S., "It's gonna be ok," *EVP Gallery 9,* <http://www.ghostpix.com/gis/evp9.html>.

50 G.I.S., "Ok," *EVP Gallery 9,* <http://www.ghostpix.com/gis/evp9.html>.

51 G.I.S., "I almost had the key," *EVP Gallery 11,* <http://www.ghostpix.com/marevpthree/evpg11.html>.

52 G.I.S., "Help, I'm in here," *EVP Gallery 11,* <http://www.ghostpix.com/marevpthree/evpg11.html>.

53 G.I.S., "Get out of here," *EVP Gallery 11,* <http://www.ghostpix.com/marevpthree/evpg11.html>.

54 G.I.S., "Knights of the Caribbean," *EVP Gallery 11,* <http://www.ghostpix.com/marevpthree/evpg11.html>.

55 G.I.S., "I'm gonna kill ya, right here," *EVP Gallery 12*, <http://www.ghostpix. com/showevpjune/evpg12.html>.

56 G.I.S., "The Boy Episode," *EVP Gallery 9*, <http://www.ghostpix.com/gis/ evp9.html>.

57 G.I.S., "Are you ok?," *EVP Gallery 12*, <http://www.ghostpix.com/showevpjune/ evpg12.html>.

58 G.I.S., "Track 8: I will kill you bastards," *EVP Gallery 17*, <http://www. ghostpix.com/march5evp/evpg17.html>.

59 G.I.S., "Track 7," *EVP Gallery 17*, <http://www.ghostpix.com/march5evp/ evpg17.html>.

60 Brendan Cook, "LeAnna Reardon / Haunted Buildings," in *Contact Beyond*, Internet Podcast (March 16, 2006), <http://www.contactbeyond.com>. The segment concerning the EVP in question begins 1:23:25 (hr:min:sec) into the show and concludes at the mark of 1:34:35.

61 James E. Alcock Ph.D, "Electronic Voice Phenomena: Voices of the Dead?," *Skeptical Inquirer* (2004): Special Articles, <http://www.csicop.org/ specialarticles/evp.html>.

62 One method for tamper-proofing an area is to lay down a tarp below the location of the recorder and sprinkle flower around the area far enough that nobody can reach the recorder without stepping in the flour. Additionally, motion detectors could be set up near any doorways or other entry points that will sound an alarm if someone triggers them by sneaking into the room.

63 Cf., Carroll, "Electronic Voice Phenomena," <http://www.skepdic.com/evp.html>.

64 Whitley Strieber, *The Key: A Conversation About The Nature and Future of Man* (San Antonio, TX: Walker & Collier, Inc., 2001), p. 51.

65 Ibid.

66 Ibid., p. 41.

67 Ibid., p. 40.

CHAPTER 9: THE UNIVERSE NEXT DOOR

1 J.B.S. Haldane, *Possible Worlds and Other Essays* (London: Chatto & Windus, 1927), p. 286.

2 Michio Kaku, *Hyperspace: A Scientific Odyssey Through Parallel Universes, Time Warps, and the Tenth Dimension* (New York, NY: Anchor Books, 1994), pp. 9–10.

3 Ibid, p. 56.

4 Ibid.

5   Ibid., pp. 69–70.

6   Ibid., pp. 70, 73–4.

7   Joseph McMaster, Director, "Part 1: Einstein's Dream," in *The Elegant Universe: Superstrings, Hidden Dimensions, and the Quest for the Ultimate Theory,* Hosted by Brian Greene, DVD (A NOVA Production for WGBH/Boston and Channel 4, 2003), originally aired: Tuesday, October 28, 2003 at 8:00 p.m. on PBS.

8   Kaku, *Hyperspace,* pp. 82–4.

9   McMaster, "Part 1," *The Elegant Universe,* DVD.

10   Ibid.

11   "The Elegant Universe Teacher's Guide," (September 22, 2003) <http://www.pbs.org/wgbh/nova/teachers/programs/3012_elegant.html>, pp. 2, 10 (in PDF version).

12   Joseph McMaster, Director, "Part 2: String's the Thing," in *The Elegant Universe: Superstrings, Hidden Dimensions, and the Quest for the Ultimate Theory,* DVD (A NOVA Production for WGBH/Boston and Channel 4, 2003), originally aired: Tuesday, October 28, 2003 at 9:00 p.m. on PBS.

13   Ibid., and also: Michio Kaku, *Parallel Worlds: A Journey Through Creation, Higher Dimensions, and the Future of the Cosmos* (New York, NY: Doubleday, 2005), pp. 192–3.

14   McMaster, "Part 2," *The Elegant Universe,* DVD.

15   Ibid.

16   Ibid.

17   Kaku, *Parallel Worlds,* pp. 211–2.

18   Ibid., pp. 216–7.

19   Joseph McMaster and Julia Cort, Directors, "Part 3: Welcome to the 11th Dimension," in *The Elegant Universe: Superstrings, Hidden Dimensions, and the Quest for the Ultimate Theory,* DVD (A NOVA Production for WGBH/Boston and Channel 4, 2003), originally aired: Tuesday, November 4, 2003 at 8:00 p.m. on PBS.

20   Ibid.

21   Ibid.

22   Ibid.

23   Ibid.

24   Max Tegmark, "Parallel Universes," *Scientific American* (New York, NY), May 2003, pp. 40-51.

25   Lewis Carroll was actually the pen name of Charles Dodgson, a professional mathematician and Oxford don (college teacher).

26 Michio Kaku, "Blackholes, Wormholes and the Tenth Dimension," Articles and Essays, (accessed: September 8, 2006) <http://www.mkaku.org/article_blackworm.htm>. See also: Kaku, Hyperspace, pp. 118-122.

27 Whitley Strieber, *The Key: A Conversation About The Nature and Future of Man* (San Antonio, TX: Walker & Collier, Inc., 2001), p. 13.

CHAPTER 10: THE COMING STORM

1 Dr. Martin Luther King, Jr., "Beyond Vietnam: A Time to Break Silence," in *A Testament of Hope: The Essential Writings and Speeches of Martin Luther King, Jr.,* ed. James Melvin Washington (New York, NY: HarperCollins Publishers, 1986), p. 243. This is one of Dr. King's least known speeches. It was delivered on April 4, 1967, at a meeting of *Clergy and Laity Concerned* at Riverside Church in New York City. For the full transcript of the speech, please see: <http://www.hartford-hwp.com/archives/45a/058.html>.

2 Whitley Strieber, *The Key: A Conversation about the Nature and Future of Man* (San Antonio, Texas: Walker & Collier, Inc., 2001), p. 68.

3 Art Bell and Whitley Strieber, *The Coming Global Superstorm* (Paperback) (New York, NY: Pocket Books, 2004), p. ix. *Author's Note:* The *Today* show interview aired on January 11, 2000. Over six years later, an amusing twist occurred when Matt Lauer hosted the two hour special *Countdown to Doomsday,* describing ten disastrous scenarios that could wreak havoc on the planet (aired: Wednesday, June 14, 2006 at 9:00 pm EST on the Sci Fi Channel). While most of the special was very good and bought up issues that we all need to recognize and address, I simply cannot pass on the opportunity to comment on the irony of the situation. The third most dangerous threat in the countdown was severe climate change brought on by global warming. As a clip from the film *The Day After Tomorrow* shows huge tornados rip through downtown Los Angeles, Matt Lauer's voice-over tells us that "[t]he movie's nightmarish scenario is not as far-fetched as it may seem." Perhaps he didn't realize the movie was based on the book written by two guys that he considered to be kooks and "doomsday" alarmists. Of course, hosting a special called *"Countdown to Doomsday"* is by no means sensationalistic.

4 Ibid., p. x.

5 Strieber, *The Key,* pp. 68–9.

6 Peter D. Ward, "Impact from the Deep," *Scientific American* (New York, NY), October 2006, pp. 64-71.

7   Ker Than, "Key Argument for Global Warming Critics Evaporates," *LiveScience* (August 11, 2005): Environment, <http://www.livescience.com/environment/050811_global_warming.html>.

8   Ibid.

9   Ibid.

10 Paul Brown, "Republicans Accused of Witch-Hunt Against Climate Change Scientists," *The Guardian* (August 30, 2005), <http://www.guardian.co.uk/usa/story/0,12271,1558884,00.html>.

11 Ibid.

12 Andrew Gumbel, "Bush Appointee at NASA Resigns Over Censorship," *The Independent Online Edition* (February 9, 2006), <http://news.independent.co.uk/world/americas/article344220.ece>.

13 Brian Berger, "Policy or Politics? NASA Accused of Intimidating Climatologist," *Space.com* (February 6, 2006): Business Report, <http://www.space.com/spacenews/businessmonday_060206.html>.

14 Terrence Joyce and Lloyd Keigwin, "Abrupt Climate Change: Are We on the Brink of a New Little Ice Age?," *Woods Hole Oceanographic Institution* <http://www.whoi.edu/institutes/occi/currenttopics/abruptclimate_joyce_keigwin.html>.

15 More information regarding how sudden climate shift may have influenced our evolution can be found in: William H. Calvin, *A Brain for All Seasons: Human Evolution and Abrupt Climate Change* (University of Chicago Press, 2002).

16 Robert B. Gagosian, "Abrupt Climate Change: Should We Be Worried?" paper presented at the World Economic Forum, January 27 Davos, Switzerland, (2003), pp. 2–3. PDF download available at: <http://www.whoi.edu/institutes/occi/images/Abruptclimatechange.pdf> or view an HTML web page version by going to: <http://www.whoi.edu/institutes/occi/currenttopics/climatechange_wef.html>.

17 Ibid., p. 4.

18 Ibid., p. 5.

19 Ibid., pp. 6–7.

20 Ibid., pp. 7–8, referring to: B. Dickson et al., "Rapid Freshening of the Deep North Atlantic Ocean Over the Past Four Decades," *Nature* Vol. 416 (April 25, 2002).

21 Strieber, *The Key*, pp. 68–9.

22 Ibid., p. 69.

23 "Reaping the Whirlwind: Extreme Weather Prompts Unprecedented Global Warming Alert," *The Independent Online Edition* (July 3, 2003), <http://news.independent.co.uk/world/environment/article94497.ece>.

24 Ibid.

25 Camille Feanny and Kiesha Porter, "Europe Recalls Lethal 2003 Heat Wave," *CNN* (August 31, 2004), <http://www.cnn.com/2004/TECH/science/08/02/heatwave.europe/index.html>.

26 Gerald Bell et al., "The 2004 North Atlantic Hurricane Season – A Climate Perspective," <http://www.cpc.ncep.noaa.gov/products/expert_assessment/hurrsummary_2004.pdf>, p. 1.

27 Tropical Storm Cindy was redesignated as a Category 1 Hurricane after post-storm analysis of the 2005 season. This technically made it the first hurricane of the season, instead of Dennis. See: Stacy R. Stewart, *Tropical Cyclone Report, Hurricane Cindy, 3–7 July 2005,* (accessed: February 14, 2006), <http://www.nhc.noaa.gov/pdf/TCR-AL032005_Cindy.pdf>.

28 National Hurricane Center, *Monthly Tropical Weather Summary (July),* (August 1, 2005), <http://www.nhc.noaa.gov/archive/2005/tws/MIATWSAT_jul.shtml?>.

29 Brett Martel, "Governor Orders Evacuations in New Orleans," *Associated Press* (August 31, 2005), <http://news.yahoo.com/s/ap/hurricane_katrina;_ylt=AofEBEAt5i9bMte6cqvFWxobLisB;_ylu=X3oDMTBiMW04NW9mBHNlYwMlJVRPUCUl>.

30 Keay Davidson, "Tragedy May Not Be Season Finale – Hurricane Period Has 3 Months to Go – Experts Predict More Big Ones Could Arrive," *San Francisco Chronicle* (September 1, 2005), <http://sfgate.com/cgi-bin/article.cgi?f=/c/a/2005/09/01/MNGGUEGGV91.DTL>.

31 National Oceanic and Atmospheric Administration, *NOAA Raises the 2005 Atlantic Hurricane Season Outlook: Bulk of This Season's Storms Still to Come* (August 2, 2005), <http://www.noaanews.noaa.gov/stories2005/s2484.htm>.

32 Ibid.

33 Ibid.

34 National Hurricane Center, *Monthly Tropical Weather Summary (September),* (October 1, 2005) <http://www.nhc.noaa.gov/archive/2005/tws/MIATWSAT_sep.shtml?>.

35 Lynn Jenner, ed., *Hurricane Season 2005: Wilma,* (October 27, 2005), Hurricane Wilma Explodes Into a Record Hurricane <http://www.nasa.gov/vision/earth/

lookingatearth/h2005_wilma.html#update>.

36 The page is no longer available, but Accuweather splashed the headline "Super Storm" on the screen during this forecast. <www.accuweather.com> (accessed: October 24, 2005).

37 MSNBC, "Early Nor'easter Coats Region with Snow," Fed by Hurricane Wilma, Storm Dumps up to 20 Inches of White Stuff, (October 26, 2005), <http://www.msnbc.msn.com/id/9827637/>.

38 Rob Gutro, *Hurricane Season 2005 Breaks All Records: Alpha Forms*, NASA (October 23, 2005), <http://www.nasa.gov/vision/earth/lookingatearth/record_breaker.html>. Each year, scientists monitoring tropical cyclones use a list of 21 short names for the Atlantic Basin region. This method allows them to quickly identify specific storms. There are six total lists, which are rotated every year. For instance, the names list for 2004 will be used again in 2010. Some letters, such as X, Y, and Z do not have enough names to fill these lists and so they are skipped. Readers interested in more information should see the National Hurricane Center's description of worldwide lists used for tropical storms at: <http://www.nhc.noaa.gov/aboutnames.shtml>.

39 National Hurricane Center, *Monthly Tropical Weather Summary (November)*, (December 1, 2005), <http://www.nhc.noaa.gov/archive/2005/tws/MIATWSAT_nov.shtml?>.

40 James L. Franklin, *Tropical Cyclone Report, Hurricane Epsilon, 29 November – 8 December 2005*, (January 7, 2006), <http://www.nhc.noaa.gov/pdf/TCR-AL292005_Epsilon.pdf>, p. 2.

41 NOAA.gov, "NOAA Reviews Record-Setting 2005 Atlantic Hurricane Season: Active Hurricane Era Likely To Continue," (November 29, 2005. Updated: February 2, 2006), <http://www.noaanews.noaa.gov/stories2005/s2540.htm>.

42 My apologies go out to my readers, the families affected by all of the devastating tropical storms and other natural disasters, and to Dan Aykroyd, Harold Ramis, Ernie Hudson, Bill Murray, and Ivan Reitman. I simply could not resist including a quotation from *Ghostbusters* here.

43 Ohio State University, *Major Climate Change Occurred 5,200 Years Ago: Evidence Suggests That History Could Repeat Itself*, (December 16, 2005), <http://www.physorg.com/news2409.html>.

44 Ibid.

45 "Tornado Hits Birmingham," *BBC News* (July 29, 2005), <http://news.bbc.co.uk/1/hi/england/west_midlands/4726703.stm>.

46 Rosamélia de Abreu, "Unable to Forecast Them, Brazil Gets Hit by Tornadoes," *Brazzil Magazine* (January 5, 2005), translated by Allen Bennett, <http://brazzilmag.com/content/view/1075/1/>.

47 John Monteverdi, "Highest Elevation Tornado Ever Observed in U.S.," *San Francisco State University,* Department of Geosciences, (August 24, 2004), <http://tornado.sfsu.edu/RockwellPassTornado/>.

48 Di Fang, "Hailstones 'as Big as Eggs' Kill 18," *China Daily* (April 4, 2004), p. 3 <http://www.chinadaily.com.cn/english/doc/2005-04/11/content_432923.htm>.

49 "Bizarre Weather Slams Japan Yet Again," (December 6, 2004), <http://www.unknowncountry.com/news/?id=4299>. *Please note:* this article refers to the original source, which is no longer available, at: <http://story.news.yahoo.com/news?tmpl=story&u=/afp/japan_weather_wind>.

50 Helen Lambourne, "Tsunami: Anatomy of a Disaster," *BBC News* (March 27, 2005), <http://news.bbc.co.uk/1/hi/sci/tech/4381395.stm>.

51 John von Radowitz, "Shocked Scientists Find Tsunami Legacy: A Dead Sea," *The Sydney Morning Herald* (December 14, 2005), <http://www.smh.com.au/articles/2005/12/13/1134236063754.html>.

52 John Pickrell, "2005: The Year in Environment," *New Scientist.com* (December 29, 2005), <http://www.newscientist.com/article.ns?id=dn8516>.

53 Bryan Walsh, "Without Warning," *TIME* (Asia Edition), (July 23, 2006), appeared in the July 31, 2006 issue of *TIME Asia* magazine <http://www.time.com/time/asia/magazine/article/0,13673,501060731-1218091,00.html>.

54 Paul Rincon, "Experts Weigh Supervolcano Risks," *BBC News* (March 9, 2005), <http://news.bbc.co.uk/2/hi/science/nature/4326987.stm>.

55 Associated Press, "Yellowstone Eruption Threat High," *Msnbc.com* (May 9, 2005), <http://www.msnbc.msn.com/id/7789918>.

56 Sandra Hughes, "Yellowstone's Explosive Secret," *CBS Evening News* (March 23, 2004), <http://www.cbsnews.com/stories/2004/03/23/eveningnews/main608243.shtml>.

57 Bruce Sterling, "Suicide by Pseudoscience," *Wired Magazine,* no. 12.06 (June 2004), <http://www.wired.com/wired/archive/12.06/view.html?pg=4?tw=wn_tophead_3>.

58 Antony Barnett, "Bush Attacks Environment 'Scare Stories': Secret Email Gives Advice on Denying Climate Change," *The Observer* (April 4, 2004), <http://www.guardian.co.uk/usa/story/0,12271,1185379,00.html>.

59 Geoffrey Lean, "Global Warming Approaching Point of No Return, Warns Leading Climate Expert," *The Independent Online Edition* (January 23, 2005),

<http://news.independent.co.uk/world/environment/article16401.ece>.

60 Mark Townsend and Paul Harris, "Now the Pentagon Tells Bush: Climate Change Will Destroy Us," *The Observer* (February 22, 2004), <http://observer.guardian.co.uk/international/story/0,6903,1153513,00.html>.

61 David Stipp, "Climate Collapse: The Pentagon's Weather Nightmare," *Fortune Magazine* (February 9, 2004), online version available at: <http://www.fortune.com/fortune/print/0%2C15935%2C582584%2C00.html>.

62 Paul Schwartz and Doug Randall, *An Abrupt Climate Change Scenario and Its Implications for United States National Security,* (October 2003), p. 3. The report is available at: <http://www.gbn.com:80/ArticleDisplayServlet.srv?aid=26231>.

63 "Have We Reached the Tipping Point?" *Unknown Country* (August 12, 2005), <http://www.unknowncountry.com/news/?id=4766>.

64 "BLIZZARD in Hawaii," *Unknown Country* (January 25, 2006), <http://www.unknowncountry.com/news/?id=5127>.

65 Jim Hansen, "Climate Change: On the Edge," *The Independent Online Edition* (February 17, 2006: Environment) <http://news.independent.co.uk/environment/article345926.ece>.

66 Bill Owens, "A Global Warning," *60 Minutes.com* (February 19, 2006) <http://www.cbsnews.com/stories/2006/02/16/60minutes/main1323169.shtml>.

67 "Sun: Solar Activity," Wikipedia (February 27, 2007), <http://en.wikipedia.org/wiki/Sun#Solar_activity>.

68 Robert Roy Britt, "Sun's String of Fury Continues as 7th Major Flare Erupts," *Space.com:* Science, (September 9, 2005), <http://space.com/scienceastronomy/050909_solar_flares.html>.

69 "Scientists Issue Unprecedented Forecast of Next Sunspot Cycle," *The National Center for Atmospheric Research & the UCAR Office of Programs,* News Releases, (March 6, 2006) <http://www.ucar.edu/news/releases/2006/sunspot.shtml>. See also: Leonard David, "Scientists Ponder Space Superstorm," *Space.com* (May 2, 2006) <http://www.space.com/scienceastronomy/060502_solar_storm.html>; and: Robert Roy Britt, "The Great Storm: Solar Tempest of 1859 Revealed," *Space.com* (October 27, 2003) <http://www.space.com/scienceastronomy/mystery_monday_031027.html>.

70 "Long Range Solar Forecast: Solar Cycle 25 Peaking Around 2022 Could Be One of the Weakest in Centuries," *Science@NASA* (May 10, 2006) <http://science.nasa.gov/headlines/y2006/10may_longrange.htm>.

71 "Maunder Minimum," Wikipedia, (May 1, 2006) <http://en.wikipedia.org/wiki/Maunder_Minimum>.

72 "Deluge (Mythology)," Wikipedia (August 24, 2005), <http://en.wikipedia.org/wiki/Deluge_(mythology)>.

73 "Sumer," Wikipedia (August 26, 2005), <http://en.wikipedia.org/wiki/Sumer>.

74 Ibid.

CHAPTER 11: FOLLOW THE YELLOW BRICK ROAD

1 Quotation from: Julia Cameron, *The Artist's Way, 10th Anniversary Edition* (New York, NY: Tarcher/Putnam, 2002), p. 64.

2 For example, consider paper money. The paper is practically worthless and there is no physical difference between a $1 bill and a $100 bill except for the declared value. The perceived value of the money can even be transferred to other items that aren't even made of paper, such as a credit card or checking account. Technically, the money is nothing more than a numerical value assigned to such accounts, and it does not physically exist until we declare that some physical object is worth the same amount.

3 *Gold in the Ancient World*, (2003), World Gold Council, 45 Pall Mall, London, SW1Y 5JG, United Kingdom <http://www.gold.org/discover/knowledge/aboutgold/ancient_world/index.html>.

4 *Gold Production through History*, (2003), World Gold Council, <http://www.gold.org/discover/knowledge/aboutgold/gold_prod/index.html>.

5 Laurence Gardner, *Lost Secrets of the Sacred Ark: Amazing Revelations of the Incredible Power of Gold* (Hammersmith, London: Element Books, Inc., 2003), p. 159. Gardner states in his notes that his information concerning David Hudson's research is taken from Hudson's own lectures given from 1994 to 1996, as well as newsletters and communiqués that were published from 1995 to 2001 by Hudson's related organization: Science of the Spirit Foundation, located in Tempe, Arizona. In addition, information is also from Hudson's talks in Phoenix, Arizona; San Diego, California; Salem, Massachusetts; Meza, Arizona; Ashland, Oregon; Tampa, Florida; Charlotte, North Carolina; Los Angeles, California; Pasadena, California, and Vancouver, British Columbia, with principal lectures given at Global Sciences, Denver, Colorado; Northwest Service Center, Portland, Oregon; The Eclectic Viewpoint, Dallas, Texas; Ramtha's School of Enlightenment, Yelm, Washington; Mt. Hood Community

College, Gresham, Oregon; Maharishi University of Management, Fairfield, Iowa; US Psychotronics Association, Columbus, Ohio, and The Ritz Carlton, Santa Barbara, California.

6   Ibid., p. 160.
7   David Hudson, *David Hudson Lectures,* "The Chemistry of M-state Elements," <http://www.asc-alchemy.com/hudson.html>.
8   Ibid.
9   Ibid.; and also: Gardner, *Lost Secrets,* p. 160.
10   Dan Sewell Ward, *David Radius Hudson,* (2003), Library of Halexandria <http://www.halexandria.org/dward467.htm>. The website author refers to a rough transcript of David Hudson's lecture in 1995 at the International Forum on New Science in Fort Collins, Colorado.
11   Gardner, *Lost Secrets,* p. 160.
12   A possible reason why the Ph.D. is unnamed is because David Hudson said that he had paid the man $22,000 to analyze the mystery substance. The man never offered to pay any of the money back after failing to identify the substance. Instead, the man requested more money for the university to carry out more tests. See: Hudson, *David Hudson Lectures,* "Chemistry of M-state," <http://www.asc-alchemy.com/hudson.html>.
13   Gardner, *Lost Secrets,* pp. 160–1.
14   The only name given by Laurence Gardner for the spectroscopic technician is "Siegfried" in ibid., p. 162. Additionally, according to a transcript of a lecture by David Hudson, the name of the Los Angeles company was Lab Test. Cf., Hudson, *David Hudson Lectures,* "Chemistry of M-state," <http://www.asc-alchemy.com/hudson.html>.
15   Gardner, *Lost Secrets,* p. 161.
16   Ibid.
17   Ibid.
18   Ibid., Chapter 11 notes: #2, p. 291.
19   Ibid., p. 161.
20   Ibid.; and also: Ward, *David Radius Hudson,* <http://www.halexandria.org/dward467.htm>.
21   Gardner, *Lost Secrets,* pp. 162, 291.
22   Ibid., p. 162; and also: Ward, *David Radius Hudson,* <http://www.halexandria.org/dward467.htm>.
23   *Platinum Metals Review,* volume 44, no. 1, January 2000.

24 Gardner, *Lost Secrets,* p. 162; and also: Ward, *David Radius Hudson,* <http://www.halexandria.org/dward467.htm>.

25 Gardner, *Lost Secrets,* p. 162.

26 Ibid., p. 163.

27 Ibid., pp. 163–4. Hudson says that he filed eleven ORMEs patents and eleven S-ORMEs patents, totaling twenty-two in all. Some of these patents can be found under the following numbers: Great Britain GB2219995; France FR2632974; Sweden SE8902258; Germany DE3920144; Switzerland CH680136; Belgium BE1003134; Australia AU3662489; Brazil BR8902984. Please note that even though there are said to be US patents filed, I have been unable to find such documents or even patent filing numbers. For the patents that have been found, I have provided archived electronic copies (some are fully searchable) of them for viewing on the website <www.gatewayofthegods.com>.

28 Ibid., p. 164.

29 Ibid.

30 Ibid.

31 Hudson, *David Hudson Lectures,* "Separating the M-state Elements," <http://www.asc-alchemy.com/hudson.html>.

32 Gardner, *Lost Secrets,* p. 164.

33 Hudson, *David Hudson Lectures,* "Separating the M-state Elements," <http://www.asc-alchemy.com/hudson.html>.

34 Ibid. *Author's Note:* There appears to be a discrepancy regarding the name of the company consulted. The name provided in the transcript is said to be the Berean Corporation from the Bay Area, but whether or not this is accurate is unknown. The person who transcribed the lecture has inserted the name of the company inside of brackets, indicating that the company's name was not provided in the source material. Internet searches have proven unsuccessful in determining if this company currently exists or did so in the past. However, Laurence Gardner says that technicians from the Varian Corporation (Varian Associates Inc., 3120 Hansen Way, Palo Alto, CA 94304-1030) were consulted. Varian is a leading maker of scientific instruments and equipment, including spectroscopy equipment like what was used by David Hudson. The company website for Varian is: <http://www.varianinc.com/>. Cf., Gardner, *Lost Secrets,* pp. 164–5, and Chapter 11 notes: #7, p. 292.

35 Ibid., Gardner, *Lost Secrets,* p. 165, citing an original article published in: *Zeitschrift für Physick Condensed Matter,* April 1986, detailing the findings of Alex Müller and Georg Bednorz at the Rüschlikon Laboratory, Switzerland.

36   Ibid., Gardner, *Lost Secrets,* p. 165.
37   "Superconductivity," Wikipedia (October 21, 2005), <http://en.wikipedia.org/wiki/Superconductivity>.
38   Gardner, *Lost Secrets,* p. 166.
39   Ibid.
40   Ibid., p. 167.
41   Ibid., pp. 167–8.
42   Ibid., Chapter notes: #10, p. 292.
43   Ibid., p. 168.
44   Ibid., p. 168–9.
45   Ibid., p. 169. Gardner also includes many other sources and publications detailing this research in ibid., Chapter 11 notes: #12, p. 292–3: "Microclusters," *Scientific American,* (December 1989), Michael A. Duncan, Dennis H. Rouvray, pp. 110–15; "New Radioactivities," *Scientific American,* (March 1990), Walter Greiner, Aurel Sandulescu, pp. 68–67; "Possible discontinuity in the octupole behavior in the Pt-Hg Region," *Physical Review C,* vol. 39 # 3, (March 1989), C.S. Lim, R.H. Spear, W.J. Vermeer, M.P. Fewell, pp. 1142–4; "Collective and single particle structure in 103Rh," *Physical Review C,* vol. 37 # 2, February, H. Dejbakhsh, R.P. Schmitt, G. Mouchaty, pp. 621–35; "Structure of Os and Pt Isotopes," *Physical Review C,* vol. 38 # 2, (August 1988), A. Ansari, pp. 953–9; "Superdeformation in 104, 105Pd," *Physical Review C,* vol. 38 # 2, (August 1988), A.O. Macchiavelli, J. Burde, R.M. Diamond, C.W. Beausang, M.A. Deleplanque, R.J. McDonald, F.S. Stephens, J.E. Draper, pp. 1088–91; "Direct Mapping of Adatom/Adatom Interactions," *Physical Review Letters,* vol. 62 # 10, (March 1989), Fumiya Watanabe and Gert Ehrlich, pp. 1146–4; "Inertias of superdeformed bands," *Physical Review C,* vol. 41 # 4, (April 1990), Y.R. Shimizu, E. Vigezzi, R.A. Broglia, pp. 1861–64; "Bound States, Cooper Pairing, and Bose Condensation in Two Dimensions," *Physical Review Letters,* vol. 62 # 9, (February 1989), Mohit Randeria, Ji-Min Duan, Lih-Yir Shieh, pp. 981–84; "Quantum size effects in rapidly rotating nuclei," *Physical Review C,* vol. 41 # 4, (April 1990), Y.R. Shimizu, R.A. Broglia, pp. 1865–8; "The Classical Vacuum," *Scientific American,* Timothy H. Boyer, pp. 79–8; "Beyond E=mc²," *The Sciences,* (November/December 1994), Bernhard Haisch, Alfonso Rueda, H.E. Puthoff, pp. 26–31; "Everything for Nothing," *New Scientist,* (28 July 1990), H.E. Puthoff; "Inertia as a zero-point field Lorentz Force," *Physical Review A,* vol. 49 # 2, (February 1994), Bernhard Haisch, Alfonso Rueda, H.E. Puthoff, pp. 678–94; "Spin Cycle: The Spectra of Super

Deformed Nuclei," *Scientific American,* (October 1991), Philip Yam, p. 26; "Evidence from Activation Energies for Superconductive Tunneling in Biological Systems at Physiological Temperatures," *Physiological Chemistry and Physics 3,* (1971), pp. 403–10; "Magnetic Flux Quantization and Josephson Behavior in Living Systems," *Physica Scripta,* vol. 40, (1989), E. Del Giudice, S. Doglia, M. Milani, C.W. Smith, G. Vitello, pp. 786–91; "Biological Sensitivity to Seak Magnetic Fields Due to Biological Superconductive Josepheson Junctions," *Physiological Chemistry and Physics 5,* (1973), pp. 173–6; "Biophysical Studies of the Modification of DNA by Antitumour Platinum Coordination Complexes," *Platinum Metals Review,* vol. 34, # 4, (1990), p. 235.

46   Miguel Alcubierre, "The Warp Drive: Hyperfast Travel Within General Relativity," *Classical and Quantum Gravity,* vol. 11 (May 1994).

47   Michael Szpir, "Space-Time Hypersurfing," *American Scientist,* vol. 82 (October 1994), pp. 422–3.

48   Gardner, *Lost Secrets,* pp. 169–70.

49   Ibid., pp. 170–1.

50   Ibid., p. 171. Cf., David Hudson, *David Hudson Lectures,* "The Chemistry of M-state Elements," <http://www.asc-alchemy.com/hudson.html>.

51   Ibid., Gardner, Chapter 11 notes: # 18, 19, p. 294: Science of the Spirit Foundation was then at P.O. Box 25709, Tempe, Arizona 85285. SOSF Newsletter #1 was issued on October 13, 1995. There were about 5,000 memberships at individual subscriptions of $500 each, totaling $2.5 million.

52   Ibid., p. 172. Cf., SOSF *Newsletters* #14 and 15, (November/December 1996).

53   Ibid. Cf., SOSF *Newsletters* # 18 and 19, (March/April 1997).

54   Ibid.

55   Ibid.

56   Ibid., pp. 172–3. Cf., SOSF *Newsletter* #29, (Fall 1998 to Fall 2000). *Author's note:* an online version of this newsletter can be found at: <http://www.subtleenergies.com/ormus/tw/enough.htm>. Also, I am unaware what became of the situation after this time or if David Hudson did ever provide refunds to members who requested them.

CHAPTER 12: SQUARING THE CIRCLE

1   As in the last chapter, the information provided within this section is primarily derived from the work of Laurence Gardner.

2   The subject of alchemy had become so popular during the late Elizabethan period that Ben Jonson was inspired to write the satirical drama, "The Alchemist," (first performed in 1610 by the King's Men) which chronicles the exploits of a group of city swindlers that trick their cohorts into believing they had discovered the secrets of the Philosophers' Stone.

3   Laurence Gardner, *Lost Secrets of the Sacred Ark: Amazing Revelations of the Incredible Power of Gold* (Hammersmith, London: Element Books, Inc., 2003), p. 83. For more information Gardner points readers to: Carl Gustav Jung, *Psychology and Alchemy* (Routledge, London), part 2, ch. 3, pp. 158–9, and part 3, ch. 5. p. 370. He also notes a commentary concerning Jung and Jason in Joscelyn Godwin's *Foreword* to: Antoine Faivre, *The Golden Fleece and Alchemy*, pp. 1–6.

4   Eirenaeus Philalethes, *Tres Tractatus de Metallorum Transmutatione — Brief Guide to the Celestial Ruby* (Amsterdam: Musaeum Hermeticum, 1668) as quoted in: Gardner, *Lost Secrets*, pp. 25–6.

5   See Note 1.

6   Gardner, *Lost Secrets*, pp. 3–4.

7   Ibid., p. 5, quoting from: David M. Rohl, *A Test of Time*, (London: Century, 1995), p. 113.

8   Ibid., p. 8.

9   Ibid., pp. 8–9. See also: Laurence Gardner, *Genesis of the Grail Kings: The Explosive Story of Genetic Cloning and the Bloodline of Jesus* (Gloucester, MA: Fair Winds Press, 2002), pp. 248–50.

10 Ibid.

11 Ibid., pp. 9–10.

12 Ibid., p. 16.

13 The Egyptians compiled an individualized book for each deceased person. The most common "Book of the Dead" that is referenced is the manuscript collected for the royal scribe, Ani, known as the *Papyrus of Ani*.

14 James Wasserman, *The Egyptian Book of the Dead (The Book of Going Forth by Day)*, 1994, translated by Dr. Raymond O. Faulkner, edited by Eva von Dassow, revised edition (San Francisco: Chronicle Books, 1998), plate 8.

15 Many times, people think of the "golden calf" as a female cow, but it was really a bull. The word used in Exodus 32 to describe it is *'egel* (עֵגֶל), a masculine noun. If it was intended to be a heifer, the feminine form, *'eglah* (עֶגְלָה), would have been used.

16 Symbols.com, "Group 28:5," *Square*. 1997–1999 <http://www.symbols.com/encyclopedia/28/285.html>. See also: "Group 9:1," Cross with Arms of Equal Length. <http://www.symbols.com/encyclopedia/09/091.html>.

17 Ibid., "Group 26:1," *Circle*. <http://www.symbols.com/encyclopedia/27/2721.html>.

18 Gardner, *Genesis of the Grail Kings*, p. 131.

19 The Tigris River actually runs through the middle of ancient Assyria, not to its east. However, since we are probably dealing with more symbolism than geographical fact, this is negligible. The discrepancy should be pointed out so as to not cause any confusion that the Biblical statement should be taken as a literal fact. It is also possible that this was a deliberate "mistake" so that anyone reading it who knew it was wrong, would recognize that Assyria is meant to be a clue.

20 Cf., John 6: 47–51.

21 John Anderson, *The Rapture: Biblical Fact... or Left Behind Fiction?* (Lighthouse World Ministries, 2004), 57 min.

22 Ibid. See also: James Whisler, "Dispensationalism Timeline," *Historicist.com*, <http://www.historicist.com/articles2/distimeline.htm>.

23 I remember reading an old edition in the early 1990s as a teenager, and it certainly did seem amusing to look over many of the prophecies that never came true, such as Jesus returning in the 1980s. That particular prophecy, by the way, has since been removed from recent editions of the book.

24 Pam Dewey, *Edgar Whisenant and His 88 Reasons*. 2001–2004 <http://www.isitso.org/guide/whise.html>.

25 *The Rapture Letters*, <http://www.raptureletters.com>.

26 It is interesting to note here that the word used here for cloud is the Greek *nephele* (νεφέλη), pronounced: nef-el-ay. This is pure speculation at this time, but the similarity in sound to the Hebrew *Nephilim* (נְפִלִים) is striking; particularly when passages involving these "clouds" are thought of as something like UFOs. While it is too early to say for certain that they are indeed referring to UFOs, there does appear to be some kind of alien/extraterrestrial connection with ancient myths and modern encounter reports. This connection will be more fully explored in a future work. For now, it would be interesting to see if a language expert can better explain the apparent connection of the term nephele with the Nephilim, or perhaps they can offer reasons why there is no real connection. For those interested in reviewing the use of this term, please refer to a website such as Crosswalk.com (http://bible.crosswalk.com) to use their study tools and quickly look up every verse that uses this term. The Strong's number for nephele is #3507.

27 Anderson, *The Rapture.*

28 The boiling point is assumed to be at standard pressure for this explanation.

29 *Author's Note:* I must offer a crucial disclaimer regarding monatomic gold and how it applies to the concepts I have just presented. By no means am I advocating that anyone, under any circumstances, should rush out and collect as much monatomic gold (or similar material) as possible and then overdose and/or kill themselves or others by ingesting or injecting it into their bodies. Until we know more about this substance, do not think for a moment that it is some magic cure-all that will eradicate cancer or give you super-human powers. While gold itself is relatively bio-friendly to the human body, too much of anything can hurt or kill you. If you still feel that you absolutely must try it, you should first consult with your doctor or other licensed medical professional before taking any such action. *The author of this book, the publisher and any associated persons or companies expressly disclaim any liability, loss, damage, or injury, and will not be held responsible for any harm you cause to yourself or others by failing to heed any of the warnings described above.*

It is extremely important that scientists perform proper and extensive tests on this material in order to determine how it can be safely and effectively utilized. Perhaps researchers will find that it does not have inter-dimensional properties as David Hudson has claimed—or perhaps maybe they will. If so, then we might be on the right track and should proceed further. Please understand that while I am excited about the potential of this theory, I must err on the side of caution and advise all of my readers to do the same.

30 Cf., Psalm 8: 4–5. It should also be noted that even though most Bibles translate the phrase "a little lower than the angels," in Psalm 8:4–5, the original Hebrew is actually "a little lower than the *elohim* (gods)."

31 Rosemary Ellen Guiley, *The Encyclopedia of Angels, 2d ed.* (New York, USA: Checkmark Books, 2004), s.v. "Elijah," p. 112.

32 One of the foremost reasons that orthodox Jews reject that Jesus was the awaited Messiah is because he was crucified on a tree. In the Old Testament book of Deuteronomy (21:22–3 NRSV), the Jewish law states: "When someone is convicted of a crime punishable by death and is executed, and <u>you hang him on a tree</u>, his corpse must not remain all night upon the tree; you shall bury him that same day, for <u>anyone hung on a tree is under God's curse</u>."

33 Stauros (σταυρός), Strong's # 4716. The following verses mention Jesus and the cross: Matthew 27:32, 40, 42; Mark 15:21, 30, 32; Luke 23:26; John 19:17, 19, 25, 31; 1 Corinthians 1:17, 18; Galatians 6:12, 14; Ephesians 2:16;

Philippians 2:8, 3:18; Colossians 1:20, 2:14; Hebrews 12:2.

34 Xulon (ξύλον), Strong's # 3586. For verses where it says that Jesus was hanged from a tree, please see: Luke 23:31; Acts 5:30, 10:39, 13:29; Galatians 3:13; 1 Peter 2:24; Notice that this word is also used to describe the "tree of life" in Revelation 22:2 and 22:14.

35 Timothy Freke and Peter Gandy, *The Jesus Mysteries: Was the "Original Jesus" a Pagan God?* (New York, NY: Harmony Books, 2000), p. 50, referring to: S.F. Dunlap, *The Mysteries of Adoni* (Williams and Norgate, 1866), p. 115.

36 Ibid., referring to: J. Harrison, *Prologemena to the Study of Greek Religion* (Princeton University Press, 1922), p. 429.

37 "Yggdrasil," Wikipedia (October 7, 2005), <http://en.wikipedia.org/wiki/Yggdrasil>.

38 Ibid.

39 "Tree of Life (Disambiguation)," Wikipedia (September 18, 2005), <http://en.wikipedia.org/wiki/Tree_of_Life>.

40 Jeremy Black and Anthony Green, *Gods, Demons and Symbols of Ancient Mesopotamia*, 1992 (Great Britain: University of Texas Press, Austin, 2003) s.v. "stylised tree and its 'rituals,'" pp. 170–1; and also: s.v. "bucket and cone," p. 46.

41 Cf., John 9:5.

42 Migene González-Wippler, *Keys to the Kingdom: Jesus and the Mystic Kabbalah* (St. Paul, Minnesota: Llewellyn Publications, 2004), p. 111.

43 Compare this to the prophecy discussed by two angels about the end of days that was overheard by Daniel (Daniel 12). The angels speak of a time of great suffering unknown in human history, but that the great prince Michael (who is confirmed in the Dead Sea Scrolls to be synonymous with Michael-Zadok, aka: Melchizedek) will arise and come to the rescue of the righteous. When this occurs, the people are said to take on a shining appearance like the angels and "stars" of heaven.

44 Daniel 3:16–27.

45 1 Enoch 18:13–16 in: *The Book of Enoch: I Enoch,* translated by R.H. Charles (Oxford: Clarendon Press, 1912), p. 42.

46 Revelation 2:7.

47 I say that this being might not actually be "God" because it seems more like it could be the Angel of Yahweh (or even some other deity as the Gnostics claimed), especially since he physically interacts with people and the environment (e.g., Genesis 3:8). I say this because if it was *really* God, then why does he have difficulty locating Adam and Eve in the garden (Genesis 3:9-11) if God is

supposed to be omniscient? Furthermore, this being routinely tries to preserve the ignorance of the human race and keep them in a subordinate position so that they will not become like the angels. Specifically, he drives Adam and Eve out of the garden so that they cannot eat from the Tree of Life (Genesis 3:22-24), and he destroys the Tower of Babel so that humans cannot reach heaven (Genesis 11:5-9).

48 Genesis 3:22–24.

49 Revelation 2:10–11.

50 Revelation 2:17.

51 Revelation 2:26–27.

52 See: Deuteronomy 32:8–9. According to the Old Testament, God allowed the other nations of the world to worship and be ruled over the other gods of the divine council. However, he specifically set aside Israel as his portion and so that they would only worship Him.

53 Revelation 3:5–6.

54 Revelation 3:12–13.

55 Revelation 3:18.

56 Chuck Missler and Mark Eastman, *Alien Encounters*, 1997, Revised and Expanded Edition (Koinonia House, 2003), p. 211.

57 See: Genesis 19:1–13.

58 Cf., 1 Enoch 1:9 in: *The Book of Enoch*, Charles, pp. 7–8.

59 John 20:11–16. It is highly significant that John's Gospel mentions that Mary mistakenly thought that Jesus was the gardener. This is yet another element adapted from similar pagan myths about the dying and rising god-man, who is commonly known as the "Green Man," a symbol for the renewal of life at springtime.

60 Cf., Luke 24:15–16; John 21:4.

61 Cf., Mark 12:25; Luke 20:34–36.

62 Cf., 1 Enoch 7:1 in: *The Book of Enoch*, Charles, p. 18.

63 The idea of angels being sexless is even humorously referenced in Kevin Smith's deliberately irreverent but entertaining film, *Dogma* (Dimension Films, 1999). When the main character, Bethany (Linda Fiorentino), is awakened to find the angel Metatron (Alan Rickman) in her bedroom she is worried that he's going to rape her. The angel removes his pants to show that he and all other angels are incapable of the act because they became as "anatomically impaired as a Ken doll" after an "incident" when the angels got a little too drunk, perhaps alluding to the events in Genesis 6.

64   Cf., Mark 13:32-37; Luke 17:26–27, 34–35; 21:34–36.

65   "Freemasonry," Wikipedia (October 7, 2005), <http://en.wikipedia.org/wiki/Freemasons>.

66   "Scottish Rite," Wikipedia (August 31, 2005), <http://en.wikipedia.org/wiki/Scottish_Rite>. See also: "York Rite," Wikipedia (July 20, 2005), <http://en.wikipedia.org/wiki/York_Rite>.

67   Hans Biedermann, *Dictionary of Symbolism: Cultural Icons and the Meanings Behind Them,* 1989, translated by James Hulbert (New York, NY: Meridian, 1994), s.v. "cube," pp. 85–6.

68   "Kaaba," Wikipedia (October 4, 2005), <http://en.wikipedia.org/wiki/Kaaba>.

69   Cf., Ezekiel 48:30–35.

70   Gardner, *Lost Secrets,* p. 257.

71   Ibid., pp. 257–8.

72   Quoted in: James N. Gardner, *Biocosm: The New Scientific Theory of Evolution: Intelligent Life is the Architect of the Universe* (Makawao, Maui, HI: Inner Ocean Publishing, 2003), p. ix.

EPILOGUE

1   Adolf Hitler, *Mein Kampf,* 1925, translated by Ralph Mannheim, (New York, NY: Mariner Books, 1999), p. 436.

APPENDIX A: PROBLEMS WITH THE THEORY

1   "Hexadactyly," Wikipedia (December 3, 2005) <http://en.wikipedia.org/wiki/Hexadactyly>. See also: "Polydactyly," (December 8, 2005) Wikipedia <http://en.wikipedia.org/wiki/Polydactyly>.

2   "Founder Effect," Wikipedia (November 26, 2005) <http://en.wikipedia.org/wiki/Founder_effect>.

3   Ibid.

4   "Russian Researchers Discover Giants' Graves in Syria," PRAVDA.Ru (December 1, 2005) <http://english.pravda.ru/science/19/94/377/16560_giants.html>.

5   Ibid.

6   Brett M. Christensen, *Giant Skeleton Hoax,* Hoax Slayer (July 2004) <http://www.hoax-slayer.com/giant-skeleton.html>.

7   For the altered image, please see: *Archaeological Anomalies 2,* Worth1000.

Com <http://www.worth1000.com/cache/contest/contestcache.asp?contest_id=447&display=photoshop>. If you would like to see the original image of the mastodon skeleton excavation, please see the Aerial View photos available at: The Cornell University Program of Computer Graphics, *Hyde Park Mastodon Photos,* (last updated: November 13, 2003) <http://www.graphics.cornell.edu/outreach/mastodon/>.

8   Dinosaur Adventure Land, 5800 N Palafox St, Pensacola, FL 32503-7614, <http://www.dinosauradventureland.com>. *From the website:* "Since 2001 Dinosaur Adventure Land has been a place where families can come to learn about God's Creation through science and the Bible. DAL is comprised of a 3 story Science Center, Creation Museum, and Theme Park, making it fun for all ages, and one of the most amazing Creation Parks in the world. Our goal is to win souls to Christ, by giving everyone another choice. You can believe that you came from a rock, or you can believe that a loving God created you for a purpose. Plan your next family vacation, to come to DAL. Thanks for visiting Dinosaur Adventure Land.com, we hope that you will enjoy the site and come to see us very soon."

9   Mt. Blanco Fossil Museum, 124 W. Main, P.O. Box 550, Crosbyton, TX 79322, <http://www.mtblanco.com>. *From the website:* "The Mt. Blanco Fossil Museum is a scientific and educational institution dedicated to a correct interpretation of Earth history and fossil remains. We believe that the fossil record speaks of catastrophic events happening several thousand years ago rather than slow processes taking place over millions or billions of years as is held by the popular establishment."

10   Carl Marychurch, *Giant Thigh Bone (Them Bones),* (accessed: December 8, 2005) <http://www.kent-hovind.com/articles/them_bones.htm>. Marychurch provides three screen captures of Hovind featuring the bone during his *Creation Seminar Series,* parts 2, 6 and 7. Referring to: Kent Hovind, 2003 (?) *Creation Seminar Series - Part 6* @ 1:15:00, Creation Science Evangelism, Pensacola, USA. A still image is available at: <http://www.kent-hovind.com/articles/pics/thigh-on-set.htm>. You can also watch the entire series of videos that have been uploaded to the Google Video service by doing a search for "Creation Seminar Series" at: <http://video.google.com>.

11   Ibid., referring to: Kent Hovind, 2003 (?) *Creation Seminar Series - Part 7* @ 1:08:00, Creation Science Evangelism, Pensacola, USA. A still image is available at: <http://www.kent-hovind.com/articles/pics/thigh-direct.htm>. Or you can watch the video at Google: <http://video.google.com> and skip

ahead to the time marker.

12   Ibid., referring to: Kent Hovind, 2003 (?) *Creation Seminar Series - Part 2* @ 0:55:00, Creation Science Evangelism, Pensacola, USA. A still image is available at: <http://www.kent-hovind.com/articles/pics/thigh-egypt.htm> or the entire video on Google <http://video.google.com>.

13   To be fair, Kent Hovind does state that this is a replica in the slide from Part 2 listed above. However, simply saying that it is a replica would lead most people to believe that it is just a copy of the real thing, and that the actual bone exists elsewhere. This could be considered deliberately misleading.

14   Joe Taylor, *Giant Tale*. Story Behind the Giant Human Femur Sculpture <http://www.mtblanco.com/html/giant_tale.html>.

15   Ibid.

16   Marychurch, <http://www.kent-hovind.com/articles/them_bones.htm>.

17   *Comparative Anatomy Topic 4: Form and Function*. Square-cube Law (December 12, 2005) <http://www.auburn.edu/academic/classes/zy/0301/Topic4/Topic4. html#square>.

18   Ibid.

19   Ibid. See also: Michael C. LaBarbera, "The Biology of B-Movie Monsters," *Fathom Archive* (2003), The University of Chicago <http://fathom.lib.uchicago. edu/2/21701757/>.

20   Marychurch, <http://www.kent-hovind.com/articles/them_bones.htm>.

21   E-mail communication between Joe Taylor and the author on October 4, 2006. See also: Taylor, <http://www.mtblanco.com/html/giant_tale.html>.

22   Controversy seems to follow Kent Hovind wherever he goes. After years of ongoing legal battles with the IRS and the U.S. government, Hovind and his wife were both arrested on July 13, 2006, and indicted in federal court on 44 counts of tax evasion. The IRS accuses them of failing to pay $473,818 in federal income, Social Security and Medicare for their employees, all of whom the Hovind's claim are "missionaries," and *not* employees. Mr. Hovind was charged with 14 additional counts (58 charges altogether) including impeding an IRS investigation, filing frivolous lawsuits, destroying records, and threatening to harm IRS investigators. Hovind plead "not guilty" under claims of "duress" and that he did not understand the charges against him because he is "employed by God and has no income or property because everything he owns belongs to God." For more information, see: Michael Stewart, "Park Owner Pleads not Guilty to Tax Fraud: Evangelist Says He's Owned by God," *Pensacola News Journal.com* (July 18, 2006) <http://www.pensacolanewsjournal.com/

23 "Hawking Says Humans Must Go Into Space," *The Associated Press* (June 14, 2006): Space News <http://www.msnbc.msn.com/id/13293390/>.

24 David J. Stewart, *Signs of Satan* (accessed: July 7, 2006) <http://www.jesus-is-savior.com/False%20Religions/Wicca%20&%20Witchcraft/signs_of_satan.htm>.

25 For people who think that changing the letters or meaning of words in the Bible is no big deal, let me assure you that many people have died over such oversights. Most of this stems from the verse in Matthew 5:18 when Jesus says: "For truly I tell you, until heaven and earth pass away, not one letter [Greek *iota*], not one stroke of a letter, will pass from the law until all is accomplished." Unfortunately, it was just such a thing—the dotting of an "i" (iota)—that began a war. This is according to the eighteenth century historian Edward Gibbon in his magnum opus *The Decline and Fall of the Roman Empire.* Gibbon writes of how an earlier transcriber had neglected to dot an "i" and so it was considered heresy for anyone to correct this error in later editions. Eventually, the undotted "i's" won—after a death toll estimated at 100,000 people. My source for Gibbon's work is contained in: Ann Moura, *The Evolution of Modern Witchcraft: The Evolution of a World Religion* (St. Paul, Minnesota: Llewellyn Publications, 2000), p. 131; referring to: Edward Gibbon, *The Decline and Fall of the Roman Empire* (Vols. I-II. New York: Henry Holt & Co., 1985).

26 Whitley Strieber, "The Majesty of the Key," *Whitley's Journal* (September 20, 2005) *Unknown Country.com* <http://www.unknowncountry.com/journal/?id=194>. *Author's note:* Whitley mistakenly mentions in this journal that the event happened in 1999, but all other accounts state that it happened in 1998.

APPENDIX B: THEORETICAL GATEWAY PHYSICS 101

1 Michio Kaku, *Parallel Worlds: A Journey Through Creation, Higher Dimensions, and the Future of the Cosmos* (New York, NY: Doubleday, 2005) pp. 338–42.

2 "Multi-verse" is a phrase sometimes used to describe a reality that has multiple universes—and yes, I realize that the phrase "multiple universes" is an oxymoron.

3 Penny Bailey, Giles Newton, and Jon Turney. *Big Picture on Nanoscience,* no. 2 (June 2005), The Wellcome Trust <http://www.wellcome.ac.uk/assets/wtd015798.pdf>, p. 2. *Author's note:* It should also be noted that some scientists currently dismiss the idea of using "nanosubs" because their diminutive size

would make them more vulnerable to being smashed into pieces by other objects floating inside the blood vessels.

4   Ibid.

5   Laurence's translation: 1 Enoch 70:13, as shown in: Elizabeth Clare Prophet, *Fallen Angels and the Origins of Evil* (USA: Summit University Press, 2000), p. 180. Cf., R.H. Charles' translation of: 1 Enoch 71:11, p. 144.

6   Daniel 3:19–25.

APPENDIX C: HOLEY(ER) THAN THOU

1   Adapted from: Michael S. Heiser, "The Meaning of the Word Nephilim: Fact vs. Fantasy," <http://www.michaelsheiser.com/nephilim.pdf>. See also: <www.sitchiniswrong.com> a site exclusively designed to discredit the work of Zecharia Sitchin.

2   Zecharia Sitchin, *The Stairway to Heaven, The Earth Chronicles,* vol. 2 (New York, NY: Avon Books, 1983), p. 111.

3   Ibid., p. 112.

4   Ibid.

5   Ibid.

6   Most historians believe that the cubit used by the Hebrews was closer to 18 inches. The origin of this particular cubit being 25.025 inches is attributed to a Victorian newspaper editor named John Taylor. Taylor was also a mathematician and amateur astronomer who was fascinated by the Great Pyramid. To prove his theories about the pyramid, he believed he needed to determine what unit of measurement was used to construct it, which is sometimes referred to as the "pyramid inch." Regardless of how intriguing the numerical associations may be using this unit of measure, it is a complete invention of Taylor and the only way to make the numbers appear to have any significance.

7   Patrick Heron, *The Nephilim and the Pyramid of the Apocalypse* (Xulon Press, 2005), pp. 11–12. *Author's note:* The final answers to the solutions have been corrected here to avoid misunderstanding. The original values in Heron's book were: 14,609.68.

8   Please note that I have obtained these measurements from several reputable online sources, but checked them against the measurements from official sources such as Dr. Zahi Hawass, the Secretary General of the Egyptian Supreme Council of Antiquities. There are some minor differences, though. For instance, I have found measurements in meters that seem more precise

than those provided by Dr. Hawass, such as the pyramid being 146.59 meters (≈ 480.94 ft) tall. But Dr. Hawass writes that the pyramid is 480 feet (≈ 146.3 m) tall. In these cases, I have decided to use the more precise measurements because they are extremely close and perhaps Dr. Hawass has simply rounded his numbers. I have noticed that there are measurements by other Egyptologists that are considerably different, but in all cases they do not match the numbers provided by Heron.

9   Heron, *Nephilim*, p. 12.

10 Ibid.

11 Ibid., p. 43.

12 Ibid., pp. 191–5.

13 Ibid., p. 191.

APPENDIX D: TRACKING THE MOVEMENTS OF VENUS

1   Trevor W. McKeown and Dr. Leigh Hunt Palmer, "Venus and the Pentagram," (March 16, 2004), <http://freemasonry.bcy.ca/anti-masonry/venus.html>.

APPENDIX E: THE RADIO EXPERIMENT

1   LEMUR Team, Understanding EVP: A Practical Demonstration. (accessed: August 8, 2006) <http://shadowboxent.brinkster.net/lemurEVP.html>.

2 Ibid.

3 Ibid.

SELECTED BIBLIOGRAPHY

Alcock, James E. "Electronic Voice Phenomena: Voices of the Dead?" *Skeptical Inquirer* (2004): Special Articles <http://www.csicop.org/specialarticles/evp.html>.

Alley, Richard B. *The Two-Mile Time Machine: Ice Cores, Abrupt Climate Change, and Our Future* (Princeton University Press, 2000).

Anderson, John. *The Rapture: Biblical Fact or Left Behind Fiction?* DVD (Lighthouse World Ministries, 2004).

Bell, Art and Whitley Strieber. *The Coming Global Superstorm* (New York, NY: Pocket Books, 1999).

Bailey, Penny, Giles Newton, and Jon Turney. *Big Picture on Nanoscience* no. 2 (June 2005). The Wellcome Trust, <http://www.wellcome.ac.uk/assets/wtd015798.pdf>.

Berger, Brian. "Policy or Politics? NASA Accused of Intimidating Climatologist." *Space.com* (February 6, 2006), <http://www.space.com/spacenews/businessmonday_060206.html>.

Biedermann, Hans. *Dictionary of Symbolism: Cultural Icons and the Meanings Behind Them,* 1989, translated by James Hulbert (New York, NY: Meridian, 1994).

Black, Jeremy and Anthony Green. *Gods, Demons and Symbols of Ancient Mesopotamia,* 1992, (Great Britain: University of Texas Press, Austin, 2003).

Boulay, R.A. *Flying Serpents and Dragons: The Story of Mankind's Reptilian Past* (Escondido, California: The Book Tree, 1999).

Brennan, Herbie. *The Secret History of Ancient Egypt* (New York, NY: Berkley Books, 2001).

Brown, Paul. "Republicans Accused of Witch-Hunt Against Climate Change Scientists." *The Guardian* (August 30, 2005), <http://www.guardian.co.uk/usa/story/0,12271,1558884,00.html>.

Calvin, William H. *A Brain for All Seasons: Human Evolution and Abrupt Climate Change* (University of Chicago Press, 2002).

Carol K. Mack and Dinah Mack. *A Field Guide to Demons, Fairies, Fallen Angels, and Other Subversive Spirits* (New York: Henry Holt and Company, 1999).

Carroll, Robert Todd. "Electronic Voice Phenomena (EVP)" *The Skeptic's Dictionary* <http://www.skepdic.com/evp.html>.

Charles, R.H., trans. *The Book of Enoch: I Enoch* (Oxford: Clarendon Press, 1912).

Childress, David Hatcher. *Lost Cities of North America* (Stelle, IL: Adventures Unlimited Press, 1992).

Collins, Andrew. *From the Ashes of Angels: The Forbidden Legacy of a Fallen Race* (Rochester, Vermont: Bear & Company, 2001).

Connolly, Robert, and Bea Connolly, producers. *The Search for Ancient Wisdom*, CD-ROM (Chatsworth, CA: Cambrix Publishing, Inc., 1995).

Dalley, Stephanie, trans. *Myths from Mesopotamia: Creation, The Flood, Gilgamesh, and Others*, 1989, Revised edition (New York: Oxford University Press, Inc., 2000).

Davidson, Gustav. *A Dictionary of Angels Including the Fallen Angels* (New York: The Free Press, 1971).

Dickson, B. et al. "Rapid Freshening of the Deep North Atlantic Ocean Over the Past Four Decades," *Nature* vol. 416 (April 25, 2002).

Downing, Barry. *The Bible and Flying Saucers*, 1968, (New York, NY: Marlowe and Company, 1997).

Dunn, Christopher. *The Giza Power Plant: Technologies of Ancient Egypt* (Santa Fe, NM: Bear & Company, Inc, 1998).

Eason, Cassandra. *A Complete Guide to Faeries & Magical Beings* (Canada: Weiser Books, 2002).

Ellis, Ralph. *Jesus: Last of the Pharaohs*, 1999, 2d ed. (Kempton, Illinois: Adventures Unlimited, 2001).

Forgione, Adriano. "The Mystery of Malta's Long-Headed Skulls." *Atlantis Rising* #43 January/February 2004 (Livingston, MT).

Gadalla, Moustafa. *Egyptian Divinities: The All Who Are THE ONE* (Egypt: Tehuti Research Foundation, 2001).

Gagosian, Robert B. "Abrupt Climate Change: Should We Be Worried?" presented at the World Economic Forum, Davos, Switzerland, (January 27, 2003).

Gardner, Laurence. *Genesis of the Grail Kings* (Gloucester, MA: Fair Winds Press, 2002).

————. *Lost Secrets of the Sacred Ark: Amazing Revelations of the Incredible Power of Gold* (Hammersmith, London: Element Books, Inc., 2003).

————. *Realm of the Ring Lords: The Myth and Magic of the Grail Quest* (Gloucester, MA: Fair Winds Press, 2002).

Gilbert, Adrian G., and Maurice M. Cotterell. *The Mayan Prophecies: Unlocking the Secrets of a Lost Civilization* (New York: Barnes & Noble, Inc., 1996).

Ginzberg, Louis. *The Legends of the Jews: Volume I — From the Creation to Jacob,* 1909–1938, translated by Henrietta Szold (Baltimore, MD: Johns Hopkins University Press, 1998).

González-Wippler, Migene. *Keys to the Kingdom: Jesus and the Mystic Kabbalah* (St. Paul, Minnesota: Llewellyn Publications, 2004).

Graham, Billy. *Angels: God's Secret Agents* (Garden City, NY: Doubleday, 1975).

Greene, Brian. *The Elegant Universe: Superstrings, Hidden Dimensions, and the Quest for the Ultimate Theory* (New York, NY: Vintage Books, 2000).

Greer, John Michael. *The New Encyclopedia of the Occult* (St. Paul, Minnesota: Llewellyn Publications, 2003).

Grimassi, Raven. *Italian Witchcraft: The Old Religion of Southern Europe* (St. Paul, Minnesota: Llewellyn Publications, 2000).

————. *The Wiccan Mysteries: Ancient Origins & Teachings* (St. Paul, Minnesota: Llewellyn Publications, 2001).

Guiley, Rosemary Ellen. *The Encyclopedia of Angels.* 2d ed. (New York, USA: Checkmark Books, 2004).

————. "A Radiance of Angels." *Fate,* (December 1993).

Hansen, Jim. "Climate Change: On the Edge." *The Independent Online Edition* (February 17, 2006: Environment) <http://news.independent.co.uk/environment/article345926.ece>.

Harrison, Jane Ellen. *Themis: A Study of the Social Origins of the Greek Religion* (London: Cambridge University Press, 1912).

Hawass, Dr. Zahi, ed. *Treasures of the Pyramids* (New York: Barnes & Noble, Inc., 2003).

Heiser, Michael S. "Ancient Ghosts, Spirits, Demons, and the Departed Dead: An Overview of the Underworld in Ancient Texts" (December 1, 2004) <www.michaelsheiser.com>.

————. "The Divine Council in the Dead Sea Scrolls: An Introductory Survey" <http://www.thedivinecouncil.com/>.

————. "The Meaning of the Word Nephilim: Fact vs. Fantasy" <http://www.michaelsheiser.com/nephilim.pdf>.

Shanks, Hershel, ed. *Understanding the Dead Sea Scrolls* (New York, NY: Vintage Books, 1993).

Heron, Patrick. *The Nephilim and the Pyramid of the Apocalypse* (Xulon Press, 2005).

Hopkins, Marilyn, Graham Simmans, and Tim Wallace-Murphy. *Rex Deus: The True Mystery of Rennes-le-Château and the Dynasty of Jesus* (Boston, MA: Element Books, Inc., 2000).

Hudson, David. *David Hudson Lectures.* The Chemistry of M-state Elements. <http://www.asc-alchemy.com/hudson.html>.

———. *David Hudson Lectures.* Sakarov's Theory of Gravity. <http://www.asc-alchemy.com/hudson.html>.

Joyce, Terrence, and Lloyd Keigwin. "Abrupt Climate Change: Are We on the Brink of a New Little Ice Age?" *Woods Hole Oceanographic Institution* <http://www.whoi.edu/institutes/occi/currenttopics/abruptclimate_joyce_keigwin.html>.

Kaku, Michio. *Hyperspace: A Scientific Odyssey Through Parallel Universes, Time Warps, and the Tenth Dimension* (New York, NY: Anchor Books, 1994).

———. *Parallel Worlds: A Journey Through Creation, Higher Dimensions, and the Future of the Cosmos* (New York, NY: Doubleday, 2005).

Knight, Christopher, and Robert Lomas. *Uriel's Machine: Uncovering the Secrets of Stonehenge, Noah's Flood, and the Dawn of Civilization* (Gloucester, MA: Fair Winds Press, 1999).

Konstantinos. *Speak with the Dead: Seven Methods for Spirit Communication* (St. Paul, Minnesota: Llewellyn Publications, 2004).

Kramer, Samuel Noah. *Sumerian Mythology: A Study of Spiritual and Literary Achievement in the Third Millennium B.C.* (Philadelphia: University of Pennsylvania Press, 1972).

Lean, Geoffrey. "Global Warming Approaching Point of No Return, Warns Leading Climate Expert" *The Independent Online Edition* (January 23, 2005) <http://news.independent.co.uk/world/environment/article16401.ece>.

Lewis, James R., and Evelyn Dorothy Oliver, with Kelle S. Sisung, ed. *Angels A to Z* (Canton, MI: Visible Ink Press, 2002).

Lincoln, Henry. *The Holy Place: Saunière and the Decoding of the Mystery of Rennes-le-Château* (New York: Arcade Publishing, Inc., 1991).

Lunn, Martin. *Da Vinci Code Decoded* (New York, NY: The Disinformation Company Ltd., 2004).

Mehler, Stephen S. *The Land of Osiris: An Introduction to Khemitology* (Adventures Unlimited Press, 2001).

Meyer, Marvin W., ed. *The Secret Teachings of Jesus: Four Gnostic Gospels* (New York: Vintage Books, 1986).

Missler, Chuck and Mark Eastman. *Alien Encounters,* 1997, Revised and Expanded Edition (Koinonia House, 2003).

Nickell, Joe. *Entities: Angels, Spirits, Demons, and Other Alien Beings* (Amherst, NY: Prometheus Books, 1995).

Oates, Joan. *Babylon: Revised Edition,* 1979, (New York, NY: Thames and Hudson, 2000).

Ohio State University. *Major Climate Change Occurred 5,200 Years Ago: Evidence Suggests That History Could Repeat Itself* (December 16, 2005) <http://www.physorg.com/news2409.html>.

Polidoro, Massimo. "The Secrets of Rennes-le-Château." *Skeptical Inquirer* 28, no. 6, November/December 2004: Notes on a Strange World <http://www.csicop.org/si/2004-11/strange-world.html>.

Prophet, Elizabeth Clare. *Fallen Angels and the Origins of Evil* (USA: Summit University Press, 2000).

RavenWolf, Silver. *Angels: Companions in Magick* (St. Paul, Minnesota: Llewellyn Publications, 2000).

"Reaping the Whirlwind: Extreme Weather Prompts Unprecedented Global Warming Alert." *The Independent Online Edition* (July 3, 2003) <http://news.independent.co.uk/world/environment/article94497.ece>.

Ronan, Margaret. *Strange Unsolved Mysteries* (New York: Scholastic Book Services, 1974).

Schwartz, Paul, and Doug Randall. *An Abrupt Climate Change Scenario and Its Implications for United States National Security* (October 2003).

"Scientists Issue Unprecedented Forecast of Next Sunspot Cycle" in *The National Center for Atmospheric Research & the UCAR Office of Programs* (March 6, 2006) <http://www.ucar.edu/news/releases/2006/sunspot.shtml>.

Silverman, David P., ed. *Ancient Egypt,* (New York, NY: Oxford University Press, Inc., 2003).

Sineath, Frederick. "Tools of the Trade: Cold Spots, or Cold Shoulders — Infrared Thermo Detection Re-Evaluated." *Ghost! Magazine* (Issue 4: 2005).

Sitchin, Zecharia. *The Stairway to Heaven.* The Earth Chronicles, vol. 2 (New York, NY: Avon Books, 1983).

————. *The Twelfth Planet.* The Earth Chronicles, vol. 1 (New York, NY: Avon Books, 1978).

Southall, Richard. *How to Be a Ghost Hunter* (St. Paul, Minnesota: Llewellyn Publications, 2003).

Starbird, Margaret. *Magdalene's Lost Legacy: Symbolic Numbers and the Sacred Union in Christianity* (Rochester, VT: Bear & Company, 2003).

Stipp, David. "Climate Collapse: The Pentagon's Weather Nightmare" *Fortune Magazine* (February 9, 2004).

Strieber, Whitley. *Communion: A True Story,* 1987, paperback (New York, NY: Avon Books, 1988).

———. *The Key: A Conversation About The Nature and Future of Man* (San Antonio, TX: Walker & Collier, Inc., 2001).

Tegmark, Max. "Parallel Universes" *Scientific American* (New York, NY: May 2003).

Than, Ker. "Key Argument for Global Warming Critics Evaporates" *LiveScience* (August 11, 2005) <http://www.livescience.com/environment/050811_global_warming.html>.

Timothy Freke and Peter Gandy. *Jesus and the Lost Goddess: The Secret Teachings of the Original Christians* (New York, NY: Harmony Books, 2001).

———. *The Jesus Mysteries: Was the "Original Jesus" a Pagan God?* (New York, NY: Harmony Books, 2000).

Toorn, Karl van der, Bob Becking & Pieter W. van der Horst. *Dictionary of Deities and Demons in the Bible DDD (2nd Extensively Rev. Ed.),* (Grand Rapids, MI: Brill; Eerdmans: Leiden, 1999).

Townsend, Mark, and Paul Harris. "Now the Pentagon Tells Bush: Climate Change Will Destroy Us" *The Observer* (February 22, 2004) <http://observer.guardian.co.uk/international/story/0,6903,1153513,00.html>.

Tyson, Donald, *The Power of the Word: The Secret Code of Creation* (St. Paul, Minnesota: Llewellyn Publications, 2004); (previously published as: *Tetragrammaton: The Secret to Evoking Angelic Powers and the Key to the Apocalypse,* 1998).

Vermes, Geza, ed. and trans. *The Complete Dead Sea Scrolls in English* (New York: Penguin Books, 1998).

Ward, Peter D. "Impact from the Deep" *Scientific American* (New York, NY: October 2006).

Warren, Joshua P. *How to Hunt Ghosts: A Practical Guide* (New York, NY: Fireside, 2003).

Wasserman, James. *The Egyptian Book of the Dead: The Book of Going Forth by Day, The First Authentic Presentation of the Complete "Papyrus of Ani"* 1994, translated by Dr. Raymond O. Faulkner, edited by Eva von Dassow. Revised edition. (San Francisco: Chronicle Books, 1998).

Waters, Frank. *Book of the Hopi* (New York, NY: Penguin Books, 1977).

INDEX

Ishtar 124, 148, 168

Jacob's Ladder 129, 145
Jehovah. *See Yahweh*
Jerusalem 102, 165, 170–1, 177–8, 190, 297, 302
Jesus 32, 50–1, 100–3, 132–4, 141, 146, 154–64, 166, 170–9, 181, 184, 190, 278–80, 283, 284, 287–9, 293–7, 299–301, 306
Jung, Carl 200, 272, 304

Kabbalah. *See Cabala*
kachinas 81, 254
Kaku, Michio 225, 328
Katrina, Hurricane 241–3, 256
The Key (Strieber) 30–1, 232, 239, 327
Ki (Sumerian Earth Goddess) 73
Kundalini 161

Laurence, Richard 56, 140–1, 333
Left Behind series 281–2
Lévi, Éliphas 166–7
Lindsey, Hal 280–2
Little Ice Age 233, 245, 250
Lucifer 135, 168, 172–3, 344, 349. *See also Venus*

M-theory 224, 227. *See also Superstring theory*
Magdalene, Mary 101, 146, 174–9, 181, 183–4, 299
magick 68, 143, 162, 188
manna 139, 276, 279, 296, 306
Master of the Key 31–2, 212, 226, 232, 238, 326, 327. *See also The Key (Strieber)*
Maunder Minimum 250
Maya 112, 129, 145, 168–70, 250
measure of the fish 157, 159
melam (garment) 100, 134, 142, 298
Melchizedek 102–3, 171
Meritaten 93
Merovingians 179, 181

Mesopotamia 44, 111, 122, 160, 278
Messiah 140–1, 154, 156, 159–61, 176–7, 293, 300
Metatron. *See angels: Metatron*
Methuselah 99, 109, 137, 147
Migdal (tower) 176, 178. *See also Magdalene, Mary*
Mithras 158
Molech 50, 72, 190
monatomic gold 257, 269, 273, 276, 286, 296, 323, 333. *See also Orbitally Rearranged Monatomic Elements (ORME)*
Morning Star 165, 168, 172–3, 344, 349. *See also Eastern Star*
Moses 100–1, 134–5, 147, 154, 158–60, 166, 273, 275–6
mountains
  Mt. Hermon 66, 87, 100, 136
  Mt. Meru 80
  Mt. Sinai 134–5, 273
  Mt. Zion 134, 177–8, 184
mušhuššu (dragon) 160. *See also Messiah*

nachash 101, 127, 160. *See also serpent*
Name of God. *See Tetragrammaton*
nanobots 330–3
nanotechnology 258, 329–30
Nebuchadnezzar 77, 131–3, 145, 294, 317, 333
Nebuchadnezzar's fiery furnace 131–3
Nephilim 20, 6–5, 68, 71–2, 80, 85–6, 107, 112, 136, 147–8, 337, 340, 348
Nephilim (etymology) 61–4
Neteru 77, 131–3, 145, 294, 317, 333
Nickell, Joe 34, 47–9
Niflheim 80, 290
Book of Noah 51, 85, 98–9
Noah 51, 59, 64–5, 78, 85, 98–101, 107, 109, 147, 300, 336. *See also Days of Noah*
Noah's flood. *See Great Flood*
Nun (letter) 153, 159
Nun (mythology) 119

CRAIG HINES is a multimedia artist with nearly two decades of experience in the fields of computer graphics, video production, and website design. His interest in computers began at an early age, and has only been rivaled by his fascination with ancient civilizations, paranormal phenomena, science, and technology. His focused research on what would later become *Gateway of the Gods* began in 1999, and continues through today. Hines believes that his training in multimedia, coupled with his knowledge of the paranormal, has given him a unique point of view, whereby he examines how to make the fantastic real and accessible.

Hines hopes that his research breathes a fresh perspective into the field, and that his methods garner the mainstream respect that has eluded other authors. He encourages discussion of the facts, not agendas, both within the scientific and historical communities, and in the population at large. "Finding the truth of the world around us," Hines states, "will depend upon our ability to be honest and open to fantastic possibilities, yet discerning enough to not blindly accept the fantastic as the only plausible explanation."

PICTURE CREDITS

The author and publisher are grateful for permission to reproduce the following photographs: *National Geographic Magazine* (p. 93); Robert Connolly (p. 94); Asbjorn Aakjaer and iStockphoto.com (p. 130); Imaginova Canada Ltd. (pp. 169, 351–7); Alan Scott (p. 183); Scott Newton (p. 245); NASA (p. 251); "IronKite" and Worth1000.com, as well as the Cornell University Program of Computer Graphics (p. 315); Joe Taylor, Mt. Blanco Fossil Museum (p. 316); Sandia National Laboratories (p. 330).

We want to hear from you! Please visit our website for more information about new products, author updates, special offers, and more!

www.NuminaMediaArts.com

Printed in the United States
83921LV00002B/1-48/A